PREPOSITIONS
AND THEOLOGY

IN THE GREEK NEW TESTAMENT

PREPOSITIONS
AND THEOLOGY

An Essential Reference Resource for Exegesis

MURRAY J. HARRIS

ZONDERVAN
ACADEMIC

ZONDERVAN ACADEMIC

Prepositions and Theology in the Greek New Testament
Copyright © 2012 by Murray J. Harris

Requests for information should be addressed to:
Zondervan, 3900 *Sparks Dr. SE, Grand Rapids, Michigan* 49546

ISBN 978-0-310-53105-0 9 (ebook)

This edition: ISBN 978-0-310-11694-3 (softcover)

Library of Congress Cataloging-in-Publication Data

Harris, Murray J.
        Prepositions and theology in the Greek New Testament / Murray J. Harris.
            p. cm.
        Includes bibliographical references (p. 17–23) and indexes.
        ISBN 978-0-310-49392-1 (hardcover)
        1. Greek language, Biblical—Prepositions. 2. Bible. N.T.—Language, style. I. Title.
PA849.H37 2011
487'.4—dc23   2011046973

All Scripture translations in the book, unless otherwise noted, are the author's own, based on the Greek New Testament text or the Septuagint.

Any internet addresses (websites, blogs, etc.) and telephone numbers in this book are offered as a resource. They are not intended in any way to be or imply an endorsement by Zondervan, nor does Zondervan vouch for the content of these sites and numbers for the life of this book.

Cover design: Tammy Johnson
Interior design: Matthew Van Zomeren

Printed in the United States of America

To Bruce and Don,
who both blazed a shining trail
in academic pursuits
for their youngest brother to follow

Contents

Preface 13
Select Bibliography and Abbreviations 17

1. Introduction 25
    A. The Phases of the Greek Language 25
    B. Terminology 26
    C. Prepositions and Adverbs. 27
    D. Prepositions and Cases. 28
    E. The Basic Meaning of Prepositions 28
    F. Principles of Choice. 30
    G. Exegeting Prepositions. 31

**2. Distinctive Features of Prepositional Usage in
New Testament Greek.** 33
    A. Characteristics in Keeping with the General
       Tendencies of Hellenistic Greek (in Comparison
       with Classical Greek). 33
    B. Possible Semitic Influence on New Testament
       Prepositional Usage 36

**3. Dangers to Be Avoided in Any Examination of
New Testament Prepositional Usage** 39
    A. Insistence on Classical Greek Distinctions. 39
    B. Failure to Make Allowance for a Writer's
       Stylistic Variation 40
    C. Disregard of Probable Distinctions 40
    D. Denial of Double Entendre 41
    E. Neglect of the Possible Significance of Items
       with Prepositions. 43

4. Ἀμφί and Ἀνά 45

    A. Ἀμφί 45

    B. Ἀνά 45

    C. Ἀνά in Compounds 48

5. Ἀντί 49

    A. Basic Idea and New Testament Use 49

    B. Equivalence 49

    C. Exchange 50

    D. Substitution 50

    E. Important New Testament Uses 51

    F. Ἀντί in Compounds 56

6. Ἀπό 57

    A. Relation of Ἀπό to Ἐκ 57

    B. Ἀπὸ θεοῦ 58

    C. Ellipses with (Pregnant) Ἀπό 60

    D. Ἀπό in Paul's Epistolary Salutations 62

    E. Other Notable Instances 62

    F. Ἀπό in Compounds 67

7. Διά 69

    A. Origin and Basic Idea 69

    B. Notable Instances of Main Uses 69

    C. Διά in Compounds 82

8. Εἰς 83

    A. Origin and New Testament Use 83

    B. Its Relation to Πρός 83

    C. Its Relation to Ἐν 84

    D. Telic Εἰς 88

    E. Consecutive/Ecbatic Εἰς 90

    F. Causal Εἰς? 90

    G. Significant Phrases Using Εἰς 92

    H. Significant Successive Instances of Εἰς 100

    I. Ambiguity of Meaning 101

    J. Εἰς in Compounds 102

9. Ἐκ 103

    A. Introduction 103

    B. Basic Signification 103

    C. Range of Figurative Uses 103

D. Important Constructions Using Ἐκ. 105
E. Other Significant Instances of Ἐκ 110
F. Ἐκ in Compounds. 113

10. Ἐν. 115
A. Extended New Testament Use and Ultimate
Disappearance. 115
B. Versatility 116
C. Encroachment on Other Prepositions 117
D. Main Uses. 118
E. Key Phrases 122
F. Ἐν in Compounds. 136

11. Ἐπί. 137
A. Basic Meaning. 137
B. Versatility 138
C. Important Constructions Using Ἐπί 138
D. Other Notable Uses of Ἐπί 141
E. Ἐπί in Compounds 145

12. Κατά 147
A. Basic Meaning. 147
B. Phrases Involving Κατά. 147
C. Κατά Denoting Correspondence or Conformity 152
D. Κατά Denoting Opposition. 154
E. Distributive Κατά 155
F. Some Ambiguous Examples. 157
G. Κατά in Compounds. 160

13. Μετά 161
A. Original Meaning and New Testament Use 161
B. Μετά with Accusative ("after") 161
C. Μετά with Genitive. 163
D. Εἶναι μετά Denoting "Presence With". 168
E. Μετά in Compounds. 170

14. Παρά 171
A. Basic Sense. 171
B. Transferred Meanings 171
C. Παρὰ (τῷ) θεῷ 172
D. Παρά and Christology in the Fourth Gospel 173
E. Παρά in Compounds 176

15. Περί 179
   A. Basic and Derived Meanings 179
   B. Περὶ ἁμαρτίας/ἁμαρτιῶν 182
   C. Περί in Compounds. 183

16. Πρό. 185
   A. New Testament Use and Basic Meaning 185
   B. Notable Uses 186
   C. Πρό in Compounds 187

17. Πρός 189
   A. New Testament Use and Basic Meaning 189
   B. Notable Instances 190
   C. Πρός in Compounds 197

18. Σύν 199
   A. Original Meaning and New Testament Incidence 199
   B. Two Basic Uses 199
   C. Relation to Μετά 200
   D. Σὺν Χριστῷ and Equivalents in Paul 200
   E. Σύν in Compounds 204

19. Ὑπέρ 207
   A. Original Meaning and New Testament Use 207
   B. Ὑπέρ with the Accusative 207
   C. Ὑπέρ with the Genitive 209
   D. Ὑπέρ and Περί. 210
   E. Ὑπέρ meaning "in the place of" 211
   F. Ὑπέρ as Expressing Both Representation/Advantage
      and Substitution 215
   G. Ὑπέρ in Compounds. 217

20. Ὑπό 219
   A. Original Meaning and New Testament Use 219
   B. Ὑπό with the Accusative 219
   C. Ὑπό with the Genitive. 220
   D. Ὑπὸ νόμον. 220
   E. Ὑπό and Other Prepositions Expressing Agency 221
   F. Ὑπό in Compounds. 223

21. Prepositions with Βαπτίζω 225
   A. Ὑπέρ 225

B. Ὑπό 226

C. Εἰς 226

D. Ἐν 230

E. Ἐν/ἐπὶ τῷ ὀνόματι. 232

22. Prepositions with Πιστεύω and Πίστις. 233

A. Nonprepositional Constructions 233

B. Prepositional Constructions. 234

C. Concluding Observations 237

23. "Improper" Prepositions 239

A. Nomenclature and Classification. 239

B. "Improper" Prepositions in Hellenistic Greek 240

C. An Annotated Alphabetical List of All 42 New Testament
"Improper" Prepositions 242

24. Notable Uses of Selected "Improper" Prepositions. 253

A. Ἄνευ – Matthew 10:29. 253

B. Ἐκτός – 1 Corinthians 6:18 and 2 Corinthians 12:2 255

C. Ἔμπροσθεν – John 1:15 (cf. 1:30). 259

D. Ἐντός – Luke 17:21 260

E. Ἕως οὗ – Matthew 1:25 262

F. Χωρίς – Hebrews 9:28 263

Index of Biblical References 267

Index of Greek Words and Expressions 287

Index of Subjects 291

Preface

The present work is not a comprehensive treatment of prepositions in the Greek New Testament. For that the reader may consult the larger grammars such as BDF or A. T. Robertson, lexicons such as BDAG, or other specialized works such as P. F. Regard's *Contribution à l'étude des prépositions dans la langue du Nouveau Testament*. Even less does it seek to relate the New Testament use of prepositions to earlier or later usage in the Greek language, although occasional references are made to Classical Greek and Modern Greek. For an examination of *Greek Prepositions from Antiquity to the Present*, we now have the recent magisterial work of that title by Pietro Bortone (Oxford: Oxford University Press, 2010). Nor does this book purport to be a "theology of the prepositions," as if prepositions in themselves can express theology. Rather, this is a study of numerous places in the Greek New Testament where prepositions contribute significantly to the theological meaning of the text. Prepositions in themselves do not carry theological meaning, but the way they are used invests them with theological import. Naturally the choice of examples is somewhat arbitrary and simply reflects the author's own theological interests and sensitivities.

What is offered here is similar in approach to the author's earlier work in a lengthy appendix in volume 3 of *The New International Dictionary of New Testament Theology*, edited by C. Brown (Exeter: Paternoster/Grand Rapids: Zondervan, 1978). But the present contribution differs from that earlier treatment in several important ways.

1. All of the 17 New Testament "proper" prepositions are dealt with.
2. There are many more verses of significance discussed under each of these prepositions.
3. There is a discussion of key repeated phrases that use a particular preposition.
4. All 42 "improper" prepositions are briefly treated, with a detailed consideration of seven theologically significant occurrences.
5. A classification of the use of prepositions in compound words is

included; "prepositions in composition often best show their original import" (Robertson 574).

6. The layout is more user-friendly and a Greek font is used.

When single verses are discussed *seriatim*, as in this work, there is the constant danger that the context may be overlooked. But the reader should find that appropriate attention has been given to the immediate literary context and the wider linguistic and theological context of a particular verse. Turner comments that "in the Koine all the prepositions become increasingly elastic and their sense has to be determined more often by the context than was earlier the case" (261). See, for example, my discussion of πρός in John 1:1 or of ἀντί in Hebrews 12:2.

I have long believed—and taught—that there are four areas of Greek grammar that produce the most handsome dividends when special attention is given to understanding them. These "Big Four" are the aorist, the genitive case, the article, and prepositions. Of prepositions it has been rightly said, "An in-depth knowledge of a language is not attained until one has total mastery of its prepositional system."[1]

Basically, a preposition is a word—usually a small word in most languages—that expresses a relationship between other words. In Greek that relationship may be as wide-ranging as purpose or result, cause or basis, concern or benefit, derivation or separation, identification or distinction, instrumentality or agency, correspondence or equivalence, representation or substitution, circumstances or sphere, incorporation or fellowship, priority or posteriority. So the significance of prepositions is immediately apparent. One is reminded of the vivid picture drawn in Jas 3:4 to illustrate the potent influence of the tongue, that "ships, though massive in size, are steered by a very small rudder" (τὰ πλοῖα τηλικαῦτα ὄντα ... μετάγεται ὑπὸ ἐλαχίστου πηδαλίου). The sentence is the πλοῖον, the preposition is often the πηδάλιον. As for prepositional influence on a vastly wider scale, the Danish linguist V. R. Brøndal believes that Greek prepositions were decisive in the development of Western philosophy, which was based on Greek and on the nuances expressed by these prepositions.[2]

To avoid a volume of inordinate length, I have resisted the temptation to supply references to sources that support the various views mentioned. Where given, documentation is generally within the text and restricted to grammars, lexicons, and English versions. For some readers it may prove refreshing to have so few footnotes! References to BDR are supplied only if this 1976 German revision of Blass's *Grammar* differs from the 1961 English revised translation (BDF) or includes additional relevant material.

---

1. "El conocimiento profundo de una lengua no se consigue en tanto no se tenga un dominio completo del sistema de las preposiciones" (M. L. López, *Problemas y métodos en el análisis de preposiciones* [Madrid: Gredos, 1972], 12, cited by Bortone 238).

2. *Praepositionernes Theori—indledning til en rationel Betydningslaere* (Copenhagen: B. Lunos, 1940), 92 (cited by Bortone 147 n.67).

This volume is offered to the reader in the hope that it may encourage close study of the Greek text of the New Testament, since interpreting the text grammatically — including giving attention to the nuances of prepositions — is the necessary prelude to understanding it theologically.

I am grateful to Dr. Stanley N. Gundry, Executive Vice President and Editor-in-Chief at Zondervan, for his ready acceptance of this manuscript for publication, and to Dr. Verlyn D. Verbrugge, Senior Editor-at-Large for Biblical and Theological Resources at Zondervan, for his skill and efficiency in guiding the book through publication.

With warm gratitude I wish to acknowledge three persons who have inspired me in my academic life. First, Jennifer, my wife of fifty years, who has constantly supported and encouraged me, latterly in the midst of her debilitating chronic multiple sclerosis. Then Bruce, my eldest brother, a Rhodes Scholar who studied classics at Balliol College, the University of Oxford, and finally served as Head of the School of History, Philosophy and Politics at Macquarie University in Sydney. And Don, an older brother, the Vinerian Scholar in law at Oxford, cofounder and formerly Director of the Centre for Socio-Legal Studies of the University of Oxford, and Emeritus Fellow of Balliol College.

To Bruce and Don I dedicate this volume with great pleasure and gratitude.

Select Bibliography and Abbreviations

1. A * indicates the writer's own preference when more than one solution is given for a particular exegetical issue and a preference is not expressed.
2. References to BDAG, LSJ, MM, *EDNT*, *GELS*, MGM, and BDB are by page number and quadrant on the page, **a** indicating the upper half and **b** the lower half of the left-hand column, and **c** and **d** the upper and lower halves of the right-hand column.
3. Abbreviations from ancient sources (Classical, Jewish, rabbinic, etc.) are not listed here; they are readily available in the *SBL Manual of Style* (Peabody, MA: Hendrickson, 1999).

AB	Anchor Bible
Abbott	Abbott, E. A., *Johannine Grammar* (London: Black, 1906).
Abel	F. M. Abel, *Grammaire du grec biblique suivie d'un choix de papyrus* (Paris: Gabalda, 1927).
Atkinson	B. F. C. Atkinson, *The Theology of Prepositions* (London: Tyndale, 1944).
Bachtin	N. Bachtin, *Introduction to the Study of Modern Greek* (Cambridge: Cambridge University, 1935).
Baldwin	H. S. Baldwin, "Improper Prepositions in the New Testament: Their Classification, Meaning, and Use, and Their Exegetical Significance in Selected Passages" (unpublished PhD diss., Trinity Evangelical Divinity School, 1994).
Barclay	W. Barclay, *The New Testament: A New Translation*. Vol. 1. *The Gospels and the Acts of the Apostles* (London: Collins, 1968); Vol. 2. *The Letters and the Revelation* (London: Collins, 1969).
BDAG	*A Greek-English Lexicon of the New Testament and Other Early Christian Literature* (rev. and ed. F. W. Danker;

Chicago/London: University of Chicago, 2000), based on W. Bauer's *Griechisch-deutsches Wörterbuch* (6th ed.) and on previous English eds. by W. F. Arndt, F. W. Gingrich, and F. W. Danker.

BDB   F. Brown, S. R. Driver, and C. A. Briggs, *A Hebrew and English Lexicon of the Old Testament* (Oxford: Clarendon, 1953; corrected 1907 ed.).

BDF   F. Blass and A. Debrunner, *A Greek Grammar of the New Testament and Other Early Christian Literature* (trans. and rev. by R. W. Funk; Chicago: University of Chicago, 1961).

BDR   F. Blass, A. Debrunner, and F. Rehkopf, *Grammatik des neutestamentlichen Griechisch* (Göttingen: Vandenhoeck & Ruprecht, 1976).

Bib   *Biblica*

Bortone   P. Bortone, *Greek Prepositions from Antiquity to the Present* (Oxford: Oxford University Press, 2010).

BT   *Bible Translator*

Buck   C. D. Buck, *Comparative Grammar of Greek and Latin* (Chicago: University of Chicago, 1933).

Burton   E. de W. Burton, *Syntax of the Moods and Tenses in New Testament Greek* (3rd ed.; Edinburgh: T&T Clark, 1898).

Buttmann   A. Buttmann, *A Grammar of the New Testament Greek* (Andover: Draper, 1873).

Caragounis   C. C. Caragounis, *The Development of Greek and the New Testament: Morphology, Syntax, Phonology, and Textual Transmission* (Tübingen: Mohr Siebeck, 2004).

Cassirer   H. W. Cassirer, *God's New Covenant: A New Testament Translation* (Grand Rapids: Eerdmans, 1989).

CBQ   *Catholic Biblical Quarterly*

CEV   Contemporary English Version (1995)

cf.   *confer* (Latin), compare

C-K   *Computer-Konkordanz zum Novum Testamentum Graece* (based on Nestle-Aland[26] and UBS[3]; Berlin: de Gruyter, 1980).

Conybeare and Stock   F. C. Conybeare and St. G. Stock, *Grammar of Septuagint Greek* (Boston: Ginn & Co., 1905; repr., Peabody, MA: Hendrickson, 1995).

Deissmann   G. A. Deissmann, *Light from the Ancient East* (2nd. ed.; New York: Doran/London: Hodder, 1927).

Deissmann, *Studies* G. A. Deissmann, *Bible Studies* (Edinburgh: T&T Clark, 1903).

DELG P. Chantraine, *Dictionnaire étymologique de la langue grecque: histoire des mots*, 4 vols. (Paris: Klincksieck, 1968–1980).

DJG *Dictionary of Jesus and the Gospels* (ed. J. B. Green, S. McKnight, and I. H. Marshall; Leicester/Downers Grove, IL: InterVarsity Press, 1992).

DLNT *Dictionary of the Later New Testament and Its Developments* (ed. R. P. Martin and P. H. Davids; Leicester/Downers Grove, IL: InterVarsity Press, 1997).

DM H. E. Dana and J. R. Mantey, *A Manual Grammar of the Greek New Testament* (New York: Macmillan, 1955).

DNTB *Dictionary of New Testament Background* (ed. C. A. Evans and S. E. Porter; Leicester/Downers Grove, IL: InterVarsity Press, 2000).

DPL *Dictionary of Paul and His Letters* (ed. G. F. Hawthorne, R. P. Martin, and D. G. Reid; Leicester/Downers Grove, IL: InterVarsity Press, 1993).

EDNT *Exegetical Dictionary of the New Testament*, 3 vols. (ed. H. Balz and G. Schneider; Grand Rapids: Eerdmans, 1990–1993).

EQ *Evangelical Quarterly*

ESV English Standard Version (2001)

EVV English versions of the Bible

ExpT *Expository Times*

GELS *A Greek-English Lexicon of the Septuagint* (eds. J. Lust, E. Eynikel, and K. Hauspie, Part I, with the collaboration of G. Chamberlain; Stuttgart: Deutsche Bibelgesellschaft, 1992); Part II (1996).

GNB Good News Bible (1976)

Goodspeed E. J. Goodspeed, *The New Testament: An American Translation* (Chicago: University of Chicago, 1923).

Goodwin W. W. Goodwin, *A Greek Grammar* (London: Macmillan, 1955).

Harris M. J. Harris, *Jesus As God: The New Testament Use of Theos in Reference to Jesus* (Grand Rapids: Baker, 1992/Eugene, OR: Wipf & Stock, 2008).

Hatzidakis G. N. Hatzidakis, *Einleitung in die neugriechische Grammatik* (Leipzig: Breitkopf & Härtel, 1892; repr., Hildesheim/New York: Olms, 1977).

HCSB Holman Christian Standard Bible (1999, 2009).

HR E. Hatch and H. A. Redpath, *A Concordance to the Septuagint and the Other Greek Versions of the Old Testament (Including the Apocryphal Books)*, 2 vols. (Graz: Akademische Druck- u. Verlagsanstalt, repr. 1975).

ICC International Critical Commentary

Jannaris A. N. Jannaris, *An Historical Greek Grammar (Chiefly of the Attic Dialect) as Written and Spoken from Classical Antiquity down to the Present Time* (London: Macmillan, 1897).

JB Jerusalem Bible (1976)

JBL *Journal of Biblical Literature*

Johannessohn M. Johannessohn, *Der Gebrauch der Präpositionen in der Septuaginta* (Berlin: Weidmannsche Buchhandlung, 1926).

KG R. Kühner, *Ausführliche Grammatik der griechischen Sprache*, Vol. 2, Parts 1 and 2 (3rd ed. by B. Gerth; Hannover and Leipzig: Hahnsche Buchhandlung, 1898–1904).

KJV King James Version (= "Authorised Version") (1611)

κτλ. καὶ τὰ λοιπά, "and the rest"

Lampe G. W H. Lampe, *A Patristic Greek Lexicon* (Oxford: Oxford University Press, 1961).

LN J. P. Louw and E. A. Nida, eds., *Greek-English Lexicon of the New Testament Based on Semantic Domains*. Vol. 1. *Introduction and Domains* (New York: United Bible Societies, 1988).

LSJ H. G. Liddell and R. Scott, *A Greek-English Lexicon* (9th ed.; rev. H. S. Jones et al.; Oxford: Clarendon, 1940). *Supplement* (ed. E. A. Barber et al.; Oxford: Clarendon, 1968).

LXX Septuagint (= Greek Old Testament)

McKay K. L. McKay, *A New Syntax of the Verb in New Testament Greek: An Aspectual Approach* (New York: Lang, 1994).

Mayser E. Mayser, *Grammatik der griechischen Papyri aus der Ptolemäerzeit*, Vol. 2, Part 2 (1934; repr., Berlin & Leipzig: de Gruyter, 1970).

Metzger B. M. Metzger, *A Textual Commentary on the Greek New Testament* (Stuttgart: Deutsche Bibelgesellschaft/New York: United Bible Societies, 1994, based on UBS[4]; original ed. of 1971 based on UBS[3]).

MGM *Moulton and Geden Concordance to the Greek New Testament*, 6th ed. (rev. and ed. I. H. Marshall; London/New York: T&T Clark, 2002).

MH   J. H. Moulton and W. F. Howard, *A Grammar of New Testament Greek.* Vol. 2. *Accidence and Word-Formation* (Edinburgh: T&T Clark, 1919).

MM   J. H. Moulton and G. Milligan, *The Vocabulary of the Greek Testament Illustrated from the Papyri and Other Non-Literary Sources* (1930; repr., Grand Rapids: Eerdmans, 1972).

Moffatt   J. Moffatt, *The Moffatt Translation of the Bible* (2nd ed.; London: Hodder, 1935).

Moule   C. F. D. Moule, *An Idiom Book of New Testament Greek* (2nd ed.; Cambridge: Cambridge University Press, 1959).

Moulton   J. H. Moulton, *A Grammar of New Testament Greek.* Vol. 1. *Prolegomena* (3rd ed., Edinburgh: T&T Clark, 1908).

MT   Masoretic Text

Muraoka   T. Muraoka, *A Greek-English Lexicon of the Septuagint, Chiefly of the Pentateuch and the Twelve Prophets* (Louvain: Peeters, 2002).

NA^{27} *Novum Testamentum Graece* (ed. B. Aland, K. Aland, J. Karavidopoulos, C. M. Martini, and B. M. Metzger, 27th rev. ed.; Stuttgart: Deutsche Bibelgesellschaft, 1993).

NAB[1]   New American Bible (1970)

NAB[2]   New American Bible: Revised New Testament (1988)

NASB[1]   New American Standard Bible (1960)

NASB[2]   New American Standard Bible (1995)

NEB   New English Bible (1970)

NET   New English Translation Bible (2005)

NewDocs   *New Documents Illustrating Early Christianity* (ed. G. H. R. Horsley and S. Llewelyn; North Ryde, NSW, Australia: Macquarie University Press, 1981 –). These will be cited by volume.

NIDNTT   *The New International Dictionary of New Testament Theology,* 3 vols. (ed. C. Brown; Grand Rapids: Zondervan, 1975 – 1978).

NIV[1]   New International Version (1983)

NIV[2]   New International Version (2011)

NJB   New Jerusalem Bible (1985)

NLT   New Living Translation of the Bible (1996)

NovT   *Novum Testamentum*

NRSV   New Revised Standard Version (1990)

NT   New Testament

NTS   *New Testament Studies*

OT   Old Testament

pace (from Latin, peace); (in stating a contrary opinion) with all due respect to (the person named)

Phillips J. B. Phillips, *The New Testament in Modern English* (London: Bles/Collins, 1958).

REB Revised English Bible (1990)

Regard P. F. Regard, *Contribution à l'étude des prépositions dans la langue du Nouveau Testament* (Paris: Gabalda, 1919).

Robertson A. T. Robertson, *A Grammar of the Greek New Testament in the Light of Historical Research* (4th ed.; Nashville: Broadman, 1934).

Robertson, *Pictures* A. T. Robertson, *Word Pictures in the New Testament*, 6 vols. (Nashville: Broadman, 1930–1933).

Rossberg C. Rossberg, *De Praepositionum Graecarum in Chartis Aegyptiis Ptolemaeorum Aetatis Usu* (Ienae: Typis G. Nevenhahni, 1909).

RSV Revised Standard Version (1952, 1973)

RV Revised Version (NT 1881)

SB H. L. Strack and P. Billerbeck, *Kommentar zum Neuen Testament aus Talmud und Midrasch*, 4 vols. (Munich: Beck, 1922–1928).

SJT *Scottish Journal of Theology*

Smyth H. W. Smyth, *Greek Grammar* (rev. G. M. Messing; Cambridge, MA: Harvard University Press, 1956).

Sophocles E. A. Sophocles, *Greek Lexicon of the Roman and Byzantine Periods (From B.C. 146 to A.D. 1100)* (New York: Frederick Ungar, 1887).

Spicq C. Spicq, *Theological Lexicon of the New Testament*, 3 vols. (trans. and ed. J. D. Ernest; Peabody, MA: Hendrickson, 1994).

s.v. *sub voce* (Latin) (under the word)

TCNT Twentieth Century New Testament (1904)

TDNT *Theological Dictionary of the New Testament*, 10 vols. (ed. G. Kittel and G. Friedrich, trans. G. W. Bromiley; Grand Rapids: Eerdmans, 1964–1974).

Thackeray H. St. J. Thackeray, *A Grammar of the Old Testament in Greek*, Vol. 1. *Introduction, Orthography and Accidence* (Cambridge: Cambridge University Press, 1909).

Thumb A. Thumb, *Handbook of the Modern Greek Vernacular: Grammar, Texts, Glossary* (trans. S. Angus; Edinburgh: T&T Clark, 1912).

TNIV Today's New International Version (2001, 2005).

TR *Textus Receptus* (Received Text).

Turner   *A Grammar of New Testament Greek*, by J. H. Moulton. Vol. 3. *Syntax*, by N. Turner (Edinburgh: T&T Clark, 1963).

Turner, *Insights*   N. Turner, *Grammatical Insights into the New Testament* (Edinburgh: T&T Clark, 1965).

Turner, *Style*   N. Turner, *A Grammar of New Testament Greek*, by J. H. Moulton. Vol. 4. *Style*, by N. Turner (Edinburgh: T&T Clark, 1976).

TynBul   *Tyndale Bulletin*

UBS/UBS[4]   *The Greek New Testament*, 4th rev. ed. (ed. B. Aland, K. Aland, J. Karavidopoulos, C. M. Martini, and B. M. Metzger; Stuttgart: Deutsche Bibelgesellschaft/ New York: United Bible Societies, 1993). 1st ed. 1966 (= UBS[1]), 2nd ed. 1968 (= UBS[2]), 3rd ed. 1975 (= UBS[3]).

v.l.   *varia lectio* (variant reading)

Voelz   J. W. Voelz, "The Language of the New Testament," in *Aufstieg und Niedergang der römischen Welt* (ed. H. Temporini and W. Haase; Berlin) 25/2 (1984): 893–977.

Wallace   D. B. Wallace, *Greek Grammar beyond the Basics: An Exegetical Syntax of the New Testament* (Grand Rapids: Zondervan, 1996).

Webster   W. Webster, *The Syntax and Synonyms of the Greek Testament* (London: Rivingtons, 1864).

Weymouth   R. F. Weymouth, *The New Testament in Modern Speech* (3rd ed.; London: Clarke, 1909).

WH   B. F. Westcott and F. J. A. Hort, *The New Testament in the Original Greek*. Vol. 1, *Text*; Vol. 2, *Introduction, Appendix* (London: Macmillan, 1881).

Williams   C. B. Williams, *The New Testament. A Translation in the Language of the People* (Chicago: Moody Press, 1937, 1952).

Winer   G. B. Winer, *A Grammar of the Idiom of the New Testament* (Andover, MA: Draper, 1872).

Zerwick   M. Zerwick, *Biblical Greek Illustrated by Examples* (trans. J. Smith; Rome: Pontifical Biblical Institute, 1963).

Zerwick, *Analysis*   M. Zerwick, *Analysis Philologia Novi Testamenti Graeci* (3rd ed.; Rome: Pontifical Biblical Institute, 1966). (Although translated [see following entry], this original contains material not appearing in the English translation and sometimes differing from it).

ZG   M. Zerwick and M. Grosvenor, *A Grammatical Analysis of the Greek New Testament*, (5th rev. ed.; Rome: Pontifical Biblical Institute, 1996).

Chapter 1

Introduction

A. The Phases of the Greek Language

The following stages may be identified:

1. *Ancient Greek*, a category that here includes both pre-Classical (especially Homer) and Classical Greek.
2. *Classical Greek*, c. 450 BC–c. 330 BC, chiefly the Attic form.
3. *Hellenistic/Koine Greek*, c. 330 BC–AD 330, ἡ κοινὴ διάλεκτος ("the common language"), in its literary and vernacular forms, is marked by a virtual absence of dialectal forms except for local differences in pronunciation, and what Bortone (239 n.3) calls "slight regional variations."[1] The six main sources for our knowledge of Hellenistic Greek are: literary texts by writers such as Polybius and Epictetus; the Septuagint; the New Testament and other early Christian literature; the Ptolemaic papyri; the inscriptions; and the observations of grammarians such as Moeris and Phrynichus. The expression "Biblical Greek" is a convenient and traditional way of referring to the Greek of the LXX and the NT, without suggesting it forms a defined dialect of Hellenistic/Koine Greek.
4. *Medieval Greek/Byzantine Greek*, AD 330 (the removal of the seat of government from Rome to Constantinople)–1453 (the conquest of Constantinople by the Turks).
5. *Modern Greek*, AD 1453–the present; but specifically, in the present work, the Greek written or spoken at the present day, "contemporary standard Greek" (Bortone 238 n.1), in which two strands are interwoven—a

---

1. Recognizing that Koine Greek was not a static entity and the probability that changes in usage occurred during the 900 or so years (on his view) of Koine Greek, J. A. L. Lee proposes a division of Koine Greek into Early (III–I BC), Middle (I–III AD) and Late (IV–VI AD), "ΕΞΑΠΟΣΤΕΛΛΩ" in *Voces Biblicae: Septuagint Greek and Its Significance for the New Testament*, ed. J. Joosten and P. J. Tomson (Leuven: Peeters, 2007), 113 n.31.

popular, vernacular strand (Demotic) and an archaizing or Atticizing "purist" strand (Katharevousa).

The five stages isolated by Caragounis (in 2004) (XIII; and for more detail XX, 1–63) are (after the Mycenaean or Linear B stage [15th–12th century BC]):

1. Archaic or Epic Greek (800–500 BC)
2. The Classical (Attic) Period (500–300 BC)
3. Post-classical Greek (c. 300 BC–AD 600)
4. Byzantine-Mediaeval Greek (AD 600–1500)
5. The Neohellenic Period (AD 1500–2000)

"Neohellenic at present (i.e., the language spoken and written today) is very broad, since it encompasses (simple) Katharevousa, moderate Demoticism and extreme Demoticism" (Caragounis 56–57). "A more cultivated Demotic is in effect a simple Katharevousa, and conversely, a simple Katharevousa, is a more cultivated Demotic" (58).

At an earlier time (1897) Jannaris (xv, xxii) delineated five periods:

1. Attic (500–300 BC)
2. Hellenistic (300–150 BC)
3. Greco-Roman (150 BC–300 AD)
4. Transitional (300–600 AD)
5. Neohellenic (600–1900 AD)
   • Byzantine (600–1000 AD)
   • Mediaeval (1000–1450 AD)
   • Modern (1450–1800 AD)
   • Restorative (1800 AD–present)

However we divide up the stages of the Greek language, all agree "that greater changes took place during the 600 years separating Polybios from Homeros than during the 2,100 years between Polybios and our time" (Caragounis 68). This shows that "in the development of Greek time-length and change do not go hand in hand: contrary to what might be expected, greater changes may take place in a briefer period, while a more protracted period may be attended by slower change" (Caragounis 89).

B. Terminology
1. "Preposition"

The term "preposition" ultimately comes from πρό-θεσις, "a placing before, a fore-placement" (a term used by the Greek grammarian Dionysius Thrax), via the Latin *prae-positio*, also meaning "a placing before." In Greek grammar it denotes an indeclinable word that is *placed before* a substantive or pronoun or *prefixed* to a verb. But originally "prepositions" followed the substantive (as still done in the NT with ἕνεκεν and χάριν) and therefore were "*post*positions"! Etymology apart, a preposition is basically a word that denotes a relationship between other words — hence the German term for preposition, *Verhältniswort*, "word of relationship." In each Greek preposition, it seems, there is an inherent, foundational meaning that is further defined by a particular context.[2]

2. "Proper" and "Improper" Prepositions

Those prepositions (such as ἐν) that can also serve as prefixes in compound words have been called "proper" prepositions (17 in the NT), and prepositions (such as ἐντός) that cannot be used this way have been called "improper" prepositions (42 in the NT). This classification is unfortunate, for most "improper" prepositions are equally "*pre*-positions" and they are functionally equivalent to "proper" prepositions. Moreover it seems arbitrary to base a classification on an external relation, that is, a word's ability to be used as a prefix to *another* word. Although "improper" prepositions are in no sense improper with regard to the Greek language, it has become customary (see, e.g., Smyth §§1647, 1699–702) to use this convenient grammatical classification, no doubt partly because "improper" prepositions usually "govern" a single case — the genitive. Robertson, however, also uses the expression "adverbial prepositions" or "prepositional adverbs" (554, 557, 636–37) to describe "improper" prepositions. See further ch. 23.

C. Prepositions and Adverbs

In the parent Indo-European language, cases probably stood alone, but later some adverbs came to be used as prepositions. Originally prepositions were locatival adverbs (Bortone xv, 140; cf. Robertson 553–54; 636–37); indeed, in Homer words like περί ("round about") and ἀμφί ("on both sides") are still used as adverbs. Also at the outset, prepositions were "post-positive" adverbs; that is, they were placed *after* the word they qualified, a usage reflected in τίνος ἕνεκα, "on account of what" = "why" (Ac 19:32; cf. Lk 4:18). So the term "preposition" reflects a later development when these adverbs *preceded* the word they qualified. Certainly, no precise distinction can be drawn between adverbs and prepositions. Words like ἐγγύς and ἔξω are used either as adverbs or as prepositions; and in Hellenistic Greek (including both the NT and the papyri) a preposition and an adverb are often combined (e.g., ἐκ πάλαι and many "improper" prepositions such as ἐπάνω [Mayser 538–42]), as also in Modern Greek (Thumb §158).

---

2. "Most linguists appear to endorse a conception of prepositional meaning as a combination of an inherent meaning with a specification supplied by the context; in the terminology diffused by [R.] Jakobson ["Beitrag zur allgemeinen Kasuslehre: Gesamtbedeutungen der russischen Kasus," *Travaux du cercle linguistique de Prague* 6 (1936): 240–88]: different *Sonderbedeutungen* in each particular context, but related through an overall *Gesamtbedeutung* in abstract, or an underlying *Grundbedeutung* at the origin" (Bortone 42).

D. Prepositions and Cases

"Both in time and at first in order" case came before prepositions (Robertson 567). From the point of view of historical development, prepositions did not "govern" the case of a noun but rather helped to define more precisely the distinctions indicated by the case forms or were added to recapture original meanings; the accusative basically denoted direction ("Whither?"); the genitive, separation ("Whence?"); and the dative, location ("Where?"). That is, cases found in prepositions a convenient means of sharpening their significance. But, in ever-increasing measure, the case ending itself came to be divested of special significance because inflection expressed such diversified relations, and the accompanying preposition, with its fixed case form, assumed part of the meaning of the case and potentially added new meanings.[3]

So it is somewhat artificial to analyze the case of a noun or pronoun in Classical or Hellenistic Greek apart from the "meaning" of the adjoining preposition; the writers themselves probably regarded prepositions as "governing" or determining the case of the noun or pronoun. Originally, then, it was the case that showed the meaning of the preposition, but ultimately the preposition was regarded as giving a particular meaning to the case. To express the point another way, at the outset cases "governed" prepositions, but in the end prepositions were thought to "govern" cases in the sense of determining the case of a noun or pronoun that would produce a specific meaning.

Since a plain case is often capable of various senses, an added preposition or prepositional phrase can clarify and reinforce the intended meaning or actually remove ambiguity. For example, a phrase such as ἡ ἀγάπη τοῦ Χριστοῦ (2Co 5:14) could mean "the love shown by Christ" (subjective genitive) or "love for Christ" (objective genitive), but ἡ ἀγάπη ἡ ὑπὸ τοῦ Χριστοῦ would express the former meaning unequivocally.

E. The Basic Meaning of Prepositions

In his comprehensive and authoritative treatment of *Greek Prepositions from Antiquity to the Present* (2010), P. Bortone has successfully defended his central thesis that "the history of Greek prepositions, if analysed in its entirety, is largely congruent with the 'localistic hypothesis' that concrete spatial meanings are the earliest ones, and entirely congruent with the 'unidirectionality hypothesis' that spatial meanings evolve into non-spatial ones but not vice-versa" (xii; cf. 52, 189, 302–3). "Spatial and non-spatial meanings seem to appear in a sequence" (170) so that "new [prepositional] items attest that spatial senses were the first

---

3. Philologists suggest that the endings of prepositions may originally have been case inflections, e.g., ἀμφί, ἐνί, ἐπί, περί, and πρός, old locatives, and ἅμα, ἀνά, διά, μετά, and κατά, old instrumentals (Bortone 141 n.57, citing earlier studies; cf. 96–97).

Diagram of the Spatial Meanings of the
Seventeen New Testament "Proper" Prepositions

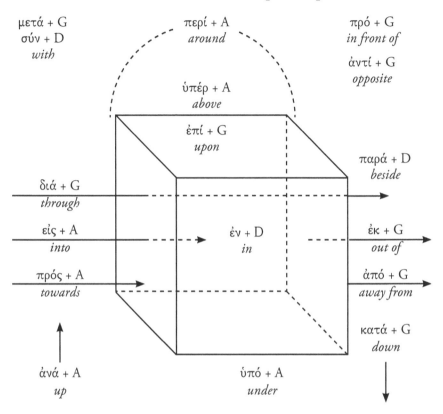

In this diagram A, D, and G indicate the case after the preposition that gives the spatial meaning indicated.

to appear, while the old items show that non-spatial senses were the last to be shed" (xvi), and "once prepositions become exclusively abstract in meaning, they never (re)acquire spatial meanings" (168). In stage 1 a preposition has only spatial meanings, in stage 2 both spatial and nonspatial senses, and in stage 3 only nonspatial meanings (see the charts in Bortone 168 and 283). On the history of the "localistic hypothesis," see Bortone 47–53.

Many prepositions can denote three relations (local/spatial, temporal, figurative/metaphorical/abstract), which apparently developed in that order but, it seems, the primary representation is always local:[4]

---

4. This primary local sense in usage was not necessarily the original local sense; e.g., πρός may originally have meant "near," and μετά "between." See the introductory remarks for each preposition.

1. motion to: εἰς (into), πρός (to[wards])
2. motion from: ἀνά (up), ἀπό (away from), διά (through), ἐκ (out of), κατά (down)
3. rest: ἀντί (opposite), ἐν (in), ἐπί (upon), ὑπέρ (above), ὑπό (under), μετά (with), παρά (beside), περί (around), πρό (in front of), σύν (with)

While the basic sense (the "root meaning") of a preposition is sometimes traceable when it is prefixed to another word, prepositions often gain additional meanings when they are prefixed. Bortone illustrates this vividly by the versatile meanings of ἀνά (basically meaning "up" as a preposition) when it is used in Classical Greek as a prefix (120).

ἀνα-κάπτω: "gulp *down*"
ἀνα-τιτράω: "bore *through*"
ἀνα-δύομαι: "shrink *back*"
ἀνα-γεννάω: "beget *anew*"
ἀνα-πυρέττω: "have fever *recurrently*"
ἀνα-κρέκομαι: "*begin* to play"
ἀνα-καλύπτω: "*un*-cover"
ἀνα-ζωγραφέω: "paint *completely*"
ἀνα-κρίνω: "examine *closely*"
ἀνα-διδάσκω: "teach *otherwise*"

Also, it is not always possible to trace a basic sense when prepositions are used figuratively. With regard to the main figurative relations, the prepositions may be grouped as follows (reflecting principal usage):

1. origin: ἀπό, ἐκ, παρά
2. cause or occasion: διά, ἐπί, ἐκ, ἀπό
3. purpose or object: εἰς, πρός, ἐπί, ὑπέρ
4. result: εἰς, πρός
5. association or identification: σύν, μετά, ἐν, διά
6. relation: περί, ὑπέρ, πρός, εἰς
7. agency: ὑπό, sometimes ἀπό, διά, παρά, or ἐν
8. instrumentality or means: διά, ἐκ, ἐν
9. correspondence: κατά, πρός
10. opposition: κατά, παρά, πρός

F. Principles of Choice

With over 10,000 NT uses of the 17 "proper" prepositions—not to speak of occurrences of the 42 "improper" prepositions—there is clearly need for some limiting criteria to determine which uses seem worthy of special examination after the introductory observations about each preposition.

Broadly speaking, there are two criteria.

1. There are two or more possible ways in which the particular preposition or prepositional phrase has been or could be understood (e.g., ἀπό in Heb 5:7);

> *or* the interpretation of the preposition or phrase has been hotly debated (e.g., ἀπό in 1Co 11:23);
> *or* there are repeated NT uses of a key prepositional phrase (e.g., ἀπὸ θεοῦ);
> *or* there are important translational matters involved (e.g., ἀπ᾽ αὐτῶν in Lk 24:31);
> *or* there are grammatical considerations at stake (e.g., ἀπὸ ὁ ὤν in Rev 1:4 or ellipses with ἀπό);
> *or* the nonuse of a second preposition is the issue (e.g., ἀπό in Paul's epistolary salutations); and

2. The particular prepositional use is deemed to be theologically significant (e.g., διά in 2Pe 1:4).

With regard to the latter criterion, there are many NT prepositional uses that are important for aspects of biblical studies other than theology. These are not discussed. For example:

provenance—ἀπό in Heb 13:24
chronology—πρό in Jn 12:1; διά in Gal 2:1
history—διά in 1Co 7:26
geography—πέραν in Jn 1:28; μέχρι in Ro 15:19

G. Exegeting Prepositions

In seeking to determine the meaning of a prepositional phrase, the NT exegete should (at least ideally) consider:

1. the primary meaning of the preposition itself (i.e., the local/spatial sense) and then its range of meanings when used with the particular case involved
2. the basic significance of the case that is used with the preposition
3. the indications afforded by the context as to the meaning of the preposition
4. the distinctive features of prepositional usage in the NT that may account for seeming irregularities

Compare with this the proposal of Robertson. "The scientific method of studying the Greek preposition is to begin with the case-idea, add the meaning of the preposition itself, then consider the context" (568). The reason I do not suggest beginning with the case idea (as Robertson proposes) is that in Hellenistic

Greek, "the meaning of the case governed by a preposition fades" (Bortone 183; cf. Regard 677, who observes that in the NT the growing role of prepositions corresponds to the decreasing role of case).

Frequency of New Testament "Proper" Prepositions

Preposition	NT Total	Percentage of total NT use	LXX	Ptolemaic papyri
ἐν	2,757	26.5%	14,276	2,245
εἰς	1,768	17.0%	7,438	1,765
ἐκ	916	8.8%	3,823	903
ἐπί	891	8.6%	7,297	1,018
πρός	699	6.7%	3,338	784
διά	668	6.4%	1,427	714
ἀπό	646	6.2%	4,150	920
κατά	476	4.6%	2,140	857
μετά	473	4.6%	2,534	211
περί	333	3.2%	852	631
ὑπό	220	2.1%	498	364
παρά	194	1.9%	879	968
ὑπέρ	150	1.4%	427	283
σύν	128	1.2%	233	134
πρό	47	0.5%	251	44
ἀντί	22	0.2%	391	89
ἀνά	13	0.1%	377	652
Totals	10,401	100%	50,331	12,582

For the NT, figures come from C-K (s.v.) and are listed in the descending order of their frequency; for the LXX, from *GELS* (s.v.); and for the Ptolemaic papyri (up to about 1909), from Rossberg 8. The inclusion of all the more recently discovered papyri, if it were possible, would probably not greatly alter, if at all, their relative incidence.

Chapter 2

Distinctive Features of Prepositional Usage in New Testament Greek

A. Characteristics in Keeping with the General Tendencies of Hellenistic Greek (in Comparison with Classical Greek)[1]

1. Prepositions are *used more frequently*, owing to a weakened sense of the original import of cases. In part they serve to reinforce or make explicit the implications of simple case usage.

2. Prepositional phrases are often *substitutes for simple cases*, which are losing their individual significance (cf. Bortone 179, 194; Turner 3, 251–53; Zerwick §§64, 70, 80, 119–20).

Mt 5:21–22	ἔνοχος ... τῇ κρίσει
	ἔνοχος ... εἰς τὴν γέενναν τοῦ πυρός
Ro 11:24	ἐνεκεντρίσθης ... εἰς καλλιέλαιον
	ἐγκεντρισθήσονται τῇ ἰδίᾳ ἐλαίᾳ
Col 2:13	νεκροὺς ... ἐν τοῖς παραπτώμασιν
Eph 2:1	νεκροὺς τοῖς παραπτώμασιν

3. *"Improper" prepositions become more numerous* and are used more frequently (cf. Bortone 180–81; Zerwick §83).

4. In general, *prepositions followed by the accusative are preferred* over prepositions used with the dative (cf. Bortone 181–83), although ἐν with the dative

---

1. Cf. Robertson 60–74; Zerwick §§78–111, 480–93; Bortone 171–94; Voelz 931–35. "Alike in Vocabulary and Grammar the language of the New Testament exhibits striking dissimilarities from Classical Greek" (MM xi).

gains ground and περί with the accusative loses ground in comparison with Classical Greek. The accusative increasingly becomes the default case with prepositions (Bortone 155). This occasions no surprise since (a) in Modern Greek (as in Medieval Greek—Browning 82), all prepositions take the accusative case ("with few exceptions," Bortone 251; cf. 263–64); and (b) the dative case, which is found in Modern Greek only in a fossilized form, had already begun to be eclipsed in the NT era (cf. BDF §203), although its disappearance was not complete until the tenth century (see the fuller discussion under ἐν, ch. 10).

5. *The variety in the use of "proper" prepositions is curtailed* (cf. Bortone 183). When a preposition has multiple uses, the least important usage tends to disappear (Regard 681). In the NT only ἐπί, παρά (and πρός: once with the genitive [Ac 27:34]) take *three cases*, although only ἐπί is used frequently with three (Regard 681). The dative is no longer used with μετά, περί, and ὑπό (as it was in Classical Greek); in addition to these three, the only other prepositions that take *two cases* (accusative and genitive) are διά, κατά, and ὑπέρ. But in the papyri ὑπό is found with three cases (Mayser 509–15). The genitive flourishes along with the "improper" prepositions, all of which take the genitive (except for ἅμα, παραπλήσιον, and ἐγγύς [which takes both the genitive and the dative]).

6. "Proper" prepositions are commonly *combined with adverbs*, especially those denoting time or place (e.g., ἀπὸ πέρυσι, "since last year," 2Co 8:10; 9:2; see Regard 679).

7. Undoubtedly the tendency of the greatest significance for NT exegesis and theology is that *the "overlap" or "confusion" between various prepositions* (when bearing certain senses) becomes more apparent.

Evidence of such *enallage* (ἐναλλαγή, interchange) may be derived from:

- parallel passages in the Synoptic Gospels (e.g., **περὶ** πολλῶν, Mt 26:28, and **ὑπὲρ** πολλῶν, Lk 22:20; or ὁ **εἰς** τὸν ἀγρόν, Mk 13:16, and ὁ **ἐν τῷ** ἀγρῷ, Mt 24:18)
- the use of two different prepositions in close proximity, apparently without distinction (e.g., ὁ θεὸς ὃς δικαιώσει περιτομὴν **ἐκ** πίστεως καὶ ἀκροβυστίαν **διὰ** τῆς πίστεως, Ro 3:30)
- the repetition of an identical noun with different prepositions within a single context or within a literary corpus (e.g., **εἰς** ἔνδειξιν ... **πρὸς** τὴν ἔνδειξιν, Ro 3:25–26)
- textual variants, which sometimes represent a scribal attempt to clarify meaning by removing imagined ambiguities or irregularities in prepositional use (e.g., παρεδέχθησαν **ἀπὸ** τῆς ἐκκλησίας, Ac 15:4 B C; 𝔓[74] ℵ A D read **ὑπό**; cf. v. 3)
- on occasion, the seemingly irregular use of a preposition (e.g., **πρὸς**

πλησμονὴν τῆς σαρκός ["against (= in combating) sensual indulgence," Col 2:23], where πρός = κατά + genitive)

Instances of this "interchange" include the following.

(1) ὑπέρ and περί (e.g., δεήσει **περὶ** πάντων τῶν ἁγίων καὶ **ὑπὲρ** ἐμοῦ, Eph 6:18–19)

(2) ἀπό and ἐκ (e.g., μήτι συλλέγουσιν **ἀπὸ** ἀκανθῶν σταφυλάς ... ; Mt 7:16)
    οὐ γὰρ **ἐξ** ἀκανθῶν συλλέγουσιν σῦκα, Lk 6:44)

(3) ἐκ and παρά (e.g., Jn 16:28, ἐξῆλθον **παρὰ** τοῦ πατρός 𝔓[5, 22] ℵ A
    ἐξῆλθον ἐκ τοῦ πατρός B C*)

(4) ἀπό and παρά (e.g., **ἀπὸ** θεοῦ ἐξῆλθεν, Jn 13:3
    παρὰ τοῦ θεοῦ ἐξῆλθον, Jn 16:27)

(5) εἰς can mean "to" (like πρός), rather than "into" (e.g., Mk 5:38–39; Jn 20:3, 4, 8 in the light of Jn 20:5b)

(6) ὑπέρ may stand for ἀντί, e.g., Phm 13, **ὑπὲρ** σοῦ, "in your place, as your proxy, substituting for you"); cf. Mayser 460.

(7) ἀπό for ὑπό (e.g., Ac 2:22, ἄνδρα ἀποδεδειγμένον **ἀπὸ** τοῦ θεοῦ)

(8) ἐκ for ὑπό (e.g., 2Co 7:9, ἵνα ἐν μηδενὶ ζημιωθῆτε **ἐξ** ἡμῶν); cf. Mayser 386.

(9) ἐν for διά (e.g., Heb 1:2, ἐλάλησεν ἡμῖν **ἐν** υἱῷ, "the ἐν signifies διά," Chrysostom)
    See also under ἐν, "Encroachment on Other Prepositions" (ch. 8 C)

While it is generally agreed that in Hellenistic Greek the distinction between some prepositions used in certain senses was becoming more and more blurred, this is not to suggest that prepositions were arbitrarily or indiscriminately substituted for one another.

Indeed, the incidence of such interchange needs to be carefully analyzed, for as Robertson comments, "each preposition had its own history and every writer his own idiosyncrasies" (569). Hellenistic Greek has obscured the distinction between motion and rest (Turner 254; cf. Bortone xiii) so that εἰς can follow verbs denoting rest and ἐν is sometimes found with verbs expressing movement. It appears that apart from Mark and Luke-Acts, where εἰς may stand for ἐν, the exegete should assume that εἰς retains its distinctive sense until the context or other considerations show that this is impossible or improbable (cf. Zerwick §106; Turner 255; and see ch. 8 C).

Given this occasional overlap between some prepositions, it is not surprising if a desire (conscious or unconscious) for stylistic variation sometimes explains why different prepositions are used in close proximity to each other without any distinction between them being intended. For example, in 1Jn 5:6 three instances of ἐν follow διά with no apparent difference of meaning ("with," of attendant circumstances) (see below under διά).

B. Possible Semitic Influence on New Testament Prepositional Use[2]

1. *Certain prepositions or prepositional uses become more frequent or assume a new significance.* It is not that the following constructions or uses are without parallel in contemporary papyri, inscriptions, or literary usage. Sometimes it is simply the greater number of instances that points to direct or indirect Semitic influence.

a. Under the influence of the Hebrew preposition *bᵉ*, ἐν often expresses

(i) accompaniment (e.g., Mk 5:2, 25; 1Co 4:21; Heb 9:25)
(ii) instrumentality (e.g., Lk 22:49; Rev 6:8)
(iii) causality (e.g., Mt 6:7; Ac 7:29; 24:16; Ro 1:24; 1Co 7:14; Col 1:21; and note the conjunction ἐν ᾧ, "because," e.g., Ro 8:3; Heb 2:18)

b. Under the influence of the Hebrew preposition *min*,

(i) a prepositional phrase with ἀπό can denote the object following verbs of fearing (cf. Dt 1:29; 7:29; Ps 3:7)

Mt 10:28 (= **Lk 12:4**) μὴ φοβεῖσθε ἀπὸ τῶν ἀποκτεννόντων τὸ σῶμα
"Do not be afraid of those who kill the body"

(ii) prepositional phrases with partitive ἐκ can act as subject or object (cf. Turner 7, 208–9)

Jn 16:17 εἶπαν οὖν ἐκ τῶν μαθητῶν αὐτοῦ … (subject)
"So some of his disciples said …"
Lk 21:16 θανατώσουσιν ἐξ ὑμῶν (object)
"They will put some of you to death"

Note also:

- the *frequent* use of prepositional phrases involving ἔμπροσθεν (162 times in the LXX, often for Hebrew *lipnē*; 48 in the NT), which is not common outside Biblical Greek. MH (465) calls οὕτως εὐδοκία ἐγένετο ἔμπροσθέν σου (lit., "this was well-pleasing before you = in your sight," "such was your gracious will," Mt 11:26 = Lk 10:21) "undeniably Semitic." Cf. Johannessohn 184–86; Turner 279.
- the temporal force of ἐν τῷ with the infinitive (a characteristically Lukan feature), reflecting the Hebrew *bᵉ* with the infinitive construct (cf. Zerwick §387)
- the gerundival use of the infinitive (with or without τοῦ, εἰς τό, or πρὸς τό; cf. the Hebrew or Aramaic *lᵉ* with the infinitive) (see Zerwick §§ 391–92; e.g., Mt 5:28, **πρὸς τὸ** ἐπιθυμῆσαι, "desiring impurely," "with lust," NRSV)

---

2. Cf. MH 460–67; Zerwick §§32, 70, 116–19, 387, 391.

- the *frequency* of prepositional phrases (using ἀπό, ἐπί, and πρός) with πρόσωπον, where "the influence of the Greek of the LXX is unmistakable" (MH 466)
- the *frequency* of a prepositional phrase with εἰς after γίνεσθαι, εἶναι, or λογίζεσθαι (cf. Heb *ľ* with *hāyâ*) instead of a predicate nominative (cf. BDF §145). See, e.g., Mt 19:5–6, ἔσονται οἱ δύο **εἰς σάρκα μίαν**. ὥστε οὐκέτι εἰσὶν δύο ἀλλὰ **σὰρξ μία** (also, e.g., Mt 21:42; Jn 16:20; Ac 19:27; Ro 2:26; 4:3; 9:8; 1Co 15:45 [2x]; 2Co 6:18 [2x]).[3] Deissmann's inscriptional parallels (120 n.10; 121 n.1) to this construction are unconvincing since they relate only to εἶναι εἰς and only to the sense "be for the purpose of." For examples from the LXX and the Apostolic Fathers, see Conybeare and Stock 81.

2. *The repetition of a preposition with each noun connected by* καί occurs so frequently in certain NT books as to be a feature of Biblical Greek attributable to Semitic influence. Of course in itself a repeated preposition need not betray Semitic practice, for any Greek writer may repeat a preposition with several substantives in one regimen in order to highlight the distinction between them. Turner has ascertained that when there is an opportunity to repeat a preposition with a series of nouns, LXX Ezekiel (B-text) accepts it 84% of the time (78 repetitions out of 93 opportunities), Revelation 63% (24:38), Romans and 1 Corinthians 58% (14:24), Ephesians 37% (6:16), Pastorals 17% (4:24), John 53% (8:15), Mark 38% (10:26), Matthew 31% (11:35), and Luke-Acts 23% (25:111) (Turner 275; *Style* 93). See the summary of debate on this matter in Voelz 920 n.158.

---

3. See further BDF §145 (1); BDAG 291b; Jannaris §1552; Robertson 595–96; and below ch. 8 G.

Chapter 3

Dangers to Be Avoided in Any Examination of New Testament Prepositional Usage

Not only is the detailed examination of NT prepositional use richly rewarding; it is also an undertaking made hazardous by several pitfalls that must be avoided. To isolate these hazards will be useful before we begin to examine some of the theologically significant uses of each of the "proper" prepositions and some of the "improper" ones.

A. Insistence on Classical Greek Distinctions

One of the principal characteristics of NT Greek in general, highlighted by all modern grammarians (e.g., Turner 2–9; Regard 688), is the relative absence of Classical Greek standards of diction. In the days before the papyri finds in Egypt were available for comparison with NT texts, it was not uncommon for commentators to find in the Johannine use (in Jn 1:1, 18) of πρός and εἰς (prepositions that generally denote direction or movement in Classical usage) proof of an intertrinitarian relationship involving either "eternal generation" or reciprocity of fellowship. J. A. Bengel, for instance, claimed that "πρός . . . denotes a perpetual, as it were, tendency of the Son to the Father in the unity of essence."[1] The papyri were unavailable to show that in Hellenistic Greek there was a blurring of the distinction between movement and rest (cf. Jannaris §§1538, 1547–48), so that both prepositions could express location; there was no need, simply because these particular prepositions were used, to find indications of motion.

---

1. J. A. Bengel, *Gnomon of the New Testament II* (1759; repr. Edinburgh: T&T Clark, 1863), 234.

Similarly, given the overlap between εἰς and ἐν in Hellenistic Greek (see ch. 8 C), it is unnecessary to distinguish between εἰς εἰρήνην and ἐν εἰρήνη after the imperative "Go!" as though εἰς always indicated movement. A. Plummer, for instance, comments on πορεύου εἰς εἰρήνην in Lk 7:50 this way: "'Depart into peace,' *i.e.* into a lasting condition of peace," noting that ἐν εἰρήνη in Ac 16:36 and Jas 2:16 "is less strong, the peace being joined to the moment of departure rather than to the subsequent life."[2]

B. Failure to Make Adequate Allowance for a Writer's Stylistic Variation

Given the general tendency in Hellenistic Greek toward relative laxity of usage and "overlap" of function with respect to prepositions, the exegete should not assume that a change of preposition, a change of case with a repeated preposition, or the use or nonuse of a preposition in successive phrases or parallel passages always marks a change of meaning. A writer may merely wish to avoid repetition or vary his style (see Turner, *Style* 76–77, for the Johannine corpus).

It seems arbitrary and unwarranted, for example, to distinguish between:

ἐξ ἀνθρώπων and ἀφ' ὑμῶν … ἀπ' ἄλλων in 1Th 2:6
οὗτος ἦν ὃν εἶπον (Jn 1:15) and οὗτός ἐστιν ὑπὲρ οὗ ἐγὼ εἶπον (Jn 1:30)
διὰ δόξης and ἐν δόξῃ in 2Co 3:11
ἐπί with the dative and ἐπί with genitive in Eph 1:10
λόγῳ and τῇ γλώσσῃ and ἐν ἔργῳ in 1Jn 3:18

C. Disregard of Probable Distinctions

This danger is the opposite of the last. A biblical writer must be allowed to alter his terminology *either* to vary his style but not change his meaning, *or* to express a distinction in sense. One should assume a writer chooses his prepositions with care. Here are examples of carefully crafted and precise distinctions.

In the interpretation of 2Jn 7, to treat ἐν σαρκί as equivalent to εἰς σάρκα would be to embrace a species of Apollinarianism. As it is, Jesus Christ came "in the flesh/in a human body," but did not come "into the flesh/into a [preexisting] human body."

In 1Pe 1:23 regeneration is said to have its origin or source in an act of immortal procreation or in imperishable seed (ἀναγεγεννημένοι … [ἐκ σπορᾶς] ἀφθάρτου), but is effected by means of the living and abiding word of God (διὰ λόγου ζῶντος θεοῦ καὶ μένοντος).

2. A. Plummer, *A Critical and Exegetical Commentary on the Gospel according to S. Luke* (ICC; Edinburgh: T&T Clark, 1896), 214 (see ch. 8 C. below).

In 2Co 3:5 Paul disowns any adequacy or qualification, in dependence on his own authority or on his own wisdom (ἀφ᾽ ἑαυτῶν), to reckon any positive result of his ministry as actually originating from himself or as belonging to himself (ἐξ ἑαυτῶν). This verse is a commentary on 1Co 15:9–11: all that Paul was as an apostle, along with all that he did as an apostle, unfit though he was for the role, was by the grace of God (1Co 15:10). So claiming anything as his own or seeking credit for his work was inappropriate. Since God alone guarantees adequacy for Christian ministry (2Co 3:5c), credit must go to God alone when it is carried out successfully. The Christian worker is ineligible to claim honor for success.

In the last clause of the Lord's Prayer (Mt 6:13b), not ἐκ but ἀπό follows ῥῦσαι. In the NT ῥύεσθαι ἐκ denotes deliverance from nonpersonal evil (7x; note esp. 2Pe 2:9, ἐκ πειρασμοῦ), never personal enemies, while (elsewhere) ἀπό with ῥύεσθαι is twice used with persons (Ro 15:31; 2Th 3:2) and once with a nonpersonal object (2Ti 4:18). In Mt 13:19, 38 and probably 5:37, as also in Jn 17:15, ὁ πονηρός refers to "the evil one" (= the devil/Satan). If τοῦ πονηροῦ in Mt 6:13 referred to "evil," we might have expected ἀπὸ παντὸς πονηροῦ ("from all/every kind of evil"; cf. πᾶν πονηρόν in Mt 5:11). Cf. 2Ti 4:18, ῥύσεταί με ὁ κύριος ἀπὸ παντὸς ἔργου πονηροῦ. The probability, then, is that τοῦ πονηροῦ means "the evil one" rather than "evil."

In 2Pe 3:5 the earth (γῆ) is said to have been formed out of the material of water or to rise from and above water (ἐξ ὕδατος) (a gloss on Ge 1:2, 6–8), and to stand amidst water or to exist by the action of water (in descending to fill low areas and ascending to form clouds, δι᾽ ὕδατος).

A distinction usually should be drawn between the same preposition used in the same sentence or in closely related passages *with different cases*. For example:

1Co 11:9 διὰ τὴν γυναῖκα "for the woman's sake"
1Co 11:12 διὰ τῆς γυναικός "through the woman"

On the other hand, there is apparently no difference of meaning between

Mt 19:28 ἐπὶ θρόνου δόξης αὐτοῦ "on his glorious throne"
ἐπὶ δώδεκα θρόνους "on twelve thrones"

D. Denial of Double Entendre

No one will doubt that a repeated preposition may bear two different senses *with the same case* within one sentence. For example:

2Co 2:12 Ἐλθὼν δὲ εἰς τὴν Τρῳάδα εἰς τὸ εὐαγγέλιον τοῦ Χριστοῦ (local and telic εἰς)
"I came to Troas in order to preach the gospel of Christ"
Heb 1:7–8 πρὸς μὲν τοὺς ἀγγέλους "about the angels"
πρὸς δὲ τὸν υἱόν "but to the Son"

Here μὲν … δέ points to a contrast not only between τοὺς ἀγγέλους and τὸν υἱόν, but also between two different meanings of πρός. See further Harris 215–16.

2Pe 1:4 ἀποφυγόντες τῆς ἐν τῷ κόσμῳ ἐν ἐπιθυμίᾳ φθορᾶς
"having escaped the corruption in the world that is caused by evil desires" (local and instrumental ἐν)
Ro 16:25–27 Three uses of κατά (expressing conformity – cause – instrumentality)
Two uses of διά (instrumentality – agency)
Three uses of εἰς (purpose – reference – goal)

But it seems illegitimate, simply on a priori hermeneutical principles, to exclude the possibility that *on occasion* an author may use *a single preposition in a dual sense.* Given the fact that in the divine omnipotence and economy a stated purpose always becomes an achieved result, εἰς and πρός could sometimes point simultaneously to a goal and an outcome. For example, εἰς ἔπαινον δόξης τῆς χάριτος in Eph 1:6 may mean both "this was aimed at extolling the splendor of his grace" (telic εἰς) and "this redounds to the praise of his glorious grace" (ecbatic εἰς).

Other possible examples include:

1Pe 3:20 διεσώθησαν δι᾽ ὕδατος
"[a few, namely eight persons,] were saved through water" (i.e., were brought safely through water [local διά]/were preserved by means of water [instrumental διά]
Col 1:17 αὐτός ἐστιν **πρὸ** πάντων
"He himself is before all things," i.e., priority of time *and* supremacy of status (so also Atkinson 8): "he is prior to all," Moffatt. The alternative accentuation, αὐτὸς ἔστιν would give the sense "he exists before everything" (NEB). See below, ch. 16 B.

Of course care needs to be exercised in determining an intended double entendre. It is tempting to see a double sense in 1Ti 2:15: σωθήσεται δὲ **διὰ** τῆς τεκνογονίας, "she will be saved through childbearing" (i.e., she will be preserved from death while giving birth [διά expressing attendant circumstances]/ she will be saved from moral ruin by bearing children [instrumental διά]), but this seems improbable because it involves giving a double meaning to σωθήσεται as well as to διά. Or again, it would scarcely be defensible to find in the phrase ἐν πνεύματι ἁγίῳ (which appears in the midst of a catalogue of moral virtues, 2Co 6:6) both the sense "in holiness of spirit" and the meaning "by gifts of the Holy Spirit" (REB). Nor could **διὰ** προφητείας in 1Ti 4:14 mean both "through a prophetic utterance" (genitive singular) and "because of prophesies" (accusative plural).

But what of prepositional phrases that may be construed either with what precedes or with what follows? Is a double entendre ever to be found here? Probably not.

The exegete must choose between "Christ is the goal of the law, and so [ecbatic εἰς] righteousness is available to every believer," and, "In the case of every believer, Christ is the end of the law viewed as a means of gaining [telic εἰς] righteousness [or, in its relation to righteousness, referential εἰς]" (εἰς δικαιοσύνην, Ro 10:4; cf. Ro 10:5; Php 3:9).

In the Pauline citation of Hab 2:4 in Ro 1:17 and Gal 3:11, ἐκ πίστεως must be taken either with ὁ ... δίκαιος ("it is the person who is righteous by faith who will live") or with ζήσεται ("the person who is righteous will live by faith"). It would hardly be permissible to affirm that Paul is saying simultaneously that faith in Christ is the means to divine approval and eternal life, *and* that faith is a characteristic of the person who is righteous before God.

Similarly, in Heb 2:9 the commentator must decide between construing the centrally placed διὰ τὸ πάθημα τοῦ θανάτου with the preceding ἠλαττωμένον or the following ἐστεφανωμένον, although both resultant concepts (i.e., the purpose of the incarnation was salvific suffering, and exaltation as the consequence of suffering) are themes present in Hebrews. Atkinson (24), however, takes the crucial phrase causally with the following words ("because of his suffering of death") *and* finally with the preceding words ("in order to suffer death"), while regarding the latter sense as primary.

Or again, word order counts against taking ἐν τῷ ὀνόματι αὐτοῦ both with πιστεύοντες and with ζωὴν ἔχετε in Jn 20:31 (ταῦτα δὲ γέγραπται ἵνα πιστεύσητε ὅτι Ἰησοῦς ἐστιν ὁ Χριστὸς ὁ υἱὸς τοῦ θεοῦ, καὶ ἵνα πιστεύοντες ζωὴν ἔχετε ἐν τῷ ὀνόματι αὐτοῦ).

There is a comparable ambiguity of construction, calling for an exegetical choice, in Lk 4:21; Jn 3:15; Ac 22:3; Ro 4:18; 1Co 3:13; 2Co 5:16; Php 2:13; Col 3:16; 1Th 4:14; Heb 9:11.

E. Neglect of the Possible Significance of Items with Prepositions

1. The Nonrepetition of the Preposition with Copulated Nouns

Generally speaking, a preposition tends to be repeated before a series of nouns joined by καί more frequently in Biblical Greek (under Semitic influence) than in nonbiblical Greek (see ch. 2 B.2). Sometimes, therefore, the nonuse of a second or third preposition in NT Greek may be theologically significant, indicating that the writer regarded the terms that he placed in one regimen as belonging naturally together or as a unit in concept or reality.

Ἐξ ὕδατος καὶ πνεύματος in Jn 3:5 shows that for the writer (or speaker) "water" and "Spirit" form a single means of that regeneration that is a prerequisite for entrance into the kingdom of God (= birth ἄνωθεν, Jn 3:3, 7). No contrast is intended between an external element of "water" and a separate inward renewal achieved by the Spirit. Conceptually, the two are aspects of a single comprehensive idea—a rebirth stemming from (ἐξ) a purification effected by the Spirit, or (less probably), a rebirth stemming from a cleansing and renewal of the (human) spirit (see further on this verse ch. 9 E).

In Mt 3:11 the phrase ἐν πνεύματι ἁγίῳ καὶ πυρί points not to two baptisms (viz., the righteous with the Holy Spirit, the wicked with fire), but to a single baptism in Spirit-and-fire, which may be interpreted either as the messianic purification and judgment that would be carried out by the Spirit (cf. Isa 4:4; 30:28) and experienced by all, or as the outpouring of the Spirit at Pentecost that would refine and inflame Jesus' followers.

On the significance of the nonrepetition of ἀπό in Paul's epistolary salutations, see below under ἀπό.

2. The Order of Nouns That Follow a Preposition

If a preposition is followed by two anarthrous substantives both in the genitive case, the preposition always seems to qualify the former. So ἐξ ἔργων νόμου (Ro 3:20; Gal 2:16 [2x]; 3:2, 5, 10) means "by the works of the law," not "by the principle of works." Thus in 2Co 3:18 ἀπὸ κυρίου πνεύματος is unlikely to mean "by the Spirit of the Lord" (KJV; similarly BDF §474[4]; also BDR §474[5]) (since inverse dependence seems to be an unparalleled NT construction), but rather means "by the Lord [= Yahweh, 2Co 3:16–17] who is [now experienced as] the Spirit" (see below, ch. 6 E), or possibly " by the Lord [Jesus] who is spirit " (cf. 1Co 15:45). See further Buttmann 343.

Even when the preposition is followed by a noun in a case other than the genitive, the limiting genitive generally follows the prepositional phrase (e.g., εἰς ἄφεσιν ἁμαρτιῶν, Mk 1:4; but note the exceptional Mt 13:33; Rev 7:17). Similarly, when the nouns involved are articular, any limiting genitive usually follows the prepositional phrase (e.g., ἀπὸ τοῦ νόμου τῆς ἁμαρτίας καὶ τοῦ θανάτου, Ro 8:2) but occasionally it may be inserted according to the ABBA word order (e.g., ἐκ τῆς τοῦ διαβόλου παγίδος, 2Ti 2:26).

Chapter 4

Ἀμφί and Ἀνά

A. Ἀμφί

Although ἀμφί ("on both sides of" [Bortone 160], "about") was one of the 18 Classical Greek "proper" prepositions, it has disappeared from Hellenistic Greek (Rossberg 11, 41; Mayser 338; Regard 683–84), including the NT (as well as from Medieval and Modern Greek, Bortone 283 n.84), in keeping with the abolition of the distinction between duality and plurality and the disappearance of the dual number in declensions and conjugations (Moulton 57, 77). Its place is taken by περί (Bortone 160–61,184), but it does appear in three NT compound verbs: ἀμφιβάλλω (Mk 1:16), "cast [a circular fishing net]" (corresponding to ἀμφίβληστρον, a casting net); and ἀμφιέννυμι (Mt 6:30) and ἀμφιάζω/ἀμφιέζω (Lk 12:28), all three of which mean "clothe."

B. Ἀνά

With only 13 NT uses, this is the least common of NT "proper" prepositions (see chart on p. 32). With its original spatial meaning of "up" or "up to," it was probably formed from ἄνω, "upward," just as κατά was probably formed from κάτω, "downward," and expresses vertical, upward motion, just as κατά expresses perpendicular, downward motion. Many of the uses of ἀνά match parallel uses of κατά (cf. Bortone 40–41).

1. NT Uses of ἀνά

Ἀνά is always used with the accusative and may be classified under two categories.

a. Fixed Compound Prepositional Phrases

(1) ἀνὰ μέσον (+ genitive), "in the middle, between"
   Common in the papyri (MM 29c-d; Mayser 403) and LXX (HR 69).

Mt 13:25 ζιζάνια ἀνὰ μέσον τοῦ σίτου
   "poisonous weeds among the wheat"

1Co 6:5 διακρῖναι **ἀνὰ μέσον** τοῦ ἀδελφοῦ αὐτοῦ
 "to judge a dispute between his brother [and an adversary]"
Rev 7:17 τὸ ἀρνίον τὸ **ἀνὰ μέσον** τοῦ θρόνου
 "the Lamb who is at the center of the throne" (see below)

(2) ἀνὰ μέρος (lit., "up to a part"), "in turn"

1Co 14:27 εἴτε γλώσσῃ τις λαλεῖ ... **ἀνὰ μέρος**
 "if anyone speaks in a tongue ... one after another/in turn"

b. Distributive, Sometimes with Numerals ("each, apiece")

This use that may have developed from the phrase ἀνὰ πᾶν ἔτος, "year by year."

Mt 20:9–10 ἔλαβον **ἀνὰ** δηνάριον
 "they received a denarius each"
Lk 10:1 ἀπέστειλεν αὐτοὺς **ἀνὰ** δύο
 "he sent them out two by two/in pairs"
Rev 4:8 ἔχων **ἀνὰ** πτέρυγας ἕξ
 "having six wings each/apiece"

Ἀνά is also used as an adverb: Rev 21:21, **ἀνὰ** εἷς ἕκαστος τῶν πυλώνων, "each one of the gates separately."

2. Ἀνὰ μέσον and ὁ θρόνος in Revelation

To judge by frequency of usage, the two principal focal points in Revelation are the throne (of God) (41x; referred to in every chapter except 2, 9–10, 15, 17–18) and "the one who sits on the throne" (11x). How various beings or entities are related to the throne is expressed by:

- the "improper" prepositions ἐνώπιον, "in front of" (11x), and κυκλόθεν, "around, encircling" (2x)
- the adverb κύκλῳ, "in a circle, all around" (3x)
- the prepositional phrase ἐν μέσῳ, "in the middle of, among" (2x)
- ἀνὰ μέσον, "in/at the center" (1x only, 7:17)

If we try to determine the relative proximity of heavenly beings to God's throne, four verses are relevant.

Rev 4:6 ἐν μέσῳ τοῦ θρόνου καὶ **κύκλῳ** τοῦ θρόνου τέσσαρα ζῷα
 "**in the middle of** the throne, that is, **encircling** the throne, were four living creatures"

That ἐν μέσῳ τοῦ θρόνου does not mean "at the very center of the throne" but "in the middle of the throne" in the sense "in close proximity to the throne" or "around (*on every side of*) the throne" (BDAG 635b), is indicated by the epexegetic καί.

Rev 5:6 εἶδον **ἐν μέσῳ** τοῦ θρόνου καὶ τῶν τεσσάρων ζῴων καί **ἐν μέσῳ** τῶν πρεσβύτερων ἀρνίον ἑστηκός
"I saw a Lamb standing **in the middle of** the throne and **among** the four living creatures and **among** the elders."

This assumes that:

(i) there is a difference between ἐν μέσῳ + the singular ("in the middle of") and ἐν μέσῳ + the plural ("among"; cf. 6:6, BDAG 635c) (cf. BDAG 635b, "on the center of the throne and among the four living creatures").

(ii) ἐν μέσῳ is to be supplied before τῶν τεσσάρων ζῴων, so that there is no need to explain the repeated ἐν μέσῳ by appeal to the Hebrew *bēn . . . ûbēn . . .*, "between . . . and . . ." (as Zerwick [*Analysis* 575] does); in any case, that Hebrew construction is regularly rendered by ἀνὰ μέσον . . . καὶ ἀνὰ μέσον in the LXX (some 17x in Genesis alone).

(iii) ἐν μέσῳ τοῦ θρόνου refers to an area immediately adjacent to the throne (see above on 4:6). LN (§83.10) suggests as an alternative translation, "in the middle of the throne area."

Rev 5:11 ἤκουσα φωνὴν ἀγγέλων πολλὼν **κύκλῳ** τοῦ θρόνου καὶ τῶν ζῴων καὶ τῶν πρεσβυτέρων
"I heard the voice of many angels **who encircled** the throne and the living creatures and the elders."
Rev 7:17 τὸ ἀρνίον τὸ **ἀνὰ μέσον** τοῦ θρόνου ποιμανεῖ αὐτούς
"the Lamb **who is at the center** of the throne will be their shepherd"

Similarly BDAG 57d. This rendering assumes the author intends a distinction to be drawn between ἐν μέσῳ (4:6; 5:6; 6:6) and his one use of ἀνὰ μέσον.

If we can plot the position of heavenly beings in relation to the central throne, there seem to be three concentric circles:

- the outer circle: angels (5:11)
- the intermediate circle: elders (5:6)
- the inner circle: living creatures (4:6)

As we try to relate 7:17 to 5:6 with regard to the location of the Lamb, two options emerge: (a) 5:6 and 7:17 are part of two separate visions with two different positions of the Lamb; or (b) the Lamb is not stationary but moves about (cf. ἦλθεν in 5:7 and ποιμανεῖ in 7:17, and note ἑστηκός, not καθήμενον, in 5:6), *with 7:17 reflecting his essential position.* Support for this latter point (and so for [b]) is as follows.

(1) 7:17 contains the only use of ἀνὰ μέσον in Revelation.
(2) 3:21 indicates that the risen Jesus (the Lamb) is seated with God on his throne.

(3) While there is only one divine throne (θρόνοι is never used of God's abode), there are two occupants (22:1, 3, ὁ θρόνος τοῦ θεοῦ καὶ τοῦ ἀρνίου).

(4) The Lord God Almighty and the Lamb jointly form the temple of the heavenly city (21:22).

(5) Worship is offered concurrently to "the one who sits on the throne" and the Lamb (5:13).

(6) The redeemed stand simultaneously "in front of the throne and in front of the Lamb" (7:9).

(7) Both the Lord God (1:8; 21:6) and Jesus Christ (22:13) are τὸ Ἄλφα καὶ τὸ Ὦ.

All of this indicates that in John's estimation Jesus Christ holds a unique and central place in the divine economy and is one with the God the Father with regard to his being and his status but is nevertheless distinct from him.

C. Ἀνά in Compounds[1]

Although infrequently used as a preposition in the NT (13x), ἀνά is common in compounds (more than 70).

1. Elevation: ἀναβαίνω, go up; ἀνίστημι, raise up, stand up
2. Return: ἀναχωρέω, go back, return, withdraw; ἀναστρέφω, turn back, overturn
3. Renewal: ἀναβλέπω, see again, regain sight; ἀναζάω, live again; ἀνασταυρόω, crucify again; ἀναγεννάω, give new life to, regenerate
4. Perfectivizing: ἀνακεφαλαιόω, sum up; ἀναπαύω, refresh, revive

In passages of high emotion there tends to be a cluster of compound words, e.g., Ro 11:33, ἀνεξεραύνητα ... ἀνεξιχνίαστοι.

---

1. MH discusses prepositions in compounds (294–328) in three categories: (a) verbal ("preverbial") compounds, (b) noun compounds and compounds developed from a phrase, and (c) "adverbial compounds or phrases that have become stereotyped as single words" (294). On occasion they give totals for category (a), by far the largest category. My own categorization, given at the end of the discussion of each preposition, relates to the meanings of compounds and is not drawn from MH.

Chapter 5

Ἀντί

A. Basic Idea and New Testament Use

With only 22 NT uses (391 in the LXX), ἀντί is the least common "proper" preposition after ἀνά, and it is relatively uncommon in the Ptolemaic papyri (89x). By Classical Greek times it had virtually ceased to have its original spatial meaning of "in front of" (Bortone 162, 167, 290) and was usually abstract (Bortone 186). This illustrates Bortone's thesis that *spatial meanings are recessive*: with time they decrease to extinction, while abstract ones increase" (168). But he notes there are a few spatial uses of ἀντί in the papyri (186), although Rossberg (18) cites only one (but cf. Mayser 373–74). Ἀντί survives in Modern Greek, with the accusative, and almost always as ἀντίς (Jannaris §1502).

On five occasions ἀντί occurs in the form ἀνθ' ὧν (lit., "in return for which things"), meaning "therefore, so then" (Lk 12:3; see also the one occurrence of ἀντὶ τούτου, Eph 5:31; cf. 2 Sa 19:22) or "because" (Lk 1:20; 19:44; Ac 12:23; 2Th 2:10; cf. Ge 22:18).

Since, then, the root sense of ἀντί is "[set] over against, opposite, facing," the preposition naturally came to denote three categories (see LSJ 153b; Regard 70):

- *equivalence*, where one entity is set over against another as its equivalent
- *exchange*, where one object, opposing or distinct from another, is given or taken in return for the other
- *substitution*, where one object, that is distinguishable from another, is given or taken instead of the other

B. Equivalence ("for, as the equivalent of")

The purpose of the *lex talionis* (Ex 21:23–25) was to limit the extent of retaliation by specifying legitimate compensation for an injury. Under this law one eye was regarded as equivalent compensation for another eye (ὀφθαλμὸν ἀντὶ ὀφθαλμοῦ) and a tooth for a tooth (ὀδόντα ἀντὶ ὀδόντος, Mt 5:38). In 1Co 11:15, arguing analogically, Paul infers from the general fact that "hair has been given to her *for/to serve as* a covering [ἀντὶ περιβολαίου]," that the more generous supply of hair that a woman has when compared with a man shows the appropriateness of her being covered when she prays or prophesies in the Christian congregation.

C. Exchange ("in return for, for the price of")

In return for evil received (ἀντὶ κακοῦ) Christians are not to do evil (Ro 12:17; 1Th 5:15; 1Pe 3:9); when abused they are not to abuse in exchange (μὴ ἀποδιδόντες ... λοιδορίαν ἀντὶ λοιδορίας, 1Pe 3:9). It was "for the price of/in exchange for" (HCSB; cf. BDAG 88b)/"in return for" (Weymouth) a single meal (ἀντὶ βρώσεως) that Esau sold his birthright (Heb 12:16).

D. Substitution ("instead of")

In its prevailing sense in the LXX (see Johannessohn 198–200), as in nonbiblical Greek (e.g., Xenophon, *Anab.* 1.1.4), including the papyri (Mayser 374–75; MM 46; Rossberg 18), ἀντί denotes a substitutionary exchange. "The idea of 'in the place of' or 'instead' comes where two substantives placed opposite to each other are equivalent and so may be exchanged" (Robertson 573).

1. Examples in the LXX

> **Ge 4:25** God grants Eve another child (Seth) "in place of Abel" (ἀντὶ Ἄβελ)
>
> **Ge 22:13** Abraham offers up a ram as a burnt offering "instead of Isaac" (ἀντὶ Ἰσαάκ)
>
> **Ge 44:33** Judah offers to remain in Egypt as Joseph's slave "instead of the boy" (ἀντὶ τοῦ παιδίου; = Benjamin)

Ge 44:33 is hardly a compelling example that "shows how the sense 'in place of' can develop into **in behalf of, for**" (BDAG 88a). When Judah is addressing Joseph, he is acting on Benjamin's behalf, but when he offers to stay on in Egypt as Joseph's slave while Benjamin "returns with his brothers," there would seem to be only substitution expressed by ἀντί, although most cases of substitution also imply representation ("on behalf of, for"). This same BDAG section (#3), with the heading "[ἀντί] indicating a process of intervention," includes Mt 17:27; 20:28; Mk 10:45.

> **Ex 29:30** ὁ ἱερεὺς ὁ ἀντ' αὐτοῦ τῶν υἱῶν αὐτοῦ
>
> "the priest from his sons who succeeds him" (Aaron)/"the son who succeeds him as priest"
>
> **2Sa 19:1** (EVV, 18:33) Lamenting the death of his son Absalom, David says, "Would that I had died instead of you (ἀντὶ σοῦ), I instead of you (ἐγὼ ἀντὶ σοῦ)!"

2. Examples in the NT

Mt 2:22 Archelaus reigns over Judea "in the place of his father Herod" (ἀντὶ τοῦ πατρὸς αὐτοῦ Ἡρῴδου)

Lk 11:11 "a snake instead of a fish" (ἀντὶ ἰχθύος ὄφιν)

Jas 4:15 "instead of your saying" (ἀντὶ τοῦ λέγειν ὑμᾶς)

E. Important New Testament Uses

1. Matthew 17:27

Ἐκεῖνον [τὸν στατῆρα] λαβὼν δὸς αὐτοῖς ἀντὶ ἐμοῦ καὶ σοῦ

"Take it [the stater] and give it to them [the collectors of the tax] for me and for you."

When a question was raised about Jesus' payment of the double drachma (= half a shekel) temple tax that was required each year of all adult Jewish males (Ex 30:13–16), Jesus directed Peter to give the collectors the stater (a Greek silver coin worth four drachmas = one shekel) he would find in the mouth of the first fish he caught, to avoid unnecessary offense to the Jewish authorities (Mt 17:24–27).

It is tempting to take ἀντὶ ἐμου καὶ σοῦ as an example of ἀντί replacing ὑπέρ and meaning "on behalf of" (BDAG 88a; Moule 71; Turner 258; *Insights* 173; F. Büchsel, *TDNT* 1:372). But this would be to overlook the OT background of the temple tax in Ex 30:11–16 (see below, "c. Possible OT Backgrounds") where the half-shekel tax is instituted and is described as "an atoning payment for himself" (the contributor) or "a ransom for his life" (Heb., *kōper napšô*; LXX, λύτρα τῆς ψυχῆς αὐτοῦ) (Ex 30:12) and as "the money of atoning payments" or "atonement money" (Heb., *kesep hakkippurîm*; LXX, τὸ ἀργύριον τῆς εἰσφορᾶς, "the money of the contribution"; Ex 30:16). This atonement money was apparently seen as a redemption tax either to redeem the payee from hypothetical slavery (Turner, *Insights* 173) or "to absolve the lives of the people from the divine wrath" (cf. Ex 30:12b).[1] For the ongoing association between this tax and ideas of atonement and ransom, see Neh 10:32–33; Josephus, *Ant.* 18.9.1; Philo, *De spec. leg.* 1.14.77 ("this contribution is called their ransom"); *m. Šeqal.* 3–4; *t. Šeqal.* 1.6 (the public sacrifices made from the half-shekel offerings "effect atonement between Israel and their Father in heaven").

I suggest that in Mt 17:27 ἀντί replaces the simple dative (of advantage) (see above, ch. 2 A) and so avoids three successive datives (i.e., αὐτοῖς ἐμοὶ καὶ σοί) and the whole phrase may be rendered "for me and for you" or "for my tax and

---

1. R. E. Davies, "Christ in Our Place—the Contribution of the Prepositions," *TynBul* 21 (1970): 79.

yours" (NIV). But then in answer to the natural question, "Why is ἀντί used and not the expected ὑπέρ or even περί?" we may suggest, further, that ἀντί alludes to the substitutionary implications of the temple tax as outlined above.

2. Mark 10:45[2] (= Matthew 20:28)

καὶ γὰρ [Μt ὥσπερ] ὁ υἱὸς τοῦ ἀνθρώπου οὐκ ἦλθεν διακονηθῆναι ἀλλὰ διακονῆσαι καὶ δοῦναι τὴν ψυχὴν αὐτοῦ λύτρον ἀντὶ πολλῶν

"For even the Son of Man did not come to be served but to serve and (in particular) to give his life a ransom for many."

a. The Meaning of Λύτρον

Everyone in the first century AD would have known about the emancipation of a slave or the freeing of a prisoner by the payment of a λύτρον, "the purchase price for release" (cf. Deissmann 327; Spicq 2:426; Horsley 3:72–75): the slave or prisoner was set free because a substitutionary payment had been made. The cognate verb λυτρόομαι means "set free by paying a ransom." Probably the closest extrabiblical parallel to the expression λύτρον ἀντί is found in Josephus, Ant. 14.107–8: Eleazar the priest gave the Roman general Crassus a gold bar "as a ransom for all [the ornaments of the temple]" (λύτρον ἀντὶ πάντων), in the hope that Crassus would keep his oath and not remove anything else out of the temple; the gold bar was offered "instead of" the ornaments.

Of the 19 uses of λύτρον in the LXX, 16 are in the plural. On the six occasions λύτρον/λύτρα renders the Hebrew kōper ("life-price, ransom, atoning payment"; Ex 21:30; 30:12; Nu 35:31, 32; Pr 6:35; 13:8), the substitutionary offering is always for a human life (ψυχή) (cf. F. Büchsel, TDNT 4:329).

b. The Parallel in 1 Timothy 2:6

| Mk 10:45 | καὶ | δοῦναι τὴν ψυχὴν αὐτοῦ λύτρον | ἀντὶ πολλῶν |
| 1Ti 2:6 | ὁ | δοὺς ἑαυτὸν | ἀντίλυτρον ὑπὲρ πάντων |

From the above comparison it is clear that (1) the 1 Timothy form of the saying is based on Mark's version; (2) ἡ ψυχὴ αὐτοῦ refers to the whole person, the self; (3) the preposition ἀντί has been taken to imply substitution—hence the apparent coinage ἀντίλυτρον ("vicarious ransom"), which has only late attestation; (4) πολλοί has been rightly understood to mean "all" (as opposed to "one" [cf. Mk 14:24; Ro 5:15, 19], rather than "many" as opposed to "few"); (5) with ἀντι- already accenting the idea of substitution (K. Kertelge, EDNT 2:366), the "more colourless" (Moulton 105) ὑπέρ is used.

---

2. On the authenticity of Mk 10:45, see S. H. T. Page, "The Authenticity of the Ransom Logion (Mark 10:45b)," in Gospel Perspectives 1 (ed. R. T. France and D. Wenham; Sheffield: JSOT, 1980), 137–61.

c. Possible OT Backgrounds

No one OT passage affords the key to the meaning of the ransom saying but it is richly allusive and seems to be deliberately so.

(1) Isaiah 52:13–53:12 (the Fourth "Servant Song")[3]

Although neither διάκονος/διακονέω nor λύτρον appears in Isa 53, there are several distinct echoes of this chapter in the ransom saying.

(a) Δοῦναι τὴν ψυχὴν αὐτοῦ is similar to παρεδόθη εἰς θάνατον ἡ ψυχὴ αὐτοῦ (53:12 LXX).

(b) The reference to the "many" is a distinctive feature of Isa 53:11–12 (πολλοῖς, πολλούς, πολλῶν).

(c) Λύτρον ἀντί and ’āšām ("guilt offering"; Isa 53:10) have in common the idea of a compensatory or substitutionary payment.

(d) Διακονῆσαι is an apt summary of the role of the Servant of Yahweh, although Mk 10:45 does not translate any part of Isa 52:13–53:12.

(e) Mk 10:43–44 shows that διάκονος and δοῦλος can be synonymous and Isa 53:11 has δίκαιον εὖ δουλεύοντα πολλοῖς.

(f) The fourth Servant Song (Isa 52:13–53:12) is cited in Mt 8:17 (Isa 53:4) while Mt 26:28 seems to allude to Isa 53:12; Mt 27:12 to Isa 53:7; Mt 27:57 to Isa 53:9; while Mk 14:24 ("This represents my blood of the covenant that is poured out for many [τὸ ἐκχυννόμενον ὑπὲρ πολλῶν]") reflects Isa 53:12 (MT), "he poured out his life unto death … he bore the sin of many."

(2) Exodus 30:11–16

In Yahweh's instructions to Moses regarding the census tax of a half-shekel, it is twice said that the payment is "to make atonement for yourselves" (ἐξιλάσασθαι περὶ τῶν ψυχῶν ὑμῶν, vv. 15–16), twice that it is "an offering for the Lord" (εἰσφορὰ κυρίῳ, vv. 13–14), and once it is described as "a [person's] ransom to the Lord for oneself" (λύτρα τῆς ψυχῆς αὐτοῦ τῷ κυρίῳ, v. 12).

(3) Psalm 49:7–9 (MT)

"No one can redeem the life of another or give to God a **ransom** (kōper) for him; the ransom for a life is costly, no payment is ever enough, that someone should live on for ever and not see decay."

What a person cannot do for anyone else—redeem one's life by paying God a costly ransom—the Son of Man did for "many" when he redeemed their

---

3. On the relation of Isa 53 to Mk 10:45, see R. E. Watts, "Jesus' Death, Isaiah 53, and Mark 10:45: A Crux Revisited," in *Jesus and the Suffering Servant: Isaiah 53 and Christian Origins* (ed. W. H. Bellinger Jr. and W. R. Farmer; Harrisburg, PA: Trinity International, 1998), 125–51.

forfeited lives through the sacrifice of his own. Their impotence was matched by his competence.

What ingredients do these three OT passages contribute to the concept of a substitutionary ransom in Mk 10:45?

Isa 53: The ransom involved the voluntary death of the Servant and his vicarious bearing of the sins of many.

Ex 30: The ransom is paid to God and made atonement for the people.

Ps 49: The ransom was costly and beyond the means of any human.

d. The Significance of Ἀντί

By its very nature a λύτρον was some form of payment, whether monetary or nonmonetary, that was made by one person to another. By one party or by both, the ransom was regarded as an equivalent to the thing or person being set free or the bond being cancelled and therefore as an adequate substitute. What λύτρον already implies, ἀντί simply reinforces—the idea of vicariousness. In this ransom saying the distinctive and predominant substitutionary sense of ἀντί applies—"for" in the sense of "in the place of."

e. Conclusion

The general meaning of the ransom saying may be stated as follows. In service to God, Jesus surrendered his life and died as "a ransom in place of many" whose lives were unconditionally forfeited to God because of their sin but who were released from indebtedness to God and therefore from guilt by Jesus' payment of their ransom. He acted on behalf of (ὑπέρ) many by taking their place (ἀντί).

Strong support for the substitutionary significance of ἀντί in Mk 10:45/Mt 20:28 is found in three important dictionary articles: F. Büchsel, *TDNT* 4:340–49 (on λύτρον) ("The ransom saying undoubtedly implies substitution," 343); 1:372–73 (on ἀντί); H. Frankemölle, *EDNT,* 1:108b–9b (on ἀντί; "The death of Jesus is interpreted as a vicarious sacrifice of life, as a substitutionary offering for the life of the many which has been forfeited through their own guilt.... In Mark [10:45] and Matthew [20:28] the idea of the universal, vicarious atonement through Jesus is unquestionable," 1:109a, b).

3. John 1:16

ὅτι ἐκ τοῦ πληρώματος αὐτοῦ ἡμεῖς πάντες ἐλάβομεν καὶ χάριν ἀντὶ χάριτος

"for from the fullness of his grace we have all received"

Here the gospel writer is confirming (ὅτι) the accuracy of John the Baptist's testimony to the superiority of Jesus (v. 15) by appealing to the uniform experience of believers. All Christians have received a share of the fullness (πλήρωμα) of Christ, who himself is filled with grace (v. 14). That fullness of provision is then defined (epexegetic καί) as χάριν ἀντὶ χάριτος.

This phrase has been variously rendered: "grace in place of grace" (NAB[2]), "grace in place of grace already given" (TNIV, NIV[2]), "grace upon grace" (NRSV, REB), "grace after grace" (Moffatt, HCSB), "one blessing after another" (GNB, NIV[1], CEV), "blessing after blessing" (Goodspeed), "one favour in place of another" (Moule 71), "(new) grace instead of (old) grace" (Turner, *Insights* 173), "gift after gift of love" (TCNT).

Certainly more is implied than a single substitutionary exchange. Because the text reads χάριν … χάριτος (and not, e.g., χάριν … ἀντὶ νόμου), the reference is to "one blessing taking the place of another in succession" (Regard 68), to replenished grace, "grace uninterrupted, unceasingly renewed" (Winer 364), to a rapid and perpetual succession of blessings, as though there were no interval between the arrival of one blessing and the receipt of the next (although LSJ 153b sees ἀντί as marking comparison, "ever-increasing *grace*"). "God's favor comes in ever new streams" (BDAG 88a), or as Robertson puts it, "As the days come and go a new supply takes the place of the grace already bestowed as wave follows wave upon the shore" (574). The nature of the constantly renewed grace remains undefined but probably refers to the multiplied spiritual benefits of the new covenant (cf. v. 17). However, those who relate each χάρις to a particular blessing find an allusion to the new covenant instead of the old, or to the spiritual presence of the Holy Spirit instead of the physical presence of Jesus, or to God's presence in Christ instead of his presence in the *Shekinah*. Abbott, for example, takes John's meaning to be that the law of Moses, the first grace, was replaced by the second grace, "the grace of freedom, or sonship" (§2286, citing Origen and Chrysostom).

4. Hebrews 12:2

Ἰησοῦν, ὃς ἀντὶ τῆς προκειμένης αὐτῷ χαρᾶς ὑπέμεινεν σταυρὸν αἰσχύνης καταφρονήσας

"Jesus, who … endured the cross, scorning its shame"

The intervening prepositional phrase may be rendered in two basic ways.

(1) "For the sake of the joy that lay ahead of him" (NEB, REB; similarly most EVV, many having simply "for the joy," which could mean "to obtain" or "because of"). This may be paraphrased as "*in order to obtain* the joy in store for him as his recompense" (cf. Cassirer), that is, his future satisfaction in seeing "the light [of life]" after his suffering (Isa 53:11), the joy of seeing the outcome of his endurance of the cross.

(2) "In place of the joy that was open to him" (NEB mg, REB mg; similarly Goodspeed, "in place of the happiness that belonged to him," NRSV mg, NLT mg; Atkinson 7). This may be paraphrased as "*instead of* the joy of heavenly bliss, of continued fellowship with God in his immediate presence, that lay before the preincarnate Son as a distinct possibility within his grasp." It is

highly improbable that the χαρά refers to the earthly "happiness" of a life free of suffering.

This second alternative seems preferable for several reasons:

(a) the prevailing substitutionary sense ("instead of") of ἀντί (apart from the compounded form ἀνθ' ὧν) in Biblical Greek
(b) the use of πρόκειμαι in Heb 6:18; 12:1 to denote a present reality, not a future acquisition
(c) the inappropriateness of any hint of personal advantage or future reward as Jesus' primary motive for submitting to suffering
(d) BDAG opts for the translation "instead of" (88a, under ἀντί; 871b, under πρόκειμαι), as also J. Schneider, *TDNT* 7:577
(e) the idea of the voluntary renunciation of personal rights for the sake of others is a common NT sentiment (e.g., Mk 8:35; Ro 15:1–3; 1Co 9:19–23; 2Co 8:9; Php 2:6–8)

On this view the author is not speaking of Jesus' motivation for his endurance of crucifixion and his scorning of its disgrace, namely, to obtain joy, but of the disregard of personal advantage that was involved in his steady submission to the cross. Jesus was like Moses (Heb 11:25) in that he chose to ignore his own pleasure in order to achieve a higher good. Jesus was unlike Moses (Heb 11:26) in that his motive for enduring disgrace was not anticipation of a future reward.[4]

The analysis of the 22 NT uses of ἀντί leads to the conclusion that apart from the six instances where this preposition joins another word to form a virtual conjunction, it always expresses (15x) or alludes to (1x, Mt 17:27) a substitutionary exchange.

F. Ἀντί in Compounds

1. Oppositeness: ἀντιπαρέρχομαι, pass by (παρά) on the opposite side (of the road)/facing, ἀντί; cf. Lk 10:31–32. This sense naturally merges into "opposition."
2. Opposition: ἀντίδικος, opponent, plaintiff; ἀντικαθίστημι, oppose; ἀντίθεσις, contradiction. The adverb ἄντικρυς, opposite, serves as a preposition + genitive (Ac 20:15).
3. Reciprocity: ἀνταποδίδωμι, repay.
4. Correspondence: ἀντίτυπος, antitype.
5. Substitution: ἀνθύπατος, proconsul.

On the relation between ἀντί and ὑπέρ, see ch. 19 E-F.

---

4. See further, in defense of this understanding, P. Andriessen and A. Lenglet, "Quelques passages difficiles de l'Épître aux Hébreux (5:7, 11; 10:20; 12:2)," *Bib* 51 (1970): 219–20; P. Andriessen, "Renonçant à la joie qui lui revenait," *La nouvelle revue théologique* 107 (1975): 424–38.

Chapter 6

Ἀπό

A. Relation of Ἀπό to Ἐκ

Ἀπό (with 646 NT uses) ranks seventh among NT prepositions in frequency, but fourth in the LXX (see the chart, p. 32). As a prefix in compound verbs it ranks fifth. In general, when expressing spatial relations, ἀπό denotes motion from the edge or surface of an object; ἐκ, motion from within. "Ἀπό and ἐξ had, in the expression of source-motion, the same functions that πρός (to[wards]) and εἰς (into) could have in the expression of goal-motion" (Bortone 164). Both prepositions have partially eclipsed the classical genitive of separation (on which see Smyth §§1392–1400), although that usage is also found in the NT (e.g., Eph 2:12, ἀπαλλοτριοῦν τινος; 1 Ti 4:1, ἀφίστασθαί τινος). Often ἀπό marks simply the general point from which movement or action proceeds. Thus "Joseph went up from [ἀπό] Galilee, out of [ἐκ] the city of Nazareth" (Lk 2:4).

It is not at all clear (*pace* Abbott §2289) that John distinguishes between ἀπό denoting place of residence ("resident in") and ἐκ denoting place of origin ("native of"), for Jesus is ἐκ Galilee and ἀπό Bethlehem (Jn 7:41–42) and is both ἀπό and ἐκ heaven (Jn 6:33, 38; cf. BDF §209[3]). The fact that ἀπό is regularly used with ἔρχομαι in Luke (13x) shows that even the broad distinction between the two prepositions is not everywhere applicable. In fact, the process by which ἀπό ultimately absorbed ἐκ has already commenced in Hellenistic Greek (cf. Bortone 184–85); in Medieval Greek ἀπό and ἐκ are synonymous (Bortone 210–11). Jannaris suggests that the synonymy of ἀπό and ἐκ "naturally led to a complete identification, and in the further process of time ἀπό, owing to its phonodynamic superiority and vocalic ending … prevailed over ἐκ and ultimately ousted it from popular speech, though the struggle lasted as late as the XVIth century" (§1506).

So it is no surprise to find that the NT uses both prepositions in the following senses:

	ἀπό	ἐκ
1. temporal	Mt 11:12	Jn 9:1
2. causal	Mt 18:7; Lk 19:3; Acts 12:14	Jn 4:6; Rev 16:10–12
3. instrumental	Mt 11:19 = Lk 7:35	Lk 16:9; Jn 6:65
4. adverbial	2Co 1:14; 2:5	2Co 9:7
5. place of origin	Jn 1:44; 11:1	Jn 1:44; 11:1
6. membership	Ac 12:1; 15:5	Ac 6:9

This illustrates the general principle that "there is a tendency for similar or identical abstract meanings to occur in pairs of prepositions with (roughly) the same spatial meanings" (Bortone 150).

Such overlapping of function between ἀπό and ἐκ makes one hesitate to distinguish between the ἀναβαίνων ἐκ τοῦ ὕδατος of Mk 1:10 (cf. Acts 8:38–39) and the ἀνέβη ἀπὸ τοῦ ὕδατος of Mt 3:16 (similarly Bortone 185), as though the later Matthean tradition testified to baptism by affusion or aspersion rather than by immersion (in the Markan tradition). This, against the suggestion of Turner that Matthew's change from ἐκ to ἀπό "may indicate a development in the gospel tradition in the method of the [Jesus'] baptism" (*Insights* 29), but earlier he had remarked that "surely nothing different is intended" (Turner 259). Perhaps the most that may be confidently said, if the prepositions are here distinguishable, is that Matthew's ἀπό does not exclude Mark's ἐκ.

On the relation of ἀπό to ὑπό, see ch. 20 E. Jannaris speaks of "a struggle among ὑπό, ἀπό, παρά, and ἐξ, which resulted in the retreat and final disappearance, one after another, of ὑπό, παρά, and ἐξ, before the victorious ἀπό" (§1628; cf. Thumb §161). For the possible influence of the Hebrew preposition *min* on the NT use of ἀπό, see MH 460–62.

B. Ἀπὸ θεοῦ

1. 1 Corinthians 1:30

Ἐξ αὐτοῦ δὲ ὑμεῖς ἐστε ἐν Χριστῷ Ἰησοῦ, ὃς ἐγενήθη σοφία ἡμῖν **ἀπὸ θεοῦ**, δικαιοσύνη τε καὶ ἁγιασμὸς καὶ ἀπολύτρωσις.

"It is as a result of his [God's] action that you have your existence in Christ Jesus, who, as God's gift, became wisdom for us, that is, both our righteousness and sanctification — our redemption" (cf. BDAG 117c).

This translation is based on four assumptions.

(1) Ὑμεῖς ἐστε is to be accented ὑμεῖς ἐστέ (WH 1:379) and construed with ἐν Χριστῷ Ἰησοῦ, rather than ὑμεῖς ἐστε and construed with ἐξ αὐτοῦ ("you are his [God's] children by being in Christ Jesus"). After

being "nonentities" or "nothings" (τὰ μὴ ὄντα, 1Co 1:28) in human estimation (κατὰ σάρκα, 1Co 1:26), the Corinthians had become "somethings" in Christ Jesus through God's redemptive action.

(2) Ἀπὸ θεοῦ should be taken with ἐγενήθη ... ἡμῖν, rather than with σοφία ("wisdom coming from God").

(3) Ἡμῖν is a dative of advantage ("for our benefit"), and δικαιοσύνη κτλ. is in epexegetic apposition to σοφία.

(4) Ἀπό echoes ἐξ, both prepositions depicting God as a causal source:
- Christians' existence in Christ Jesus is God's doing
- Christ's becoming wisdom for believers' benefit is God's doing.

2. James 1:13

Μηδεὶς πειραζόμενος λεγέτω ὅτι Ἀπὸ θεοῦ πειράζομαι· ὁ γὰρ θεὸς ἀπείραστός ἐστιν κακῶν, πειράζει δὲ αὐτὸς οὐδένα.

"When tempted, no one should say, 'My temptation comes from God,' for God is incapable of being tempted by evil; indeed, he himself tempts no one."

In light of v. 13b (πειράζει δὲ αὐτὸς οὐδένα), it is appealing to regard ἀπὸ θεοῦ as equivalent to ὑπὸ θεοῦ ("I am being tempted by God," NRSV, NASB[2], HCSB; or "God is tempting me," NLT, NIV[1,2]) since ἀπό sometimes expresses agency with a passive verb (e.g., Acts 4:36, TR ὑπό; cf. Jannaris §1507, citing Jas 1:13). But elsewhere in James ἀπό expresses source (Jas 1:17; 5:4) or separation (Jas 1:27; 4:7; 5:19), so we should assume, not that here ἀπό = ὑπό, but rather that ἀπό probably has its most common nonspatial meaning—source or origin. But it is a case of "indirect origination" (BDAG 107b); Webster (152, citing Jas 1:13), less appropriately, calls this usage "subordinate agency." Winer renders the phrase "*I am tempted* (through influences proceeding) *from God*" (371 n.1). "The temptation is caused by God, though not actually carried out by God" (BDAG 107b).

In this verse, then, James is affirming that God is never the originator of any enticement to do wrong, whether acting directly (Jas 1:13b) or indirectly (Jas 1:13a).

Other examples of ἀπό expressing "indirect origination" (and often suitably rendered by "at the hands of" or "on the part of") include the following.

Mt 11:19 ἐδικαιώθη ἡ σοφία ἀπὸ τῶν ἔργων αὐτῆς

Mt 16:21 (= Lk 9:22; Mk 8:31 has ὑπό) πολλὰ παθεῖν ἀπὸ τῶν πρεσβυτέρων κτλ.

Lk 17:25 ἀποδοκιμασθῆναι ἀπὸ τῆς γενεᾶς ταύτης

Ac 12:20 διὰ τὸ τρέφεσθαι αὐτῶν τὴν χώραν ἀπὸ τῆς βασιλικῆς [χώρας]

Jas 5:4 ὁ μισθὸς τῶν ἐργατῶν ... ὁ ἀπεστερημένος **ἀφ᾿ ὑμῶν**
Rev 12:6 τόπον ἡτοιμασμένον **ἀπὸ** τοῦ θεοῦ
(possibly) **Ro 9:3** ηὐχόμην γὰρ ἀνάθεμα εἶναι αὐτὸς ἐγὼ **ἀπὸ** τοῦ Χριστοῦ

3. 2 Peter 1:21

Οὐ γὰρ θελήματι ἀνθρώπου ἠνέχθη προφητεία ποτέ, ἀλλὰ ὑπὸ πνεύματος ἁγίου φερόμενοι ἐλάλησαν **ἀπὸ θεοῦ** ἄνθρωποι.

"For no prophecy ever originated in human impulse, but prophets, though human, spoke words from God as they were carried along by the Holy Spirit."

The best proto-Alexandrian witnesses ($\mathfrak{P}^{72}$ B 1739) read ἀπὸ θεοῦ. The reading ἅγιοι θεοῦ (ἄνθρωποι), "holy men of God" (ℵ K Ψ 33 *Byz*), probably arose from palaeographical confusion (ΑΠΟΘΥ → ΑΓΙΟΙΘΥ) (cf. Metzger 632).

In 2Pe 1:20–21 Peter is affirming the divine inspiration of OT prophecy against opponents who apparently argued that OT prophecies were simply the product of prophets' own interpretation (2Pe 1:20) of their signs or visions or dreams. Peter's rejoinder is that though the prophets were mere humans, they delivered messages that came directly from God, all the while being swept along (cf. the sense of φέρομαι in Ac 27:15, 17) or impelled by God's Spirit.

Ἀπὸ θεοῦ belongs with ἐλάλησαν, not with ἄνθρωποι; "men from God" would require ἄνθρωποι *οἱ* ἀπὸ θεου. The dramatic juxtaposition of θεοῦ and ἄνθρωποι is emphatic: prophecy had its origin in God, not in mere human reflection. The unexpressed object of ἐλάλησαν is probably τὰ (ἀπὸ θεοῦ) (this combination occurs in Mt 16:23; 22:21), "words from God," although if ἀπό is simply a stylistic variation of the earlier ὑπό, it could mean "by God's power" or "under God's inspiration." However ἀπό is taken, the two prepositions ἀπό and ὑπό introduce a twofold emphasis on the divine origin of OT prophecy.

C. Ellipses with (Pregnant) Ἀπό
1. After Transitive Verbs
Jn 21:10 "Bring [some] of the fishes" (ἐνέγκατε **ἀπὸ** τῶν ὀψαρίων)
Ac 2:17–18 "I will pour out [a portion of] my Spirit" (ἐκχεῶ **ἀπὸ** τοῦ πνεύματός μου).

2. With the Notion of Separation or Severance or Alienation (BDF §211) Implied
Ro 9:3 ηὐχόμην γὰρ ἀνάθεμα εἶναι αὐτὸς ἐγὼ **ἀπὸ** τοῦ Χριστοῦ.

"Indeed, I could wish that I myself were cursed [and cut off] from Christ" (similarly most EVV).

Ηὐχόμην is a "potential" imperfect (Robertson 886; *Pictures* 4:380), replacing the classical potential optative (εὐξαίμην ἄν, Ac 26:29) and expressing an unattainable wish (BDR §359[5]). "I could almost pray" (Turner 65). So eager was Paul for the salvation of his Jewish compatriots that he would have been willing to be eternally damned and to forfeit his relationship to Christ if such a wish were permissible and could achieve their salvation.

2Co 11:3 φοβοῦμαι δὲ μή πως ... φθαρῇ τὰ νοήματα ὑμῶν **ἀπὸ τῆς** ἁπλότητος καὶ τῆς ἁγνότητος τῆς εἰς τὸν Χριστόν
"But I am afraid that ... your minds may somehow be corrupted [and lured away] from your single-mindedness and your purity in relation to Christ."

The main danger confronting the Corinthian church was intellectual deception—their adulterous flirting with a false gospel (2Co 11:4c) and their countenancing of a different Jesus and an alien Spirit (2Co 11:4a-b). If such deception took place, the casualty would be their singleness of outlook and purpose and their original virginity as a church betrothed to Christ, her heavenly bridegroom and one husband (2Co 11:2).

Col 2:20 εἰ ἀπεθάνετε σὺν Χριστῷ **ἀπὸ** τῶν στοιχείων τοῦ κόσμου
"if you died with Christ [and were thus freed] from the elemental spirits of the universe"

Christians' baptismal identification with Christ in his crucifixion (Ro 6:3, 5, 8) effects deliverance from the control of the στοιχεῖα, severing bondage to their malevolent and enslaving influence (Gal 4:8–9).

2Th 1:9 οἵτινες δίκην τίσουσιν ὄλεθρον αἰώνιον **ἀπὸ** προσώπου τοῦ κυρίου καὶ **ἀπὸ** τῆς δόξης τῆς ἰσχύος αὐτοῦ
"These people will be punished with everlasting destruction, [being excluded] from the presence of the Lord and the mighty glory that is his."

At his second advent the Lord Jesus will execute vengeance (διδόντος ἐκδίκησιν) on those who have no knowledge of God and refuse to submit to the gospel (2Th 1:8), with that punishment defined in v. 9 as eternal ruin, involving banishment from his presence (cf. Mt 7:23; 25:41) and from his mighty glory. There will be both retribution (ἐκδίκησιν ... ὄλεθρον αἰώνιον) and deprivation (ἀπό ... ἀπό ...).

In two cases there seems to be an ellipsis *after* ἀπό. Mt 1:21, αὐτὸς γὰρ σώσει τὸν λαὸν αὐτοῦ **ἀπὸ** τῶν ἁμαρτιῶν αὐτῶν: "For he will save his people from [the consequences of] their sins." Ac 2:40, σώθητε **ἀπὸ** τῆς γενεᾶς τῆς σκολιᾶς ταύτης: "Rescue yourselves from the doom awaiting this crooked generation" (Cassirer).

D. Ἀπό in Paul's Epistolary Salutations

Eight of Paul's letters (Ro 1:7; 1Co 1:3; 2Co 1:2; Gal 1:3; Eph 1:2; Php 1:2; 2Th 1:2; Phm 3) begin with a standard salutation:

Χάρις ὑμῖν καὶ εἰρήνη **ἀπὸ** θεοῦ πατρὸς ἡμῶν καὶ κυρίου Ἰησοῦ Χριστοῦ

In 1Ti 1:2 and 2Ti 1:2, Paul addresses an individual, and (i) there is no ὑμῖν; (ii) it reads χάρις ἔλεος εἰρήνη before ἀπὸ θεοῦ πατρός; and (iii) it ends with καὶ Χριστοῦ Ἰησοῦ τοῦ κυρίου ἡμῶν. Tit 1:4 also has no ὑμῖν, but reads χάρις καὶ εἰρήνη before ἀπὸ θεοῦ πατρός and ends καὶ Χριστοῦ Ἰησοῦ τοῦ σωτῆρος ἡμῶν. In 1Th 1:1 we read simply χάρις ὑμῖν καὶ εἰρήνη. So then, *a single ἀπό stands before two coordinated proper names on 11 occasions.* The theological significance of this fact is twofold.

(1) The absence of ἀπό before the second unit, which ἀπό also governs, does not indicate that God the Father and the Lord Jesus Christ are one and the same person (as though καί were epexegetic), since Paul always distinguishes the person of the Father from the person of the Son. In this regard, compare 2Jn 3 (ἔσται μεθ' ἡμῶν χάρις ἔλεος εἰρήνη **παρὰ** θεοῦ πατρὸς **καὶ παρὰ** Ἰησοῦ Χριστοῦ τοῦ υἱοῦ τοῦ πατρός), where the repetition of the preposition serves to emphasize the distinctiveness and duality of the sources (cf. the threefold ἀπό in Rev 1:4–5; see below).

(2) The single ἀπό standing before both personal names points to the unity and singularity of the source. God the Father and the Lord Jesus Christ jointly form a single source of divine grace, mercy, and peace. They sustain a single relation—not two diverse relations, such as source and channel—to the grace and peace that come to believers. A monotheistic Jew would never claim that a mere human being, together with God, is a fount of spiritual blessing; the deity of Christ is thus implicitly affirmed.

E. Other Notable Instances

1. Luke 24:31

αὐτῶν δὲ διηνοίχθησαν οἱ ὀφθαλμοὶ καὶ ἐπέγνωσαν αὐτόν· καὶ αὐτὸς ἄφαντος ἐγένετο ἀπ' αὐτῶν

"Then their eyes were opened and they recognized him. And he became invisible and parted from them."

Although γίνεσθαι ἀπό τινος can mean "withdraw from someone," ἄφαντος cannot here be adverbial: "he withdrew from them without being seen." Accordingly, ἐγένετο must be construed with ἄφαντος ("he became invisible"). This adjective is not found elsewhere in the Greek Bible. The more common adjective ἀφανής occurs with γενέσθαι in 2 Macc 3:34 of angels disappearing, and the cognate verb ἀφανίζειν is used with ἀπό in Ex 8:5 (LXX): "Moses said to

Pharaoh, 'Set a time for me, when I might pray for you and your servants and your people in order to **cause** the frogs **to disappear** from you and your people [ἀπὸ σοῦ καὶ ἀπὸ τοῦ λαοῦ σου].' " Here ἀπό seems to mean "from the sight of."

Ἀπ᾽ αὐτῶν in Lk 24:31 can be taken in three ways.

(1) "[He vanished] from their sight" (so many EVV), where ἀπ᾽ αὐτῶν = ἀπὸ τῶν ὀφθαλμῶν αὐτῶν (Ac 1:9). The Vulgate has *evanuit ex oculis eorum*, "he vanished from their eyes."

(2) In Ac 10:40 the expression ἐμφανῆς γενέσθαι ("to become visible") occurs: "God raised Him up on the third day and granted that He become visible," NASB[2]. Significantly, this phrase is followed (in Ac 10:41) by two datives: οὐ παντὶ τῷ λαῷ, ἀλλὰ μάρτυσιν κτλ. This suggests that in Lk 24:31 ἀπ᾽ αὐτῶν may stand for αὐτοῖς, "he became invisible to them."

(3) Perhaps here too we have an ellipsis after ἀπό: "he became invisible [and parted] from them" (διέστη ἀπ᾽ αὐτῶν, Lk 24:51). This also has the advantage of retaining the literal meaning of ἄφαντος ἐγένετο: "he became invisible" was the means by which he "vanished," or suddenly disappeared, from their sight.

Ἄφαντος γενέσθαι is the opposite of ἐμφανῆς γενέσθαι. Both of these expressions, unique in the Greek Bible, are found in statements about the resurrected Jesus. Apparently one of the earthly characteristics of the resurrection body of Jesus was his ability to become visible or invisible at will.

2. 1 Corinthians 11:23

Ἐγὼ γὰρ παρέλαβον ἀπὸ [D E have παρά] τοῦ κυρίου, ὃ καὶ παρέδωκα ὑμῖν, ὅτι ὁ κύριος Ἰησοῦς ...

"For I received from the Lord what I also passed on to you, that the Lord Jesus ..."

The issue here is whether Paul received the narrative of the institution of the Lord's Supper (1Co 11:23–25) by a *tradition* that reached him "from the Lord" through an unbroken and reliable transmission, or by a special *revelation* from the Lord himself. Clearly there was a threefold chain: the Lord (ὁ κύριος) – Paul (ἐγώ) – the Corinthians (ὑμῖν); but were there intermediaries between the Lord and Paul?

Several observations are relevant.

(1) Contrary to the view of some, the matter is not settled by the preposition used, as though ἀπό implies a greater distance from a source than does παρά. It is true that παρά often implies immediate communication in Paul's letters (e.g., 1Th 2:13; 4:1) and elsewhere (e.g., Jn 8:40; 10:18; Ac 10:22), but ἀπό also can be used of direct, unmediated relations (e.g., Col 1:7 and Mt 11:29; 1Jn 1:5). Moreover, Paul may have used ἀπό in 1Co 11:23 to avoid a threefold use of παρά.

(2) The prominent presence of ἐγώ and the singular παρέλαβον, as opposed

to the plural παρελάβομεν, point to a strong personal element in the receipt of the information.

(3) That intermediaries were involved in Paul's "receiving" is suggested by the two verbs παραλαμβάνω (= Heb. *qibbēl*) and παραδίδωμι (= Heb. *māsar*), which were technical terms for the transmission of tradition.

Perhaps it is not necessary to choose between tradition and revelation. If the factual content about the institution of the Lord's Supper came to Paul via the apostles or others (cf. Gal 1:18–19), there still could have been a confirmation or explanation of that content by a direct revelation to Paul through some unspecified means such as a vision, so that he could accurately say he received the tradition ἀπὸ τοῦ κυρίου, understandably overlooking the human intermediaries; but he had not received the information δι᾽ ἀποκαλύψεως Ἰησοῦ Χριστοῦ ("by a revelation from Jesus Christ"), as he had the gospel (Gal 1:11–12). If there had been no specific divine element, he could have said simply παρέλαβον, as in 1Co 15:3.

3. 2 Corinthians 3:18

ἡμεῖς δὲ πάντες ἀνακεκαλυμμένῳ προσώπῳ τὴν δόξαν κυρίου κατοπτριζόμενοι τὴν αὐτὴν εἰκόνα μεταμορφούμεθα **ἀπὸ** δόξης εἰς δόξαν καθάπερ **ἀπὸ** κυρίου πνεύματος

"And all of us, with unveiled faces, looking at the glory of the Lord as in a mirror, are being transformed into the same image, from one degree of glory to another. Appropriately, this transformation comes from the Lord who is the Spirit."

The progressive nature of the Christian's present transformation is expressed by the phrase **ἀπὸ** δόξης εἰς δόξαν. If ἀπό denotes source and εἰς result, there are several possible identifications of this beginning and this end:

- *from* the splendor of the Lord *to* the splendor of the believer
- *from* initial glory already received through regeneration *to* final glory to be gained at the parousia
- *from* glory beheld *to* glory reflected

If, however, the two prepositions together express the nature or direction of the μεταμόρφωσις, the meaning will be:

- "with ever-increasing glory" (NIV[1,2], REB), or
- "from one degree of glory to another" (RSV, NRSV)

On this latter view (which is to be preferred), there is a stark contrast between the radiance on Moses' face that gradually faded (2Co 3:7, 13) and the glory of the Lord, now reflected in believers' lives, which gradually increases. Justified at regeneration, believers are progressively sanctified until they finally bear the likeness of "the man from heaven" (Ro 8:29–30; 12:2; 1Co 15:49; 2Co 4:16;

Col 3:10) in a transformed, resurrection body suffused with divine glory (1Co 15:43–44). For Paul, "transformation," like salvation, was past (Gal 2:20; 3:27), present (Ro 12:2), and future (1Co 15:51; Php 3:21).

The origin (ἀπό) of this progressive transformation of the Christian into Christ's likeness is "the Lord who is the Spirit" (Goodspeed, RSV, NAB[1], NJB, NAB[2], REB). Less probably, ἀπό could denote agency or cause. If we take v. 17a to mean "Now this 'Lord' [= 'Yahweh' in Ex 34:34] is in the present era experienced as the Spirit," v. 18c may be seen as a restatement of this affirmation: "[This transformation comes from] the Lord [= Yahweh], who is [now experienced as] the Spirit." The new era is the era of the Spirit, for as a result of conversion to the Spirit (vv. 16–17a), there is liberation through the Spirit (v. 17b), and also transformation originating (ἀπό) in the work of the Spirit (v. 18).

4. Hebrews 5:7

εἰσακουσθεὶς ἀπὸ τῆς εὐλαβείας

There are two interrelated issues here: whether εὐλάβεια refers to Jesus' anxious fear or to his reverent piety; and whether ἀπό is locatival, meaning "from" (after an ellipsis supplied from the preceding σῴζειν, "and thus was rescued"; cf. ἀπό in Col 2:20), or causal, "because."

Two possible translations emerge from these options.

"He [Jesus] was heard

(1) [and rescued] **from fear** [of death]

(2) **because of his godly fear**"[1]

Translation (2) is to be preferred for several reasons.

(a) It is difficult to justify the meaning "fear" for εὐλάβεια (see LSJ 720a).

(b) "Fear of death" is expressed in Heb 2:15 by φόβος θανάτου. And had Jesus succumbed in any measure to such fear, with divine deliverance being needed and given to him in answer to his prayers, it is difficult to see how he himself could bring deliverance to those enslaved by fear of death. Jesus was never overtaken by a fear of dying, but he was "overwhelmed by sorrow … to the point of death" (ἕως θανάτου, Mk 14:34), not by fear as he faced death.

(c) In the only other NT use of εὐλάβεια (Heb 12:28), it is joined to δέος ("awe, godly fear"), perhaps forming a hendiadys: μετὰ εὐλαβείας καὶ δέους, "with reverential awe." LSJ (720a) renders the word by "godly fear" in both Heb 5:7 and 12:28 (similarly BDAG 407c). In Heb 11:7 the cognate verb (εὐλαβέομαι, a NT *hapax legomenon*) refers to Noah's reverent regard for God (cf. the use of

---

1. Alternative interpretations are unconvincing: that ἀπὸ τῆς εὐλαβείας is to be construed with the following ἔμαθεν ("he learned obedience from his anxiety, from what he suffered"); that ἀπό is temporal ("he was heard after experiencing anguish"); that we must assume a scribal omission of an original οὐκ before εἰσακουσθείς ("he was not heard in spite of his fear").

this verb in Na 1:7) or possibly his pious attentiveness to the divine will, not to any apprehension (cf. BDAG 407d) about the impending flood or general cautiousness. Also the Lukan adjective εὐλαβής (Lk 2:25; Ac 2:5; 8:2; 22:12) means "God-fearing."

(d) It is true that in none of the other 22 uses of ἀπό in Hebrews does this preposition bear the sense of "because," but such usage is not uncommon in Classical Greek (see LSJ 192b, s.v. III.6) and the LXX (e.g., Ge 9:11; Nu 22:3; Ps 75:7; see Johannessohn 2:281–82), it is found elsewhere in the NT (e.g., Mt 14:26; Lk 22:45; Jn 21:6; Ac 22:11), and it is common in Modern Greek (e.g., γίνεται ἀπὸ ἀνάγκη, "it happens of necessity"; see Thumb §161.5). A causal sense for ἀπό in Heb 5:7 is recognized by BDAG 106c; Robertson 580; MH 461; ZG 663; Turner, *Style* 111, and earlier Turner 251 (tentatively); not by BDF §211, but cf. §210 (1) and BDR §210[1]; but by many commentators and EVV. The Vulgate, too, has *exauditus est pro sua reverentia*.

If ἀπό is causal, the probable sense of the verse is this. In answer to Jesus' anguished prayers, God delivered him, not from actual death although he had the power to do so, but from the permanent grip of death through his resurrection (Heb 13:20; cf. Ro 6:9, Χριστὸς ἐγερθεὶς ἐκ νεκρῶν οὐκέτι ἀποθνῄσκει, θάνατος αὐτοῦ οὐκέτι κυριεύει). "He was heard on account of his reverent submission" to the will of his Father (Mk 14:36). "The main result of Jesus' entreaty had been achieved, namely, conformity to his Father's will" (Zerwick, *Analysis* 499).

5. Revelation 1:4–5

> Χάρις ὑμῖν καὶ εἰρήνη **ἀπὸ** ὁ ὢν καὶ ὁ ἦν καὶ ὁ ἐρχόμενος
> καὶ **ἀπὸ** τῶν ἑπτὰ πνευμάτων ...
> καὶ **ἀπὸ** Ἰησοῦ Χριστοῦ

"Grace and peace to you from him who is, and who was, and who is to come, and from the seven spirits ... and from Jesus Christ."

This salutation is unique in the NT in that:

(1) It is trinitarian (assuming "the seven spirits" or "the sevenfold Spirit" refers to the Holy Spirit).
(2) God the Father is not named.
(3) The Holy Spirit is included as a source of "grace and peace."
(4) Ἀπό is repeated before each source (cf. 2Jn 3).
(5) The nominative follows ἀπό in the first line.

This latter feature, remarkable as it is, was clearly intended by the author, because the second and third lines have the expected genitive, and he could have written ἀπὸ **τοῦ** ὁ ὢν κτλ., ("from the one called 'He who is'"), which would have been perfectly acceptable Greek, even if awkward. Various explanations have been given for this apparent solecism.

(1) The seer's reverence for the divine name (see Ex 3:14) kept him back from submitting it to declensional change.[2]

(2) The phrase ὁ ὤν κτλ. is a paraphrase of the indeclinable tetragrammaton YHWH.[3]

(3) It is a nominative apposition that was originally preceded by four dots standing for the tetragrammaton: that is, ἀπὸ . . . . ὁ ὤν became ἀπὸ ὁ ὤν, which was then shortened to ἀπὸ ὁ ὤν κτλ. by subsequent copyists for whom the space was meaningless.[4]

*(4) The easiest and most common explanation is that this threefold title of Yahweh is an indeclinable noun that by its very form effectively highlights the unchangeable and eternal character of God.

The same threefold title of God is found in Rev 1:8 and in 4:8 (with ὁ ὤν and ὁ ἦν transposed) and without ὁ ἐρχόμενος in Rev 11:17; 16:5. Ὁ ἦν is used because there is no past particple of εἰμί; it is used instead of ὅς ἦν to preserve the titular parallelism; and the forms ὁ γεγονώς or ὁ γενόμενος would be open to the misinterpretation that God had "come into being." Ὁ ἐρχόμενος was preferred over ὁ ἐσόμενος ("the one who will [always] be"), the rare future participle of εἰμί, since there is a sense in which God himself "comes" in the coming of Christ (see Rev 1:7; 22:7, 12).

F. Ἀπό in Compounds

About 40 of the 90 NT verbal compounds with ἀπό have the local force of "off/away" (MH 297).

1. Separation: ἀποκόπτω, cut off/away; ἀπεκδύομαι, strip off, disarm
2. Return: ἀποδίδωμι, give back; ἀποκαθιστάνω, restore
3. Perfectivizing: ἀποτέλεω, finish; ἀπεκδέχομαι, await eagerly
4. Liberation: ἀπολύω, release; ἀπολύτρωσις, a buying back, a setting free, redemption; ἀπελεύθερος, freed person
5. Departure: ἀποβαίνω, go away
6. Cessation: ἀποψύχω, stop breathing

---

2. R. H. Charles, *The Revelation of St. John* (Edinburgh: T&T Clark, 1920), 1:10.
3. J. M. Ford, *Revelation* (AB; Garden City, NY: Doubleday, 1975), 376.
4. G. Mussies, *The Morphology of Koine Greek as Used in the Apocalypse of St. John* (Leiden: Brill, 1971), 93–94.

Chapter 7

Διά

A. Origin and Basic Idea

With its 668 NT uses, διά ranks sixth in frequency among NT "proper" prepositions (see the chart on p. 32).

There is uncertainty about the origin of **διά**, which has "no clear Indo-European etymon" (Bortone 140 n.56; cf. 158 n.78). Robertson suggests it originated from δύο, "two," which developed into the idea of "in two"/"between" (cf. Ac 15:9, where μεταξύ ["between"] explains δι[-έκρινεν]), pointing to an interval when used in expressions of time. Accordingly, δι᾽ ἡμερῶν (Mk 2:1) means "days between, after some days" (Robertson 580–81; cf. Bortone 167 n.88). An alternative proposal is that διά originally signified "passing through and out from," a sense reflected in Mt 4:4 ("every word that proceeds from [ἐκπορευομένῳ διά] the mouth of God") and 1Co 3:15 ("he himself will be saved, but only as one who escapes through fire," διὰ πυρός); cf. Lk 18:25. When this notion of "extension through" is applied to temporal categories, the meaning is "during the course of" (e.g., διὰ νυκτός, Ac 23:31).

Whichever putative origin of διά be preferred, διά moved beyond the categories of space and time to express the idea of "intervention," the idea of any cause, whether direct or indirect, primary or secondary, that comes between the beginning and end of an action. For Modern Greek use of γιά (= διά in ancient Greek), see Thumb §163.

B. Notable Instances of Main Uses

1. Temporal

Ac 1:3 οἷς καὶ παρέστησεν ἑαυτὸν ζῶντα μετὰ τὸ παθεῖν αὐτὸν ἐν πολλοῖς τεκμηρίοις, **δι᾽ ἡμερῶν** τεσσεράκοντα ὀπτανόμενος αὐτοῖς

"After his suffering he presented himself to them [the apostles] with many convincing proofs that he was alive, appearing to them at intervals during forty days."

In itself δι' ἡμερῶν τεσσεράκοντα could mean either "continuously throughout a forty-day period" (although this would more commonly be expressed by τεσσεράκοντα ἡμέρας) or "intermittently (or repeatedly) during the course of forty days" (cf. Ac 13:31, Jesus appeared [ὤφθη] "over a period of [ἐπί] many days," BDAG 367b; cf. BDAG 224b; Moule 56). But the references to "many (separate) convincing proofs" (1:3a) and to various self-presentations (1:3a; παρέστησεν is a constative aorist) and repeated appearances (ὀπτανόμενος implies iteration; cf. 1Co 15:5 – 8) show that the preposition here signifies "intermittently throughout" (so also BDF §223[1]; Robertson 581, "at intervals within the forty days"; A. Oepke, *TDNT* 2:66 n.3).[1] If the heavenly exaltation of Jesus dates from his resurrection (Mt 28:18; Ac 2:32 – 33), all his appearances lie on the other side of his enthronement, and he appears from heaven as the triumphant plenipotentiary of God.

2. Means/Instrument/Agent

From the local/spatial sense of διά there naturally developed the instrumental sense, which marks the medium *through* which an action passes before its accomplishment. Thus, in the expression πίστις δι' ἀγάπης ἐνεργουμένη (Gal 5:6), love is specified as the instrument by which faith becomes visibly effective. Demonstrations of love (= good works) constitute the means by which faith is operative. In contrast to the insignificance (οὔτε ... τι ἰσχύει) of circumcision and uncircumcision, it is only "faith operating/working [RV] through love" that has any meaning (τι ἰσχύει). Both the priority of faith and its natural and necessary expression in good works are implied, a view that is consonant with Jas 2:14 – 26.

Sometimes, however, διά with the genitive expresses not the efficient means but the ultimate cause, not instrumentality but sole agency, as in Ro 11:36, where God the Father is designated the source (ἐκ), sole cause (διά), and goal (εἰς) of all things. Similarly, ὁ θεός, δι' οὗ ἐκλήθητε (1Cor 1:9); κληρονόμος διὰ θεοῦ (Gal 4:7); ἔπρεπεν γὰρ αὐτῷ ... δι' οὗ τὰ πάντα (Heb 2:10).

It follows, as Zerwick observes, that when the role of Christ as creator (e.g., Jn 1:3, 10) or redeemer (e.g., Ro 5:9) is expressed by διά, the idea of his mediation may not be prominent (§113). Accordingly, in Col 1:16c (τὰ πάντα δι' αὐτοῦ καὶ εἰς αὐτὸν ἔκτισται) there may be no special emphasis on Christ's mediatorial or cooperative role in creation; he is creation's sole and ultimate cause. By contrast, in 1Co 8:6 the function of God the Father as the source of creation (ἐξ οὗ τὰ πάντα) is distinguished from Christ's role as mediator of creation (δι'

---

1. Pointing out that Luke uses διά with the genitive, not the accusative of "time throughout which," Chrysostom interpreted the prepositional phrase to mean "from time to time during forty days" (*The Nicene and Post-Nicene Fathers of the Christian Church* [ed. P. Schaff; Grand Rapids: Eerdmans, 1956], 5).

οὗ τὰ πάντα), while in 2Co 5:18 God is the reconciler and Christ the divinely appointed "efficient means" (διὰ Χριστοῦ) of reconciliation.

On the relation between διά and ὑπό, see ch. 20 E.

a. Acts 20:28

ποιμαίνειν τὴν ἐκκλησίαν τοῦ θεοῦ, ἣν περιεποιήσατο **διὰ** τοῦ αἵματος τοῦ ἰδίου

"to shepherd the church of God, which he obtained with the blood of his own Son" (cf. GNB, NJB, NRSV)

The Greek text printed above is the result of preferring θεοῦ over κυρίου and αἵματος τοῦ ἰδίου over τοῦ ἰδίου αἵματος (see Metzger 425–27; Harris 133–37). This verse forms the center and climax of Paul's "farewell speech" delivered to the Ephesian elders at Miletus and recorded by Luke in abbreviated form in Ac 20:18–35.

Ὁ ἴδιος may be regarded as a christological title ("his own one") and as an abbreviation of ὁ ἴδιος υἱός (cf. Ro 8:32; just as in Jn 1:18 μονογενής probably stands for [ὁ] μονογενὴς υἱός, so that the sense is "the only Son, who is God [θεός])."

Since περιεποιήσατο is followed by διὰ τοῦ αἵματος and not by ἐν τῷ αἵματι (indicating price, as in Rev 5:9) or simply τοῦ αἵματος (genitive of price; see BDF §179), αἷμα should probably be regarded, not as the price of acquisition, but as the means by which the acquisition was made (so also BDAG 224c; LN §57.61). Just as God had originally acquired a people to be his treasured possession through a covenant ratified by blood (Ex 19:5–6; 24:3–8), so now he had secured for himself the church to be his distinctive people by means of the shed blood of his own Son.

b. 2 Peter 1:4

τὰ τίμια καὶ μέγιστα ἡμῖν ἐπαγγέλματα δεδώρηται, ἵνα **διὰ** τούτων γένησθε θείας κοινωνοὶ φύσεως ἀποφυγόντες τῆς ἐν τῷ κόσμῳ ἐν ἐπιθυμίᾳ φθορᾶς

"Magnificent and precious promises have been bestowed on us, so that through these you may become sharers in the divine nature, having escaped the corruption that is in the world because of sinful desire."

Two questions arise from this verse, which has figured so prominently in the theological discussion of "deification" or "divinization" (θεοποίησις, θέωσις).

(1) What is involved in Christians' sharing in the divine nature? A distinction must be drawn between inherent participation in the divine essence, a function reserved for the three persons of the Trinity, and an unmediated participation in

the very life of God, a sharing in his absolute immortality. This "sharing in the divine nature" is not an intrinsic characteristic of humans; it is a contingent and derived immortality, a gracious gift of the divine will (cf. Ro 2:7; 6:23), involving, as God's immortality does, inviolable holiness and so freedom from all decay and death (God "alone has immortality and dwells in unapproachable light," 1Ti 6:16). Just as resurrected persons can be described as ἰσάγγελοι ("like the angels") because "they can no longer die" (Lk 20:36), so also those who can be described as θείας κοινωνοὶ φύσεως are "like God" in having become immortal but without in any sense sharing in the divine essence.[2]

(2) When does this occur? The case for believing that this sharing in the divine nature is a future experience, not a past act and present possession, is as follows.

(a) There can be little doubt that **διὰ τούτων** ("through these") refers to ἐπαγγέλματα, the immediate antecedent. These "magnificent and precious promises" are promises about the second advent of Christ (2Pe 3:4, ἐπαγγελία; 3:9, ἐπαγγελίας), the future day of the Lord (3:10), and the future day of God (3:12–13, ἐπάγγελμα).

(b) The Christian hope can certainly confirm and strengthen faith and love (Col 1:4–5), and the future expectation of seeing Christ can prompt present holiness (1Jn 3:2–3). But it is difficult to see how promises have the intrinsic power to enable present participation in the divine nature.

(c) "Through these" must therefore mean "through these promises, when fulfilled" or "after seeing the fulfillment of these promises."

(d) "Deliverance from the corruption that is in the world" must precede participation in the divine nature (ἀποφυγόντες is an aorist participle). Whether this "deliverance" refers to a past baptismal renunciation of sin or *points to a future escape from the human proneness to decay and death (φθορά) that marks life in the world, the future time of the γένησθε κτλ. remains unaltered.

3. Cause or Ground

The two main nonlocal meanings of διά are:

(1) "by means of, through" (+ genitive; 58% of NT uses of διά [cf. Moulton 105] and 71% in the Ptolemaic papyri [cf. Rossberg 9])

(2) "on account of, because of, for the sake of" (+ accusative; 42% of NT uses of διά [cf. Moulton 105] and 29% in the papyri [cf. Rossberg 9])

The relation between these two most common uses is illustrated by the textual variants in Ro 8:11, where the revivification of mortal bodies is attributed to

---

2. On these issues see M. J. Harris, *Raised Immortal: Resurrection and Immortality in the New Testament* (London: Marshall, 1983; Grand Rapids: Eerdmans, 1985), 189–201, 273–75.

the *agency* of God's indwelling Spirit (διά + genitive; **διὰ** τοῦ ἐνοικοῦντος αὐτοῦ πνεύματος), who is already active in the transformation of character (2Co 3:18); or, in the inferior reading (διά + accusative; **διὰ** τὸ ἐνοικοῦν αὐτοῦ πνεῦμα; see Metzger 456), the revivification is *grounded* in the fact that a life-giving Spirit (Ro 8:2; 1Co 15:45; 2Co 3:6) indwells believers, the Spirit of him who raised Jesus from the dead.

Occasionally there is an overlap between these two constructions with διά, so that

(1) διά with the accusative may denote means or "efficient cause" (BDAG 226a), as in Jn 6:57a (ζῶ **διὰ** τὸν πατέρα, "I have life through the Father," Cassirer), where God the Father is the source of the Son's life (cf. Jn 5:26b).

(2) διά with the genitive can express cause, as in Ro 12:3, **διὰ** τῆς χάριτος τῆς δοθείσης μοι, "by virtue of [BDF §223(4)] the grace given me" (the parallel in Ro 15:15 has **διὰ** τὴν χάριν τὴν δοθεῖσάν μοι ὑπὸ τοῦ θεοῦ, "because of the grace God gave me"), and 2Co 9:13, **διὰ** τῆς δοκιμῆς τῆς διακονίας ταύτης, "because of the evidence that this service provides."

a. Romans 11:36

ὅτι ἐξ αὐτοῦ καὶ **δι᾿** αὐτοῦ καὶ εἰς αὐτὸν τὰ πάντα

"For from him and through him and for him are all things."

Paul ends his review of God's past, present, and future dealings with the nation of Israel with an exuberant rhapsody (Ro 11:33–36) that celebrates the ineffable wisdom, knowledge, and sovereignty of God. He is the source (ἐκ), sole cause (διά), and goal (εἰς) of all that exists. Here διά points to God's sole or ultimate agency in creating and preserving the universe, not to any intermediate or secondary agency. NEB paraphrases these three relations God sustains toward the universe as "Source, Guide, and Goal of all that exists."

When we consider what other prepositions might have been used in this construction that ends with the emphatic subject τὰ πάντα, we realize that ἀπό and πρό could be regarded as subsumed under ἐκ; πρός under εἰς; and ἐν and ὑπό under διά. Paul's affirmation differs from the comparable sentiments of the Stoic emperor-philosopher Marcus Aurelius (ἐκ σοῦ πάντα, ἐν σοὶ πάντα, εἰς σὲ πάντα [*Meditationes* 4.23]), in three notable regards: (1) for Paul the referent is the personal God of Israel and the Father of the Lord Jesus Christ, not an impersonal φύσις (nature); (2) there is no pantheistic ἐν αὐτῷ; (3) the articular τὰ πάντα refers to "all things collectively," the universe in its totality, while πάντα focuses on "all things, everything" in a distributive sense.

b. 1 Corinthians 8:6

In 1Co 8:4–6 Paul is contrasting the unreality of idols and the plurality of so-called gods and lords with the reality and singularity of God and Jesus Christ, with a view to showing that although food sacrificed to idols is not defiled (cf. 1Co 10:25–26), it should be avoided if consuming it wounds the weak conscience of a Christian brother or sister.

ἀλλ' ἡμῖν εἷς θεὸς ὁ πατὴρ ἐξ οὗ τὰ πάντα καὶ ἡμεῖς εἰς αὐτόν, καὶ εἷς κύριος Ἰησοῦς Χριστὸς δι' οὗ τὰ πάντα καὶ ἡμεῖς δι' αὐτοῦ

For us there is
   one God, who is the Father,
      from whom all things proceed
      and for whom we exist; and
   one Lord, who is Jesus Christ,
      through whom all things exist
      and through whom we exist.

1. Singularity of person	εἷς θεός	εἷς κύριος
2. Description (apposition)	ὁ πατήρ	Ἰησοῦς Χριστός
3. Relationship to τὰ πάντα	ἐξ οὗ	δι' οὗ
4. Relationship to ἡμεῖς	εἰς αὐτόν	δι' αὐτοῦ

With regard to #1 and #2, the LXX version of the beginning of the Shema (Dt 6:4) reads κύριος ὁ θεὸς ἡμῶν κύριος εἷς ἐστιν. Paul concurs with the Corinthians in this basic affirmation ("We know … there is no God but one," 1Co 8:4), but he proceeds to restate the undifferentiated generic εἷς θεός of the Shema in a binitarian formulation: εἷς θεὸς ὁ πατὴρ … καὶ εἷς κύριος Ἰησοῦς Χριστός, which indicates that in Paul's view ὁ πατήρ + Ἰησοῦς Χριστός = εἷς θεός. That is, Paul did not regard εἷς κύριος as an addition to the Shema but as a constituent part of a christianized Shema. Apparently, then, the solution Paul proposed to the theological problem posed by the Christ event was to use the expression εἷς θεός only of the Father (cf. Eph 4:6), never of Jesus, although θεός could occasionally be used of Jesus (Ro 9:5; Tit 2:13), while the expression εἷς κύριος was applied exclusively to Jesus (cf. Eph 4:5), never to the Father, although κύριος was often applied to the Father. All this is foundational to the distinction between ἐξ οὗ and δι' οὗ.

With regard to #3 and #4, God and Christ both operate in the spheres of creation and redemption, nature and grace, cosmology and soteriology, but their function in these realms is distinguished: the Father is the origin or source or fount (ἐξ οὗ) of creation, and the purpose and goal (εἰς αὐτόν, "for/to him") of Christians' existence, so that they live/exist to serve him; while the Son was and is God's intermediary (δι' οὗ) (BDAG 225b) in creation and is God's agent (δι' αὐτοῦ) in maintaining the existence of Christians. Each use of διά in reference to Christ implies he acts as an intermediate agent on God's behalf. Further, his agency with respect to τὰ πάντα implies his personal existence prior to creation and therefore to time (cf. Ro 8:3; 2Co 8:9; Gal 4:4; Php 2:6).

Since this Greek sentence is verbless, we may supply with the phrase δι᾽ αὐτοῦ τὰ πάντα various verbs: "[through him all things] were created" (GNB)/"came to be" (NEB), referring to his role as creator, or "come" (TCNT, NJB), or "exist" (Weymouth, cf. Moffatt), alluding to his role as both creator and sustainer. Similarly, with ἡμεῖς δι᾽ αὐτοῦ we may supply "[through him we] exist" (NRSV, REB, NASB[2])/"live" (NAB[1]; NIV[1,2]) (both physically and spiritually), or even "have been given life" (NLT).

c. 2 Corinthians 4:5

οὐ γὰρ ἑαυτοὺς κηρύσσομεν ἀλλὰ Ἰησοῦν Χριστὸν κύριον, ἑαυτοὺς δὲ δούλους ὑμῶν **διὰ** Ἰησοῦν

"For we do not proclaim ourselves; no, we proclaim Jesus Christ as Lord, and ourselves as your slaves for Jesus' sake."

In 2Co 4:1–6 Paul describes the Christian gospel, which in its essence relates to the lordship of Jesus the Messiah, as God's agent for the dispelling of the spiritual darkness created by Satan, the god of the present age. The parallelism between "Jesus Christ as Lord" and "ourselves as your slaves," along with the natural sequence of thought from lordship to slavery (κύριον … δούλους), suggests that acknowledgment of the lordship of Jesus leads naturally and inevitably (δέ here has the sense "and therefore") to lowly, unquestioning service to one's fellow believers. For Paul and his coworkers, slavery to Christ was exhibited in slavery to other Christians.

But there were two important differences between the vertical and the horizontal "slavery." (1) Paul was not obligated always and everywhere to obey and please the Corinthians in the way he was obligated to obey and please his heavenly Lord. (2) The Corinthians were not Paul's lord any more than he was their lord (cf. 2Co 1:24). His unconditional obligation to serve them was "for Jesus' sake" (διὰ Ἰησοῦν), that is, on account of him and for his benefit, because only Jesus was Lord. There were clear limits to mutual slavery (cf. Gal 5:13b).

d. Colossians 1:4–5

ἀκούσαντες τὴν πίστιν ὑμῶν ἐν Χριστῷ Ἰησοῦ καὶ τὴν ἀγάπην ἣν ἔχετε εἰς πάντας τοὺς ἁγίους **διὰ** τὴν ἐλπίδα τὴν ἀποκειμένην ὑμῖν ἐν τοῖς οὐρανοῖς

"because we heard of your faith in Christ Jesus and of the love you show to all God's people. Both stem from the hope stored up for you in heaven."

Unlike πίστις and ἀγάπη, ἐλπίς here is objective, not subjective, in this sense: hope is not an inward disposition but denotes, by metonymy, the object of hope (cf. BDAG 320c; 739b), whether inheritance (cf. 1Pe 1:4), eternal life (cf. Tit 1:4), or "the totality of blessing that awaits the Christian in the life to come" (BDAG 113a). By the phrase διὰ τὴν ἐλπίδα ("because of the hope") Paul is not suggesting that hope in itself initially produces faith and love. Rather, awareness of the inheritance of Christians has the effect of stimulating in them stronger faith and deeper love. An objective fact produces subjective attitudes. The function of eschatology, rightly understood, is to stimulate virtue, not satisfy curiosity.

e. Hebrews 2:10

ἔπρεπεν γὰρ αὐτῷ, δι᾽ ὃν τὰ πάντα καὶ δι᾽ οὗ τὰ πάντα, πολλοὺς υἱοὺς εἰς δόξαν ἀγαγόντα τὸν ἀρχηγὸν τῆς σωτηρίας αὐτῶν διὰ παθημάτων τελειῶσαι.

"Indeed, in leading many sons to glory, it was appropriate that God, for whom and through whom all things exist, should bring the author of their salvation to perfection through his sufferings."

Here the two main uses of διά are dramatically juxtaposed in a circumlocution for God (αὐτῷ κτλ.; cf. Heb 1:3; 8:1), with paronomasia and parallelism (διά + relative + τὰ πάντα). The author's point is that it was entirely congruous with God's role in the universe for him to lead humans to their intended goal through the sufferings of the princely pioneer who secured their salvation.

In reference to God δι᾽ οὗ does not refer to intermediate agency or mediation (as it does when used of Jesus Christ in 1Co 8:6—see above, 3.b) but to his role as originator and creator of all things (BDAG 225b, d), being equivalent to ἐξ οὗ (1Co 8:6; cf. ἐξ αὐτοῦ in Ro 11:36).

If δι᾽ ὃν meant "because of whom [all things exist]," it would be redundant with the following δι᾽ οὗ, both phrases then expressing primary causation. It must therefore mean "for the sake of whom" or simply "for whom," being equivalent to εἰς αὐτόν (in Ro 11:36; 1Co 8:6) and pointing to God as the "ultimate goal or purpose of life" (BDAG 225d). Expressed in Aristotelian or Thomist categories, δι᾽ ὃν and δι᾽ οὗ denote "final cause" and "efficient cause" (respectively; cf. ZG 657). Stated in other terms, God here is described as "the Final Goal and the First Cause of the universe" (Williams), provided we include in the word "universe" at least the material and the moral/spiritual worlds. GNB interprets δι᾽ οὗ more specifically and inverts the order: "God, who creates and preserves all things."

We suggest that this dual description of God in relation to τὰ πάντα is equivalent to saying ὅς ἐστιν τὸ Ὦ καὶ τὸ Ἄλφα, ὁ ἔσχατος καὶ ὁ πρῶτος, τὸ τέλος καὶ ἡ ἀρχή (cf. Rev 1:8, 17; 2:8; 21:6; 22:13).

4. Attendant/Accompanying/Prevailing Circumstances and Manner

Not infrequently διά expresses the circumstances that accompany an action or state, and in this function the preposition overlaps with ἐν. For example, Abraham "received the sign of circumcision as a seal of the faith-righteousness that he had while he was as yet uncircumcised [ἐν τῇ ἀκροβυστίᾳ], thus becoming the father of all who are believers while being uncircumcised [δι᾽ ἀκροβυστίας]" (Ro 4:11).

Since διά may denote accompaniment as well as instrumentality, it is special pleading to distinguish between μετά in 1Ti 4:14 (used of the elders' imposition of hands) and διά in 2Ti 1:6 (used of Paul's imposition of hands) in regard to the consecration of Timothy, as if an apostolic laying on of hands were a prerequisite for "ordination" while the imposition of presbyters' hands was simply a desirable concomitant. Διὰ τῆς ἐπιθέσεως τῶν χειρῶν μου (2Ti 1:6) may well mean "when I laid my hands upon you" (Goodspeed; διά of attendant circumstances). But even if διά here does denote the instrumental cause of Timothy's receipt of his gift, the actual participation of the body of elders in this imposition of hands need not be excluded; the presbytery and the apostle may have acted conjointly. The use of μετά rather than διά in 1Ti 4:14 may be explained by the presence of another διά phrase (διὰ προφητείας) in this verse: "Do not neglect your gift, which was given you through a prophetic message when the body of elders laid their hands on you" (NIV[1]). Even with διὰ προφητείας some EVV find a διά of accompaniment: (e.g.) "under the guidance of prophecy" (REB), "amidst prophesyings" (Cassirer).

This use of διά extends even to marking circumstances that turn out not to help but sometimes even to hinder an action. "Even with" (= "in spite of one's having") the written code and circumcision (διὰ γράμματος καὶ περιτομῆς), transgression of the law occurs (Ro 2:27), although one would expect such circumstances to aid in keeping the precepts of the law (cf. Turner, *Insights* 105–6).

a. Acts 21:4

οἵτινες τῷ Παύλῳ ἔλεγον διὰ τοῦ πνεύματος μὴ ἐπιβαίνειν εἰς Ἱεροσόλυμα

"Through the Spirit [or, while under the inspiration of the Spirit] [the Tyrian disciples] urged Paul not to keep on going to Jerusalem."

We need to compare this verse with two others in Acts: (1) Ac 19:21: "Paul resolved in the Spirit [ἐν τῷ πνεύματι] to go through Macedonia and Achaia, and then to go on to Jerusalem" (NRSV); and (2) 20:22–23: "And now, compelled by the Spirit [τῷ πνεύματι], I am on my way to Jerusalem, not knowing what will happen to me there, except that the Holy Spirit testifies to me in every city that imprisonment and persecutions are waiting for me." The advice given to Paul by the Tyrian disciples in Ac 21:4 "through the Spirit" (διὰ τοῦ πνεύματος) not to persist in going to Jerusalem seems to conflict (a) with his own resolve "in the Spirit" to go there (19:21), and (b) with the constraint and testimony of the Spirit (20:22–23).

It is noteworthy that Agabus's subsequent prophecy at Caesarea (Ac 21:11) that predicted Paul's suffering in Jerusalem and begins "The Holy Spirit says" (λέγει τὸ πνεῦμα τὸ ἅγιον) does not include an injunction or exhortation to Paul not to go on to Jerusalem, although those who heard Agabus's prophecy "pleaded with Paul not to go up to Jerusalem" (21:12), only then to receive Paul's vigorous rejoinder (21:13). Perhaps, therefore, the crucial phrase διὰ τοῦ πνεύματος should be rendered "while under the inspiration of the Spirit" (but Moule [57] tentatively suggests "as a spiritual insight").

In his condensed statement Luke has not distinguished between a prophecy regarding Paul's suffering at Jerusalem (doubtless given by the Tyrian disciples [= prophets?; cf. Ac 11:28; 21:9] before their exhortation—else why their exhortation) that was delivered at the direction of the Spirit (cf. 21:11) and their own urgent plea (ἔλεγον, iterative imperfect) (cf. 21:12) that was occasioned by the prediction and immediately followed it. The verse may be paraphrased thus: "Prompted by a prediction of the Spirit, they urged Paul not to persist in going to Jerusalem."

This seems a more satisfactory solution than the proposal of Robertson (*Pictures* 3:360): "In spite of this warning [Ac 21:4b] Paul felt it his duty as before (Ac 20:22) to go on. Evidently Paul interpreted the action of the Holy Spirit as information and warning although the disciples at Tyre gave it the form of a prohibition. Duty called louder than warning to Paul even if both were the calls of God."

b. 2 Corinthians 5:7

διὰ πίστεως γὰρ περιπατοῦμεν, οὐ διὰ εἴδους

"For we walk in the realm of faith, not of sight."

The difficulty concerning διά here is occasioned by the fact that while, in Pauline usage, διὰ πίστεως ("through faith") specifies the means by which the benefits of salvation are received (e.g., Ro 3:22, 25; Gal 2:16; Eph 2:8), περιπατεῖν is usually followed by κατά (e.g., 1Co 3:3; 2Co 10:2), ἐν (e.g., Ro 6:4; Eph 2:2), the simple dative (2Co 12:18; Gal 5:16), or an adverb or adverbial phrase (e.g., Col 1:10; 1Th 2:12) when the manner, means, or time of the περιπατεῖν is designated. Because this περιπατεῖν διά combination is unique in Paul, διὰ πίστεως need not bear its customary sense of "by means of faith," especially since no object (such as Ἰησοῦ Χριστοῦ) is expressed. With περιπατεῖν, the modal sense ("with") of διά would be appropriate, but to explain (περιπατεῖν) διὰ εἴδους in this way is difficult. But if both prepositional phrases describe accompanying circumstances ("in the realm of faith, not [in the realm] of sight"), διά bears an identical sense with the two abstract nouns, both of which carry an active sense.

Paul is here contrasting seeing with believing, in much the same way as Jn 20:29 and 1Pe 1:8 contrast ὁρᾶν and πιστεύειν. It is faith, not sight, that determines and guides Christian conduct (περιπατεῖν). But the verse is not simply a Christian maxim, for it has particular relevance to "the Lord" of 2Co 5:6, 8: "we lead our lives in the sphere of faith, without yet seeing him."

c. 1 John 5:6

οὗτός ἐστιν ὁ ἐλθὼν **δι'** ὕδατος καὶ αἵματος, Ἰησοῦς Χριστός, οὐκ **ἐν** τῷ ὕδατι μόνον ἀλλ' **ἐν** τῷ ὕδατι καὶ **ἐν** τῷ αἵματι

"This is the one who came with water and blood — Jesus Christ; he came not with the water only, but with the water *and* with the blood."

The nonrepetition of διά in v. 6a suggests that "water" and "blood" here form a conceptual unit, "water-and-blood" (cf. ἐξ ὕδατος καὶ πνεύματος in Jn 3:5), whereas the repetition of the preposition and of the (anaphoric) articles in v. 6b shows that "water" and "blood" are now being conceived of as separate entities. If ὕδωρ is taken literally, it will refer either to amniotic fluid (as evidence of Jesus' natural birth and real humanity) or to the water that came from Jesus' pierced side at his crucifixion (Jn 19:34). But more probably "water" is here used figuratively (by metonymy) of Jesus' baptismal water, either his experience of John's baptism (Mt 3:13 – 17; cf. Jn 1:26, 31, 33) as the fulfillment of all righteousness (Mt 3: 15) or his own ministry of baptizing in water (Jn 3:22, 26; 4:1 – 2).

Αἷμα (hardly literal here, *pace* BDAG 224a) will refer not only to Jesus' life surrendered in death (Jn 10:11, 15, 17 – 18), but in particular to his death as an "atoning sacrifice" (ἱλασμός, 1Jn 2:2; 4:10; cf. 3:16) that purifies from all sin (1Jn 1:7). The secessionists (cf. 2:19) apparently denied the reality of Jesus' death or its atoning efficacy while acknowledging his "coming with water," his humanity; hence the οὐκ ... μόνον ἀλλά construction (cf. 1Jn 2:2). On the textual issue involving αἵματος (which had a "B" rating [some doubt] in UBS[1–3] but an "A" rating [certain] in UBS[4]), see Metzger 646.

Ὁ ἐλθών may imply the incarnation (1Jn 4:2, 14) but has special reference to Jesus' "appearance" at the beginning and end of his public ministry with his baptism and death. "The one who was promised to come" (ὁ ἐρχόμενος) has now appeared and so has become "the one who came" (ὁ ἐλθών).

Some EVV distinguish between διά and the threefold ἐν: "with ... by" (NEB, REB), "by ... with" (RV, NASB[1,2], JB, NJB, RSV, NRSV), "through ... in" (NAB[1]), "through ... by" (NAB[2]). But since ἐν τῷ ὕδατι μόνον refers back (with the anaphoric article) to δι' ὕδατος, it seems antecedently probable that the first two cases of ἐν have the same meaning as διά. Similarly ἐν τῷ αἵματι picks up δι' ... αἵματος. If, then, διά and ἐν are here likely to have the same sense (thus many commentators), they may express instrumentality ("by, " as KJV, Goodspeed, Moffatt, NIV[1,2], NLT, HCSB, ESV) or *attendant circumstance/

manner ("with," as Weymouth [671 n.1]; GNB; Moule 57 ["possibly"]; cf. BDF §223[3] and Robertson, *Pictures* 6: 239).

On this latter view John is affirming, against the secessionists, that Jesus Christ's "coming" in fulfillment of messianic promises was accompanied and characterized by not simply one but two significant events. He "came with the water of his baptism and the blood of his death" (GNB). These two events, both crucial for the carrying out of his messianic vocation, can be considered in unison ("water-and-blood") as a summary of his public ministry with reference to its beginning and end, or separately ("the water and the blood") as the two most crucial events in his messianic life.

5. Purpose?

Just as there has been debate whether εἰς ever bears a retrospective (= causal) sense in the NT (see below), so there is no unanimity concerning the alleged prospective (= telic) sense of διά. If sometimes it were to bear this meaning in the NT, it should occasion no surprise since: (a) διά with the accusative exceptionally has a prospective sense in Classical Greek (= ἕνεκα) (see LSJ 389 s.v. διά B.III.3; Smyth 375 note c) and Hellenistic Greek (e.g., Polybius 2.56.12; Mayser 426 for the papyri); (b) in Modern Greek γιά (= διά; cf. Bortone 215) with the accusative, "for," can express purpose (Hatzidakis 212–13; Thumb §163.2; Bortone 285); (c) conceptually, "with a view to" is not a great advance on "for the sake of." There are, in fact, a few examples where διά could be rendered "for the benefit of" and so approaches a prospective sense (Mt 24:22; Mk 2:27; Jn 11:42; 12:30; Ro 11:28a; 1Co 11:9; Zerwick [§112] compares the διὰ τοῦτο ... ἵνα formula in Ro 4:16; 1 Ti 1:16; Phm 15), but the alleged instances that are most regularly adduced are Ro 3:25 and 4:25.

a. Romans 3:25–26a

> ὃν προέθετο ὁ θεὸς ... εἰς ἔνδειξιν τῆς δικαιοσύνης αὐτοῦ διὰ τὴν πάρεσιν τῶν προγεγονότων ἁμαρτημάτων ἐν τῇ ἀνοχῇ τοῦ θεοῦ

> "God presented Christ ... to demonstrate his righteousness, because in his forbearance he had passed over sins committed previously."

In this verse διὰ τὴν πάρεσιν seems to mean "because he had passed over" or "on account of his passing over" (similarly BDAG 225c) rather than "with a view to his forgiving." Paul is observing that the purpose or outcome of God's provision of Christ as a propitiatory sacrifice was the demonstration of his own righteousness, a righteousness that needed vindication because in his patience (not his indifference) God had refrained from exacting the full and proper penalty for acts of sin committed previously. He had not always left sin unpunished, but he had temporarily suspended, withheld, or set aside appropriate punishment in light of his eternal purpose to provide an altogether adequate basis for the forgiveness of sin in the atoning death of Christ. Πάρεσις (= remission of punishment or debt) should be distinguished from ἄφεσις (= remission of sin; cf. MM 493d) and an unusual telic sense need not be given to διά with the accusative when the more normal causal meaning accords with the context.

b. Romans 4:25

ὃς παρεδόθη **διὰ** τὰ παραπτώματα ἡμῶν καὶ ἠγέρθη **διὰ** τὴν δικαίωσιν ἡμῶν

"He was delivered over to death because of our transgressions and was raised to life because of our justification."

Both verbs, παρέδοθη and ἠγέρθη, are theological passives, with God as the implied agent (cf. Ro 8:32, where God is the subject of παρέδωκεν). The precise parallelism between the two διά phrases might suggest *prima facie* that διά should bear the same sense (either prospective or retrospective) in each case, but this is not necessarily so, especially when, as here, there is a contrast between a negative concept (παραπτώματα) and a positive (δικαίωσις). Three interpretations may be mentioned (in ascending order of probability).

(1) *Διά is final in both clauses*: "Jesus 'was given up to death to atone for our offences' [cf. Is 53:5, 12, LXX], and was raised to life that we might be pronounced righteous" (TCNT).

(2) *Διά is causal in v. 25a* ("because of") *but final/telic in v. 25b* ("in order to achieve" or "to confirm/guarantee"): "Because of our sins he was handed over to die, and he was raised to life in order to put us right with God" (GNB). Many EVV have "for" in both cases (e.g., KJV, NAB[1,2], NRSV, NIV[1,2]), where the first "for" means "because of" and the second, "with a view to" (so Turner 268; similarly BDAG 225c, "on account of … in the interest of," and G. Schrenk, *TDNT* 2:224). Taking this view, some commentators find here a case of the antithetical parallelism of Hebrew poetry, so that Jesus' death and his resurrection — inseparable events in Paul's thought — are related both to sin-bearing/forgiveness/atonement and to justification.

(iii) *Διά is causal in both clauses*: "He who was delivered over because of our transgressions, and was raised because of our justification" (NASB[2]; similarly Weymouth, NASB[1]; NEB mg, "because we are now justified"; Atkinson 24, "justification was the *cause*, not the purpose, of the resurrection"). Just as the delivering up of Jesus to death was the consequence of human sin, so his resurrection by God was the consequence of the justification that had been achieved by his death (Ro 5:9–10). The conceptual sequence would then be: human sin — Jesus' death — human justification — Jesus' resurrection, with the resurrection here seen as the proof of Christ's procurement of human justification (see Ro 8:33–34; 1Co 15:17; 1Ti 3:16; cf. Isa 53:11; Heb 1:3b) and as the seal of divine approval on that procurement.

Such a view has the advantage of giving διά in v. 25b its most common meaning with the accusative and of understanding the preposition the same way in both of these parallel clauses. When the usual meaning of a preposition yields a satisfactory sense that does not contravene a writer's thought, that meaning should be preferred over an appeal to possible exceptional usage.[3]

C. Διά in Compounds

MH (300) notes that 200 of the 343 uses of the 79 NT διά compounds occur in Luke-Acts.

1. "(Right) through": of space: διαβαίνω, go through
   of time: διαγρηγορέω, keep awake
2. Transfer: διερμηνεύω, translate
3. Continuance: διαμένω, remain
4. Completeness: διαφθείρω, destroy completely
5. Intensity: διακαθαρίζω, thoroughly cleanse
6. Mediation: διαλλάσσομαι, become reconciled
7. Distribution: διαιρέω, distribute, divide

---

3. Vigorous defenses of this third interpretation on linguistic grounds are found in Weymouth 407 n.1 (one of the longest notes in his heavily annotated translation) and H. G. Meecham, "Romans iii. 25f., iv. 25 — the Meaning of διά c. acc.," *ExpT* 50 (1938–39): 564.

Chapter 8

Εἰς

A. Origin and New Testament Use

Εἰς was originally ἑνς (= ἐν + ς, where ς was added to ἐν on the analogy of ἐκ + ς = ἐξ) (cf. Bortone 162 n.81). When the ν was dropped, ἑνς became ἐς (an Ionic, old Attic, and Doric form of εἰς) or εἰς.

At first only ἐν existed, and it could express either position or direction, but gradually εἰς took over the latter usage (with the accusative case) and ultimately ousted ἐν itself, so that in Modern Greek εἰς (usually in the form σέ or 'ς before the article—see Thumb §160; Hatzidakis 210–11) expresses both position and direction, as ἐν originally did (Robertson 584, 591).

After ἐν, εἰς is the most common preposition in the NT, the LXX, and the Ptolemaic papyri (see the chart on p. 32), and accounts for 17% of NT "proper" prepositions. It is found in all strands of the NT but is more common (by comparison) in the parts (such as Mark and Luke-Acts) where it often overlaps with ἐν (see below, C). It expands its sphere, not only sometimes replacing ἐν to denote position or rest but also standing for the dative case (Bortone 181 n.26; Regard 224; A. Oepke, *TDNT* 2:425).

B. Its Relation to Πρός

Although the distinctions are not uniformly maintained, it is generally true that with regard to literal movement εἰς denotes entry ("into") and πρός approach ("up to"), and (correspondingly) that εἰς is used with impersonal objects and πρός with personal.[1] So in 2Co 1:15–16 we find **πρὸς ὑμᾶς ἐλθεῖν** ... **καὶ δι' ὑμῶν διελθεῖν εἰς** Μακεδονίαν. That these are simply tendencies is apparent from passages such as Mk 5:38–39; Lk 19:29; Jn 20:3–6, 8; Ro 11:36; Phm 5. As

---

1. See the argument of E. de Witt Burton (*A Critical and Exegetical Commentary on the Epistle to the Galatians* [ICC; Edinburgh: T&T Clark, 1921], 96–99), based on Paul's twofold use of εἰς (not πρός) in Gal 2:9, that the apostolic division of labor was primarily territorial (Jewish lands/Gentile lands) rather than racial (Jews/Gentiles).

for metaphorical use, both prepositions may express purpose (e.g., εἰς ἔνδειξιν ... πρὸς τὴν ἔνδειξιν, "in order to demonstrate," Ro 3:25–26) and result (e.g., εἰς τὸ εἶναι αὐτοὺς ἀναπολογήτους, "so that they are without excuse," Ro 1:20; πρὸς θάνατον, "resulting in death," 3x, 1Jn 5:16–17; cf. BDAG 290c-d for further examples of these two uses of εἰς).

C. Its Relation to Ἐν

There are two reasons why it is not surprising that εἰς and ἐν shared some common territory in Hellenistic Greek. (1) Etymologically εἰς was a later variant of ἐν (see above). Under the heading "Original Static Use" (of εἰς), Robertson observes that "in itself εἰς expresses the same dimension relation as ἐν, viz. *in*" (591, citing KG 2.1.468). (2) Hellenistic Greek is marked by a general tendency to confuse the categories of linear motion ("to") and punctiliar rest ("in"). The confusion was in both directions: εἰς denoting position (e.g., Ge 37:17a, second use; Jos 7:22, third use; Mayser 373 for the papyri) and ἐν implying movement (e.g., Ex 4:21; Tob 5:5; Mayser 372 for the papyri). Examples of this interchange are not lacking in Classical Greek but they are relatively infrequent, especially in narrative.

It was observed in ch. 2 that the interchange of εἰς and ἐν is not promiscuous in NT Greek and that the idiosyncrasies of each author must be examined. An examination of places where εἰς may encroach on the domain of ἐν produces the following results.

> Matthew: 3:11 Ἐγὼ μὲν ὑμᾶς βαπτίζω ἐν ὕδατι εἰς μετάνοιαν (see below, ch. 21 C); 5:35 εἰς Ἱεροσόλυμα (amid three cases of ἐν after μὴ ὀμόσαι, vv. 34–36; BDF §206[2]; BDAG 706a); this could be stylistic variation; in 10:9 εἰς τὰς ζώνας ὑμῶν probably means "for/to fill your purses."
>
> Mark (9x): 1:9, 39; 5:14, 34; 6:8; 10:10; 13:3, 9, 16.
>
> Luke (13x): 1:20; 4:23, 44; 7:50; 8:34, 48; 9:61; 10:36; 11:7; 13:9; 14:8, 10; 21:37.
>
> John (3x): 1:18 εἰς τὸν κόλπον τοῦ πατρός (see below); 19:13 ἐκάθισεν ἐπὶ βήματος εἰς τόπον λεγόμενον Λιθόστρωτον; 20:7 τὸ σουδάριον ... ἐντετυλιγμένον εἰς ἕνα τόπον[2]
>
> Acts (21x): 2:5; 4:3, 5; 7:4, 12, 53; 8:40; 9:21, 28; 13:42; 14:25; 16:24; 19:3 (2x), 22; 20:14; 21:13; 22:5; 23:11 (2x); 25:4; in 2:27 (citing Ps 15:10[LXX]; cf. Ac 2:31) οὐκ ἐγκαταλείψεις τὴν ψυχήν μου εἰς ᾅδην

---

2. All the apparent exceptions in the gospel of John to the classical use of εἰς and ἐν have been examined by J. J. O'Rourke, who concludes that only in Jn 1:18 and 19:13 does εἰς possibly stand for ἐν (1.09% of John's 183 uses of εἰς) and only in Jn 3:35 is ἐν (218 uses) possibly used for εἰς ("ΕΙΣ and ΕΝ in John," *BT* 25 [1974]: 139–42).

could as easily mean "you will not abandon me *to Hades*" (since εἰς ᾅδην in Ps 15:10 LXX renders the Hebrew *lišᵉʾôl*, "to Sheol"), as (BDAG 273c; similarly Moule 68) "you will not allow me to remain *in Hades*."

1 Peter (2x): 3:20 κιβωτοῦ **εἰς** ἣν ὀλίγοι ... διεσώθησαν; 5:12 ἀληθῆ χάριν τοῦ θεοῦ **εἰς** ἣν στῆτε

Revelation: 1:11 ὃ βλέπεις γράψον **εἰς** βιβλίον (cf. 22:19, ἐν τῷ βιβλίῳ τούτῳ).

In such cases εἰς may stand for:

- locatival ἐν – Lk 10:36 **εἰς** τοὺς λῃστάς, "among robbers"
  Ac 19:22 **εἰς** τὴν Ἀσίαν, "in Asia"
  1Pe 5:12 **εἰς** ἣν στῆτε, "stand fast in it [the grace of God]"
- temporal ἐν – Lk 1:20 **εἰς** τὸν καιρὸν αὐτῶν, "at their proper time"
  Lk 13:9 **εἰς** τὸ μέλλον, "[in the] next year" (BDAG 628b, c)
  Ac 13:42 **εἰς** τὸ μεταξὺ σάββατον, "on the next Sabbath"
- instrumental ἐν – Mt 5:35 **εἰς** Ἱεροσόλυμα, "[do not swear ...] by Jerusalem"
  Ac 7:53 **εἰς** διαταγὰς ἀγγέλων, "by directions of angels" (BDAG 237c) = ἐν διαταγαῖς (BDF §206 1); cf. Gal 3:19 διαταγεὶς δι᾿ ἀγγέλων
- circumstantial ἐν – Mk 5:34 ὕπαγε **εἰς** εἰρήνην, "go in peace!"
  Lk 7:50; 8:48 πορεύου **εἰς** εἰρήνην, "go in peace!" = ἐν εἰρήνῃ (BDAG 291b)

For LXX influence in this last category, see MH 463. Note ὑπάγετε ἐν εἰρήνῃ in Jas 2:16 and πορεύεσθε ἐν εἰρήνῃ in Ac 16:36; also μετ᾿ εἰρήνης ("with [the blessing of] peace") in Acts 15:33.

Other alleged examples of εἰς = ἐν are often better explained on different grammatical grounds.

1. Εἰς can mean "with respect/reference/relation to, in, about, for" (see BDAG 291a for this use of εἰς). E.g., Mt 12:18; Ro 16:19 (2x); 2Co 2:9; Php 1:5; 2:22; 2Pe 1:8, 17 and especially uses of the phrase εἰς Χριστόν (2Co 1:21; Eph 4:15; Phm 6).
2. Εἰς is sometimes found where a verb of motion is implied. (cf. LSJ 491c). E.g., Jn 21:4; 2Th 2:4; Heb 11:9; and the phrase εἰς (τὸ) μέσον, "in the midst" in Mk 3:3; 14:60; Lk 6:8; Jn 20:19, 26 ("he [came and] stood among them," BDAG 289a; similarly Moule 68).
3. Εἰς sometimes occurs where a verb of motion is explicit. E.g., ἐλθὼν κατῴκησεν **εἰς** in Mt 2:23 and 4:13, "He came to X and lived there"; Jn 9:7 ὕπαγε νίψαι **εἰς** τὴν κολυμβήθραν.

If the above analysis is defensible, we may conclude that Mark and Luke–Acts are not averse to using εἰς in the place of ἐν; that this use is rare in John's gospel and 1 Peter; and that apart from two instances in Matthew and one in Revelation, the rest of the NT—including the whole of the Pauline corpus—has no example of this usage and conforms to the general differentiation between εἰς and ἐν found in Classical Greek. Clearly there are two extremes to be avoided in any discussion of the relationship between εἰς and ἐν: to treat them as everywhere synonymous, and always to insist on a distinction between them.

John 1:18

Μονογενὴς θεὸς ὁ ὢν εἰς τὸν κόλπον τοῦ πατρὸς ἐκεῖνος ἐξηγήσατο

"The only Son, who is God and is always near the Father's heart, has revealed him."

Each part of this verse has prompted extensive discussion. There are compelling reasons for: (1) preferring the reading μονογενὴς θεός; (2) regarding μονογενής as equivalent to (ὁ) μονογενὴς υἱός; (3) construing θεός as standing in epexegetic apposition to this substantival μονογενής; (4) translating μονογενὴς θεός as "the only Son, who is God" or "the only Son, by nature God"; and (5) understanding ὤν as an "atemporal present of 'characterization' (generality)" (Zerwick §372), "indicating the eternal presence proper to the Son" (ZG 287).[3]

The imagery behind εἰς τὸν κόλπον could be festal (of reclining at a meal, cf. Jn 13:23), familial (of the child on a parent's lap or in a parent's or nurse's embrace), or conjugal (of the embrace of husband and wife). Whatever the source of the image, it denotes the exclusive and privileged intimacy of a deeply affectionate interpersonal relationship.

In this phrase the preposition εἰς has been given three main senses.

(1) Both Static and Dynamic

Before the influence of the papyri finds had been felt, B. F. Westcott (in 1880) claimed: "There is the combination (as it were) of rest and motion, of a continuous relation, with a realization of it (comp. i.1, ἦν πρός). The 'bosom of the Father' (like heaven) is a state and not a place."[4] Moulton (234–35) declares this interpretation of εἰς in Jn 1:18 "impossible," noting that "there are many NT passages where a real distinction between εἰς and ἐν is impossible to draw without excessive subtlety" (63).

(2) Dynamic

I. de la Potterie renders the whole phrase "turned towards the Father's bosom" and finds two theological truths expressed: a personal distinction between Father

---

3. For a detailed defense of each of these positions, see Harris 74–96.

4. *The Gospel according to St. John* (1880; repr. London: T&T Clark, 1958), 15. Abbott develops Westcott's thought still further, arguing for a "mystical" or "spiritual" understanding of εἰς (§§2308, 2706, 2712).

and Son, and "the constant orientation of the Son toward the bosom of the Father as toward his origin (εἰς not πρός), as toward the source of his own life (εἰς τὸν κόλπον)."[5] For de la Potterie it is not simply a matter of "filiation" (as in Jn 1:1b and 1Jn 1:1), but of "eternal generation" (cf. ὤν and Jn 6:57),[6] "the eternal act of receiving divine life from the Father."[7]

But the idea of eternal generation would comport better with the prepositions παρά (cf. Jn 6:46, ὁ ὢν παρὰ τοῦ θεοῦ) or ἐκ (cf. the reading ἐκ τοῦ κόλπου reflected in syr[c]). If any element of movement is implied in εἰς, its direction is in effect reversed on de la Potterie's view. Moreover, the connotation "source of life" for κόλπος appears to be unparalleled.

*(3) Static

Given the obscuring of the distinction between motion and rest in Hellenistic Greek (Turner 254; Bortone 186) and the fact that John may occasionally use εἰς to denote position (Jn 19:13; 20:7; see above), it is perfectly defensible to hold that in 1:18 εἰς τὸν κόλπον is equivalent to ἐν τῷ κόλπῳ (13:23). This, in fact, is the prevailing view among grammarians,[8] lexicographers,[9] and commentators,[10] and the view to be preferred.

Yet few scholars are content to affirm that the phrase denotes simply the personal juxtaposition of Son and Father. But it is not a case that εἰς implies an earlier entrance *into* the Father's bosom or points to the Son's *return* to his preincarnate state through the ascension, for the preceding ὁ ὤν depicts a supratemporal condition that had no beginning. Nor can we follow those Greek fathers who, while giving εἰς a static sense, believed that the verse described the consubstantiality of the Father and Son. Chrysostom, for example, speaks of the Son's dwelling (ἐνδιαιτᾶσθαι) in the Father's bosom as involving "affinity of essence": "the Father would not have in his bosom one of another essence."[11] Any notion of a dynamic interpersonal relationship that may be found in 1:18 stems from the nouns κόλπος and πατήρ, not from the preposition εἰς. Since the κόλπος is a place of privileged and affectionate intimacy where secrets can be shared (cf.

---

5. "L'emploi dynamique de εἰς dans Saint Jean et ses incidences théologiques," *Bib* 43 (1962): 366–87 (quotation from p. 386).
6. Ibid., 385.
7. Ibid., 386.
8. E.g., Jannaris §1548; Abel §47(a); BDF §205; Moulton 234–35 (apparently); Robertson 535–36, 559, 593; Turner 254.
9. E.g., BDAG 289b, 557a; Regard 157, 548; A. Oepke, *TDNT*, 2:433; W. Elliger, *EDNT*, 1:399b; MM (xiv, 186b, c), who cite the classic instance from P.Oxy. 2.294, lines 3 and 6: A certain Sarapion writes (AD 22) to his brother Dorion, "On coming to Alexandria [ἐπὶ τῷ γεγονέναι ἐν Ἀλεξανδρίᾳ] ... I learned from some fishermen at Alexandria [εἰς Ἀλεξάνδρι(αν)] that...."
10. E.g., W. Bauer, M. Lagrange, R. Bultmann, E. C. Hoskyns, R. Schnackenburg, C. K. Barrett, R. E. Brown, J. R. Michaels.
11. Chrysostom, *Homilies on the Gospel of St. John* 15.2.

Jn 13:23–26; Lk 16:22–23) and the relationship is between persons (the only Son and his Father), the whole phrase—not εἰς in itself—points to direct, uninhibited interactive fellowship.

In the whole of John's gospel, 1:18 has a twofold function. It links the prologue and the remainder of the gospel by highlighting the dual themes of the Father as fully and directly known to the Son, and the Son as the unique Exegete of the Father—themes that are prominent throughout the gospel. Having had eternal access to the inmost thoughts of the Father, Jesus is perfectly and uniquely qualified to disclose the Father's nature and character (cf. Jn 3:31–32).

D. Telic Εἰς

Εἰς can also express metaphorical direction, i.e., goal or purpose (final or telic εἰς). There are two significant examples of a telic εἰς αὐτόν in Colossians 1.

1. Colossians 1:16

τὰ πάντα δι' αὐτοῦ καὶ εἰς αὐτὸν ἔκτισται

"All things have been created through him and he is their goal."

While εἰς here may mean "for him," i.e., for his benefit or glory (thus being equivalent to αὐτῷ), more probably the sense is "to him [as their goal]." The whole universe has been created and now exists (ἔκτισται) with Christ as both its sole cause (διά) and its ultimate goal (εἰς). Just as there is creatorial coherence in the sustaining power of Christ (Col 1:17b, τὰ πάντα ἐν αὐτῷ συνέστηκεν), so there is a teleological convergence of reality on Christ, what Eph 1:10 calls the unification of the entire universe under the headship of Christ (ἀνακεφαλαιώσασθαι τὰ πάντα ἐν τῷ Χριστῷ).

2. Colossians 1:19–20

εὐδόκησεν πᾶν τὸ πλήρωμα ... δι' αὐτοῦ ἀποκαταλλάξαι τὰ πάντα εἰς αὐτόν

"God in all his fullness was pleased ... through him [Christ] to reconcile all things for himself."

Πᾶν τὸ πλήρωμα (v. 19) should probably be conceived of personally ("God in all his fullness," REB, NLT) in light of the personal expressions εὐδόκησεν and ἀποκαταλλάξαι, the reflexive αὐτόν, and the masculine participle εἰρηνοποιήσας (Col 1:20).

If v. 16 traces the existence of the universe to the preincarnate Christ as cause, v. 20 depicts the agency (διά) of the incarnate Christ in God's work of reconciliation. As in v. 16, so in v. 20, εἰς αὐτόν could refer to Christ (as NAB[2], "for him"), but since reconciliation for Paul was always reconciliation "to God" (τῷ θεῷ, Ro 5:10; 2Co 5:20; Eph 2:16; or ἑαυτῷ, 2Co 5:18–19), the referent is more probably God (so most EVV). Evidently in Hellenistic Greek αὐτόν could function as a reflexive (cf. Metzger 616 in the first edition), although it would also be possible to print αὐτόν (= ἑαυτόν by contraction; cf. Moule 119). But why did Paul not write ἑαυτῷ ("to himself")? Perhaps he wanted to say more than that reconciliation is directed toward God as the offended party to whom other people or things must be reconciled. He himself was one of the beneficiaries of the reconciliation he initiated. It was "for himself," i.e., "to promote his glory," so that εἰς αὐτόν = εἰς δόξαν αὐτοῦ. Or is this a case of double entendre (see above, ch. 3 D) — "to and for himself"?

If Christ is the culminating focal point of all reality (Col 1:16), God the Father is himself the ultimate goal of the reconciliation achieved by Christ. Salvation not only has its genesis in God; it also finds its consummation in God.

Εἰς can also mark *divine appointment*, reflecting divine purpose. Believers were destined to have eternal life (τεταγμένοι εἰς ζωὴν αἰώνιον, Ac 13:48), while it is the appointed lot (ἐτέθησαν) of unbelievers who deliberately reject the message of salvation to "stumble" over the Stone (1Pe 2:8, where the antecedent in the phrase εἰς ὅ is the stumbling because of unbelief, not the unbelief itself).

In the context of the notoriously difficult Ro 9:22 Paul is illustrating the absolute sovereignty of God, his freedom to act as he chooses (Ro 9:14–21, esp. v. 18). Although God was ready (θέλων) to display his wrath and make known his power, he bore most patiently with the objects who deserved his wrath (σκεύη ὀργῆς) and so were "ripe and ready to be destroyed" (Moffatt) (κατηρτισμένα εἰς ἀπώλειαν). But those once "fit for destruction" — including both Jews and Gentiles (Ro 9:24) — have now become "recipients of his mercy" (σκεύη ἐλέους), those whom he prepared from the first to share his glory (ἃ προητοίμασεν εἰς δόξαν, Ro 9:23).

A similar "then-now" contrast is found in Eph 2:3–5, where τέκνα φύσει ὀργῆς ("by nature subjects who deserved his wrath," 2:3) corresponds to σκεύη ὀργῆς in Ro 9:22. In the latter passage there is a contrast not only between εἰς ἀπώλειαν and εἰς δόξαν but also between κατηρτισμένα and ἃ προητοίμασεν. Some may be or may have been "fit only to be destroyed," but only those who have received God's mercy are "prepared beforehand" (cf. 2Th 2:13); Paul does not say σκεύη ὀργῆς ἃ προητοίμασεν εἰς ἀπώλειαν. Also, God would hardly be said to have "tolerated most patiently" a situation he himself had ordained.

In 1Pe 1:11 τὰ εἰς Χριστὸν παθήματα could mean "the sufferings of Christ," given the fact that εἰς can replace the genitive (so A. Oepke, *TDNT* 2:434) but more probably εἰς is telic, "the sufferings destined for Christ" (Goodspeed, NAB[2], NRSV).

On εἰς αὐτόν in reference to God (Ro 11:36; 1Co 8:6), see ch. 7. B. 3.

E. Consecutive/Ecbatic Εἰς

As well as expressing a goal that is simply aimed at, εἰς can express a purpose that is actually realized (consecutive or telic or resultative εἰς). For instance, in Ro 10:9–10 belief in the heart that God raised Jesus from the dead leads to righteousness (εἰς δικαιοσύνην, "and so obtains righteousness/and so is justified"), just as to confess with the mouth Jesus as Lord results in salvation (εἰς σωτηρίαν, "and so obtains salvation/and so is saved"). Yet earlier (10:4) the same phrase εἰς δικαιοσύνην may bear a telic sense, "[Christ is the end of the law] viewed as a means of gaining righteousness" (cf. Moule 70). There is a similar alternation of senses for εἰς τό with the infinitive in Ro 4:11 (ecbatic, 2x), 4:16 (telic), 4:18 (ecbatic).

In a thorough article that deals with "The Articular Infinitive with εἰς" in both Classical and Hellenistic Greek (*JBL* 15 [1896]: 155–67), I. T. Beckwith concludes that in eight NT passages (Ro 1:20; 7:5; 12:2; 2Co 8:6; Gal 3:17; Php 1:10; Heb 11:3; Jas 3:3), a consecutive sense for εἰς with the articular infinitive is highly probable. Further, there are examples (e.g., Ro 13:4; 1Co 11:17, 34; 2Co 7:9–10) where ecbatic εἰς is followed by articular or anarthrous substantives.

If the consecutive sense of εἰς is recognized in Ro 12:2, Paul's point is not that the aim of the transformation of character is the discernment of God's will (= telic εἰς), but rather that the Christian's ability to ascertain (δοκιμάζειν, "determine by scrutiny," cf. Lk 12:56) God's will naturally results from the renewal of the mind (cf. ecbatic εἰς with verbs denoting renewal in Col 3:10; Heb 6:6).

F. Causal Εἰς?

It is striking the entries under εἰς in LSJ, BDAG, *EDNT*, BDF, MM, and Rossberg do not include any reference to a causal use. Of course this does not show that such a use is nonexistent, but it certainly makes the exegete hesitant to classify a passage that way, especially if recognized uses of this preposition satisfactorily account for the particular use. Yet it would not occasion surprise if there were such cases, since εἰς can be shown to overlap with at least four of the principal uses of ἐν (see above), another being causal. The best approach would seem to be to examine the proposed examples with a questioning yet open mind. The translation preferred will be given with each verse.

> **Mt 10:41a** εἰς ὄνομα προφήτου, "*as* a prophet" or "*because* he is a prophet"
> **Mt 10:41b** εἰς ὄνομα δικαίου, "*as* a righteous person" or "*because* he is a righteous person"
> **Mt 10:42** εἰς ὄνομα μαθητοῦ, "*as* my disciple" or "*because* he is my disciple"
> **Mt 12:41** (= Lk 11:32) εἰς τὸ κήρυγμα Ἰωνᾶ, "*at* the preaching of Jonah" (cf. BDAG 291c)
> **Mt 14:31** (cf. Mk 15:34) εἰς τί ἐδίστασας; "*why* did you doubt?" (literally, "in order to what?")

Ac 7:53 εἰς διαταγὰς ἀγγέλων, "*by* directions of angels" (BDAG 237c) = ἐν διαταγαῖς (BDF §206[1])

Ro 4:20 εἰς δὲ τὴν ἐπαγγελίαν τοῦ θεοῦ διεκρίθη, "yet he did not waver *with regard to* God's promise"

Ro 11:32 συνέκλεισεν γὰρ ὁ θεὸς τοὺς πάντας εἰς ἀπείθειαν "for God has consigned all *to* disobedience" (cf. Ps 77:62 LXX)

2Co 10:16 οὐκ ... εἰς τὰ ἕτοιμα καυχήσασθαι, "not to boast *about* work already done"

Gal 6:4 τότε εἰς ἑαυτὸν μόνον τὸ καύχημα ἕξει καὶ οὐκ εἰς τὸν ἕτερον, "then he will take pride *with regard to/in* himself alone, and not somebody else"

2Ti 2:25 μετάνοιαν εἰς ἐπίγνωσιν ἀληθείας, "repentance *leading to* a knowledge of the truth"

2Ti 2:26 ἐζωγρημένοι ὑπ᾽ αὐτοῦ εἰς τὸ ἐκείνου θέλημα, "entrapped by him *to do* his will"

Tit 3:14 εἰς τὰς ἀναγκαίας χρείας, "*to relieve* the pressing needs of others"

Heb 12:7 εἰς παιδείαν ὑπομένετε, "endure hardship *as* discipline/it is *for the benefits of* discipline that you have to endure"

1Jn 5:10 οὐ πεπίστευκεν εἰς τὴν μαρτυρίαν, "he has not believed the testimony"

From this analysis we conclude that although there are as many as 15 instances where εἰς could be construed as causal, in no case is εἰς in itself unambiguously causal; alternative and preferable renderings always present themselves.[12] In Mt 10:41–42 it is not εἰς in itself that justifies the rendering "because," but the phrase εἰς ὄνομα, which may be a Semitism, representing a causal use of *ĕšēm* (cf. Zerwick §106); or it may be a case where ὄνομα means "category," so that εἰς ὄνομα προφήτου has the sense "*within the category [of his being a] 'prophet,*' i.e. because he is a prophet, *as a prophet*" (BDAG 714b; similarly LN §58.22). In that case, εἰς = ἐν ("within"). H. Bietenhard takes εἰς here as an accusative of respect — "with respect to the fact that" (*TDNT* 5:274).

If there are no conclusive NT cases of εἰς used causally, we should not expect to find such usage in two theologically important verses (Mt 3:11 and Ac 2:38),

---

12. See the vigorous debate on this issue in the *JBL* (1951–1952) between J. R. Mantey ("The Causal Use of *Eis* in the New Testament," *JBL* 70 [1951]: 45–48; "On Causal *Eis* Again," ibid., 309–11) and R. Marcus ("On Causal *Eis*," ibid., 129–30; "The Elusive Causal *Eis*," *JBL* 71 [1952]: 43–44). Mantey has not adduced any convincing example from extrabiblical Hellenistic Greek where εἰς expresses "immediate and direct cause." The one example he cites from the LXX is Gen 4:23: ἄνδρα ἀπέκτεινα εἰς τραῦμα ἐμοὶ καὶ νεανίσκον εἰς μώλωπα ἐμοί; "I killed a man for wounding me and a young man for striking me." Here εἰς renders the Hebrew "*lamed* of specification" ("regarding"), which exceptionally (as here) can be almost causal. As the Greek stands, εἰς could mean simply "regarding [his wounding me] ... regarding [his striking me]."

which are discussed in detail below (ch. 21 C). It is significant that A. Oepke, who allows a "very occasional" causal εἰς in the NT, finds εἰς to be telic/final in both of these verses (*TDNT* 2:429). For the uses of εἰς with βαπτίζω, see ch. 21 C; for its use with πιστεύω, see ch. 22 B.

G. Significant Phrases Using Εἰς
1. Εἰς (τὴν) δόξαν (τοῦ) θεοῦ (πατρός)

In this phrase εἰς may indicate purpose ("in order to promote") or result ("that leads to"); only the context will determine which meaning is appropriate. Just as δοξάζω can mean "glorify" in the sense of "recognize someone's status and give appropriate honor," so, correspondingly, in reference to God δόξα can refer to the recognition of God's majesty and the ascription to him of appropriate praise, as it does in this phrase (which BDAG [258a] simply renders "to the praise of God").

a. Purpose

Ro 15:7 "Welcome one another, then, just as Christ welcomed you, *in order to bring praise to God.*"

1Co 10:31 "So whether you eat or drink or whatever you do, do everything *in order to promote God's glory.*"

b. Result

Ro 3:7 "[Someone might argue,] 'If God's truthfulness is enhanced by my falsehood *and so increases his glory,* why am I still condemned as a sinner?'"

2Co 4:15 "Yes, all this is for your benefit, so that when grace has widened its scope through more and more people, it may increase thanksgiving, *and so lead to God's glory.*"

Php 1:9–11 "And this is my prayer: that your love will keep on growing ever richer in knowledge and insight of every kind, so that you can discern what really matters and may be pure and blameless until the day of Christ, yielding the full harvest of righteousness that comes through Jesus Christ—all this *advancing God's glory and praise.*"

Cf. εἰς ἔπαινον δόξης αὐτοῦ ("leading to the extolling of his majesty," Eph 1:12, 14); πρὸς δόξαν (2Co 1:20); πρὸς τὴν αὐτοῦ τοῦ κυρίου δόξαν (2Co 8:19).

Philippians 2:10–11

ἵνα ἐν τῷ ὀνόματι Ἰησοῦ πᾶν γόνυ κάμψῃ ... καὶ πᾶσα γλῶσσα ἐξομολογήσηται ὅτι κύριος Ἰησοῦς Χριστὸς εἰς δόξαν θεοῦ πατρός

"that at the name of Jesus every knee should bow ... and every tongue confess that Jesus Christ is Lord—leading to the glory of God the Father"

What resulted in the glorifying of God the Father? With what ideas or words should εἰς δόξαν θεοῦ πατρός be construed? There are three possibilities.

1. The whole drama of redemption described in Php 2:6–11, i.e., the preexistence (v. 6), incarnation (v. 7), death (v. 8), and exaltation (vv. 9–11) of Christ. This would be the widest contextual antecedent.
2. ὅτι κύριος Ἰησοῦς Χριστός, i.e., Christ's installation as κύριος. This is the immediate and narrowest antecedent.
3. ἵνα … κάμψῃ … ἐξομολογήσηται, i.e., the universal acknowledgement, by both action and word, of Christ's lordship. Syntactically, this is the most likely antecedent.

There can be little doubt that the climax of the "hymn" is found in the universal confession κύριος Ἰησοῦς Χριστός, but the four words that follow are certainly no anticlimax or afterthought, no merely formal appendage. Rather, they testify to Paul's unwavering belief in the ultimacy of God the Father. The worship of the Son ultimately redounds to the glory of the Father, enhancing the divine prestige (cf. BDAG 257d); "wherever the Son is glorified, the Father is glorified" (Chrysostom). If the Son represents penultimacy in the divine economy, the Father represents ultimacy: at the end, God the Father will be "all in all," utterly supreme (1Co 15:27–28). Paul can affirm not only that τὰ πάντα ἐκ τοῦ θεοῦ (2Co 5:18) or ἐξ αὐτοῦ … τὰ πάντα (Ro 11:36), but also that εἰς αὐτὸν τὰ πάντα (Ro 11:36). Yet the Father himself has endowed Jesus Christ with the name (κύριος) that surpasses every name so that the title εἷς κύριος can be applied to Jesus (1Co 8:6; Eph 4:5). Paul has clearly reformulated his inherited Jewish monotheism so as to include Christ within the Godhead.

2. Βλασφημεῖν εἰς τὸ πνεῦμα τὸ ἅγιον

Εἰς can express two opposite relationships between people:

a. friendly	Ro 12:16	τὸ αὐτὸ εἰς ἀλλήλους φρονοῦντες "have equal regard for one another"
	1Pe 4:9	φιλόξενοι εἰς ἀλλήλους "show hospitality to one another"
b. hostile	2Co 10:1	θαρρῶ εἰς ὑμᾶς "I deal boldly with you"
	Col 3:9	μὴ ψεύδεσθε εἰς ἀλλήλους "do not lie to one another"

Mark 3:29

Ὃς δ᾽ ἂν βλασφημήσῃ εἰς τὸ πνεῦμα τὸ ἅγιον, οὐκ ἔχει ἄφεσιν εἰς τὸν αἰῶνα, ἀλλὰ ἔνοχός ἐστιν αἰωνίου ἁμαρτήματος

"But whoever blasphemes against the Holy Spirit remains unforgiven for eternity; he is guilty of an eternal sin."

In an emphatic and solemn affirmation (ἀμὴν λέγω ὑμῖν, v. 28a) Jesus distinguishes sins and slander that God will (= can) forgive (v. 28), and one particular sin—blasphemy or slander against the Holy Spirit—that God will not forgive and so has "unending consequences" (αἰωνίου). This teaching arose from the accusation of the Pharisees that Jesus was exorcizing demons by the power of Beelzebub (v. 22). Their blasphemy apparently consisted of verbally crediting Satan with what was clearly God's work through Jesus—the emancipation of people from Satan's influence by the power of the Spirit (ἐν πνεύματι θεοῦ, Mt 12:28). Their repeated accusations (note the iterative imperfect ἔλεγον in Mk 3:22 and 30) that Jesus was "possessed by Beelzebub" (v. 22) and had "an evil spirit" (v. 30) reflected a mind-set that rejected God's redemptive action through his Spirit. "Speaking a word against the Son of Man" was a forgivable sin (Mt 12:32; Lk 12:10)—Peter's rebuke of Jesus (Mt 16:22–23) was subsequently forgiven (cf. Jn 21:15–17)—but the willful and open rejection of the Spirit's overtures was beyond forgiveness.

In this verse and in the Lukan parallel (Lk 12:10) εἰς clearly means "against," as is shown by Matthew's expression ἡ δὲ τοῦ πνεύματος βλασφημία (Mt 12:31), where τοῦ πνεύματος is an objective genitive, "directed at/against the Spirit," and by his twofold use of κατά in the following verse (Mt 12:32).

3. Uses of Εἰς with (ὁ) Αἰών

a. Εἰς τὸν αἰῶνα

In Jewish and early Christian circles in the first century AD, history was divided into two ages:

"the present age" (Heb. *hā'ôlām hazzeh*), variously called:	ὁ αἰὼν ὁ ἐνεστώς (e.g., Gal 1:4)
	ὁ νῦν αἰών (e. g., 1 Ti 6:17)
	ὁ αἰὼν οὗτος (1Co 1:20)
"the age to come" (Heb. *hā'ôlām habbā'*), variously called:	ὁ αἰὼν ὁ μέλλων (Mt 12:32)
	ὁ αἰὼν ὁ ἐρχόμενος (Lk 18:30)
	ὁ αἰὼν ὁ ἐπερχόμενος (Eph 2:7)

Since the term αἰών can refer to either a limited or an unlimited period of time, the phrase εἰς τὸν αἰῶνα has no uniform meaning and does not always mean "for [= throughout] the age [to come]"; its sense depends on the referent and the context.

- "Permanently/for a lifetime"—of a son's place in his family (Jn 8:35)
- "In perpetuity"—of the presence of the Spirit in believers (Jn 14:16)
- "To eternity/eternally" (BDAG 32b)/"for ever" (BDAG 289d):
  of Jesus' resurrected life (Heb 7:24)
  of Christ's priesthood (Heb 5:6; 6:20; 7:17)
  of the word of the Lord (1Pe 1:25)
  of the believer's life (Jn 6:51, 58; 1Jn 2:17)

But when the phrase is negated, it has the attenuated meaning of "never again" (e.g., Mt 21:19), "never" (e.g., Jn 10:28), or "not ever" (Jn 13:8)

b. Εἰς τοὺς αἰῶνας

The plural τοὺς αἰῶνας may be explained as "generalizing" (cf. BDF §141[1]; Zerwick §7) or as "Semitic" (where αἰῶνες reflects *'ôlāmîm*; Turner 25) or even as a stylistic variation of the singular τὸν αἰῶνα.

Here the meaning is always "to all eternity (BDAG 32b)/eternally/for ever:"

- of the blessedness or praiseworthiness of God (Ro 1:25; 2Co 11:31) and of Christ (Ro 9:5)
- of the glory that belongs to God (Ro 11:36)
- of the future reign of Jesus (Lk 1:33)

c. Εἰς τοὺς αἰῶνας τῶν αἰώνων

The meaning of this phrase is "for ever and ever/for evermore" (BDAG 32b). The added genitive τῶν αἰώνων simply emphasizes the unendingness or eternality already expressed by εἰς τοὺς αἰῶνας (or εἰς τὸν αἰῶνα). But the two juxtaposed plurals suggest that from one perspective eternity may be considered an interminable accumulation of endless "ages" (αἰῶνες) (cf. H. Sasse, *TDNT* 1:199). This extended phrase is a common formula in doxologies (Gal 1:5; Php 4:20; 1Ti 1:17; 2Ti 4:18; Heb 13:21; 1Pe 4:11; 5:11; also Ro 16:27, 𝔓[61vid] ℵ A D P 81 lat) and occurs 13 times in Revelation.

Hebrews 13:8

Ἰησοῦς Χριστὸς ἐχθὲς καὶ σήμερον ὁ αὐτὸς καὶ **εἰς** τοὺς αἰῶνας

"Jesus Christ, the same yesterday, today—and for ever"

In contrast with church leaders who once guided church members in accordance with the word of God (Heb 13:7) but who through death were now unable to give that guidance, Jesus Christ is permanently available, as the unchanging one (1:12b, citing Ps 101:28 LXX)—"yesterday," as the one who offered up prayers and petitions during his earthly life (5:7) and effected cleansing from sin (1:3); "today," as a great and sympathetic high priest (4:14–15) with a permanent priesthood (7:24), who constantly meets his people's needs (7:26); "and for ever," as the one who is eternally alive and who intercedes for his people (7:24–25). Church leaders may come and go and "all sorts of outlandish teachings" (REB) may gain currency, but Christ himself represents personal continuity and permanency as the essence of the gospel message ("the word of God"). Εἰς τοὺς αἰῶνας is not an afterthought but a climax "—yes, and for eternity!" Being immutable, Christ will never be superseded or supplanted.

No NT letter speaks more often of the eternality of Christ and the phrase εἰς τοὺς αἰῶνας (and parallels) sums up this prominent feature of the letter.

- "Your throne, O God, is for ever and ever [εἰς τὸν αἰῶνα τοῦ αἰῶνος, Heb 1:8]" affirms that Christ's personal rule is eternal and implies that Christ, as ruler, is also eternal.
- Εἰς τὸν αἰῶνα τοῦ αἰῶνος here reflects the phrase εἰς τὸν αἰῶνα of Ps 109:4 LXX that is cited three times by the author in reference to the eternality of the Melchizedekian order of priesthood (Heb 5:6; 6:20; 7:17). Jesus is a priest "forever" in the succession of Melchizedek, and the treatment in Hebrews of the relationship between these two figures constitutes the culmination and essence of the whole letter.
- "You are the same and your years will never end" (Heb 1:12).
- "One who has become a priest ... on the basis of the power arising from an indestructible life [ζωῆς ἀκαταλύτου]" (Heb 7:16).
- "He lives for ever [εἰς τὸν αἰῶνα] ... he has the power for all time (εἰς τὸ παντελές) to bring salvation to those who approach God through him, since he is always alive (πάντοτε ζῶν) to plead on their behalf" (Heb 7:24–25).

2 Peter 3:18

Αὐτῷ ἡ δόξα καὶ νῦν καὶ εἰς ἡμέραν αἰῶνος

"Glory belongs to him [Jesus Christ] both now and to the day of eternity."

This is the only NT use of the remarkable expression ἡμέρα αἰῶνος.[13] The genitive could be epexegetic, "the day, which is eternity," or adjectival, "the eternal day" that will dawn at the parousia (2Pe 1:19); but more probably it is a "general" genitive/genitive of reference, "the Day [of the Lord (Jesus), 2Pe 3:10] that ushers in [future] eternity." If so, this doxology is ascribing glory to Christ both in the present age and in the eternal age to come. The parousia is both the culminating day and the last "day" of all.

Jude 25

—μόνῳ θεῷ σωτῆρι ἡμῶν διὰ Ἰησοῦ Χριστοῦ τοῦ κυρίου ἡμῶν δόξα μεγαλωσύνη κράτος καὶ ἐξουσία πρὸ παντὸς τοῦ αἰῶνος καὶ νῦν καὶ εἰς πάντας τοὺς αἰῶνας, ἀμήν

"—to the only God, our Savior, is glory, majesty, power, and authority, through Jesus Christ our Lord, before all time, and now, and for ever and ever."

---

13. The expression also occurs in Sir 18:9–10: "The number of a person's days are at most 100 years. In comparison with the day of eternity [ἐν ἡμέρᾳ αἰῶνος] a few years are like a drop of water from the sea or a pebble from the sand" (cf. 2Pe 3:8).

A timeless ἐστιν should be supplied with δόξα κτλ. But to avoid the conceptually awkward "is [as opposed to 'was'] ... before all time," we could supply "[to the only God, our Savior] be ascribed [through Jesus Christ our Lord, glory ...]" (as TCNT, Cassirer) and continue "as it was before all time, is now, and shall be for ever and ever."

If διὰ Ἰησοῦ Χριστοῦ τοῦ κυρίου ἡμῶν belonged with the preceding σωτῆρι ἡμῶν (as in Moffatt, RSV, JB, NLT), we might have expected the more natural μόνῳ θεῷ τῷ σώσαντι ἡμᾶς or μόνῳ θεῷ τῷ σῴζοντι ἡμᾶς (JB in fact has "to God, the only God, who saves us"); the sequence, "our Savior, through the Savior" (Jesus) seems somewhat inelegant. Rather, this phrase should be construed with the following δόξα κτλ., as TCNT, Goodspeed, NEB, NAB[1], NIV[1,2], Cassirer, REB; and, with a comma after "Savior," RV, ASV, NASB[1,2], Barclay, GNB, NJB, NAB[2], NRSV, HCSB, ESV. "Glory, majesty, power, and authority" belonged to God through Jesus Christ "before time began" (BDAG 32a; cf. πρὸ τῶν αἰώνων), that is, in eternity past, and these attributes belong to God at present (νῦν) and will do so "to all eternity" (BDAG 32b)/"for evermore." This unique eternal mediatorial work of Christ in ascribing all glory, majesty, power, and authority to God implies both his preexistence and his deity.

Jude's inclusion of past, present, and future in his doxology is unique among Jewish and early Christian doxologies, although threefold temporal descriptions of Christ (Heb 13:8) and God (Rev 1:4; 4:8) are found outside doxologies.

4. Τοῦτο ποιεῖτε εἰς τὴν ἐμὴν ἀνάμνησιν (Lk 22:19; 1Co 11:24–25)

"Do this so that you might remember me."

Several matters seem clear.

a. Τοῦτο ποιεῖτε means "Do this" in the sense "Perform these acts," not "Offer this sacrifice," which would require τοῦτο προσφέρετε or the equivalent. The actions to be carried out were taking the bread and the wine, giving thanks, breaking the bread and pouring the wine, and reciting the words of institution.

b. Εἰς is telic, equivalent to a ἵνα clause, "in order that, with a view to." The literal rendering "for the remembrance of me" is more naturally expressed as "in memory/remembrance of me" (BDAG 68b; 323a; and most EVV). It is not impossible, however, that εἰς = ὡς, "as a memorial of me" (NEB, in 1Co 11:24–25; Lk 22:19 mg).

c. As an attributive adjective, ἐμός can be equivalent to an objective genitive (BDAG 323a), here μου. Significantly, an objective genitive (ἁμαρτιῶν) follows the only other NT use of ἀνάμνησις ("a reminder of sins," Heb 10:3).

But the crucial question is whether the ἀνάμνησις is (1) *God's remembering*: "Do this, that God may remember me (as his Messiah)" and bring in the kingdom at the parousia;[14] or (2) a *human remembering*. It is unlikely both senses are intended or that Paul's understanding of the phrase is to be distinguished from Jesus' intended sense.

In favor of (2), the following points may be made.

(a) In the context Paul is instructing the Corinthians how they ought to conduct themselves as they celebrate the Lord's Supper (1Co 11:17–34). By reminding them of the circumstances of the meal's institution according to Christian tradition (vv. 23–25), he is demonstrating that the purpose of the Supper was to enable Jesus' followers to "remember" him, not to satisfy human appetite for food and drink (vv. 20–21, 34). The way the Corinthians were behaving at the Supper was contradicting the very purpose of the celebration.

(b) This "remembering" of Christ involved primarily a human "proclaiming" of Christ's death (v. 26; note the explanatory γάρ) to other humans by the recounting of the events surrounding his death, including (presumably) his resurrection and exaltation (since the instruction was to "remember me"). That the Lord's Supper commemorates Christ's resurrection as well as his death is shown by the early association of Sunday (not Friday) with the celebration.

(c) The idea that God needs to be "reminded" in any sense of the need to bring in the kingdom or of the efficacy of his Son's atoning death betrays an anthropomorphic view of God's knowledge and ignores the fact that the very presence of Christ before God as believers' "friend at court" (Ro 8:34) is a potent reminder, if such were needed, of the adequacy of the atonement.

5. Λογίζεσθαι εἰς

This phrase, which in the LXX renders *ḥāšab l* (BDB 363b), occurs in a quotation of Ge 15:6 in three NT passages.

MT: "He [Abram] believed Yahweh, and he [Yahweh] reckoned it [Abram's faith] to him as righteousness."

LXX: καὶ ἐπίστευσεν Ἀβραμ τῷ θεῷ, καὶ ἐλογίσθη αὐτῷ εἰς δικαιοσύνην
"And Abram believed God, and [Abram's faith] was credited to his account [by God] as righteousness."

Εἰς δικαιοσύνην has been understood in various ways:

1. "as equivalent to/standing in the place of righteousness"[15]
2. "as a righteous, meritorious act" (the prevalent Jewish view—see, e.g., Philo, *Quis Rer. Div. Her.* 90–95; Mekilta 40[b] [on Ex 14:31] speaks of the "merit of faith" while citing Gen 15:6; SB 3:199–201)

---

14. So J. Jeremias, *The Eucharistic Words of Jesus* (London: SCM, 1966), 244–55.
15. W. Sanday and A. C. Headlam, *A Critical and Exegetical Commentary on the Epistle to the Romans* (ICC; Edinburgh: T&T Clark, 1902), 100.

3. "as giving a status of righteousness"[16]

This last view (faith is recorded in God's ledger *as bringing righteousness*) seems to be reflected in the three NT citations.

a. Romans 4:3

In Ro 4:1–25 Paul finds in the case of Abraham an OT precedent for the principle of righteousness on the basis of faith apart from observing the law (3:28; 4:6). Paul can say both that "faith was reckoned to Abraham as righteousness" (4:9; cf. 4:3, 5, 22) and that righteousness was reckoned to the account of Abraham on the basis of his faith (4:6, 11, 13, 23; cf. 9:30; Php 3:9) because he regarded faith and righteousness as correlatives.[17]

b. Galatians 3:6

Here Paul is appealing to Scripture: (1) to validate the implied answer to the question he posed in vv. 2 and 5: "Did God give you the Spirit because of your law-observance or because of your faith in the gospel?"; and (2) to preface his demonstration in vv. 6–14 that those who believe are children of Abraham (v. 7) and that "the righteous will live by faith" (v. 11) and receive the promised Spirit (v. 14). As in Ro 4:3, Abraham's faith was his unswerving acceptance of God's promise that his own son would be his heir and that his descendants would be as numerous as the stars of heaven (Ge 15:4–5).

c. James 2:23

In Jas 2:14–26 the author is seeking to establish the inseparability of faith and actions. Abraham's example (v. 23) shows that the two are complementary (v. 22), since Abraham "offered his son Isaac on the altar" (v. 21; cf. Ge 22:1–18) in an "obedience inspired by faith" (Ro 16:26) and he had already acted on the basis of faith in departing from Ur and traveling to Canaan in obedience to God's call (Ge 12:1–3; 13:1).

6. Εἰς αὐτὸ τοῦτο

Literally, this phrase means "for this itself," thus "for just this" (cf. BDAG 153a), "for this very reason" (BDAG 290d). If the τοῦτο is prospective, the reason may be defined ("namely, that") by a following ἵνα clause (as in Col 4:8//Eph 6:22) or ὅπως clause (as in Ro 9:17). If it is retrospective, the context will indicate the implied or explicit antecedent, as is the case in 2Co 5:5.

---

16. Douglas J. Moo, *The Epistle to the Romans* (NICNT; Grand Rapids: Eerdmans, 1996), 262.
17. Cf. J. Murray, *The Epistle to the Romans* (NICNT; Grand Rapids: Eerdmans, 1959), 1:343, 359.

2 Corinthians 5:5

ὁ δὲ κατεργασάμενος ἡμᾶς εἰς αὐτὸ τοῦτο θεός, ὁ δοὺς ἡμῖν τὸν ἀρραβῶνα τοῦ πνεύματος

"Now the one who has prepared us for this very destiny is God, who gave us the Spirit as a pledge."

The immediate antecedent of τοῦτο here is ἵνα καταποθῇ τὸ θνητὸν ὑπὸ τῆς ζωῆς, "so that what is mortal may be swallowed up by life." If τὸ θνητόν is a case of "abstract for concrete" ("what is mortal" = "this mortal body" [τὸ θνητὸν τοῦτο, 1Co 15:53–54]) and καταπίνω implies absorption (cf. NEB, REB) rather than annihilation, Paul is referring to the transformation of the mortal, earthly body by "(eternal) life," by "what is immortal" (= ἀθανασία, 1Co 15:53–54), by immortality. Such a resurrection transformation forms the climax, we suggest, of the incessant process of inward renewal (2Co 4:16b). For Paul, resurrection consummates rather than inaugurates the process of spiritual re-creation, being the acceleration and completion of the process of "Christification."

Verse 5b specifies the means God used to prepare believers for this climactic change, for "the redemption of the body" (Ro 8:23; cf. Eph 1:14; 4:30). He gave them his Spirit as the pledge (ἀρραβών) of the receipt of their future inheritance (Eph 1:14), a resplendent resurrection body comparable to Christ's (Php 3:21). The same Spirit who empowers the daily re-creation of believers (2Co 3:18; 4:16; Eph 3:16) will also effect their resurrection transformation (Ro 8:11; cf. 1Co 6:14; Gal 6:8) and sustain their resurrection life (Ro 1:4). Paul found the continuity between the present age and the age to come in the possession and activity of the Spirit. In 2Co 3:18 Paul may allude to these two stages of the Spirit's work. There is the ongoing present metamorphosis of character, and also the creation of the final "degree of glory" when Christians come to bear perfectly the image of the man from heaven (Ro 8:29; 1Co 15:49).

H. Significant Successive Instances of Εἰς

1. Ephesians 1:3–14

- εἰς υἱοθεσίαν (v. 5, telic εἰς): "In love God predestined us *to be installed as his sons*."
- εἰς αὐτόν (v. 5, telic): "*for himself*"/"*to promote his own pleasure*"; or εἰς could be a substitute for the dative of advantage (ἑαυτῷ; cf. BDAG 290d)
- εἰς ἔπαινον δόξης τῆς χάριτος αὐτοῦ (v. 6), either telic ("*this was aimed at extoling the splendor of his grace*") or ecbatic/consecutive/resultative ("*this redounds to the praise of his glorious grace*"); or both senses may be present (see ch. 3. D)

- εἰς οἰκονομίαν (v. 10, telic): (v. 9) "God has made known to us his will, formerly hidden, in harmony with his good pleasure which he purposed within himself—[v. 10] (*a purpose destined to be put into effect* when the times reach their fulfillment)."
- εἰς τὸ εἶναι ἡμᾶς ... εἰς ἔπαινον δόξης αὐτοῦ (v. 12, telic ... telic): (v. 11) "By our union with Christ, too, we have been made God's inheritance for we were predestined for this ... [v. 12] *so that we* who were the first to place our hope in Christ *should be devoted to praising his glorious majesty.*" For the construction εἰμὶ εἴς τι, "serve as something," see BDAG 290c.
- εἰς ἀπολύτρωσιν τῆς περιποιήσεως, εἰς ἔπαινον τῆς δόξης αὐτοῦ (v. 14, temporal εἰς, then ecbatic and/or telic): (v. 13) "You were sealed with the promised Holy Spirit, [v. 14] who is a deposit guaranteeing our inheritance *until our redemption* as those who are God's possession—*leading to the praise of his glory/for the extoling of his glorious majesty.*"

2. 2 Thessalonians 2:13–14

- εἰς σωτηρίαν (v. 13, telic εἰς): "From the first God chose you *to be saved*"
- εἰς ὅ (v. 14, telic): "It was *to gain this salvation* that he called you through our preaching of the gospel"
- εἰς περιποίησιν (v. 14, telic, redefining the purpose of the divine choice and calling, or defining the goal of the σωτηρία): "*So that you may share in* the majestic splendor of our Lord Jesus Christ."

3. 1 Peter 1:3–5

- εἰς ἐλπίδα ζῶσαν (v. 3) telic: "In his great mercy God has caused us to be born anew *so that we may possess* a life-giving hope" or ecbatic: " ... *and so we have* a living hope" or both—defining the purpose and/or outcome of divine regeneration
- εἰς κληρονομίαν ... εἰς ὑμᾶς (v. 4) telic, defining the content of the vibrant hope; and telic, indicating the beneficiaries of the inheritance, or εἰς equivalent to a dative of advantage (ὑμῖν): "a life-giving hope, *namely, an inheritance* ... reserved in heaven *for you/for your benefit*"
- εἰς σωτηρίαν (v. 5) ecbatic, defining the outcome of God's powerful protection: "you who, through faith, are being protected by God's power, *and so acquire a salvation* that is ready to be disclosed at the final time"; or telic, " ... *so that you may acquire a salvation* that is ready to be disclosed at the final time." If both senses are present, "*for a salvation.*"

I. Ambiguity of Meaning

Not infrequently the import of εἰς is unclear and all the exegete can do is to opt for an accepted sense of the preposition that accords with the context and with the writer's usage and theology. For instance, in Col 3:10 the phrase εἰς ἐπίγνωσιν that follows ἐνδυσάμενοι τὸν νέον [ἄνθρωπον] τὸν ἀνακαινούμενον ("for you have put on the new nature, which is being renewed") has been understood as

1. expressing direction: "towards true knowledge" (NJB)
2. equivalent to a locatival ἐν: "in knowledge" (BDAG 369d, 572d; TCNT, NRSV, NIV[1,2]) = "in the sphere of knowledge" or "with respect to knowledge"
3. telic: "for full knowledge" (BDAG 64d)
4. consecutive: "leading to knowledge" (ZG 609)
5. temporal: "until it reaches fullness of knowledge" (Barclay)

J. Εἰς in Compounds

Compounds with εἰς are few (only about 13 in the NT — MH 304) in comparison with ἐν, since εἰς was originally a variant of ἐν (see above, C). Nine of the 10 verbal compounds occur only a total of 50 times (MH 304). Not surprisingly, the idea of *entrance* (cf. εἴσοδος, in-coming, entrance) is found in many of the compounds — e.g., εἰσέρχομαι (191 uses), go into; εἰσφέρω, bring into; εἰσκαλέομαι, invite into; εἰσδέχομαι, receive into, welcome.

Chapter 9

Ἐκ

A. Introduction

Ἐκ (ἐξ before vowels) is the third most common preposition in the NT after ἐν and εἰς, accounting for 8.8% of NT "proper" prepositions. More than a third of the NT uses are in the Johannine corpus. Although its uses are varied, they are less varied than those of ἀπό (Regard 416), which has displaced ἐκ in Modern Greek. Yet ἐκ is more common than ἀπό in the NT (916x vs. 646x), but not in the LXX (3823x vs. 4150x) or the Ptolemaic papyri (903x vs. 920x).

B. Basic Signification

Originally ἐκ signified an exit "from within" something with which there had been an intimate connection, so that ἐκ expressed the severance of some relationship. It is the opposite of εἰς, "to the inside of." So, more generally, in reference to geography, we read that Jesus had come ἐκ τῆς Ἰουδαίας εἰς τὴν Γαλιλαίαν (Jn 4:47).

From this original spatial idea there naturally developed the primary non-spatial/metaphorical notion of *origin*, which in turn prompted the use of ἐκ to express source, agency, basis, cause, and means—to mention the main figurative uses. For example, the transition from origin to cause or occasion is easy to understand, both meaning "arising from." To illustrate this MM cites P.Oxy. VII. 1020 line 5 (AD 198–201), τὴν ἐκ τῆς ἡλικίας ... β[οήθιαν], "the assistance due to immature age" (189d).

C. Range of Figurative Uses

1. Origin

Mt 28:2 ἄγγελος γὰρ κυρίου καταβὰς ἐξ οὐρανοῦ
"For the angel of the Lord descended from heaven."

Php 3:5 Ἑβραῖος ἐξ Ἑβραίων

"a Hebrew, the son of Hebrews" (Moulton 10; BDAG 296c) (of familial origin; not "a Hebrew of Hebrews" = "a thorough Hebrew")

2. Source

2Co 2:4 Ἐκ γὰρ πολλῆς θλίψεως καὶ συνοχῆς καρδίας ἔγραψα ὑμῖν

"For I wrote you out of deep distress and anguish of heart."

1Co 9:14 ὁ κύριος διέταξεν τοῖς τὸ εὐαγγέλιον καταγγέλλουσιν **ἐκ** τοῦ εὐαγγελίου ζῆν

"The Lord directed that those who proclaim the gospel are to get their livelihood from [proclaiming] the gospel."

3. Agency

Jn 6:65 οὐδεὶς δύναται ἐλθεῖν πρός με ἐὰν μὴ ᾖ δεδομένον αὐτῷ **ἐκ** τοῦ πατρός

" No one can come to me unless enabled by the Father."

2Co 8:7 τῇ **ἐξ** ἡμῶν ἐν ὑμῖν ἀγάπῃ (𝔓⁴⁶ B 1739 1881)

"the love we inspired in you"

4. Basis

1Co 7:5 μὴ ἀποστερεῖτε ἀλλήλους, εἰ μήτι ἂν **ἐκ** συμφώνου πρὸς καιρόν

"Do not deprive one another [of sexual intercourse], unless perhaps on the basis of/by mutual consent and for a time."

2Co 8:11 ὅπως καθάπερ ἡ προθυμία τοῦ θέλειν, οὕτως καὶ τὸ ἐπιτελέσαι **ἐκ** τοῦ ἔχειν

"so that your eager desire may be matched by your completion [of the project], on the basis of/according to your means"

5. Cause

Jn 4:6 ὁ οὖν Ἰησοῦς κεκοπιακὼς **ἐκ** τῆς ὁδοιπορίας

"so Jesus, exhausted because of/from the journey"

2Co 7:9 ἐν μηδενὶ ζημιωθῆτε **ἐξ** ἡμῶν

"You suffered no harm at all because of us/at our hands."

6. Means

Lk 16:9 ἑαυτοῖς ποιήσατε φίλους **ἐκ** τοῦ μαμωνᾶ τῆς ἀδικίας

"Win friends for yourselves by means of money, tainted though it be."

Heb 11:35 ἔλαβον γυναῖκες **ἐξ** ἀναστάσεως τοὺς νεκροὺς αὐτῶν

"Women received back their dead through their being resurrected/as a result of their resurrection."

D. Important Constructions Using Ἐκ

1. Ἐκ (τοῦ) θεοῦ

With the ubiquitous NT portrayal of God as both creator and redeemer, it is not surprising that this phrase points to God as the *origin or source* of a wide variety of entities, whether actions, benefits, or people:

- Jesus' teaching (Jn 7:17)
- Jesus' appearance on earth (Jn 8:42)
- the person who hears what God says (Jn 8:47)
- the many great miracles Jesus performed (Jn 10:32)
- the praise of the person whose heart is circumcised (Ro 2:29)
- people's existence as believers (1Co 1:30; 1Jn 4:4, 6; 5:19)
- the gift of the Spirit (1Co 2:12)
- spiritual gifts (1Co 7:7)
- all human life (1Co 11:12)
- those who sincerely proclaim God's Word (2Co 2:17)
- Paul's empowering to carry out his divine commission (2Co 3:5)
- the resurrection body of believers (2Co 5:1)
- a new and right standing before God (Php 3:9)
- every spirit that acknowledges that Jesus Christ made his appearance in bodily form (1Jn 4:2)
- true love (1Jn 4:7)
- the person who does what is good (3Jn 11)

Two Pauline affirmations that are all-embracing and unqualified sum up God's role as source: ἐξ αὐτοῦ ... τὰ πάντα (Ro 11:36) and εἷς θεὸς ὁ πατὴρ ἐξ οὗ τὰ πάντα (1Co 8:6).

When God is identified as the source of some benefit, it is often permissible to infer that he is also the agent in its provision. For example, if spiritual conversion or "the new creation" is traceable to God (τὰ δὲ πάντα ἐκ τοῦ θεοῦ, 2Co 5:18; cf. 2Co 5:17), we may legitimately assume he is also the agent who produces this alteration of attitude, conduct, and motivation in humans. Also, when spiritual renewal is depicted as God's work, the apostle John frequently employs the metaphor of rebirth or regeneration, either γεννᾶσθαι ἐκ [τοῦ] θεοῦ (Jn 1:13; 1Jn 2:29; 3:9 (2x); 5:1 (2x); 5:4, 18a) or γεννᾶσθαι ἐκ [τοῦ] πνεύματος (Jn 3:5, 6, 8).

John 1:12c–13

τοῖς πιστεύουσιν εἰς τὸ ὄνομα αὐτοῦ, οἳ οὐκ **ἐξ** αἱμάτων οὐδὲ **ἐκ** θελήματος σαρκὸς οὐδὲ **ἐκ** θελήματος ἀνδρὸς ἀλλ' **ἐκ** θεοῦ ἐγεννήθησαν[1]

"to those who believe in his name—children born not of bloodlines, nor of human instincts or a husband's initiative, but born of God"

The three negated ἐκ phrases are simply a foil for the climactic and positive ἐκ θεοῦ. Whether the plural αἵματα, unique in the NT, is a generalizing (cf. Zerwick §7) or idiomatic (Robertson 408) plural (= "blood," RV, ESV) or an actual plural, referring to "bloodlines," αἵματα is a case of "concrete for abstract," the allusion being to human parentage or "human descent" (Weymouth). In the phrase ἐκ θελήματος σαρκός, the term σάρξ refers to the purely natural or physical sphere and is adjectival in import; thus "human instincts" (TCNT; = sexual desire?), "human choice" (NAB[2]). The third negative phrase (**ἐκ** θελήματος ἀνδρός) excludes spiritual rebirth as arising from human initiative, which occurs in natural procreation.

The privileged experience of becoming God's children (Jn 1:12b)—which John later calls the new birth (3:3, 5, 7)—comes through receiving Jesus Christ (1:12a), that is, believing in his person (1:12c), and it owes nothing to special ancestry or natural instincts or human creativity but everything to God's initiative. Ἐκ θεοῦ may be paraphrased "as a result of God's initiative and action."

On ἐξ αὐτοῦ in reference to God (Ro 11:36; 1Co 8:6), see ch. 7.

2. Ἐκ δεξιῶν τοῦ θεοῦ/μου

It was the language and symbolism of Ps 110:1 (109:1 LXX) that shaped the thought of the early Christians as they reflected on the exaltation of Jesus. Given the crucial nature of Christ's enthronement as evidence of God's acceptance of Christ's "offering for sins a single sacrifice of permanent efficacy" (Heb 10:12), it is not surprising that NT writers quote (e.g., Mt 22:44; Ac 2:34; Heb 1:13) or allude to (e.g., Mk 14:62; Heb 8:1) this OT verse more than any other.

---

1. All Gk. mss. and most versional and patristic witnesses read the plural, οἳ ... ἐγεννήθησαν, "[those who believe in his name] who were born...." But some (mainly Latin) witnesses read the sg., ὃς ... ἐγεννήθη, "[the name of him] who was born ...," referring either to Christ's being eternally "begotten" by God or to his virginal conception or birth. A few scholars defend the singular reading (also found in JB, but not NJB), but most commentators and textual critics (e.g., NA[27]; UBS[1-4] [all with an A rating]) prefer the plural reading, on the basis of the uniform Greek testimony and the likelihood that the singular reading arose from a desire to have the Fourth Gospel refer to the virginal conception or birth of Christ or under the influence of the preceding singular αὐτοῦ (see Metzger 168–69), or, possibly, because some scribe took ἐξ αἱμάτων to mean "as a result of [ἐκ] the [shedding of the] blood [of Christ]."

Εἶπεν ὁ κύριος τῷ κυρίῳ μου· Κάθου ἐκ δεξιῶν μου,
ἕως ἂν θῶ τοὺς ἐχθρούς σου ὑποπόδιον τῶν ποδῶν σου

"The Lord said to my Lord, 'Sit at my right hand until I make your enemies a footstool for your feet'."

To be or to sit at someone's right hand is to be in the position of unparalleled honor and privilege (1Ki 2:19). In the case of Christ this meant sharing God's throne (Rev 3:21; 22:1, 3) or occupying the second throne alluded to in Da 7:9 and Mk 14:62 (cf. Heb 1:8). When Paul speaks of Christians' spiritual identification with Christ, he can say, "God has enthroned us with him [Jesus] in the heavenly realms"(Eph 2:6), but significantly he does not add "at his right hand [ἐν δεξιᾷ αὐτοῦ]," a phrase that *is* applied to Christ in a comparable statement in Eph 1:20. Christ's exalted status cannot be shared. Angels stand or fall down in worship in God's presence (1Ki 22:19; Rev 4:10); the enthroned Son sits.

The full phrase ἐκ δεξιῶν τοῦ θεοῦ is found only twice in the NT (apart from Mk 16:19), in connection with Stephen's seeing Jesus "standing at God's right hand" (Ac 7:55–56). Certainly the use of ἐκ to denote position is uncommon (cf. BDAG 296b) except in the stereotyped pair of phrases ἐκ δεξιῶν ("on the right [side]") and ἐξ εὐωνύμων/ἀριστερῶν ("on the left [side]"; see, e.g., Mt 20:21, 23; Mk 10:37; 15:27). Ἐν δεξιᾷ is the form preferred by Paul (Ro 8:34; Eph 1:20; Col 3:1), the author of Hebrews (Heb 1:3; 8:1; 10:12; 12:2), and Peter (1Pe 3:22). This same locatival sense could be expressed by the plain dative, τῇ δεξιᾷ τοῦ θεοῦ/αὐτοῦ (Acts 2:33 and 5:31; so BDF §199; P. von der Osten-Sacken, *EDNT* 1:286c), although these are probably instrumental datives, "by God's/his right hand" (BDAG 218a) or even in the case of Acts 2:33, "by the power of God" (BDAG 1046a). Cf. Ps 117:16 LXX, "The Lord's right hand has exalted me."

Instead of the qualifier τοῦ θεοῦ after ἐκ δεξιῶν or ἐν δεξιᾷ, sometimes we find "of the Mighty One" (Mt 26:64; Mk 14:62), "of God Almighty" (Lk 22:69), "of the Majesty in heaven" (Heb 1:3), "of the throne of God" (Heb 12:2), or "of the throne of the Majesty in heaven" (Heb 8:1).

3. Ἐκ ... Εἰς
a. Romans 1:17

Δικαιοσύνη γὰρ θεοῦ ἐν αὐτῷ ἀποκαλύπτεται ἐκ πίστεως εἰς πίστιν, καθὼς γέγραπται, Ὁ δὲ δίκαιος ἐκ πίστεως ζήσεται.

"For in it [the gospel] a righteousness from God is revealed, a righteousness that is based on faith and leads to faith, just as it stands written, 'The righteous person will live by faith.'"

In the crucial phrase ἐκ πίστεως εἰς πίστιν, the two prepositions may be considered as together forming a single idiomatic sense or as expressing two separate ideas. If ἐκ and εἰς are construed together ("from … to"), the whole phrase may express:

- *progression*, from OT faith with the law to NT faith with the gospel, from God's faithfulness to his covenant promises to human response in faith
- *exclusiveness*, emphasizing "the elimination of other possibilities": God's righteousness is revealed in the gospel "as exclusively a matter of faith" (LN §78.48)
- *rhetorical emphasis* (cf. BDAG 298b), with εἰς πίστιν intensifying the effect of ἐκ: from smaller to greater degree of faith (cf. ἀπὸ δόξης εἰς δόξαν, 2Co 3:18); "by faith from first to last" (NIV[1,2]); "by faith and nothing but faith"

If ἐκ πίστεως εἰς πίστιν qualifies δικαιοσύνη and the prepositions are considered separately, ἐκ will specify the basis ("on the basis of") or the means ("through/by") for the receipt of righteousness, and εἰς the purpose ("for [ever-increasing] faith," whether individual or worldwide) or the effect ("leading to [a life of] faith") of the receipt of righteousness.

We suggest that four distinct affirmations are made in Romans 1:17 regarding the believer's right standing in the heavenly court:

1. It is provided by God (taking θεοῦ as a subjective genitive; cf. τὴν ἐκ θεοῦ δικαιοσύνην, Php 3:9).
2. It is made known for acceptance in the message of the gospel (ἐν αὐτῷ [= τὸ εὐαγγέλιον, Ro 1:16] ἀποκαλύπτεται).
3. It is received on the basis of faith (ἐκ πίστεως).
4. It leads to more and more faith (εἰς πίστιν), which illustrates Hab 2:4.

An expanded paraphrase of the verse will summarize these points.

"In the gospel and its preaching, a new and right relationship with God, provided by him, is made known and made available—a righteousness that is received on the basis of faith and that leads to a life of faith, as it stands written in Scripture, 'The person who is righteous before God will lead a life that is characterized by faith.'"

b. 2 Corinthians 2:16

οἷς μὲν ὀσμὴ ἐκ θανάτου εἰς θάνατον, οἷς δὲ ὀσμὴ ἐκ ζωῆς εἰς ζωήν

"To the latter group it is a deadly stench that leads to death, but to the former it is a vitalizing fragrance that leads to life."

The two groups here referred to are described in v. 15 as οἱ σῳζόμενοι ("those who are being saved") and οἱ ἀπολλύμενοι ("those who are perishing"). In a chiastic construction (ABBA) involving vv. 15 and 16, οἳ ἀπολλύμενοι are those for whom the gospel is ὀσμὴ ἐκ θανάτου εἰς θάνατον, while οἳ σῳζόμενοι are those to whom the gospel is ὀσμὴ ἐκ ζωῆς εἰς ζωήν. In each case εἰς expresses a result or effect: "leading to/resulting in [death or life]." Ἐκ, on the other hand, could denote source ("arising from, issuing from") or, consequently, quality ("characterized by" death or life, simply "of death, of life," or "deadly, life-giving"). If we give the neutral term ὀσμή ("smell, odor") a sense appropriate in the context, we arrive at the rendering suggested above.

Whether we regard the ὀσμή as the gospel as proclaimed by the apostles or the apostles themselves as proclaimers, Paul is envisaging a message or a group of messengers as creating, inevitably, a dual effect: the possession of eternal life (ζωή) as the final outcome of present σωτηρία, and the experience of eternal death (θάνατος) as the outcome of present ἀπώλεια. "Life" results from a positive response to the apostolic preaching, "death" from a negative response (cf. Lk 2:34; Jn 3:36). One aspect of the potency of the cross of Christ (cf. 1Co 1:17) is its power to attract and convert those who repent and to repulse and harden those who are unrepentant. To the former group the cross is a ground for boasting (Gal 6:14), to the latter it is an occasion for offense (1Co 1:23). Compare 1Pe 2:6–8, where one and the same "stone" (= Jesus Christ) is a foundation stone (λίθος ἀκρογωνιαῖος) and a stumbling stone (λίθος προσκόμματος).

On ἐκ ... εἰς in reference to God (Ro 11:36; 1Co 8:6), see ch. 7.

4. Ὁ/οἱ ἐκ + Noun

A distinctive and important use of ἐκ is found in constructions where the singular or plural article is followed by ἐκ and a noun (in the genitive). The uses fall into two categories, with the context, not the number of the article and not always the nature of the noun, determining the category.

1. The whole phrase sometimes has a *neutral* sense, with ἐκ simply signifying "belonging to, connected with" or "member(s) of."

- **Ac 6:9** οἱ ἐκ τῆς συναγωγῆς, "members of the synagogue"
- **Ro 3:26** ὁ ἐκ πίστεως Ἰησοῦ, "believers in Jesus"
- **Ro 4:12** οἱ οὐκ ἐκ περιτομῆς μόνον, "those who are not circumcised merely"
- **Ro 9:6** οἱ ἐξ Ἰσραήλ, "Israelites"
- **Gal 3:7, 9** οἱ ἐκ πίστεως, "those who have faith"
- **Php 4:22** οἱ ἐκ τῆς Καίσαρος οἰκίας, "those who belong to Caesar's household"

But those who share a common origin or membership usually have similar characteristics such as beliefs or conduct, so this use of ὁ/οἱ ἐκ naturally developed into a description of particular groups with shared views or standards. For instance, οἱ ἐκ τοῦ Περιπάτου (Lucian, *Pisc.* 43) means "the Peripatetics," those belonging to the school of Aristotle.

2. The whole phrase sometimes has a *pejorative* sense, determined by the context, with ἐκ signifying not simply connection with or adherence to but often active propagation of a viewpoint.

- Aeschines, *Tim.* 54 οἱ ... ἐκ τῆς διατριβῆς ταύτης, "those characterized by this way of life"
- **Ac 11:2** οἱ ἐκ περιτομῆς, "the circumcision party"
- **Ro 4:14** οἱ ἐκ νόμου, "partisans of the law" (BDAG 296d), "nomists," "those who place reliance on the law" (Cassirer)
- **Ro 4:16** ὁ ἐκ τοῦ νόμου, "those who rely on the Law" (Weymouth), "those who hold by the law" (Cassirer)
- **Gal 2:12** οἱ ἐκ περιτομῆς, "those who belonged to the circumcision group" (NIV[1,2]), "the advocates of circumcision" (Cassirer), who apparently were insisting that Gentile converts should adhere to the Mosaic law, especially circumcision, as a condition of Christian fellowship.

E. Other Significant Instances of Ἐκ
1. John 3:5

Ἐὰν μή τις γεννηθῇ ἐξ ὕδατος καὶ πνεύματος, οὐ δύναται εἰσελθεῖν εἰς τὴν βασιλείαν τοῦ θεοῦ

"Unless a person is born by water and Spirit, he cannot enter the kingdom of God."

In his conversation with Nicodemus (Jn 3:1–15), Jesus solemnly affirms (with ἀμὴν ἀμὴν λέγω σοι, Jn 3:3, 5) the necessity of the new birth for entry into God's kingdom.

Those who regard ὕδωρ and πνεῦμα as *separate entities* in the phrase ἐξ ὕδατος καὶ πνεύματος usually see "born of [the] water" as a reference to physical birth (the "water" being amniotic fluid at birth or semen at conception) and "born of the Spirit" as an allusion to the agent of spiritual birth; or "water" as pointing to proselyte baptism or John the Baptist's baptism or Christian baptism as the instrumental cause of rebirth, and "the Spirit" denoting the primary cause of regeneration.[2]

A dual reference would be incontestable if John had written ἐξ ὕδατος καὶ ἐκ τοῦ πνεύματος. But the difference between the anarthrous [ἐκ] πνεύματος in

---

2. There is no textual justification for the suggestion that ὕδατος καί is a copyist's interpretation or a redactional alteration added to an original ἐκ πνεύματος to ensure that reference is made to Christian baptism in connection with spiritual birth.

v. 5 and the articular ἐκ τοῦ πνεύματος in vv. 6 and 8, along with the nonrepetition of the preposition in v. 5, suggests that "water" and "Spirit" form a single conceptual unit (not a hendiadys),[3] "water-and-Spirit," with the focus being on the personal Spirit, not the impersonal water (only the Spirit is referred to in vv. 6 and 8). The Spirit operates through water in producing rebirth.

A direct association between "water" as the agent of cleansing from impurity and the "Spirit" as the agent who creates a new responsive heart and a new spirit of obedience to the divine decrees is explicit in Eze 36:25–27. Indeed, ἐξ ὕδατος καὶ πνεύματος would be an apt summary of these three verses in Ezekiel that speak of spiritual renewal.

I conclude that ἐξ ὕδατος καὶ πνεύματος in Jn 3:5 refers to the cleansing and renewing role of the Spirit in producing rebirth that is a prerequisite for entrance into the kingdom of God, and it expounds both the γεννηθῆναι ἄνωθεν ("be born again/from above") of Jn 3:3 and the γεννηθῆναι ἐκ θεοῦ of 1:13 so that ἐκ θεοῦ = ἐκ [τοῦ] πνεύματος.

2. Romans 1:3–4

περὶ τοῦ υἱοῦ αὐτοῦ τοῦ γενομένου **ἐκ** σπέρματος Δαυὶδ κατὰ σάρκα, τοῦ ὁρισθέντος υἱοῦ θεοῦ ἐν δυνάμει κατὰ πνεῦμα ἁγιωσύνης **ἐξ** ἀναστάσεως νεκρῶν, Ἰησοῦ Χριστοῦ τοῦ κυρίου ἡμῶν

"about his Son, Jesus Christ our Lord: with regard to his physical descent he was born of David's line; he was designated Son of God with power by the Spirit of holiness through the resurrection of the dead"

Paul is here depicting neither the two coexistent natures of Christ (human-divine) nor two successive forms of sonship (Davidic-divine), but rather two successive stages of his "career." Christ's earthly existence had its beginning in his descent from David, whereas his open installation as Son of God took its rise, temporally and instrumentally, in his resurrection from the dead (ἐξ ἀναστάσεως νεκρῶν). Not only "from the time of" the resurrection but also "through" (or "as a result of") the resurrection itself, Jesus was visibly designated Son of God.

Two special points call for comment. First, it was not the sonship of Christ but his sonship "with power" that was inaugurated at the time of and by his resurrection, since (a) there is a single referent—"his [= God's] Son"—in both verses; (b) the phrase ἐν δυνάμει implies a previous concealment or "weakness" of the sonship; (c) elsewhere Paul affirms that Jesus was God's Son before the resurrection occurred (e.g., Ro 8:3, 32; Gal 4:4). Through the resurrection what had been a secret reserved for the few (e.g., Mk 9:2, 7, 9) became open for all to see.

Second, in the crucial phrase ἐξ ἀναστάσεως νεκρῶν the primary allusion in

---

3. Δι' ὕδατος καὶ αἵματος (1Jn 5:6) does not form a counterargument, for there the two elements are immediately explicitly distinguished.

the context must be to Christ's own resurrection from the dead, but the absence of ἐκ before νεκρῶν (cf. 1Pe 1:3, δι' ἀναστάσεως Ἰησοῦ Χριστοῦ ἐκ νεκρῶν) and the use of the plural νεκρῶν suggest that Paul envisaged the resurrection of all believers as ideally achieved in the resurrection of Christ (cf. 1Co 15:20, 23; Col 1:18). The general, inclusive category, "the resurrection of the dead," includes the first, determinative instance, "his resurrection from the dead."

3. Romans 3:30

εἴπερ εἷς ὁ θεὸς ὃς δικαιώσει περιτομὴν **ἐκ πίστεως** καὶ ἀκροβυστίαν **διὰ τῆς πίστεως**

"since there is only one God, who will justify the circumcised by faith and the uncircumcised by that same faith"

In Ro 3:21–31 Paul is establishing that God has graciously made provision for a right standing (δικαιοσύνη) with himself by means of the redemption accomplished by Christ, a right standing that is to be appropriated by Jew and Gentile alike through faith in Christ apart from observing the law.

Many efforts have been made to define the presumed distinction between the two prepositions (ἐκ and διά) used with πίστις. But none has proved convincing to the majority of scholars. If any distinction is intended between these two prepositional phrases, it is formal, not substantial: God justifies the Jew *as a result of* his faith (ἐκ πίστεως) and the Gentile on same ground, namely, *by means of* that same kind of faith (διὰ τῆς πίστεως, the article being anaphoric), faith in Jesus (ἐκ πίστεως Ἰησοῦ, Ro 3:26).

Against there being any substantial difference between the justification of Jew and the justification of Gentile, several points may be urged.

a. Both prepositional phrases may mean "through faith" or "by faith," since both prepositions may express either the effective means or the efficient cause (see BDAG 296d–297b for ἐκ; BDAG 224c-d for διά).

b. Elsewhere Paul uses ἐκ or διά to denote the immediate means or cause of justification or salvation (ἐκ—Ro 1:17 [2x]; 3:26; 5:1; 9:30, 32; Gal 2:16; διά—Ro 3:22, 25; Gal 2:16; 3:26; Eph 2:8).

c. There is a comparable change from διὰ [τῆς] πίστεως to ἐκ πίστεως in Ro 3:25–26 and in Gal 2:16 (in reference to ἄνθρωπος, Jew or Gentile).

d. In Gal 3:8 Gentiles are said to be justified ἐκ πίστεως.

e. In Gal 3:26 the Jews and Gentiles of the Galatian churches (πάντες; cf. Gal 3:28) are described as sons of God διὰ τῆς πίστεως; similarly Ro 3:22, 25.

f. Any suggestion that there are two distinct means or grounds of justification (mentioned in Ro 3:30) would tend to undermine Paul's earlier insistence that there is no difference between Jew and Gentile with respect to sinfulness (Ro 3:22–23) or the ultimate ground (= grace) and means (= redemption) of justification (Ro 3:24).

  g. Stylistic or rhetorical variation is not untypical of Paul (e.g., Ro 4:11, ἐν and διά; 10:17, ἐκ and διά).

4. 2 Corinthians 13:4

Καὶ γὰρ ἐσταυρώθη ἐξ ἀσθενείας, ἀλλὰ ζῇ ἐκ δυνάμεως θεοῦ

"For indeed he was crucified because of his weakness, but he lives because of God's power."

If we assume that it is more likely that ἐκ bears the same sense in each part of this sentence than a different sense, it would be difficult to give ἐξ ἀσθενείας the meaning "from a position of weakness" or "out of a condition of weakness," because such senses do not suit the phrase ἐκ δυνάμεως θεοῦ. The most appropriate meaning for ἐκ in both cases is either "through" (RV, where that word means "under the conditions of") or "due to," or, better, "as a result of" (BDAG 142b, 297b, for ἐξ ἀσθενείας), "because of" (NASB; similarly Robertson 598; Turner 260). Some take that weakness to be his helplessness or defenselessness before unjust accusation or "his vulnerability as a human being" (BDAG 142b), but if Paul is emphasizing that this ἀσθένεια was self-imposed, it would refer to the "weakness" — in human eyes — of his obedience to God "all the way to death" (μέχρι θανάτου, Php 2:8 GNB), including his nonretaliation or nonaggressiveness during his passion (cf. Mt 26:52, 67–68; 27:11–14, 27–31; 1Pe 2:23).

In this verse Paul is asserting that Christ's career is the pattern for his own ministry. Just as Christ was crucified because of his "weakness" and now lives because of God's power, so Paul, as a result of his faith union with Christ, shares the "weakness" of Christ's passion and the effective power of God (cf. 2Co 10:1–2, 10–11; 11:20–21, 30; 12:9–10; 13:4b, 9–10).

F. Ἐκ in Compounds

There are 94 verbal compounds with ἐκ in the NT, and in more than half of them there is evidence of the sense "out" (e.g., ἐκτείνω, stretch out) (MH 308–9).

  1. Separation/emission: ἐκβάλλω, drive out, release; ἐκχέω, pour out
  2. Thoroughness/completeness: ἐξαπατάω, utterly deceive; ἀπεκδύομαι, strip completely; ἐκζητέω, search diligently
  3. Fulfillment (cf. BDF §318 [5]): ἐκκαθαίρω, clean out, make clean; ἐκνήφω, sober up, "of sobriety attained *out of* drunkenness" (MH 309); come to one's senses

Chapter 10

’Εν

A. Extended New Testament Use and Ultimate Disappearance

From the chart above (p. 32) it is clear that ἐν is by far the most common preposition not only in the NT (where it accounts for 26.5% of the use of all "proper" prepositions) but also in the Septuagint and the Ptolemaic papyri, two of the main sources for Hellenistic Greek. In comparison with Classical Greek, ἐν has a remarkable elasticity of use in the NT (as well as in the Septuagint). N. Turner (261) isolates three factors that contributed to its extended NT use:

- the increasing imprecision of the dative case
- Septuagintal usage, where ἐν generally rendered the diversified Hebrew preposition *b* (to illustrate Turner's point, see BDB 88a–91b and *GELS* 149)
- the influence of distinctively Christian ideas, such as ἐν Χριστῷ (on which see below, E)

More should be said about the first of these. Greek is one of the sister languages that make up a putative original Indo-European language that is assumed to have flourished around 3000 BC (see Buck 1–4). This parent language seems to have had eight cases: nominative, vocative, accusative, genitive, dative, ablative, instrumental (or sociative), and locative. Greek assimilated the genitive and ablative functions into its genitive case, while the dative case absorbed the Indo-European dative, instrumental, and locative functions (cf. Bortone 153–54). From the outset, then, the Greek dative case was burdened with three onerous functions: expressing the indirect object (its "true" function), instrumentality, and location—all functions capable of many variations.

As the dative case gradually weakened with its increasing load, the role of prepositions became more and more significant as a means of clarifying the meaning intended by the case ending. As a result of these influences, by the end of the tenth century AD the dative case had disappeared and with it the preposition ἐν (cf. Bachtin 42–44). The whole process has been carefully documented, stage by stage, by J. Humbert in his book, *La disparition du datif en grec (1er au Xe siècle)* (Paris: Champion, 1930; see also Regard 525–76, 677). Thus in modern demotic Greek the preposition ἐν, so prominent in Biblical Greek, is no longer used, except in some fossilized Classical or Hellenistic prepositional phrases using ἐν + dative that have been borrowed from Katharevousa, such as ἐν πρώτοις, "in the first place" or ἐν μέρει, "in part" (Bortone 253; cf. 245, 252, 300–301).

Commenting on this ultimate demise of ἐν owing to its extremely diversified use in Hellenistic Greek, P. F. Regard notes that in the case of the infinitive also, there was an extension of usage simultaneously with signs of its ultimate eclipse; the more a linguistic form is employed, the more it is subject to weakening (323–24, 524). J. H. Moulton aptly observes that in "late Greek [ἐν] has become so much a maid-of-all-work that we cannot wonder at its ultimate disappearance, as too indeterminate" (103).

B. Versatility

Two passages where ἐν occurs several times in close succession well illustrate its versatility.

1. 2 Corinthians 6:4b–7a

Paul begins his catalogue of hardships and triumphs (vv. 4b–10) with these words: "As God's servants, we try to commend ourselves in every way by our steadfast endurance [ἐν ὑπομονῇ πολλῇ]." This phrase, an instrumental dative, stands as a general heading for the following 17 instances of ἐν that describe first his outward circumstances (vv. 4b–5), then his qualities of character (v. 6) and spiritual equipment (v. 7). Nine instances of a locatival dative, grouped in three triads (vv. 4b–5), are followed by eight cases of the instrumental dative in a pair of tetrads (vv. 6–7a).

Locatival		Instrumental	
		ἐν ὑπομονῇ πολλῇ	v. 4b
ἐν θλίψεσιν ἐν ἀνάγκαις ἐν στενοχωρίαις	v. 4b	ἐν ἁγνότητι ἐν γνώσει ἐν μακροθυμίᾳ ἐν χρηστότητι	v. 6
ἐν πληγαῖς ἐν φυλακαῖς ἐν καταστασίαις	v. 5	ἐν πνεύματι ἁγίῳ ἐν ἀγάπῃ ἀνυποκρίτῳ ἐν λόγῳ ἀληθείας ἐν δυνάμει θεοῦ	v. 6 v. 7a
ἐν κόποις ἐν ἀγρυπνίαις ἐν νηστείαις	v. 5		

2. 1 Timothy 3:16

		Type of dative	Referent
Ὅς ἐφανερώθη he was manifested	ἐν σαρκί in human form	Locatival	Incarnation/ earthly life
ἐδικαιώθη he was vindicated	ἐν πνεύματι by the Spirit	Agent	Resurrection
ὤφθη he appeared	ἀγγέλοις to angels		Ascension/ exaltation
ἐκηρύχθη he was proclaimed	ἐν ἔθνεσιν among the nations	Locatival	Proclamation
ἐπιστεύθη he was believed on	ἐν κόσμῳ in the world	Locatival	Response
ἀνελήμφθη he was taken up	ἐν δόξῃ amid glory	Attendant circumstances	Ascension/ parousia

If line six refers to the parousia—which would preserve a chronological sequence for the six lines—ἀνελήμφθη is a proleptic aorist, comparable to ἐδόξασεν in Ro 8:30, which also occurs after several preterite aorists (Ro 8:29–30).

C. Encroachment on Other Prepositions

In its diversification ἐν encroached on the territory of:

1. εἰς, in being employed with verbs of motion (e.g., Lk 23:53; 2Co 8:16)
2. διά with the accusative, in expressing the ground of an action (e.g., Mt 6:7)
3. διά with the genitive, in expressing instrumentality or agency (e.g., Lk 22:49; Mt 9:34)
4. μετά or διά with the genitive, in denoting attendant circumstances (e.g., Col 2:7c; 4:2c)
5. σύν, in expressing accompaniment (e.g., Lk 14:31)
6. κατά, in indicating a standard of judgment (e.g., Eph 4:16; see Weymouth)

It is not that the distinction between ἐν and any other preposition was obliterated, but the area and frequency of overlap in usage became greater in Hellenistic and especially Biblical Greek than it had been earlier.

Each potential example of such overlapping needs to be carefully weighed. For example, in Jas 5:3 we should render ἐν ἐσχάταις ἡμέραις by "[you have piled up wealth] in the last days" rather than "for the last days" (KJV) (as if ἐν = εἰς), given the fact the James does not confuse εἰς and ἐν, and the NT conviction that with the coming of Jesus the "last days" had dawned (Ac 2:16–17; 2Ti 3:1; Heb 1:2; 1Pe 1:20). On the relation of ἐν to εἰς, see below, 8.

D. Main Uses

1. Locatival

a. Of places: ἐν πόλει Δαυίδ (Lk 2:11), "in the city of David"
ἐν τῇ ἀμπέλῳ (Jn 15:4), "in the vine"
ἐν δεξιᾷ τοῦ θεοῦ (Col 3:1), "at God's right hand"
b. Of persons: ἐν τοῖς ἡγεμόσιν Ἰούδα (Mt 2:6), "among the rulers of Judah"
ἐν ἐμοί (Ro 7:8, 17–18, 20), "[with]in me"
ἐν τῷ πονηρῷ (1Jn 5:19), "in the grip of the evil one, under the control of the evil one"
c. Of things: ἐν τῇ καρδίᾳ αὐτοῦ (Mt 5:28), "in his heart"
ἐν τοῖς ἐπουρανίοις (Eph 1:20), "in the heavenly realms"
ἐν τῷ θρόνῳ μου (Rev 3:21), "on my throne"

Notes

a. Ἐν τοῖς τοῦ πατρός μου (Lk 2:49) should be rendered "in/at my Father's house" (BDAG 326c) rather than "about my Father's business" (KJV), since τά τινος is normal Greek idiom for "so-and-so's house" (see LSJ 1195b), so that ἐν τοῖς means "in the house of" (Moulton 103, with illustrations from the papyri). Similarly, ἐν τοῖς Ἀντιπάτρου (Josephus, *Ant.* 16.10.1) means "at Antipater's house."
b. Those who defend the reading ὁ ὢν ἐν τῷ οὐρανῷ in Jn 3:13 see in it a reference to the preexistence or postexistence of the Logos, or believe the phrase depicts heaven as the true and timeless abode of the earthly Son of Man. But against the originality of this reading, see Metzger 174–75. The majority of the UBS[4] committee regarded the phrase as "an interpretative gloss, reflecting later Christological development" (Metzger 175).
c. An example of the basic locatival sense of ἐν is found in Gal 1:16, where Paul is describing how he received his gospel. Ἐν ἐμοί here means "in me" (NIV[1,2], NJB), "within me" (Weymouth), "in [the sphere of] my soul," not "through me" (which would more commonly be δι' ἐμοῦ; REB has "in and through me," similarly Cassirer), since (i) a personal revelation is to be distinguished from a public proclamation; (ii) the revelation was visual as well as verbal (Ac 9:17, 27; 22:14; 26:16, 19; 2Co 4:4); (iii) it is the following statement of purpose (ἵνα εὐαγγελίζωμαι) that points to Paul's agency in proclaiming

the revelation he had received. By ἐν ἐμοί Paul is stressing the inward and intensely personal character of God's revelation to him of the risen Jesus, an inward revelation that matched and coincided with his external vision. But it is not impossible that the phrase could mean "to me" (NAB², NRSV), involving a pleonastic ἐν, a proleptic ἐν, or the influence of the ἐν τοῖς ἔθνεσιν that follows.

2. Temporal

a. Of specific time: ἐν ἡμέρᾳ κρίσεως (Mt 10:15), "on the day of judgment"

ἐν σαββάτῳ (Jn 7:23), "on the Sabbath"

ἐν τῇ ἐσχάτῃ σάλπιγγι (1Co 15:52), "at [the sounding of] the last trumpet"

b. Of a period of time in the course of which, or within which, something happens: ἐν τῇ στάσει (Mk 15:7), "during the uprising"

ἐν τῷ εἶναι αὐτούς (Lk 2:6), "while they were there"

ἐν τρισὶν ἡμέραις (Jn 2:19–20), "within three days"

3. Instrumental

a. ἐν παραβολαῖς ἔλεγεν αὐτοῖς (Mk 3:23), "he spoke to them by means of/using parables"

b. ἐν πυρὶ ἀποκαλύπτεται (1Co 3:13), "[each person's work] will be revealed by [the application of] fire"

c. ἐν πάσῃ δυνάμει δυναμούμενοι (Col 1:11), "equipped with full power"

Notes

a. Bortone observes that "the most frequent non-spatial sense of ἐν in Biblical Greek is instrumental/causal." Such use is rare in Homeric Greek and in lofty Attic Greek (192). It is the *frequency* of instrumental ἐν in Biblical Greek that is traceable to the extensive and varied uses of the Hebrew *bᵉ* (193).

b. In the NT instrumental ἐν has curtailed the use of the instrumental dative (BDF §195). For example, ἐν μαχαίρῃ ("by the sword") is found in Mt 26:52; Lk 22:49; Rev 13:10 (2x), but without the preposition in Ac 12:2.

c. Closely associated with instrumental ἐν is modal ἐν (e.g., ἐσμὲν ἐν τῷ ἀληθινῷ, **ἐν** τῷ υἱῷ αὐτοῦ Ἰησοῦ Χριστῷ [1Jn 5:20], "we are in him who is true, *by being in* his Son, Jesus Christ"), and adverbial ἐν expressing manner (ἐν δικαιοσύνῃ [Ac 17:31] = δικαίως, "with justice/justly").

d. Nine times we find the expression ἐν τῷ αἵματι τοῦ Χριστοῦ (or the equivalent—αὐτοῦ, μου, σου, Ἰησοῦ): Lk 22:20; Ro 3:25; 5:9;

1Co 11:25; Eph 2:13; Heb 10:19; Rev 1:5; 5:9; 7:14. Usually the phrase can be satisfactorily translated "by/through/sealed by the blood of Christ," referring in each context to some spiritual benefit accruing to the believer "by means of" the sacrificial death of Christ. (Note the six uses of διὰ τοῦ αἵματος αὐτοῦ – or equivalents — in Ac 20:28; Eph 1:7; Col 1:20; Heb 9:12; 13:12; Rev 12:11.)

Turner, however, claims that in three of these cases (Ro 3:25; 5:9; Rev 5:9) we have a literal rendering of the Semitic *beth pretii* (= "*bᵉ* denoting price") construction (cf. BDB 90a-b), so that ἐν τῷ αἵματι αὐτοῦ/σου means "at the cost of his/your blood" (Turner 253; *Style* 156; "The Preposition *en* in the New Testament," *BT* 10 [1959]: 119). But there seems to be no need to appeal to Semitic influence. Expressions of cost or price *could* be seen as a "distinguishable extension" of instrumental ἐν (Moule 77, tentatively—see 205); Robertson regards these three cases as simply instrumental ἐν denoting price (*Pictures* 4:348; 6:336). We can be more confident about the translation "at the cost of" when a verb denoting purchase is used, as in Rev 5:9, ἠγόρασας τῷ θεῷ ἐν τῷ αἵματι σου. Interestingly, when we do find the expression τιμῆς ἠγοράσθητε (1Co 7:23; also 1Co 6:20), "You were bought at a price," the price is simply implied, as being well-known. The crucially important verse Ro 3:25 can be rendered "By the shedding of Christ's blood, God presented him as a propitiatory sacrifice, to be received by faith."

4. Agency

a. Ἰησοῦς ... ἤγετο ἐν τῷ πνεύματι (Lk 4:1), "Jesus ... was led by the Spirit"

b. ὁ θεός ... μέλλει κρίνειν ... ἐν ἀνδρί (Ac 17:30–31), "God ... will judge ... by a man"

c. εἰ ἐν ὑμῖν κρίνεται ὁ κόσμος (1Co 6:2), "If the world is to be judged by you"

5. Causal

a. ἐν τῇ πολυλογίᾳ αὐτῶν (Mt 6:7), "because of their many words"

b. ἐν τούτῳ πιστεύομεν (Jn 16:30), "because of this we believe"

c. ἐχθροὺς τῇ διανοίᾳ ἐν τοῖς ἔργοις τοῖς πονηροῖς (Col 1:21), "enemies in your minds because of your evil deeds"

6. Attendant Circumstance /Accompaniment

a. ἐν ἀγαλλιάσει καὶ ἀφελότητι καρδίας (Ac 2:46), "with glad and sincere hearts"

b. ἐν ἀκροβυστίᾳ (1Co 7:18), "while uncircumcised"

c. ἐντολὴ πρώτη ἐν ἐπαγγελίᾳ (Eph 6:2), "the first commandment with a promise attached"[1]

7. Respect

a. ἐν βρώσει καὶ ἐν πόσει (Col 2:16), "with regard to food and drink"

b. διδάσκαλος ἐθνῶν ἐν πίστει καὶ ἀληθείᾳ (1Ti 2:7), "a teacher of the Gentiles regarding faith and truth/a teacher of the true faith to the Gentiles"

c. ἐν μηδενὶ λειπόμενοι (Jas 1:4), "lacking in nothing"

Notes

a. In the NT the dative of respect is far more common than the accusative of respect, whereas in Classical Greek the reverse is true (BDF §197).

b. The three examples Moule cites of an extension of the instrumental use that he terms "exemplary" (ἐν ἡμῖν in 1Co 4:6, and ἐν ἐμοί in 1Co 9:15 and 1Ti 1:16) could appropriately be classified as datives of respect: *with regard to us/me*, or *in our/my case*. Ideally, grammatical categories should be kept to a minimum.

8. Ἐν = Εἰς

a. ἐπιστρέψαι καρδίας πατέρων ἐπὶ τέκνα καὶ ἀπειθεῖς ἐν φρονήσει δικαίων (Lk 1:17), "to turn the hearts of parents towards their children and the disobedient to the wisdom of the righteous"

b. ὁδηγήσει ὑμᾶς ἐν τῇ ἀληθείᾳ πάσῃ (Jn 16:13), "[the Spirit of truth] will guide you into all the truth" (note that A B K Δ Π Ψ f^{13} *al* read εἰς + accusative)

c. πνεῦμα ζωῆς ... εἰσῆλθεν ἐν αὐτοῖς (Rev 11:11), "the breath of life ... entered them." Here, surprisingly, the εἰς of Eze 37:10 (LXX) has become ἐν.

Notes

a. In Biblical Greek ἐν stands for εἰς far less frequently than εἰς for ἐν, but in neither case is there promiscuous interchange. Cf. Jannaris §§1549, 1564–65.

b. Where ἐν follows δίδωμι (e.g., Lk 12:51; Jn 3:35; 2Co 1:22; 8:1, 16), ἐν is pregnant (Robertson 585; Zerwick, *Analysis* 405), presupposing εἰς, with the emphasis not on the direction of the giving but on the final location of the gift.

---

1. For LXX examples, see Conybeare and Stock 82.

9. Exegetical Ambiguities

A corollary of the versatility of ἐν is the exegetical ambiguity that often attaches to its use. Three examples will illustrate the point.

a. Ἐν δὲ εἰρήνῃ (1Co 7:15), which is emphatic by position, provides the reason (δέ, "for," RSV) a Christian partner in a mixed marriage is under no compulsion (οὐ δεδούλωται) to persist in seeking a reconciliation when the non-Christian partner has initiated a separation: God has called believers (i) into a state of peace *in* which they should now live (pregnant or proleptic ἐν; cf. 1Th 4:7, οὐ γὰρ ἐκάλεσεν ἡμᾶς ὁ θεὸς ἐπὶ ἀκαθαρσίᾳ ἀλλ᾽ ἐν ἁγιασμῷ); or (ii) *in the sphere of/in a spirit of* (Christian) peace (locatival ἐν).

b. Paul affirms (in Col 3:4) that when Christ appears at his second coming, believers too will appear along with him ἐν δόξῃ. This ἐν could denote attendant circumstances ("attended by glory," "in a blaze of glory" [Cassirer]), or it could be instrumental ("clothed with glory," Zerwick, *Analysis* 452), but it is probably locatival ("in glory" = "glorified" or "in glorified bodies" [cf. 1Co 15:43; Php 3:21]).

c. In Col 3:16 Paul exhorts the Colossians, "Let the message of Christ dwell in you [ἐν ὑμῖν] in all its richness." As often in Paul's letters, this prepositional phrase is ambiguous, for it could mean "within you" (NASB[2]), "in your hearts" (NLT), or, in a corporate sense, "among you" (HCSB), "in your midst" (Moffatt). The exegete is hesitant to exclude either sense, since both are appropriate, but only a paraphrase such as "in your hearts and in your midst" can incorporate both options.

E. Key Phrases

1. Ἐν (τῷ) Χριστῷ (Ἰησοῦ) in Paul

This is a distinctly Pauline expression, with about 170 examples in the Pauline corpus if we include the phrases ἐν αὐτῷ and ἐν ᾧ when they refer to Christ. Never do we find the expression ἐν Ἰησοῦ Χριστῷ in Paul, and only once ἐν τῷ Ἰησοῦ (Eph 4:21; cf. Rev 1:9). Only 1 and 2 Thessalonians have the fuller phrase ἐν κυρίῳ Ἰησοῦ Χριστῷ (1Th 1:1; 2Th 1:1; 3:12) while the Pastorals have only ἐν Χριστῷ Ἰησοῦ (9x).[2] Although John lacks the actual expression εἶναι ἐν Χριστῷ, he comes close when he says ἐσμὲν ἐν τῷ ἀληθινῷ, ἐν τῷ υἱῷ αὐτοῦ Ἰησοῦ Χριστῷ (1Jn 5:20).

Ἐν Χριστῷ qualifies nouns (e.g., Ro 16:3; 1Co 3:1; 1Ti 3:13), verbs (e.g., Ro 9:1; 1Co 1:2; Eph 4:17), and adjectives (e.g., Col 1:28).

---

2. See the treatment of the linguistic data in W. Kramer, *Christ, Lord, Son of God* (London: SCM, 1966), 141–46.

From a theological viewpoint, Paul's uses of ἐν [τῷ] Χριστῷ fall into two classes:

1. where Christ is an individual person, distinct from others, e.g., Eph 1:10; 2:15 – 16; Php 2:5 (see below); Col 1:19; 2:9
2. where Christ is a corporate person (cf. ὁ Χριστός in 1Co 12:12), including others, e.g., Ro 8:1; 12:5; Gal 1:22

In the former case, ἐν Χριστῷ often bears the sense "in personal, intimate fellowship with/joined closely to the exalted Christ"; in the latter case, "in/part of the [spiritual] body of Christ." The distinction may be illustrated by the difference between οἱ νεκροὶ ἐν Χριστῷ (1Th 4:16), which refers to "the dead" as currently being in intimate fellowship with the risen Christ, and οἱ κοιμηθέντες ἐν Χριστῷ (1Co 15:18), which refers to "those who fell asleep" as members of the body of Christ.

a. Range of Uses

From a grammatical standpoint, the uses may be conveniently, even if somewhat arbitrarily, grouped into the following six categories. A paraphrase will bring out the import of ἐν in the examples cited. There is no rigid division between the categories; some instances could appropriately be classified in another category. How, for example, should we translate ἐν Χριστῷ in Phm 8 (πολλὴν ἐν Χριστῷ παρρησίαν ἔχων ἐπιτάσσειν σοι τὸ ἀνῆκον διὰ τὴν ἀγάπην μᾶλλον παρακαλῶ)? "In the name of Christ" (NLT), "in Christ's service," "as a Christian" (Goodspeed), "as your brother in Christ" (GNB), "because of your union with Christ," or "with Christ's authority" (Weymouth)?

(1) Incorporative Union

Ro 8:1 "There is therefore now no penal servitude for those who are **in union with** Christ Jesus."

1Co 15:18 "Then indeed those who fell asleep **as members of the body of** Christ have perished."

2Co 5:17 "Consequently, if anyone **has been incorporated into** Christ, there is a new creation."

1Th 4:16 "The dead who are **united with the exalted** Christ will rise first"

(2) Agency

Ro 3:24 "They are justified freely by his grace through the redemption **accomplished by** Christ Jesus."

2Co 3:14 "That same veil remains there because only **through** Christ is it abolished."

Gal 2:17 "If, while seeking to be justified **by** Christ ..."

Eph 4:32 "Be kind to one another, tenderly affectionate, and forgive each other, just as God **through** Christ forgave you."

(3) Mode

Ro 12:5 "**By our union with** Christ we form one body, though we are many."

1Co 1:4 "The grace of God that was given to you **by means of** Christ Jesus."

2Co 5:21 "so that, **by being in** him [Christ], we might become righteous before God."

Gal 3:28 "You are all one **by being in** Christ Jesus."

(4) Cause

Ro 6:11 "In the same way, consider yourselves dead to sin but alive to God **because of your union with** Christ Jesus."

1Co 15:22 "All will be made alive **by virtue of their connection and solidarity with** Christ."

Gal 2:4 "This issue arose because certain false brothers had been smuggled in, who sneaked in to spy out the liberty we enjoy **because of** Christ Jesus."

Col 2:10 "You have your completeness **as a result of being in** him [Christ]."

(5) Location

Ro 8:39 "the love of God **that is focused in** Christ Jesus our Lord"

Ro 16:9 "Greet Urbanus, our fellow worker **in the service of** Christ."

Php 2:5 "In your relations with one another, adopt this attitude that was also **displayed in** Christ Jesus."

2Ti 2:10 "I endure everything for the sake of the elect, that they too may obtain the salvation **that is found in** Christ and comes with eternal glory."

(6) Sphere of Reference

In this usage, ἐν Χριστῷ is equivalent to the adjective χριστιανός, -ή, -όν, "Christian."

Ro 16:7 "They were **Christians** before I was."

1Co 4:15a "even though you may have ten thousand **Christian** instructors"

2Co 12:2 "I know a **Christian** man ..."

Gal 1:22 "I was personally unknown to the **Christian** churches of Judea."

For the literature on the subject, see J. D. G. Dunn, *The Theology of Paul the Apostle* (Grand Rapids; Eerdmans, 1998), 390 n.1. Behind the corporate aspects of Paul's ἐν Χριστῷ formula may lie the concept of Christ as a universal personality (A. Oepke, *TDNT* 2:542), an inclusive personality,[3] or a corporate

---

3. See C. D. F. Moule, *The Phenomenon of the New Testament* (London: SCM, 1967), 26; idem, *The Origin of Christology* (Cambridge: Cambridge Univ. Press, 1977), 54–69.

personality.[4] Alternatively, "Paul's references to 'in Christ' and 'in the Lord' appear to be a special extension of the common and almost unnoticed practice of symbolically representing exclusivity or definition as a locality" (M. A. Seifrid, *DPL* 434, citing [435] the expressions "into Moses" [1Co 10:2]; "in Abraham" [Gal 3:8–9]; "in him" [Ro 9:15]; "in me" [Php 1:30]; "in his wife" [1Co 7:14]).

In the complementary expression, [Ἰησοῦς] Χριστὸς ἐν ὑμῖν (Ro 8:10; 2Co 13:5; Col 1:27; cf. Gal 2:20), the notion of a direct relation between two individuals is to the fore; reciprocity of fellowship between the believer and Christ is implied. It is the risen and exalted Christ, not the corporate Christ, who indwells the believer (through the Spirit). Only in Johannine thought do we find the idea of personal co-inherence (Jn 6:56; 14:20; 15:4–5; 1Jn 3:24; 4:13, 15–16), patterned on the archetype of divine co-inherence (Jn 10:38; 14:10–11, 20; 17:21, 23). It is noteworthy that Paul more often depicts Christians as being ἐν Χριστῷ and the Spirit as ἐν ὑμῖν than Christ as ἐν ὑμῖν and Christians as ἐν πνεύματι.

b. Notable Instances

(1) 2 Corinthians 5:19a

θεὸς ἦν ἐν Χριστῷ κόσμον καταλλάσσων ἑαυτῷ

This statement has been translated in two basic ways.

(a) "God, through Christ, was reconciling the world to Himself" (Barclay). This rendering, along with the variation, "In Christ God was reconciling the world to himself" (NRSV, and many EVV), takes ἦν … καταλλάσσων as a periphrastic imperfect and ἐν Χριστῷ as either instrumental ("through Christ") or locatival ("in Christ").

(b) "God was in Christ, reconciling the world unto himself" (KJV). In this case there is no periphrastic construction; ἐν Χριστῷ is an adverbial predicate after ἦν, and καταλλάσσων is temporally undefined.

Each translation coheres with the context and expresses Pauline sentiments. However, the following considerations favor the second rendering.

• In the other three uses of the periphrastic imperfect in the Pauline corpus (Gal 1:22, 23; Php 2:26), no words (other than the inconsequential δέ in Gal 1:22) intervene between the copula and the participle.

• With regard to non-Pauline uses of this periphrastic imperfect construction, where words are found between the copula and participle (Ac 2:5;

---

4. See E. Best, *One Body in Christ: A Study of the Relationship of the Church to Christ in the Epistles of the Apostle Paul* (London: SPCK, 1955), 29. On this whole theme, see the recent work by Constantine R. Campbell, *Paul and Union with Christ* (Grand Rapids: Zondervan, 2012).

10:30; 11:5; 16:12; 19:14), (i) in only one case (Ac 19:14) does the participle govern a direct object (cf. κόσμον in 2Co 5:19), and then it is the colorless τοῦτο, and (ii) the intervening words should be construed with the copula when they can be (as in Ac 11:5; 19:14); "God was in Christ" as a thought-unit is certainly not incomprehensible.

- Elsewhere when Paul uses the verb καταλλάσσειν and specifies Christ as God's agent in effecting reconciliation, the διά phrase used to express the latter idea either precedes (as in Col 1:20; cf. Ro 5:12) or follows (as in Ro 5:10; 2Co 5:18; cf. Col 1:22) the fixed order: verb (καταλλάσσειν) – object(s) of reconciliation – goal of reconciliation. This would lead us to expect, if ἐν Χριστῷ in v. 19 specified or implied agency and ἦν … καταλλάσσων were a periphrastic imperfect, that ἐν Χριστῷ would precede θεός or follow ἑαυτῷ (although, on any view, κόσμον is not in its normal position). That is, ἐν Χριστῷ would be likely to be placed outside the verbal unit ἦν … καταλλάσσων.
- It would be repetitious to have the notion of agency expressed twice (if ἐν Χριστῷ is merely a stylistic variant of διὰ Χριστοῦ) within one sentence, although if ἐν Χριστῷ = "in and through Christ," this difficulty is partially relieved.
- To treat ἦν as an independent verb (i.e., translation 2) avoids the difficulty of explaining the change from the aorist participle (καταλλάξαντος) in v. 18 to the *ex hypothesi* periphrastic imperfect in v. 19 in describing the identical past act of reconciliation (quite apart from its ongoing dimensions).
- Given Col 1:19; 2:9 (see the detailed discussion below), there can be no theological objection to Paul's having asserted that God was personally present in Christ.

On this view θεὸς ἦν ἐν Χριστῷ does not refer to the incarnation (as if ἦν were equivalent to ἐσκήνωσεν, "took up residence") but to the entire life of Christ on earth in which God was personally present and through which he revealed himself. Further, it seems that the finite verb (ἦν) and the participle (καταλλάσσων) are related as cause to effect; it was only because God in all his fullness had chosen to dwell in Christ (Col 1:19), only because there dwelt embodied in Christ the total plenitude of deity (Col 2:9), that reconciliation was accomplished. God was in Christ and therefore acted through Christ (cf. Jn 14:10b, "the Father who dwells in me does his works"). A functional Christology presupposes and finds its ultimate basis in an ontological Christology.

(2) Philippians 2:5

Whether Php 2:6–11 is seen (a) as a potent reminder to the Philippian believers of how they came to be "in Christ" (the "kerygmatic" view); or (b) as a powerful appeal to the ethical example of the earthly Jesus (the "ethical" view), is largely determined by the interpretation of the phrase ἐν Χριστῷ Ἰησοῦ at the end of v.5. These two views are represented by two translation options.

τοῦτο φρονεῖτε ἐν ὑμῖν ὃ καὶ **ἐν Χριστῷ Ἰησοῦ**

(a) "Let this disposition be yours which it is necessary to have as those who are in Christ Jesus."[5]

(b) "In your relations with one another, adopt this attitude that was also in Christ Jesus."

The latter interpretation of the crucial phrase is to be preferred for the following reasons.

- Ἐν Χριστῷ can refer to the earthly Jesus (2Co 5:19a; Col 1:19; 2:9).
- Paul elsewhere appeals to the example afforded by Jesus' known character (1Co 1:10) or his specific qualities (Ro 15:1 – 3; 1Co 10:31 – 11:1; 2Co 8:9; and esp. 2Co 10:1, where διά bears the sense "by means of [the example of]" = "on the basis of").
- The addition of Ἰησοῦ to ἐν Χριστῷ supports the idea that Paul is here appealing to the normative paradigm of Jesus' life.
- The "kerygmatic" view ignores the significance of καί after τοῦτο [τὸ φρόνημα] ... ὅ: "this attitude that was *also*...."
- The "kerygmatic" view would be more convincing if the text had read ἐν ὑμῖν τοῖς ἐν Χριστῷ Ἰησοῦ (cf. 1Pe 5:14, εἰρήνη ὑμῖν πᾶσιν τοῖς ἐν Χριστῷ).
- Verse 5b is elliptical on any view. It seems preferable to add the innocuous ἦν (as so often in Gk.) rather than the more colorful εὑρέθη or the various proposed forms of φρονέω (e.g., ἐφρονεῖτο, ἐφρονήθη, φρονεῖτε [indic.], φρονεῖν δεῖ).

c. Ἐν αὐτῷ (= ἐν Χριστῷ)

(1) Colossians 1:19

> Ἐν αὐτῷ εὐδόκησεν πᾶν τὸ πλήρωμα κατοικῆσαι
> "In him God in all his fullness was pleased to dwell."

The subject of εὐδόκησεν could be God (implied from Col 1:15 or 1:13): "God was pleased to have all His fullness dwell in Him [Christ]" (HCSB). But it is preferable to take πᾶν τὸ πλήρωμα as the subject, conceived of impersonally, "all the fullness" (BDAG 404b, 829d; NAB[2]), or personally, "God in all his fullness" (REB, NLT). Support for the latter rendering is twofold: (i) the expressions εὐδόκησεν and ἀποκαταλλάξαι ... εἰς αὐτόν ("to reconcile ... to himself") suggest a personal subject; (ii) the masculine singular participle εἰρηνοποιήσας in

---

5. R. P. Martin, *Philippians* (Grand Rapids: Eerdmans, 1980), 92.

v. 20 and the close parallel to Col 1:19 in 2:9 ("all the fullness of the Godhead" = "the Godhead in all its fullness," TCNT) show that "all the fullness" may be construed personally.

If κατοικῆσαι is an ingressive aorist ("God in all his fullness was pleased [or resolved] to take up residence in him"), this residence began at the incarnation. But more probably the infinitive is a constative aorist, with the time of the residence left undefined, though it would certainly include the incarnation and risen life of Christ: "In him God in all his fullness was pleased to dwell." That is, it was God's good pleasure that all divine attributes and powers should reside in the person of Jesus.

(2) Colossians 2:9

Ἐν αὐτῷ κατοικεῖ πᾶν τὸ πλήρωμα τῆς θεότητος σωματικῶς

"In him there dwells the whole fullness of deity in bodily form."

This verse, like Col 1:19, speaks of Christ himself, not the believer, so ἐν αὐτῷ does not have either of its most common meanings, that is, "in union with him" and "incorporate in him." Rather, it means "in his person." Κατοικεῖ is a timeless present, "permanently dwells, continues to live." As in 1:19, πᾶν τὸ πλήρωμα means "all the fullness, the entire fullness," no aspect of the fullness being excepted (cf. Zerwick §188). The genitive θεότητος may be epexegetic, "all the fullness, namely, the Godhead," but is more probably possessive, "all the fullness that constitutes/characterizes deity," "the entire Fulness of deity" (Moffatt), "the full measure of deity" (BDAG 829d), "the Godhead in all its fullness" (TCNT, REB).

Σωματικῶς describes the permanent (cf. κατοικεῖ) postincarnational state of Christ, that is, "in bodily form" (so most EVV). The separation of κατοικεῖ from σωματικῶς suggests that two distinct affirmations are being made: that the total plenitude of the Godhead dwells in Christ eternally, and that this fullness now permanently resides in Christ in bodily form. It is true that before the incarnation the πλήρωμα did not reside in Christ σωματικῶς; it is not true that before the incarnation the πλήρωμα did not reside in him at all. Thus Paul implies both the eternal deity and the permanent humanity of Christ. Moreover, κατοικεῖ ... σωματικῶς implies that both before and after his resurrection Christ possessed a σῶμα (cf. 1Co 15:44; Php 3:21; Col 1:22).

2. Ἐν (τῷ) κυρίῳ (Ἰησοῦ) in Paul

Paul's main variant for ἐν Χριστῷ is ἐν (τῷ) κυρίῳ Ἰησοῦ (9x in 1 Corinthians alone; note especially 1Co 4:17, where these two phrases are juxtaposed). Ἐν κυρίῳ (Ἰησοῦ) is often found in exhortations (e.g., Php 3:1; 4:1–2; 1Th 4:1) or contexts where Christ's authority or power is at the fore (e.g., 1Co 7:22, 39; 2Co 2:12). In generalized terms, ἐν Χριστῷ often appears in contexts that speak of believers' actual status, ἐν κυρίῳ in settings that describe their appropriate and required conduct. This distinction broadly corresponds to the indicative-imperative or doctrine–practice poles of Paul's theology. There are two significant differences between ἐν κυρίῳ and ἐν Χριστῷ:

a. (ὁ) κύριος never stands for the whole body of Christians in the way ὁ Χριστός does in 1Co 12:12.

b. Κύριος may occasionally refer to Yahweh, as in the citation of Jer 9:23 (LXX) in 1Co 1:31; 2Co 10:17, whereas ὁ Χριστός never does. But normally the κύριος in ἐν κυρίῳ is identical with the Χριστός (i.e., the Lord Jesus Christ).

Not surprisingly, most of the 48 uses of ἐν κυρίῳ in Paul may be classified under headings similar to those used above for ἐν Χριστῷ, with the addition of "Authoritative Basis." Again, a paraphrase will highlight the significance of ἐν in the examples cited.

a. Personal Relationship

1Co 7:22 "the person who was a slave when God called him **to be united to** the Lord"

Gal 5:10 "I am confident about you **as those who belong to** the Lord that you will not take a different view."

Col 3:18 "Wives, be subject to your husbands, as is appropriate **for those who belong to** the Lord."

1Th 3:8 "Now we gain fresh life if you are standing firm **in your union with** the Lord."

b. Agency

1Co 11:11 "**By the Lord's assignment**, woman is not independent of man, nor is man independent of woman."

2Co 2:12 "A door had been opened for me **by the Lord's providence**."

Eph 6:10 "Be strong **through** the Lord and his mighty power."

Php 4:1 "That is how you should stand firm **through the Lord's help**."

c. Mode

1Co 9:1 "Are you not the result of my work **by the Lord's enabling?**"

Eph 5:8 "Once you were darkness but now, **by being united to** the Lord, you are light."

Php 4:2 "I plead with Euodia and I plead with Syntyche to agree with each other **by recognizing their oneness in** the Lord."

2Th 3:4 "**By the Lord's reassurance** we have confidence in you that you are doing and will continue to do what we command."

d. Cause

1Co 9:2 "You are the seal of my apostleship **because you belong to** the Lord."

1Co 15:58 "You know that your labor is not in vain **because it is for** the Lord."

Eph 4:1 "I urge you, as a prisoner **for the Lord's sake** ..."

Phm 20 "Yes, brother, let me derive some profit from you **because you belong to** the Lord."

e. Location

Ro 16:12a "Greet Tryphaena and Tryphosa who labor **in the Lord's service.**"

Php 2:19 "It is my hope—**grounded in** the Lord Jesus—to send Timothy to you soon."

Col 4:7 "Tychicus ... a fellow slave **in the Lord's service** ..."

1Th 5:12 "We ask you, brothers and sisters, to respect those who ... are set over you **in the Lord's fellowship.**"

f. Sphere of Reference

In this usage, ἐν κυρίῳ is equivalent to the adjective χριστιανός, -ή, -όν, "Christian."

Ro 16:8 "Greet Ampliatus, my dear **Christian** friend."

1Co 7:39 "If a woman's husband dies, she is free to marry anyone she wishes—but from **within the Lord's people.**"

1Co 16:19 "Aquila and Prisca send you their warmest **Christian** greetings."

Php 2:29 "Give him a very joyful **Christian** welcome."

g. Authoritative Basis

Ro 14:14 "I know, I am convinced **on the authority of the Lord Jesus** that no kind of food is 'unclean' in itself."

Eph 4:17 "This is what I mean and insist on **in the Lord's name.**"

1Th 4:1 "Finally, brother and sisters, we ask and urge you **in the name of the Lord Jesus** ..."

2Th 3:12 "**With the authority of the Lord Jesus Christ** we command and urge such people to do their work quietly and eat food they have earned for themselves."

Example: Romans 14:14a

To illustrate the subjective and rather arbitrary nature of any classification of uses, below are the renderings of ἐν κυρίῳ in Ro 14:14a (οἶδα καὶ πέπεισμαι ἐν κυρίῳ Ἰησοῦ ὅτι οὐδὲν κοινὸν δι' ἑαυτοῦ) in 27 major English translations.

a. Personal Relationship
- "as one who is in the Lord Jesus" (NIV[1])
- "in union with the Lord Jesus" (Weymouth)
- "as a man united to the Lord Jesus" (Cassirer)

b. Agency
- "by the Lord Jesus" (KJV, HCSB)
- "The Lord Jesus has made it clear." (CEV)

c. Mode
- "through my union with the Lord Jesus" (TCNT)
- "My union with the Lord Jesus makes me certain." (GNB)
- "All I know of the Lord Jesus convinces me." (REB)

d. Cause
- "as a follower of the Lord Jesus" (Goodspeed)

e. Location
- "in the Lord Jesus" (RV, ASV, Moffatt, RSV, NASB[1,2], NJB, NAB[2], NRSV, ESV, NIV[2], NET)

f. Sphere of Reference
- "as a Christian" (NEB)
- "My Christian faith gives me the knowledge." (Barclay)

g. Authoritative Basis
- "on the authority of the Lord Jesus" (NAB[1], NLT)
- "I speak for the Lord Jesus." (JB)

3. Καυχᾶσθαι ἐν

If used intransitively, καυχᾶσθαι means "boast," either in a positive sense, "be proud of," or in a negative sense, "brag, glory [in]." Only the context will indicate whether a translation such as "pride oneself on" has a positive or a negative sense. (In 2Co 5:12 both senses are present.)

a. Attendant Circumstances

Jas 4:16 "But as it is, you boast **in arrogance** [ἐν ταῖς ἀλαζονείαις ὑμῶν]" (= "you make arrogant boasts," BDAG 40d).

b. Cause

Ro 2: 23 "You who brag **because you have the law** [ἐν νόμῳ]"/"You who boast **on the basis of your law-keeping**."

c. Content or Object

(1) Things

Ro 5:3 "We take pride **in our sufferings** [ἐν ταῖς θλίψεσιν]."

2Co 5:12 "Those who pride themselves **on externals and not on the heart** [ἐν προσώπῳ … καὶ μὴ ἐν καρδίᾳ]."

2Co 10:15 "We do not boast beyond due measure **of work done by others** [ἐν ἀλλοτρίοις κόποις]."

2Co 11:12 " **in the matter about which** [ἐν ᾧ] they boast."

2Co 12:5 "But I will not boast about [ὑπέρ] myself, except **about my weaknesses** [ἐν ταῖς ἀσθενείαις]."

2Co 12:9 "Therefore I will boast all the more gladly **about my weaknesses** [ἐν ταῖς ἀσθενείαις μου]."

Gal 6:13 "so that they may boast **about something in your outward condition/about some bodily mark you have** [ἐν τῇ ὑμετέρᾳ σαρκί]."

Gal 6:14 "May I never boast except **about the cross** [ἐν τῷ σταυρῷ] of our Lord Jesus Christ"

Jas 1:9 "The brother in humble circumstances should take pride **in his high position** [ἐν τῷ ὕψει αὐτοῦ]."

(2) Persons: Divine, Human

1Co 3:21 "No one should boast **about what men can do** [ἐν ἀνθρώποις]."

Ro 2:17 "if … you boast **about your knowledge of God** [ἐν θεῷ]"

Ro 5:11 "We boast about **what God has done** [ἐν τῷ θεῷ]."

Php 3:3 "We make our boast **about what Christ Jesus has done** [ἐν Χριστῷ Ἰησοῦ]."

1Co 1:31 and **2Co 10:17** "The one who boasts must boast **in the Lord**" (ὁ [δὲ] καυχώμενος ἐν κυρίῳ καυχάσθω).

With regard to the latter two verses, the following observations may be made. Both verses are citing (1Co 1:31 has the introductory formula καθὼς γέγραπται) a line from the LXX of Jer 9:23 (EVV, 9:24), which reads:

ἀλλ᾽ ἢ ἐν τούτῳ καυχάσθω ὁ καυχώμενος, συνίειν καὶ γινώσκειν ὅτι ἐγώ εἰμι κύριος ποιῶν ἔλεος καὶ κρίμα καὶ δικαιοσύνην ἐπὶ τῆς γῆς, ὅτι ἐν τούτοις τὸ θέλημά μου, λέγει κύριος.

"But rather, the one who boasts must boast in this: that he understands and knows that I am the Lord who exercises kindness, justice and righteousness on the earth, for my pleasure resides in these things, says the Lord."

In adapting the LXX text Paul has omitted the initial ἀλλ᾽ ἤ, has advanced ὁ καυχώμενος, and has substituted ἐν κυρίῳ for ἐν τούτῳ. The contrast in Jeremiah 9 is between proper and improper boasting, between illegitimate boasting of one's wisdom, strength, and riches as though these blessings were derived from oneself, and legitimate boasting that focuses on who Yahweh is ("I am the Lord … my pleasure") and what he does ("who exercises kindness, justice and righteousness"). Ἐν κυρίῳ, then, is shorthand for the character and deeds of the Lord. In both Corinthian passages κύριος refers to Christ: the prepositional phrase ἐν κυρίῳ regularly refers to Christ in Paul's letters; the concept of "boasting in Christ" is found in Php 3:3 ("we pride ourselves only on Christ Jesus"); Paul is not averse to applying to Christ OT passages that refer to Yahweh (e.g., Isa 28:16 in Ro 9:33; 10:11).

If we link the Old Testament context of Jeremiah 9 with the identification of κύριος as Christ, we may conclude that Paul's twice-cited aphorism has the sense that "the person who boasts should boast solely about who Christ is or what he has accomplished" (cf. τὴν καύχησιν ἐν Χριστῷ Ἰησοῦ, Ro 15:17). In 1Co 1:31 the aphorism serves to counteract prideful boasting in human wisdom, power, pedigree, and strength (1:26–29). "Boasting in the Lord" is taking pride in the salvific work of "righteousness, sanctification, and redemption" that Christ accomplished as believers' true Wisdom (1:30). In 2Co 10:17, by contrast, the purpose of the OT citation is to counteract any prideful boasting about someone else's successful ministry carried out in someone else's God-assigned sphere of activity (10:13–16).

In Paul's view, then, for boasting to be legitimate, it must have two characteristics. It must not be about personal status or accomplishments but only about who Christ is and what he has done in securing redemption, that is, his character and his exploits; and it must be confined to taking pride in the Lord's accomplishments within one's divinely allotted assignment or domain of service.

4. Ἐν (τῇ) ἀληθείᾳ περιπατεῖν

The Johannine corpus has 11 uses of the phrase ἐν (τῇ) ἀληθείᾳ (Jn 4:23–24; 17:17, 19; 1Jn 3:18; 2Jn 1, 3, 4; 3Jn 1, 3 4), but only three when it modifies a form of περιπατεῖν:

2Jn 4 Ἐχάρην λίαν ὅτι εὕρηκα ἐκ τῶν τέκνων σου **περιπατοῦντας ἐν ἀληθείᾳ**
"I was overjoyed to find some of your children walking in the truth."

3Jn 3 Ἐχάρην γὰρ λίαν ἐρχομένων ἀδελφῶν καὶ μαρτυρούντων σου τῇ ἀληθείᾳ, καθὼς σὺ **ἐν ἀληθείᾳ περιπατεῖς**
"I was overjoyed when some brothers came and told me about your loyalty to the truth, just as you continue to walk in the truth."

3Jn 4 Μειζοτέραν τούτων οὐκ ἔχω χαράν, ἵνα ἀκούω τὰ ἐμὰ τέκνα **ἐν τῇ ἀληθείᾳ περιπατοῦντα**
"I have no greater joy than to hear that my children are walking in the truth."

That there is no significant difference between ἐν ἀληθείᾳ and ἐν τῇ ἀληθείᾳ is suggested by Jn 17:17, 19, where both forms are found with the same verb (ἁγνίζω), and the fact that the articular form could not be adverbial in meaning ("truly, in reality, authentically"): "Sanctify them by the truth" (ἐν τῇ ἀληθείᾳ, v. 17); "For them I sanctify myself, so that they also may be sanctified by the truth" (ἐν ἀληθείᾳ, v. 19).

In the 2 and 3 John passages ἐν is not instrumental, as it certainly is in Jn 17:17. Rather, it states the sphere or realm in which the "walking" takes place. In its metaphorical use, περιπατεῖν means "conduct oneself, live one's life," referring to a characteristic outlook on life and pattern of behavior. Ἀλήθεια here denotes "the content of Christianity as the ultimate truth" (BDAG 42b). As these three elements are put together, we conclude that ἐν (τῇ) ἀληθείᾳ περιπατεῖν describes a way of life, embracing both thought and action, that is informed, molded, and regulated by Christian truth. It is "believing and acting as a Christian" (R. Bergmeier, *EDNT* 3:75d). It is to have a mind-set and lifestyle molded by the gospel, although John, unlike Paul (in Col 1:5), does not explicitly equate "truth" with the "gospel." While it is not common, our phrase is a happy blend of a characteristic Johannine term (ἀλήθεια) and a favorite Pauline verb (περιπατεῖν), aptly summing up the ideal Christian life and encapsulating Christian ethics.

A similar thought is expressed with ἐν in Ps 85:11 (LXX; EVV, 86:11): "Guide me in your way, O Lord, and I will walk in your truth [πορεύσομαι ἐν τῇ ἀληθείᾳ σου]." This is comparable to John's "walking in the light" (ἐν τῷ φωτὶ περιπατεῖν, 1Jn 1:7). Similar ideas in John with constructions other than ἐν include "living by the truth" (ποιεῖν τὴν ἀλήθειαν, Jn 3:21; 1Jn 1:6) and "walking in obedience to his commands" (περιπατεῖν κατὰ τὰς ἐντολὰς αὐτοῦ, 2Jn 6). Not dissimilar concepts are found in Paul's πνεύματι περιπατεῖν (Gal 5:16), living a life empowered and directed by the Spirit; in Paul's κατὰ ἀγάπην περιπατεῖν (Ro 14:15), conduct governed by love; and in Peter's ἡ ὁδὸς τῆς ἀληθείας (2Pe 2:2), belief and conduct (= the way) characterized by truth.

5. Μένειν ἐν in John

When used in a literal sense, μένειν ἐν refers to "staying in/at" a particular place for a shorter or longer time, whether it be a house (Lk 10:7), a city (Ac 9:43), or a district (Jn 7:9). Other prepositions are used with μένειν in the Johannine corpus (such as εἰς, Jn 6:27; ἐπί, Jn 1:32; 3:36; μετά, 1Jn 2:19; παρά, Jn 1:39; 14:17), but it is John's use of ἐν with μένειν that is theologically significant.

a. Statistics and Meaning

There are 40 uses of μένειν in John's gospel, 24 in 1 John, and 3 in 2 John. Within these uses, μένειν ἐν occurs 17x in John's gospel (plus three implicit instances—6:56b; 15:4a, 5b), 22 times in 1 John, and 3 times in 2 John.

As an intransitive verb, μένειν may be translated "remain/stay/continue/persist, endure," or even "live/dwell," depending on the context. Ideas of continuance, permanency, and adherence regularly attach to the word. When μένειν has a personal subject and there is a personal referent after the locatival ἐν, the verb implies an intimate and reciprocal fellowship, a mutual indwelling, a reciprocal immanence between the two parties ("remain united to").

b. Μένειν ἐν and Reciprocity

The following table shows the extent of the reciprocal relations between God/the Father, Jesus/Christ/the Son, and Jesus' followers/believers/Christians in John's gospel and his letters.

God in Christ	Jn 14:10c	Christ in God	Jn 15:10c (in the Father's love)
God in believers	1Jn 3:24; 4:12, 13, 15, 16	Believers in God	1Jn 2:6, 24; 3:24; 4:13, 15, 16
Christ in believers	Jn 6:56; 15:4, 5	Believers in Christ	Jn 6:56; 15:4, 5, 6, 7; 1Jn 2:24, 27, 28; 3:6

When ἐν αὐτῷ is found with μένειν, it is sometimes unclear whether God or Christ is being referred to (see, e.g., 1Jn 2:5–6), but since 1Jn 2:24b speaks of the believer as remaining "in the Son and in the Father," any decision is not of crucial import. Rather, just as there are not two competing objects of human faith — God and Christ — so too there are not two distinct divine figures in whom the believer must "remain"; it is impossible to remain in God without also remaining in Christ.

Two further points are noteworthy. First, the intimate and reciprocal relationship that God and Christ enjoy as Father and Son is the pattern for a comparable relationship between Christ and the believer (cf. Jn 17:21: Christian unity mirrors Father-Son unity). Indeed, as the member common to both relationships, Christ acts as the mediator of the paradigm.

Second, the mutual indwelling of God and Christ, and of Christ and the believer, does not involve the loss of personal identity or the forfeiture of individual distinctives. The Father indwells the Son, and the Son indwells the Father, but neither is "absorbed" by the other. (The classical doctrine of *circumincessio* denotes the "co-inherence" of the persons of the Trinity in the shared divine essence, and [as here] in each other.) Similarly, Christ indwells the believer, and the believer indwells Christ, but neither surrenders individual distinctiveness by this mutuality. But when μένειν (ἐν) is imperative (Jn 15:4; 1Jn 2:28; cf. Jn 15:9), the responsibility for preserving this intimate fellowship is clearly seen to rest with the believer: "You must remain united to me and I will remain united to you" (Jn 15:4, Goodspeed).[6]

---

6. See the Goodspeed translation; also his *Problems of New Testament Translation* (Chicago: Univ. of Chicago Press, 1945), 112–14.

But John applies the expression μένειν ἐν to things as well as to persons. Believers are to "remain" in love (Jn 15:9–10; 1Jn 4:16), in light (1Jn 2:10), and in the teaching of Christ (Jn 8:31; 2Jn 9), while a wide range of items "remain" in the believer—things heard from the beginning (1Jn 2:24), Christ's words (Jn 15:7), God's word (Jn 5:38; 1Jn 2:14), truth (1Jn 1:8; 2Jn 2), God's love (1Jn 3:17), God's seed (1Jn 3:9), and the anointing (1Jn 2:27). What is more, unbelievers "remain" in darkness (Jn 12:46) and in death (1Jn 3:14).

c. Relation of μένειν ἐν to εἶναι ἐν

Εἶναι ἐν appears 13x in John's gospel and 18x in 1 John (apart from places where the verb is understood). These two phrases, "remaining in" and "being in," share much common territory in John's usage and often seem synonymous, especially where μένειν ἐν may be appropriately rendered by "living in" (see, e.g., 1Jn 2:6; 3:24 [2x]). Significantly, in Jn 14:10 the expression ὁ δὲ πατὴρ ἐν ἐμοὶ μένων precisely parallels the earlier ὁ πατὴρ ἐν ἐμοί ἐστιν. As to the difference between the two phrases, μένειν ἐν presupposes εἶναι ἐν: only those who are already "in" can be encouraged to "continue in." In other words, "being in" depicts a status that should be recognized and appreciated; "remaining in" points to a status that should be maintained. Also, μένειν ἐν emphasizes the durability and permanency of the relationship under discussion. The idiom ἔχειν τι μένον (cf. its use in 1Jn 3:15) means "have something continually/permanently" (cf. BDAG 631b).

We suggest that the phrase μένειν ἐν became one of John's favorite ways of describing personal relations between the Father and the Son and between believers and Christ because it aptly expresses a permanent and reciprocal immanence, a dynamic symbiotic union in which personal identity is not compromised. Like μένειν μετά (see 1Jn 2:19; cf. BDAG 631c), the phrase μένειν ἐν means "remain in fellowship with."

F. Ἐν in Compounds

In the NT there are 55 verbal compounds with ἐν, "which seem about equally divided between the forces of εἰς and ἐν" (MH 305).

1. Location: ἐγκαταλείπω, abandon (in adverse circumstances)
   ἐγκρατής, having inner strength, self-controlled
2. Direction: ἐντρέπομαι, turn toward
   ἐγκαλέω, bring charges against, accuse
3. Quality: ἔννομος, in accordance with law, legal
   ἔνδοξος, with glory, distinguished, splendid

Chapter 11

Ἐπί

A. Basic Meaning

Basically denoting position *on* something that forms a support or foundation, ἐπί is the opposite of ὑπό ("under") and differs from ὑπέρ ("above") in implying actual rest on some object. In this primary local sense of "on" or "upon," ἐπί is followed by the accusative, the genitive, or the dative, sometimes without distinction in meaning. Take, for example, the use of ἐπί with ὁ καθήμενος and θρόνος in Revelation, in a circumlocution for God's majestic name.

> ὁ καθήμενος ἐπὶ τοῦ θρόνου (Rev 4:10; 5:1, 7; 6:16; 7:15)
> ἐπὶ τὸν θρόνον (Rev 4:2)
> ἐπὶ τῷ θρόνῳ (Rev 4:9; 5:13; 7:10; 19:4; 21:5)

Or again, in marking "power, authority, control of or over someone or someth[ing]" (BDAG 365c), ἐπί is found with:

the accusative (Lk 12:14), "as judge *over* you"
the genitive (Lk 12:42), "*over* his household servants"
the dative (Lk 12:44), "set *over* all his possessions"

The overlap between ἐπί with the accusative and ἐπί with the genitive may be illustrated by two observations.

1. Ἐπί + accusative need not imply linear motion but may simply denote punctiliar rest. E.g., 2Co 3:15, κάλυμμα ἐπὶ τὴν καρδίαν αὐτῶν κεῖται, "a veil rests over their hearts"; Jn 1:32, τὸ πνεῦμα ... ἔμεινεν ἐπ᾽ αὐτόν, "the Spirit ... remained on him."
2. Ἐπί + genitive may indicate motion ("toward") rather than rest, as in the phrase ἐπὶ τῆς γῆς, "toward land/to the ground" (Mk 9:20; 14:35; Jn 6:21; Ac 10:11).

The overlap between ἐπί with the accusative and ἐπί with the dative is clear from two Matthean uses of οἰκοδομέω:

Mt 7:24, ᾠκοδόμησεν αὐτοῦ τὴν οἰκίαν ἐπὶ τὴν πέτραν, "he built his house on the rock"

Mt 16:18, ἐπὶ ταύτῃ τῇ πέτρᾳ οἰκοδομήσω μου τὴν ἐκκλησίαν, "I will build my church on this rock"

In keeping with the general tendency in Hellenistic Greek for the accusative to become the default case with prepositions, ἐπί with the accusative is by far the most common NT use (464x), with ἐπί followed by the genitive next in frequency (216x), then ἐπί with the dative (176x). These statistics are from Moulton 107; Turner's corresponding figures [271] for the LXX are 4629x, 1730x, and 1219x.

B. Versatility

In frequency among NT "proper" prepositions, ἐπί ranks fourth after ἐν, εἰς, and ἐκ, accounting for 8.6% of these prepositions. Not surprisingly, the uses of ἐπί are even more varied than the uses of ἐν, since ἐπί is the only NT preposition regularly followed by three cases (cf. Mayser 462). From the simple spatial meaning of ἐπί ("upon") there naturally developed a multitude of derived senses, so that the preposition may express, *inter alia*:

1. basis: Mt 4:4 ; Lk 5:5; 1Ti 5:19; ἐπὶ τῇ πίστει, "on the basis of faith" (BDAG 364d), Ac 3:16 and Php 3:9
2. cause: Mk 12:17; 2Co 9:13; Phm 7
3. circumstance: Ro 8:20; 1Co 9:10; Tit 1:2
4. superintendence: Mt 2:22; Lk 12:44; Ac 6:3
5. addition: Lk 3:20; 2Co 7:13; Php 2:27
6. purpose: Mt 3:7, ἐπὶ τὸ βάπτισμα αὐτοῦ, "for baptism by him/to have themselves baptized by him" (similarly BDAG 366a); Gal 5:13, ἐπ' ἐλευθερίᾳ ἐκλήθητε, "you were called to/for freedom," "freedom claimed you when you were called" (R. Knox), a statement epitomizing the argument of this letter that has been called "the charter of Christian liberty"; also Eph 2:10; 1Th 4:7

Of special interest is the use of ἐπί (with the accusative) to denote individuals or groups on whom some spiritual blessing comes or rests—blessings such as the word of God (Lk 3:2), the kingdom of God (Mt 12:28; Lk 10:9), the grace of God (Lk 2:40), the Holy Spirit (Lk 2:26; Ac 1:8; 2:17–18; 10:45; Tit 3:6; 1Pe 4:14), and the power of Christ (2Co 12:9).

C. Important Constructions Using Ἐπί

1. Ἐπί τὸ αὐτό

In the LXX (e.g., 2Sa 2:13; Pss 2:2; 33:4) the meaning of this prepositional phrase is "together, with one accord, at/in the same place," or "at the same time," while in the papyri it is frequent in the sense "in all" (denoting the sum total of an account; cf. Mayser 418 and n.2; MM 234d; Moulton 107, citing Ac 1:15; 2:47 as examples).

The phrase has the sense of "together" in Ac 4:26 (quoting Ps 2:2) and in Mt 22:34; Lk 17:35. As a euphemism for sexual intercourse ἐπὶ τὸ αὐτὸ εἶναι occurs in 1Co 7:5. Adducing illuminating parallels from the Qumran Manual of Discipline (e.g., 1QS 5:7), M. Wilcox has shown that in Ac 2:47 (as in 1:15; 2:44, 46 D) the phrase is not a mistranslation of the Aramaic *lahdā'* (as C. C. Torrey maintained; see MH 473) but a quasitechnical expression denoting the union of the Christian fellowship: "the Lord was day by day incorporating into the Fellowship those who were being saved."[1] BDAG (363c) proposes simply "to their number" for ἐπὶ τὸ αὐτό in Ac 2:47 (so also Goodspeed); JB and NJB have "to their community."

That ἐπὶ τὸ αὐτό and ἐν ἐκκλησίᾳ are sometimes virtually synonymous, signifying "in church fellowship" or "in the assembly," seems evident from the parallelism of 1Co 11:18 and 11:20. Such a sense (or "together in fellowship"), common in the *Apostolic Fathers* (e.g., *1 Clem* 34:7; Ign. *Eph.* 5:3; 13:1; *Mag.* 7:1; *Phil.* 6:2; 10:1; *Barn.* 4:10),[2] should be given to the phrase in Ac 2:1, 44 *v.l.*, 46 D, 47; 1Co 11:20; 14:23 (BDAG 363c suggests "to the same place" for the last two passages) and possibly Ac 1:15. The "togetherness" of the early Christians was expressed mainly in their meeting for public worship "in church fellowship" or "in the assembly."

2. Ἐφ' ᾧ

There is general unanimity among grammarians that ἐφ' ᾧ means "because," "inasmuch as," or "in view of the fact that," where ἐφ' ᾧ = ἐπὶ τούτῳ ὅτι, "on the basis of this reason, namely that," or = διότι/διὰ τοῦτο ὅτι, "because" (see BDF §235[2]; Moulton 107; Robertson 604, 722, 963; Zerwick §127; *Analysis* 399; Turner 272, 319; so also BDAG 365a-b; cf. 727c). Such a sense certainly fits the context in Ro 5:12; 2Co 5:4; Php 3:12, although some have doubts about Php 4:10 (e.g., BDF §235[2], "for"; BDAG 365b "for, indeed"; Turner 272, "whereon"; and Moule 132 suggests "with regard to which" [i.e., τὸ ὑπὲρ ἐμοῦ φρονεῖν, "your concern for me"]).

a. Romans 5:12

Διὰ τοῦτο ὥσπερ δι' ἑνὸς ἀνθρώπου ἡ ἁμαρτία εἰς τὸν κόσμον εἰσῆλθεν καὶ διὰ τῆς ἁμαρτίας ὁ θάνατος, καὶ οὕτως εἰς πάντας ἀνθρώπους ὁ θάνατος διῆλθεν, ἐφ' ᾧ πάντες ἥμαρτον

"Therefore, just as sin entered the world through one man, and death entered as a consequence of that sin, and so death has spread to all people, because all have sinned [with Adam]."

---

1. M. Wilcox, *The Semitisms of Acts* (Oxford: Clarendon, 1965), 93–100.
2. Cited by E. Ferguson, "'When You Come Together': *Epi to Auto* in Early Christian Literature," *Restoration Quarterly* 16 (1973): 205–6.

In Romans 5:12–21 Paul is comparing (with both similarities and differences) Christ, the sole author of righteousness and life, with Adam, the author of sin and death. Verse 12 is anacoluthic—the true conclusion matching the ὥσπερ would probably have been "so righteousness came into the world through one man, and life through that righteousness."

Few phrases in Paul's writings have generated more controversy than ἐφ' ᾧ πάντες ἥμαρτον. J. A. Fitzmyer lists no fewer than eleven proposed meanings for ἐφ' ᾧ;[3] he himself opts for "with the result that" (cf. LSJ 622c, "wherefore"). The numerous interpretations of the verse fall into two main grammatical categories:

1. those that construe ᾧ as a relative pronoun (whose antecedent may be either ὁ θάνατος, "death," or ἑνὸς ἀνθρώπου, "one man"), with ἐπί meaning "in" or "because of"
2. those that treat ἐφ' ᾧ as a conjunction, equivalent to ἐπὶ τούτῳ ὅτι, "because"

The former alternatives are improbable since elsewhere in Paul (2Co 5:4; Php 3:12; 4:10), ἐφ' ᾧ is conjunctional, whatever its precise nuance.

Thus, the focus of exegetical attention naturally moves to πάντες ἥμαρτον, which may refer to human beings' corporate involvement in the transgression of Adam, or to their personal sin either in imitation of Adam or as a result of inheriting a corrupt Adamic nature. Since some nexus between Adam and his descendants regarding sin seems demanded by Paul's Adam-Christ analogy (see Ro 5:18–19; cf. 1Co 15:22), the most likely options seem to be:

1. "death spread to all people because all sinned" (either actually in Adam's primal transgression or in their federal representative, Adam, ἥμαρτον being a constative aorist)
2. "death spread to all people because all do sin" (as those who have inherited Adam's nature, ἥμαρτον being a gnomic aorist)
3. *"death spread to all people because all [since the time of Adam] have sinned" (ἥμαρτον being a constative aorist).

b. 2 Corinthians 5:4

καὶ γὰρ οἱ ὄντες ἐν τῷ σκήνει στενάζομεν βαρούμενοι, **εφ' ᾧ** οὐ θέλομεν ἐκδύσασθαι ἀλλ' ἐπενδύσασθαι, ἵνα καταποθῇ τὸ θνητὸν ὑπὸ τῆς ζωῆς

"For indeed, as tent-dwellers, we sigh with a sense of oppression because, not wishing to become disembodied, we desire to put on our heavenly dwelling as an overgarment, so that what is mortal may be swallowed up by life."

In 2Co 5:1–10 Paul is reckoning with the probability of his own pre-parousia decease and is recounting the sources of divine comfort afforded the believer who

---

3. J. A. Fitzmyer, *Romans* (AB; New York: Doubleday, 1993), 413–17.

stands within the shadow of death. Both the term γυμνοί in v. 3 and ἐκδύσασθαι here in v. 4 seem to be direct allusions to the view of certain Corinthian proto-gnostics for whom ἀθανασία as disembodied immortality represented the *summum bonum* and was the object of their eager longing (ἐκδύσασθαι ἐπιποθοῦμεν, cf. v. 2). Paul repudiates this aberrant view by asserting in vv. 2–4 that his long-ing or desire was for "superinvestiture" followed by permanent embodiment; the object of his ἐπιπόθησις (v. 2) or θέλησις (v. 4) was not γυμνότης but an ἐπένδυσις, the putting on of his heavenly dwelling as an overgarment. If v. 3 defines the outcome of the ἐπένδυσις negatively—it is not disembodied immortality—v. 4 defines it positively: it is the transformation of the mortal body by immortal life.

Clearly there is parallelism between στενάζομεν ... ἐπενδύσασθαι ἐπιποθοῦντες in v. 2 and στενάζομεν ... εφ' ᾧ ... θέλομεν ... ἐπενδύσασθαι in v. 4: "we sigh ... *because we long* to put on [our heavenly dwelling as an overgarment]" and "we sigh ... *because* ... we wish ... to put on [our heavenly dwelling as an overgarment]." The origin of Paul's groaning or sighing, that is, his sense of frustration under the limitations of a σάρξ-dominated σῶμα, is not to be traced to a Hellenistic depre-ciation of corporeality but to his yearning or wish for the acquisition of a spiritual body (cf. 1Co 15:44). And if Paul "groaned" in physical embodiment *because* he longed for spiritual corporeality, that longing arose because God had given him the Spirit as the pledge of the resurrection transformation (2Co 5:4b, 5).

D. Other Notable Uses of Ἐπί
1. Matthew 16:18

Κἀγὼ δέ σοι λέγω ὅτι σὺ εἶ Πέτρος, καὶ ἐπὶ ταύτῃ τῇ πέτρᾳ οἰκοδομήσω μου τὴν ἐκκλησίαν, καὶ πύλαι ᾄδου οὐ κατισχύσουσιν αὐτῆς

"And I also tell you: your name is Peter [a stone]; but upon this rock foundation I will build my church and the powers of Hades will not triumph over it."

If Peter's confession in Mt 16:16 about the person of Jesus ("You are the Messiah, the Son of the living God") was the result of divine revelation, not natural intuitive powers ("flesh and blood," v. 17), here in v. 18 Jesus himself gives a second revelation (implied by κἀγώ, "I also"), this time about his work—his building of his community and its withstanding of the incontestable power of Satan, evil, and death (αὐτῆς refers back to ἐκκλησίαν, not πέτρᾳ). Σὺ εἶ Πέτρος mirrors Σὺ εἶ ὁ Χριστός in v. 16 and further underlines the link between vv. 18–19 and v. 16.

If there is an Aramaic substratum to this logion, the wordplay would have involved the term *kepaʾ*, since this word can mean both "stone" and "rock." But the exegete must engage with the Greek as it stands, not with a putative Aramaic original. Some distinction must be intended between πέτρος and πέτρα, between "stone" and "[bed]rock" (of some massive rock formation), for καὶ ἐπὶ τούτῳ τῷ πέτρῳ might have been expected after Πέτρος.

There are two main identifications of the πέτρα (other proposals include Jesus himself, Jesus' teaching, or the revelation given to Peter).

(1) *Peter himself*, as the leader and representative of the apostles (*primus inter pares*), to whom special teaching and disciplinary roles in the church were given (v. 19; but see also 18:18), or as a representative of the church to be formed by Jesus, or as the first confessor of Jesus as Messiah.

This last option (Peter as first confessor) has the advantage of tying v. 18 to vv. 16–17. As the first among the Twelve to enunciate what had been revealed by the Father (v. 17), Peter and his confession formed the bedrock for the edifice of Christ's church. On this view Petrine primacy is temporal, not official. Peter himself later explicitly distinguishes between Christ as the "cornerstone" (ἀκρογωνιαῖος) of the church (a view shared by Paul, 1Co 3:11; Eph 2:20), and all believers (including Peter himself) as "living stones" (λίθοι ζῶντες) who together constitute the "spiritual temple" (οἶκος πνευματικός), the church (1Pe 2:4–6).

It must be observed that Jesus does not say ἐπί σοι ("on you") or ἐπί σοι ὡς πέτρᾳ ("on you as a rock"). And there is the antecedent improbability that so significant an edifice as a messianic community, constructed by the Messiah himself, should be erected on so insecure a foundation as a mere mortal, even though Peter was the recipient of divine revelation.

(2) *The messianic confession of Peter* (v. 16). The Greek does not require that the referent in πέτρος and πέτρα be identical; indeed, the presence of the demonstrative ταύτῃ is decidedly awkward (in a move from second to third person) if it refers back to Πέτρος. Rather, it looks back to an implied τοῦτο (= the content of the confession of v. 16) with ἀπεκάλυψεν in v. 17 in a case of "construction according to sense." Significantly, the early history of the church indicates that the earliest, foundational christological confession was in fact "Jesus is the Messiah" (ὁ Χριστὸς Ἰησοῦς, Ac 18:5, 28; cf. 2:36; 9:22; 17:3).[4]

2. Matthew 19:9

λέγω δὲ ὑμῖν ὅτι ὃς ἂν ἀπολύσῃ τὴν γυναῖκα αὐτοῦ μὴ ἐπὶ πορνείᾳ καὶ γαμήσῃ ἄλλην μοιχᾶται

"I tell you that anyone who divorces his wife, except for marital unfaithfulness, and marries another woman commits adultery." (NIV[1])

In itself the crucial phrase μὴ ἐπὶ πορνείᾳ (lit., "not on the basis of immorality") in this famous Matthean divorce saying could conceivably be interpreted

---

4. This view, held (with variations) by Ambrose, Chrysostom, Calvin, and Zwingli, has recently been defended by C. C. Caragounis, *Peter and the Rock* (Berlin: de Gruyter, 1989).

as parenthetical, providing a negative explanatory refinement: "it is also not allowed on the ground of fornication" (a view cited in *TDNT* 6:592 n.75), "not [even] in the case of immorality [can he divorce her]," making 19:9 an absolute prohibition of divorce. But this view accords better with μηδέ ("not even") in place of μή, as does an appeal to preterition: "the ground of fornication being left out of account" (Cassirer) or "I am not speaking of an illicit marriage" (NJB).

But in light of the unambiguous parallel in Mt 5:32, παρεκτὸς λόγου πορνείας, "except for the reason of immorality/apart from the ground of immorality" (cf. BDAG 601b, 774d; Zerwick §128 n.8), the μή of 19:9 should be treated as equivalent to εἰ μή, introducing an exception, "except on the basis of immorality" (cf. BDAG 364d), "except for immorality." (Under the influence of 5:32 some witnesses such as B D f f[13] 33 read παρεκτὸς λόγου πορνείας in 19:9.) The difference between the two Matthean phrases (παρεκτὸς λόγου πορνείας and μὴ ἐπὶ πορνείᾳ) is formal rather than substantial. To treat μὴ ἐπί as meaning "not in addition to" yields no satisfactory sense in the context.

Many identifications have been made of the πορνεία (here mentioned in descending order of probability):

- adultery
- marriage (entered into in good faith) within the prohibited degrees of consanguinity (Lev 18:6–18; cf. Ac 15:20, 29; 1Co 5:1, where incest = πορνεία), where πορνεία = Heb. z[e]nût
- premarital unchastity discovered after marriage (cf. Dt 22:13–21)
- moral or spiritual adultery (since figuratively z[e]nût can denote apostasy or violation of the covenant, e.g., Nu 14:33)
- λόγος πορνείας (Mt 5:32) = Heb. 'erwat dābār, lit., "nakedness of a thing" (Dt 24:1, LXX ἄσχημον πρᾶγμα), "some indecency."

3. Colossians 3:14

ἐπὶ πᾶσιν δὲ τούτοις τὴν ἀγάπην, ὅ ἐστιν σύνδεσμος τῆς τελειότητος

"And in addition to all these garments, put on love, which is the bond that perfects them all."

In the context Paul is exhorting the Colossians to put off (ἀπόθεσθε) various vices and put on (ἐνδύσασθε) various Christian virtues (3:8–14). This verse well illustrates the variety of possible meanings of ἐπί.

- "Above" (NRSV, HCSB; ZG 610; cf. NEB, "to crown all"), where "above all" = "first and foremost"
- "Over" (= "on top of" [Zerwick, Analysis 453]), developing the clothing imagery (NJB, NAB[2], NIV[1,2])
- "In addition to" (BDF §235[3]; Robertson 605; Zerwick §128; similarly BDAG 365b; GNB, NASB[2])

With τὴν ἀγάπην we should probably supply ἐνδύσασθε, "put on," from v. 12, although more general verbs could be supplied, such as "add" (on the basis of ἐπί = "in addition to") or "there must be" (REB). The article with ἀγάπην suggests that concrete expressions of love, love dramatized, is in mind (cf. Zerwick §176).

Any one of these possible renderings of ἐπί hints at the primacy and superiority of love, a sense that becomes explicit in the affirmation that follows. Ὅ ἐστιν may be explanatory ("which is/that is to say," the vernacular equivalent of the literary τοῦτ᾽ ἔστιν), or, more probably, the antecedent of ὅ may be the general concept of "the putting on of love" or of "love put on," i.e., love in action (cf. Robertson 713). In the phrase that follows, the genitive τῆς τελειότητος could be qualitative, "the perfect bond" (NJB, NASB[2], NET) or, better, objective, "the bond that unites [all the virtues] in perfect harmony" (BDAG 966c), "the bond that produces perfection" (BDF §163, citing Fridrichsen); but BDR §166[1] classifies it as a genitive of pur[pose]), or "the bond that perfects [them all]." On this showing, the Christian's obligation is to display love in specific actions, for such love-in-action binds together all Christian virtues and brings them to harmonious perfection.

4. 1 Peter 2:24a

Ὅς τὰς ἁμαρτίας ἡμῶν αὐτὸς ἀνήνεγκεν ἐν τῷ σώματι αὐτοῦ ἐπὶ τὸ ξύλον

"He himself, in his own body, carried our sins up on to the cross."

Most EVV render this statement in a way similar to the NRSV: "He himself bore our sins in his body on the cross." Although it is true that ἀναφέρω may mean nothing more than φέρω (cf. LXX Isa 53:4 φέρει, 53:12 ἀνήνεγκεν, both rendering Heb. *nāsā᾽*) and ἐπί with the accusative can denote location (BDAG 363b-c; LSJ 622d), there are two reasons for preferring the proposed translation.

a. If, as is probable, 1Pe 2:24a is a combination of Isa 53:12 (αὐτὸς ἁμαρτίας πολλῶν ἀνήνεγκεν) and Dt 21:23 (κεκατηραμένος ὑπὸ θεοῦ πᾶς κρεμάμενος ἐπὶ ξύλου, "cursed by God is everyone who hangs on a tree"), Peter's change to ἐπὶ τὸ ξύλον is significant.

b. It is the combination of ἀνα- and ἐπί with the accusative that is remarkable. A distinction should be drawn between (ἀν)ήνεγκεν ἐπὶ τοῦ ξύλου and Peter's ἀνήνεγκεν ... ἐπὶ τὸ ξύλον, "he carried up on to the cross." "On a/the cross" is expressed by ἐπὶ ξύλου in Ac 5:30; 10:39; Gal 3:13, while in the only other NT case of ἐπὶ τὸ ξύλον (Rev 22:14), the reference is to a right of access (ἐξουσία) to approach or feed on the tree of life (τὸ ξύλον τῆς ζωῆς).

Two EVV reflect this understanding: "who his own self carried up our sins in his body to the tree" (RV margin); "in his own body he carried our sins up to the cross" (Cassirer).

Although ἀναφέρω is a technical term describing the priest's task of bringing a sacrifice and placing it on the altar (ἀναφέρειν ἐπὶ τὸ θυσιαστήριον, e.g., Lev 14:20), in 1Pe 2:24a the verb does not mean "offer up in sacrifice" (as it does in Heb 7:27; Jas 2:21; cf. 1 Pet 2:5) since sins could never be conceived of as an offering to God and Peter has preferred the term ξύλον ("cross") over θυσιαστήριον ("altar"). Rather, the verb should be understood in a nontechnical sense, "carry up." The picture is not of Christ as priest (and victim) and the cross as an altar, but of Christ as the sin-bearer (cf. Jn 1:29) and the cross as the place where sin was destroyed (cf. Col 2:14–15; BDAG 685d). E. G. Selwyn finds a possible allusion to Peter's actually having seen Jesus ascend Golgotha as the sin-bearer.[5] For the view that ἀναφέρω ἐπί is a forensic technical expression for the laying of one person's debt on another, see Deissmann, *Studies* 88–91.

On the use of ἐπὶ τῷ ὀνόματι after βαπτίζω, see below, ch. 21 E; and of ἐπί with πιστεύω, ch. 22 B.

E. Ἐπί in Compounds

1. Position: ἐπίγειος (= ἐπὶ γῆς), earthly; ἐπιγραφή, inscription, superscription
2. Movement: ἐπιβάλλω, place upon; ἐπίθεσις, laying on (of hands)
3. Direction: ἐπικαλέομαι, appeal to; ἐπεκτείνομαι, stretch toward, reach for
4. Intensity/perfectivizing: ἐφάπαξ, once for all; ἐπιμελῶς, thoroughly
5. Addition: ἐπενδύομαι, put on over

---

5. E. G. Selwyn, *The First Epistle of Peter* (London: Macmillan, 1946), 96, 181.

Chapter 12

Κατά

A. Basic Meaning

With regard to frequency of usage, κατά ranks eighth among NT and LXX "proper" prepositions. Its primary spatial meaning seems to have been "down (from or upon), downward." Just as ἀνά corresponds to ἄνω, so the preposition κατά answers to the adverb κάτω, "down(ward)." Instances of this spatial sense of κατά (with the genitive) are Mt 8:32 (κατὰ τοῦ κρημνοῦ, "down the steep bank"; Ac 27:14, "a tempestuous wind swept down from it" (κατ' αὐτῆς)" = the island of Crete with its mountain ravines. Paul in 2Co 8:2 affords a clear example of the developed metaphorical sense: ἡ κατὰ βάθους πτωχεία αὐτῶν (lit., "their poverty reaching down to the depths") — thus, "their extreme/abysmal poverty."

B. Phrases Involving Κατά

1. Κατὰ σάρκα

Like the term σάρξ itself (see 2Co 10:3), the phrase κατὰ σάρκα has both (a) a neutral sense, and (b) a pejorative sense. The literal, colorless yet common rendering of κατὰ (τὴν) σάρκα as "according to the flesh" or "after the flesh" evades the exegete's responsibility to determine from the context the particular shade of meaning that attaches to this expression, which is exclusively Pauline (19x) except for Jn 8:15 ("by human/outward standards").

a. Neutral Sense

No one translation fits all contexts, but the general, nonspecific sense is "with respect to what is physical/natural/external."

Romans 9:5

> [Ἰσραηλῖται] ἐξ ὧν ὁ Χριστὸς τὸ **κατὰ σάρκα**, ὁ ὢν ἐπὶ πάντων θεὸς εὐλογητὸς εἰς τοὺς αἰῶνας, ἀμήν

"[the people of Israel] from their ranks, as far as human descent is concerned, came Christ, who is supreme over all as God blessed forever"

In Ro 9:4–5 Paul is reviewing the unique privileges enjoyed by the people of Israel that intensify his sorrow (vv. 1–3) that his fellow Jews as a whole have failed to embrace Jesus as their Messiah. The substantivized κατὰ σάρκα (unique in the Greek Bible) emphasizes the limitation: "insofar as the physical is concerned " (BDF §266[2]; similarly Moule 58), "with respect to his human lineage." Although neither an adversative δέ nor a formal antithesis such as τὸ δὲ κατὰ πνεῦμα (cf. Ro 1:3–4) follows τὸ κατὰ σάρκα, there are compelling reasons for thinking that ὁ ὤν κτλ. expresses an informal contrast.

(1) If there was no sense in which ὁ Χριστός was not purely of Jewish stock, Paul would have concluded his statement simply with Χριστός. As it is, τὸ κατὰ σάρκα suggests there is an aspect of Christ's person to which the category of human descent is inapplicable.

(2) With the addition of τὸ κατὰ σάρκα after ὁ Χριστός, there would be a diminution of the stated Israelite privileges unless a complementary contrast followed that testified to the elevated status of the Messiah.

(3) The substantivizing τό relates κατὰ σάρκα back to ἐξ ὧν [ἦλθεν]; Paul is not here writing about "the human Christ," ὁ Χριστὸς [ὁ] κατὰ σάρκα. But it also looks forward, not to a suppressed τὸ κατὰ πνεῦμα, but to ὁ ὤν ἐπὶ πάντων θεός. What is being contrasted is not two disparate origins of the Messiah, human and divine, but, on the one hand, his Jewish descent (ἐξ ὧν) and his universal supremacy (ὁ ὤν ἐπὶ πάντων) and, on the other hand, his humanity (κατὰ σάρκα) and his deity (θεός), the human side of his being and the divine.

Colossians 3:22

Οἱ δοῦλοι, ὑπακούετε κατὰ πάντα τοῖς **κατὰ σάρκα** κυρίοις

"Slaves, obey your earthly masters in everything."

The second element in Paul's third pair of "household" exhortations in Colossians is οἱ κύριοι (Col 4:1), who are directed to treat their slaves fairly and justly "because you know that you too have a Master—in heaven [καὶ ὑμεῖς ἔχετε κύριον ἐν οὐρανῷ]." If Christian slaves are accountable to their earthly (κατὰ σάρκα) masters and so must obey them "in all respects" (κατὰ πάντα), Christian masters must remember they also are accountable for their conduct—to a heavenly κύριος. If the context in Ro 9:5 (see above) points to a human-divine contrast, in Colossians it adverts to an earth-heaven antithesis.

b. Pejorative Sense

In this case the general, nonspecific sense of κατὰ σάρκα may be expressed as "with respect to what is self-centered/sinful/purely worldly." That ἐν σαρκί may have the same sense as the pejorative κατὰ σάρκα is clear from Ro 8:4–5, 8–9.

2 Corinthians 1:17

ἢ ἃ βουλεύομαι **κατὰ σάρκα** βουλεύομαι;

"Or the decisions that I make—do I make them impulsively?"

Aware that he had altered his announced travel plans that involved the Corinthians, Paul is responding to a charge of "fickleness" (ἡ ἐλαφρία) that evidently had been leveled against him. The context suggests several possible meanings for κατὰ σάρκα. If it alludes to the earlier phrase ἐν σοφίᾳ σαρκικῇ (v. 12), it could mean "like an unprincipled worldling." If it anticipates what immediately follows ("So that with me it is first 'Yes, yes,' and then 'No, no,'" v. 17c), the sense may be "according to the mood of the moment." Or if the expression looks forward to the charge of domineering (v. 24), it may mean "on the basis of self-interest" or "for personal advantage." But it probably looks back to the immediately preceding term τῇ ἐλαφρίᾳ (v. 17a) and means "whimsically" or "impulsively."

2 Corinthians 5:16

Ὥστε ἡμεῖς ἀπὸ τοῦ νῦν οὐδένα οἴδαμεν **κατὰ σάρκα**· εἰ καὶ ἐγνώκαμεν **κατὰ σάρκα** Χριστόν, ἀλλὰ νῦν οὐκέτι γινώσκομεν

"So then, from now on we regard no one from a human perspective. Even though we once viewed Christ from a human perspective, yet now we no longer do so."

For some scholars this verse affords proof that Paul disavowed interest in the historical Jesus or regarded such knowledge as irrelevant or relatively unimportant; he no longer valued knowledge about "Christ as a man, the human Christ, Christ in the flesh" (κατὰ σάρκα Χριστόν).

There are, however, at least four reasons for construing κατὰ σάρκα with ἐγνώκαμεν and so treating it as adverbial, not adjectival: "as far as externals are concerned" (BDAG 916a), "from a solely human point of view."

1. Although Paul elsewhere uses κατὰ σάρκα as a modifier of both nouns and verbs, when the expression qualifies a noun, it usually follows the noun (Ro 1:3; 4:1; 9:3; 9:5, with τό; 1Co 1:26; 10:18),[1] whereas when it qualifies a verb it either precedes (e.g., 2Co 10:3) or follows (e.g., 2Co 11:18).
2. In v. 16a κατὰ σάρκα follows and qualifies the verb (οἴδαμεν).

---

1. In Ro 8:5 οἱ … κατὰ σάρκα ὄντες = οἱ ὄντες οἱ κατὰ σάρκα, and in Eph 6:5/Col 3:22 τοῖς κατὰ σάρκα κυρίοις = τοῖς κυρίοις τοῖς κατὰ σάρκα.

3. If κατὰ σάρκα functioned as an adjective, we would have expected Χριστὸν τὸν κατὰ σάρκα.

4. It is doubtful whether κατὰ σάρκα is ever equivalent to the neutral sense of ἐν [τῇ] σαρκί (see 2Co 10:3) or to ὡς ἄνθρωπος.

Since the time of his conversion (ἀπὸ τοῦ νῦν) Paul had ceased making superficial judgments about human beings based on external appearances (cf. 2Co 5:12). He now repudiated as totally erroneous his sincere yet superficial preconversion estimate of Jesus as a misguided messianic pretender whose followers must be exterminated (Ac 9:1–2; 26:9–11). So too, he regarded the time-honored division of people into Jew and Gentile (2Co 5:16a) as less significant for him than the believer-unbeliever distinction (see, e.g., Ro 2:28–29; 10:12–13; 1Co 5:12–13; Gal 6:10). Both people and events were now seen in the light of the new creation. Two basic and profound changes had been brought about in Paul's attitude as a result of his Damascus encounter with the risen Jesus: he now acclaimed Jesus as Messiah and Lord (Ac 9:22; 17:3; Ro 10:9); and he now viewed Gentile believers as Abraham's offspring, fellow citizens in the kingdom of God, brothers in Christ (Gal 3:26–29; Eph 2:11–21), and Jewish unbelievers as needing salvation in Christ (Ro 10:1–4).

2 Corinthians 10:2b–3

… ἐπί τινας τοὺς λογιζομένους ἡμᾶς ὡς **κατὰ σάρκα** περιπατοῦντας. ἐν σαρκὶ γὰρ περιπατοῦντες οὐ **κατὰ σάρκα** στρατευόμεθα

"… against certain people who reckon that we conduct our lives by worldly principles. For though we live in the world, we do not wage war with human resources."

In v. 2a Paul is pleading with the Corinthians to avoid forcing him to act boldly in a display of his confidence as an apostle having the Lord's authority. Apparently a segment of the Corinthian church had sided with the intruders from Judea and were infected with their negative attitudes toward Paul. The "catch-all" charge leveled against Paul was that his whole life was being lived κατὰ σάρκα, "by worldly principles, from worldly motives" (Goodspeed), "on the purely physical level," apart from the Spirit's direction, without the Spirit's power, or devoid of the Spirit's gifts.

In Paul's response to this charge, two opposing uses of σάρξ are juxtaposed. In the phrase ἐν σαρκί it refers to life on earth in its totality, the universal human condition shared by believer and unbeliever alike. Ἐν σαρκὶ περιπατεῖν is materially equivalent to (τὸ) ζῆν ἐν σαρκί (Gal 2:20; Php 1:22). Κατὰ σάρκα, by contrast, here means "by human methods" (NJB) or "with human resources," and points forward to the next verses that describe divine resources and methods of warfare.

2. Κατὰ σάρκα *and* κατὰ πνεῦμα

In Paul's writings, whenever the phrases κατὰ σάρκα and κατὰ πνεῦμα are found in close proximity, they are always antithetical, not complementary.[2] Again, we suggest that the general, nonspecific meaning of these phrases, when opposed, is "pursuing the desires/following the promptings of the sinful human nature" and "pursuing the desires/following the promptings of the Spirit."

a. Romans 8:4–5

... τοῖς μὴ **κατὰ σάρκα** περιπατοῦσιν ἀλλὰ **κατὰ πνεῦμα**. οἱ γὰρ **κατὰ σάρκα** ὄντες τὰ τῆς σαρκὸς φρονοῦσιν, οἱ δὲ **κατὰ πνεῦμα** τὰ τοῦ πνεύματος.

"... those whose lives are not ruled by the sinful nature but by the Spirit. For those who follow the sinful nature focus their attention on what that nature desires, but those who follow the Spirit focus their attention on what the Spirit desires."

What is being contrasted here are two diametrically opposed patterns of conduct and thinking (περιπατοῦσιν): on the one hand, a life lived under the control of the unregenerate human nature pursues what that nature wants and is preoccupied with satisfying those desires; on the other, a life lived under the domination of the Spirit pursues the things the Spirit desires and is preoccupied with satisfying the Spirit's desires. The same contrast is expressed differently in Gal 6:8 by ὁ σπείρων εἰς τὴν σάρκα ("the person who sows to please his sinful nature") and ὁ σπείρων εἰς τὸ πνεῦμα ("the person who sows to please the Spirit"); and in 5:19, 22, in reference to outcomes, τὰ ἔργα τῆς σαρκός ("actions prompted by the sinful nature") and ὁ καρπὸς τοῦ πνεύματος ("fruit produced by the Spirit").

b. Galatians 4:21–31

Nowhere in Galatians, Paul's charter of Christian freedom, is the theme of "liberty in Christ" (cf. Gal 2:4) more in evidence than in the section 4:21–31, where Paul interprets the Hagar-Sarah story of Ge 16:1–16; 21:1–21 in an analogical fashion to illustrate his point that believers are emancipated from all spiritual slavery: "For the enjoyment of this freedom, Christ has set us free. Stand firm, therefore, and do not be tied again to a yoke of slavery" (Gal 5:1). The paragraph presents a series of antitheses between slavery and freedom.

Contrasted with Hagar, the slave woman, is Sarah, the free woman, Abraham's freeborn wife, although she is not explicitly named. Ishmael too

---

2. On the other hand, when the simple terms σάρξ and πνεῦμα are juxtaposed, they may occasionally be complementary, signifying the physical and the spiritual, the outward and the inward (e.g., 2 Co 7:1; Col 2:5).

remains unnamed; he is depicted simply as Abraham's "son by the slave woman" (v. 23a), someone born κατὰ σάρκα (v. 23a), "in the ordinary course of nature" (Goodspeed), "in the usual way" (GNB), "by natural human processes" (Barclay). Isaac stands opposite Ishmael as Abraham's "son by the free woman," born not only δι' ἐπαγγελίας, "in fulfillment of the promise/as a result of a promise" (v. 23b), but also κατὰ πνεῦμα (v. 29), "under the Spirit's guidance" (Cassirer), "by the power of the Spirit." Then there is the covenant of law that is "from Sinai and bears children for slavery" (v. 24), which is implicitly contrasted with the covenant of promise (cf. Gal 3:17) that produces children for freedom. Finally, we have "the present city of Jerusalem" (= Judaism) that "is in slavery along with her children" (= the Judaizers; v. 25), which is paired against "the Jerusalem that is above," that is free and is the mother of the free (v. 26).

Clearly κατὰ σάρκα and κατὰ πνεῦμα derive their distinctive meanings here from the context. Two types of birth (γεγέννηται, v. 23; γεννηθείς, v. 29) are described: birth by natural procreation (κατὰ σάρκα) and birth under the influence of the Spirit (κατὰ πνεῦμα) in fulfillment of a divine promise.

C. Κατά Denoting Correspondence or Conformity

Often the substantive that follows κατά specifies the criterion, standard, or norm in the light of which a statement is made, an action is performed, or a judgment is passed. In these cases the preposition will mean "according to, in conformity/keeping with, corresponding to, in a manner consistent with, on a scale that matches." In the Lukan account of the institution of the Lord's Supper, Jesus declares that "the Son of Man is setting out on his road, in accordance with what has been decreed [κατὰ τὸ ὡρισμένον]" (Lk 22:22, Cassirer).

To encourage Corinthian generosity in contributing to his collection for "the poor among the saints in Jerusalem" (Ro 15:26), Paul appeals to the example of the liberality of the Macedonians. "They gave according to their means/as they were able [κατὰ δύναμιν], as I can affirm, and even beyond their means/even more than they were able (καὶ παρὰ δύναμιν), of their own accord" (2Co 8:3). Giving should not be reckless but it may be sacrificial.

This use is common in reference to the precise and impartial standard of judgment that will be applied in the final Assize, where ἕκαστος emphasizes the individual nature of the assessment and reward or penalty.

- **Mt 16:27** ἑκάστῳ **κατὰ** τὴν πρᾶξιν αὐτοῦ
- **Ro 2:6** ἑκάστῳ **κατὰ** τὰ ἔργα αὐτοῦ
- **1Co 3:8** ἕκαστος ... **κατὰ** τὸν ἴδιον κόπον
- **1Pe 1:17** **κατὰ** τὸ ἑκάστου ἔργον
- **Rev 2:23** ὑμῖν ἑκάστῳ **κατὰ** τὰ ἔργα ὑμῶν

The same thought is expressed in 2Co 5:10 using πρός: ἕκαστος ... πρὸς ἃ ἔπραξεν, "in accordance with/in proportion to what he has done." See below, ch. 17 B.

In 1Pe 3:7 Peter encourages Christian husbands to live with their wives κατὰ γνῶσιν, which may mean *(1) in conformity with Christian knowledge about husband-wife relations in general and sexual relations in particular (cf. 1Co 7:3–5); (2) in light of the knowledge of God's will and character; or (3) in a considerate and tactful manner.

1. Κατὰ θεόν

a. 2 Corinthians 7:9–11a

In this passage Paul is reflecting on the Corinthians' reaction to a stern letter he had recently sent to them, calling on them to discipline one of his vocal detractors. His initial regret that the letter had caused his converts pain (v. 8) had now altogether disappeared before the joyful realization that their temporary sorrow had led to a sincere repentance. Three times he speaks of pain or sorrow (ἐλυπήθητε, λύπη, τὸ λυπηθῆναι) that is κατὰ θεόν (9b, 10a, 11a). Since this sorrow is contrasted with ἡ δὲ τοῦ κόσμου λύπη (v. 10b), "worldly sorrow," it is tempting to render κατὰ θεόν by a matching "godly" (as Moule 59). But the context suggests a more expressive rendering, such as "[sorrow] borne in God's way" or "[sorrow] experienced as God intends." God's intent was that the λύπη should lead to repentance (εἰς μετάνοιαν, v. 9a), "a repentance that results in salvation and so is not regretted" (μετάνοιαν εἰς σωτηρίαν ἀμεταμέλητον, v. 10a). When sorrow or grief is experienced "in a godly way" or "as God intends" (κατὰ θεόν), spiritual benefit results and spiritual harm is avoided (cf. vv. 9b, 10b).

b. 1 Peter 4:6

Here two κατά phrases are contrasted. Addressing a concern some believers evidently felt about the fate of Christian martyrs (cf. 1Th 4:13–18), Peter observes that the very reason for the proclamation of the good news to such people who were now deceased is that, although "in human estimation" (κατὰ ἀνθρώπους) they had been physically judged by death, they should live in a spiritual state (ζῶσι ... πνεύματι) "as God does" (κατὰ θεόν). There is no need to insist that κατά should bear an identical sense in both parts of the verse.

2. Κατὰ τὰς γραφάς

1 Corinthians 15:3–4

Here Paul is reminding the Corinthians (in c. AD 55) of the gospel he had preached to them during his first visit to Corinth (c. AD 50–52), which he himself had received, probably at Damascus immediately after his conversion (c. AD 33). In vv. 3b–5 a fourfold creedal ὅτι introduces four verbs (ἀπέθανεν, ἐτάφη, ἐγήγερται, ὤφθη) that summarize the essence of early Christian preaching—the death, burial, resurrection, and appearances of Christ. Of these four pillars of Christian tradition, the first and third appear in a triadic structure:

ἀπέθανεν	ὑπὲρ τῶν ἁμαρτιῶν ἡμῶν	**κατὰ τὰς γραφάς**
ἐγήγερται	τῇ ἡμέρᾳ τῇ τρίτῃ	**κατὰ τὰς γραφάς**

The OT passages that from a Christian perspective predicted the death of the Messiah as an atonement for sin included Isa 53:4–6, 10–12, but the appeal may be to the general thrust of the OT sacrificial system as a whole, especially the Day of Atonement (Lev 16:1–34). With regard to the resurrection of Christ "on the third day," κατὰ τὰς γραφάς may allude to Hos 6:1–2, where the resurrection of the nation after its "burial" in exile occurs on the third day; or to 2Ki 20:5, where King Hezekiah is promised restoration to health and an ascent to the house of the Lord on the third day; or even to Ex 19:10–11, where the Lord promises to appear to his people on Mount Sinai on the third day. But again, the plural τὰς γραφάς could refer to the general tenor of OT teaching (cf. Lk 24:46) that God relieves the distress of the righteous "on the third day," that is, "after a brief interval, without delay."

Whatever the actual content of κατὰ τὰς γραφάς in each case, Paul's appeal to the OT Scriptures serves to confirm the reliability of the NT kerygma and the continuity of God's action in the two ages. Both the death and the resurrection of Christ formed part of the agelong plan of God (cf. Ac 2:23–32; 13:34–37).

D. Κατά Denoting Opposition

An obvious development from the local meaning "down upon" is where κατά expresses the idea of hostile movement directed against someone or something. The opposition involved ranges from a simple accusation laid against someone to aggressive hostility between irreconcilable adversaries.

Gal 5:17 "For the cravings of the sinful nature [ἡ γὰρ σάρξ ἐπιθυμεῖ] are in conflict with [κατά] the Spirit and the desires of the Spirit are in conflict with [κατά] the sinful nature—these two are diametrically opposed to each other [ἀλλήλοις ἀντίκειται]."

Col 2:14 God cancelled "the bond that stood against us [ἐξαλείψας τὸ καθ᾽ ἡμῶν χειρόγραφον]" (BDAG 254b), "the certificate of indebtedness that stood to our debit," and set it aside by nailing it to Christ's cross.

1Ti 5:19 "Do not entertain an accusation against [κατά] an elder, except on the evidence of two or three witnesses."

1Pe 2:11 "Dear friends, I appeal to you, as aliens and exiles here, to refrain from indulging the cravings of your sinful nature that are always at war with the soul [αἵτινες στρατεύονται κατὰ τῆς ψυχῆς]."

2 Corinthians 13:8

οὐ γὰρ δυνάμεθά τι **κατὰ** τῆς ἀληθείας ἀλλὰ ὑπὲρ τῆς ἀληθείας

"For we cannot do anything to oppose the truth but only to support the truth."

At first sight this might seem to be an aphorism: "Truth is impregnable but thrives on validation." But the context indicates Paul is here explaining when disciplinary action is or is not justified. When "truth" (= pure and authentic Christian behavior) prevails, when there is repentance and uprightness (cf. 2Co 12:21; 13:7), no discipline is required; but when "truth" is absent, when disobedience and impenitence are present, disciplinary action is demanded. "We could never act against the truth, but only in support of it." Paul was both able and willing, if necessary, to act decisively to reestablish "truth," that is, to work toward restoring the Corinthians to wholeness (cf. v.9b) in attitude and behavior.

Alternatively, or in addition, we could treat ἀλήθεια as a synonym for the gospel (cf. Eph 1:13; Col 1:5). As an agent of Christ (cf. 2Co 5:20; 13:3) in whom the truth resided (2Co 11:10), Paul was unable to act in a way that compromised the gospel, and he refused to alter its content (2Co 2:17; 4:2). Positively, he was under compulsion to propagate it, for it had been entrusted to him as a precious deposit (1Co 9:16–17; Gal 2:7).

E. Distributive Κατά

1. In Reference to Location

Sometimes κατ' οἶκον simply means "in the house" (Ro 16:5; 1Co 16:19; Col 4:15; Phm 2), but the expression can also mean "from house to house" or "by households." For κατ' οἰκί[αν] ἀπογρ[αφήν] referring to a "house-by-house census" conducted under Hadrian (AD 133), see *NewDocs* 6 §119. Accordingly, Acts 2:46 affords evidence that, at least in the earliest days of the Jerusalem church, there was a daily (**καθ' ἡμέραν**) celebration of the Lord's Supper "in various houses" (**κατ' οἶκον**), just as there was daily (πᾶσαν ἡμέραν, "every day") teaching and preaching in the temple courts and "from house to house" (**κατ' οἶκον**) (5:42; cf. 20:20). And with regard to ecclesiastical polity, in Acts 14:23 the phrase **κατ' ἐκκλησίαν** ("in each individual congregation/assembly," BDAG 304b) implies that every Pauline church in south Galatia had a plurality of elders (Paul and Barnabas "appointed elders [πρεσβυτέρους] for them, church by church"; cf. Php 1:1).

2. In Reference to Time

The expressions **κατ' ἔτος** (Lk 2:41; see MM 323b for use in the papyri) and **κατ' ἐνιαυτόν** (Heb 9:25; 10:1, 3) both mean "year by year, every year." Those who speak in tongues during a congregational meeting must do so **κατὰ** δύο ἢ τὸ πλεῖστον τρεῖς (1Co 14:27), "two or, at the most, three at a time" (BDAG 512b), that is, on any one occasion. Or again, Paul faced the pressure of his anxiety for all the churches "every day" (**καθ' ἡμέραν**, 2Co 11:28), or, more colloquially, "on a daily basis, day in and day out."

1 Corinthians 16:2

κατὰ μίαν σαββάτου ἕκαστος ὑμῶν παρ' ἑαυτῷ τιθέτω θησαυρίζων ὅ τι ἐὰν εὐοδῶται

"On the first day of every week, each one of you should set aside at home and store up some money in proportion to how he is prospering."

In preparation for his forthcoming visit (1Co 4:18 – 19; 16:5 – 6), Paul is repeating directions concerning his collection "for the poor among the saints in Jerusalem" (Ro 15:26) that he had already given to his Galatian churches (cf. Ac 18:23), so that no special collections would need to be made in Corinth after his arrival (1Co 16:1, 2b).

From these directions we may deduce Paul's concept of giving, at least for one of the churches he founded. It should be:

(1) *Regular.* Literally, **κατὰ μίαν σαββάτου** means "on each first day of the week" = "on the first day of every week" (BDAG 512b) = "every Sunday, Sunday by Sunday." In expressing the day of the week, the cardinal numeral εἷς regularly replaces the ordinal numeral πρῶτος, following LXX usage (Winer 248; Robertson 671 – 72; here μίαν for πρώτην; cf. Mk 16:2). Also, τιθέτω is a present imperative; "let this be your habit." "The first day of the week" (Jn 20:1, 19; Ac 20:7), "the Lord's Day" (Rev 1:10), had become or was becoming the holy day for Christians, being the day of Christ's resurrection.

(2) *Individual.* Although any collecting of the offerings before Paul arrived might be done in public, the "setting aside" was an individual act. Note a similar use of ἕκαστος in the same connection in 2Co 9:7.

(3) *Voluntary.* As a third person imperative τιθέτω is an exhortation ("each one of you should ..."), not a formal command (such as τίθετε ἕκαστος ὑμῶν); giving cannot be mandated. The imperatival ποιήσατε in v. 1 relates to following directions (cf. διέταξα, v. 1) about procedures and assumes the willingness and desire of the Corinthians to give. This is in keeping with his later directions regarding the same collection: "I am not commanding you" (2Co 8:8); "I am simply giving you my advice" (2Co 8:10).

(4) *Financial.* The term λογεία (v. 1) relates to the collection of money (BDAG 597b; Deissmann, *Studies* 142 – 43), just as τιθέτω refers to the laying aside of money (BDAG 1004a).

(5) *Private.* Because τίθημι as a commercial technical term can itself mean "put *aside*" (BDAG 1004a), it is unlikely that παρ᾽ ἑαυτῷ has the sense "aside" here (*pace* BDAG 268d; several EVV such as NRSV, NASB[2]). Rather, this phrase means "at home" (so BDAG 757a, citing Philo, *Cher.* 48; *Legat.* 271; and BDAG 1004a). A regular setting aside of unspecified sums of money *at home* would avoid any competitiveness and ensure privacy.

6. *Proportional.* Literally, ὅ τι ἐὰν εὐοδῶται means "with regard to whatever way he is prospering." The verb εὐοδῶται, probably present passive subjunctive (so Moulton 54; Robertson 343) rather than (as εὐόδωται) perfect passive indicative, refers not to profit ("in proportion to his gains," NEB, GNB) or to "income" (cf. "in keeping with your income," NIV[2]), which would be anachronistic given the presence of slaves in the Corinthian church, or to what one can afford (cf. "whatever he can afford," REB; "as much as each can spare," NJB), but to general financial prospering week by week. The "proportion" is not some percentage but conformity to whatever degree of prosperity an individual has enjoyed. Paul expresses the similar sentiment in 2 Corinthians 8: giving is to be ἐκ τοῦ ἔχειν, "as resources permit" (8:11) or καθὸ ἐὰν ἔχῃ, "according to/in proportion to whatever one has" (8:12).

F. Some Ambiguous Examples

Four passages will illustrate the difficulty of deciding the sense of κατά in some contexts.

1. Galatians 5:23

κατὰ τῶν τοιούτων οὐκ ἔστιν νόμος

"There is no law that restrains such virtues!"

This tantalizingly abbreviated statement follows a list of Christian virtues that are described as "the fruit produced by the Spirit" (ὁ καρπὸς τοῦ πνεύματος).

a. Κατά Denoting Opposition

*(1) *With τῶν τοιούτων construed as neuter.* Most EVV translate the statement as "There is no law against such things," or, reflecting the Greek word order, "Against such things there is no law," renderings that beg for clarification. It is unlikely the sentiment is banal ("Christian virtues do not flout the Mosaic law") or purely axiomatic ("no law exists that bans virtues such as these"). More probably the affirmation is *ironical ("No law forbids things like that" [Barclay]; "of

course the law is not against such virtues"). In contrast to the role of the Mosaic law to restrain wrongdoing (cf. 1Ti 1:9–10), "there is no law restricting the operation of virtues like these"; they may be freely developed! Perhaps reflecting such a view, some EVV end the statement with an exclamation mark (TCNT, Goodspeed, NAB[1], NLT). But Paul's remark also could be a case of litotes, with κατά ... οὐκ ἔστιν = ὑπέρ ... ἔστιν: the law actually endorses such virtues.

(2) *With τῶν τοιούτων construed as masculine.* "There is no law against those who practise such things" (Moffatt), that is, against those who exhibit the fruit of the Spirit (Gal 5:22–23a), since by leading lives ruled by the Spirit they are in fact fulfilling the law (Ro 8:4).

b. Κατά Denoting Relationship (cf. BDAG 513b-c)

(1) *With τῶν τοιούτων construed as neuter.* "There is no law dealing with such things as these" (NEB); virtue cannot be legislated. Or, "the law is not related to such manifestations of the Spirit."

(2) *With τῶν τοιούτων construed as masculine.* "There is no need for law with regard to such people" as exhibit the fruit of the Spirit.

2. Colossians 1:11

ἐν πάσῃ δυνάμει δυναμούμενοι **κατὰ** τὸ κράτος τῆς δόξης αὐτοῦ

"being equipped with full power through his majestic strength"

Δυναμούμενοι is the third of four circumstantial present participles in vv. 10–12 that describe four traits typical of believers as they lead a life that is worthy of the Lord (v. 10).

The preposition κατά may here express:

(1) *conformity* ("in accordance with"; "according to," RV, RSV, NASB[2]), in which case κατά κτλ. points to the level of the resources available for the equipping with power

(2) *basis* ("based on [his own glorious power]," JB)

*(3) *cause* ("as a result of/because of," "that comes from" (NRSV), and thus "through"; see BDAG 513a), in which case the ἐν phrase denotes that with which the Colossians are empowered and the κατά phrase that through which they are empowered: God's glorious strength equips them with a full measure of power.

3. Colossians 2:8

βλέπετε μή τις ὑμᾶς ἔσται ὁ συλαγωγῶν διὰ τῆς φιλοσοφίας καὶ κενῆς ἀπάτης **κατὰ** τὴν παράδοσιν τῶν ἀνθρώπων, **κατὰ** τὰ στοιχεῖα τοῦ κόσμου καὶ οὐ **κατὰ** Χριστόν

"Take care that no one carries you off as spoil by an empty, deceptive philosophy derived from human tradition and centered on the elemental spiritual forces of the universe, but not based on Christ."

In Col 2:4–8 Paul is issuing an urgent warning against a twofold danger: the danger of being talked into error by specious argument (vv. 4–7), and the danger of being taken captive by a philosophy that is empty deceit (v. 8).

The first κατά sets out the basis ("based on," REB; "which depends on," NIV) or *source ("derived from, which comes from," GNB) of the "philosophy," namely, "the tradition of humans, man-made/human tradition" (rather than divine revelation).

Some EVV take κατά in an identical sense in each of its three occurrences in this verse: RV, "after"; Weymouth, "following"; NASB[2], "according to"; NIV[1,2], "[which depends] on." But it is preferable, whether τὰ στοιχεῖα τοῦ κόσμου refers to "the elemental spirits of the universe" (REB, NRSV) or to "the elemental spiritual forces of this world" (NIV[2]), to take the first κατά as denoting the origin or source of the "philosophy," the second κατά as describing its content or substance (τὰ στοιχεῖα τοῦ κόσμου), and the third κατά as introducing the negation of the two preceding clauses (the essential weakness of this "philosophy" was that Christ was neither its source nor its substance).

4. Titus 1:1

Παῦλος δοῦλος θεοῦ, ἀπόστολος δὲ Ἰησοῦ Χριστοῦ **κατὰ** πίστιν ἐκλεκτῶν θεοῦ καὶ ἐπίγνωσιν ἀληθείας τῆς **κατ᾽** εὐσέβειαν

"Paul, a slave of God and an apostle of Jesus Christ called to promote the faith of God's chosen people and the knowledge of the truth that leads to godliness."

Whereas Paul introduces himself in Ro 1:1 as δοῦλος Χριστοῦ Ἰησοῦ, κλητὸς ἀπόστολος, here he is God's slave and Jesus Christ's apostle. The first κατά phrase probably relates to both δοῦλος and ἀπόστολος (δέ here is conjunctive, not adversative), while the second κατά phrase relates only to ἀληθείας, given τῆς (and not τήν or ὅ [referring to the general idea of the knowledge of the truth]).

Κατὰ πίστιν κτλ. may bear one of two senses.

  a. *conformity* ("in agreement with the faith held by God's elect and their knowledge of the truth"). But it is difficult to see how slavery and apostleship "accord with" this faith, unless one supplies "[roles exercised] in agreement with...."

  *b. *purpose* ("to arouse faith in those whom God has chosen, and the comprehension of religious truth," Goodspeed; "charged to strengthen the faith of God's Chosen People, and their knowledge of that Truth which makes for godliness," TCNT; cf. BDAG 512c). A general expression such as "to promote" could include a dual purpose, "to instill . . ." and "to further. . . ."

Κατ᾽ εὐσέβειαν may express:

a. *conformity* ("[the truth] which accords with godliness," RSV, ESV)
b. *relationship* ("[the truth] as our religion embodies it," NAB[1]; "[the truth] enshrined in our religion," REB; "[the truth] taught by our religion," GNB)
*c. *purpose* ("[the truth] that leads to godliness," HCSB, NIV[1,2]); "[the truth] that leads to true religion," JB, NJB; so also Robertson, *Pictures* 4:597)

G. Κατά in Compounds

With its 107 NT verbal compounds, κατά is second in frequency to σύν (123 verbal compounds; MH 316, 324). Most compounds fall into one of two categories.

1. Downward movement ("down/downwards"), although sometimes merely strengthening the simplex with "perfectivizing" force
   καταπίπτω, fall (down)
   κατεσθίω, eat up, swallow, devour
   κατακολουθέω, follow (closely)
   καταγράφω, write (down), draw figures
2. Opposition ("against")
   καταλαλέω, speak against, slander
   κατακρίνω, pass judgment on, condemn
   κατεξουσιάζω, exercise authority (over), tyrannize

Chapter 13

Μετά

A. Original Meaning and New Testament Use

Most scholars agree that originally μετά bore a local sense, "amid" or "between," signifying a middle or intervening space that, when crossed, naturally prompts ideas of "change" and sequence ("after") (cf. MH 318; Bortone 151, 166). This basic spatial sense is reflected in words such as μέτωπον, "forehead" (the space *between* the eyes) and μετεωρίζομαι (from the adjective μετέωρος, "suspended in mid-air, in suspense [between hope and fear]"), which in Classical Greek meant "buoy up with false hopes" but is used only once in the NT (Lk 12:29), probably in the sense "be worried/upset." Compare our idiom in English, "be up in the air." Basically, the preposition expresses the idea of "association," ranging in sense from loose connection to accompaniment to companionship to intimate union.

In NT usage μετά + genitive occurs over three times more often than μετά + accusative (364 to 109 uses). Μετά survives in Modern Greek as a result of purism, for example in the fossilized set expression μετὰ χαρᾶς, "with joy" (Bortone 207, 251). The demotic Modern Greek μέ (+ accusative) is probably not a new preposition but a new form of μετά (Bortone 207; cf. Thumb §162).

B. Μετά with Accusative ("after")

Robertson explains how "after" developed from the root idea of "midst": "You pass through the midst of this and that event and come to the point where you look back on the whole. This idea is 'after'" (612). In the NT this construction is probably only temporal. BDAG (637d) and Robertson (612) regard the one possible exception (μετὰ τὸ δεύτερον καταπέτασμα, Heb 9:3) as local ("behind [the second curtain]"), but BDF (§226) proposes "after the second curtain one comes to...." Common is μετά followed by the substantival infinitive (always aorist), as in Acts 10:41, μετὰ τὸ ἀναστῆναι αὐτὸν ἐκ νεκρῶν, "after he rose from the dead."

1 Peter 1:11

ἐραυνῶντες εἰς τίνα ἢ ποῖον καιρὸν ἐδήλου τὸ ἐν αὐτοῖς πνεῦμα Χριστοῦ προμαρτυρόμενον τὰ εἰς Χριστὸν παθήματα καὶ τὰς μετὰ ταῦτα δόξας

"They [the prophets] tried to discover the time and the circumstances which the Spirit of Christ within them was indicating when he predicted the sufferings destined for Christ and the splendors that would follow them."

In 1Pe 1:10–12 Peter is describing the salvation (σωτηρία, 1:5, 9–10) accomplished by Christ, which was revealed to OT prophets and preached by NT evangelists as constituting the essence of the gospel, namely, τὰ εἰς Χριστὸν παθήματα καὶ τὰς μετὰ ταῦτα δόξας. There is clear parallelism between τὰ εἰς Χριστὸν παθήματα and the preceding phrase τῆς εἰς ὑμᾶς χάριτος (v. 10) in the same sentence. In each case εἰς means "intended/destined for" and depicts destinies ordained by God. Moreover, the two expressions are related as cause and effect: "grace" was destined for believers precisely because sufferings were destined for Christ. Here χάρις denotes the blessings or benefits of God's beneficence and is virtually equivalent to the preceding term σωτηρία (1:5, 9b–10a).

In two of the three NT cases of the plural δόξαι, the meaning is "majestic beings" or "illustrious persons" (2Pe 2:10; Jude 8; BDAG 258a). But here in 1Pe 1:11 the sense is "splendors," referring to the "glorious events" or "spectacular results" that followed (μετὰ ταῦτα) the sufferings divinely intended for Christ. That concrete instances of δόξα are in mind is shown by the use of the article (cf. Zerwick §176) and of the plural (cf. BDF §142). These multiple consequences of Christ's passion will include his resurrection (1:3, 18, 21; 3:18, 21), his resurrection appearances (Ac 1:3, to the apostles Jesus "presented himself alive after his suffering" [μετὰ τὸ παθεῖν αὐτόν]), his ascension, session, and universal lordship (1Pe 3:22), and his parousia (1Pe 1:7, 13; 5:1, 4). Whether or not εἰς Χριστόν is understood as applying also to τὰς μετὰ ταῦτα δόξας, these "splendors" are those of Christ, although believers are the direct beneficiaries. For instance, when Christ's δόξα is revealed, believers themselves will rejoice and exult (1Pe 4:13).

From the viewpoint of NT theology, few passages are more important than 1Pe 1:10–12.

1. These verses highlight the continuity between the OT and NT eras: what OT prophets predicted and what NT evangelists proclaimed were identical—the sufferings destined for Christ and the glorious events that followed as a result.

2. There is a golden linguistic thread running through vv. 11 and 12, represented by τὰ εἰς Χριστὸν παθήματα καὶ τὰς μετὰ ταῦτα δόξας ... αὐτά ("these truths" regarding the παθήματα and the δόξαι), ἅ ... ἅ, namely, the passion of Christ and its spectacular results.

3. **Μετὰ ταῦτα** ("after these [sufferings]"; cf. **μετὰ τὸ παθεῖν αὐτόν,** Ac 1:3) points to an important and constant NT theme—that δόξα follows παθήματα, glory follows suffering, or (expressed as an aphorism) "no cross, no crown." See, e.g., Ro 8:18–25; 2Ti 2:12; and elsewhere in 1Pe (1:5–7; 4:12–13), although Peter can also speak of the simultaneity of suffering and glory (4:14). If grace and freedom are summarizing catchwords for Paul, suffering and glory are for Peter.

C. Μετά with Genitive

In this construction μετά has two basic meanings—"among" and "with"—but in the latter case it has many different nuances including those listed below.

1. "Among"

Mk 1:13 ἦν **μετὰ** τῶν θηρίων, "he was among the wild animals"
Lk 22:37 καὶ **μετὰ** ἀνόμων ἐλογίσθη, "and he was classed among the criminals"

2. "With"

a. "Together with, in the company of"

Mt 20:20 Τότε προσῆλθεν αὐτῷ ἡ μήτηρ τῶν υἱῶν Ζεβεδαίου **μετὰ** τῶν υἱῶν αὐτῆς
"Then the mother of Zebedee's sons came to Jesus with her sons."
Rev 20:4 ἐβασίλευσαν **μετὰ** τοῦ Χριστοῦ χίλια ἔτη, "they reigned with Christ a thousand years"

b. "Accompanied by"

Mt 24:30 **μετὰ** δυνάμεως καὶ δόξης πολλῆς, "with power and great glory"
1 Ti 6:6 ἔστιν δὲ πορισμὸς μέγας ἡ εὐσέβεια **μετὰ** αὐταρκείας, "godliness with contentment is indeed great gain"

c. "Present with"

Mt 28:20 καὶ ἰδοὺ ἐγὼ **μεθ'** ὑμῶν εἰμι πάσας τὰς ἡμέρας, "and remember, I am with you every day"
See further below, D.

d. "Having"

Lk 22:52 **μετὰ** μαχαιρῶν καὶ ξύλων, "with swords and clubs"
Php 2:12 **μετὰ** φόβου καὶ τρόμου τὴν ἑαυτῶν σωτηρίαν κατεργάζεσθε, "continue working with reverence and awe to complete your salvation"

e. "Combined with"

Eph 6:23 ἀγάπη **μετὰ** πίστεως, "love with faith"

1Pe 3:15–16 ἕτοιμοι ἀεὶ πρὸς ἀπολογίαν ... ἀλλὰ **μετὰ** πραΰτητος καὶ φόβου, "always be ready to make your defense ... but do this with gentleness and respect"

f. "Using"

Mt 14:7 μεθ' ὅρκου ὡμολόγησεν, "he promised with an oath"

g. "Against"

1Co 6:6 ἀδελφὸς **μετὰ** ἀδελφοῦ κρίνεται, "one brother goes to law with another"

3. Significant Examples

a. Matthew 1:23

Ἰδοὺ ἡ παρθένος ἐν γαστρὶ ἕξει καὶ τέξεται υἱόν, καὶ καλέσουσιν τὸ ὄνομα αὐτοῦ Ἐμμανουήλ, ὅ ἐστιν μεθερμηνευόμενον **Μεθ'** ἡμῶν ὁ θεός

"Look! The virgin will be with child and will give birth to a son, and they will call him Immanuel, which means 'God is with us'."

Matthew 1:23 is the first of Matthew's "formula citations" (see v. 22) and reflects the LXX version of Isa 7:14, to which the evangelist has added ὅ ἐστιν μεθερμηνευόμενον **Μεθ'** ἡμῶν ὁ θεός. These last four words may be legitimately rendered in one of two ways:

- "God with us" (KJV, RV, Weymouth, Goodspeed, RSV, NASB[1,2], NIV[1,2], ESV, NET)
- "God is with us" (TCNT, Moffatt, NAB[1,2], NEB, JB/NJB ["God-is-with-us"], GNB, Cassirer, NRSV, REB, CEV, NLT, HCSB).

In favor of the latter rendering the following points may be made.

(1) There are only three occurrences of *'immānû 'ēl* in the OT, all in Isaiah. Twice the LXX translates the expression by μεθ' ἡμῶν [κύριος] ὁ θεός (Isa 8:8, 10), and once it transliterates the phrase (Ἐμμανουήλ, Isa 7:14). Matthew cites the transliteration found in Isa 7:14, but when he adds a translation he uses the rendering found in Isa 8:8, 10, verses where, according to BDB, *'immānû 'ēl* is a "declaration of trust and confidence, *with us is God!*" (769a). That is, the meaning of μεθ' ἡμῶν ὁ θεός seems almost indistinguishable from ὁ θεὸς ὑπὲρ ἡμῶν (cf. Ro 8:31).

(2) While it is true that the translation of *'immānû 'ēl* / Ἐμμανουήλ that Matthew supplies, μεθ' ἡμῶν ὁ θεός, simply reproduces the word order of the Hebrew, if ὁ θεός were in fact a title of Jesus, one might have expected the trans-

lation to be either ὁ **μεθ'** ἡμῶν θεός or ὁ θεὸς **μεθ'** ἡμῶν (or the more correct Greek ὁ θεὸς ὁ **μεθ'** ἡμῶν. That is, the word order suggests that **μεθ'** ἡμῶν is predicative rather than attributive.

(3) It is unlikely that Matthew, whose favorite designation for Jesus is υἱὸς θεοῦ (9x), would preface his gospel with ὁ θεός as a christological title.

(4) The closest verbal parallel in the NT to **μεθ'** ἡμῶν ὁ θεός is found in 2Co 13:11: ὁ θεὸς ... ἔσται μεθ' ὑμῶν. In both texts εἶναι μετά denotes divine aid and favor (cf. BDAG 636c-d).

Μεθ' ἡμῶν ὁ θεός signifies that in Jesus God is *present with* (μετά) his people to bring them salvation from their sins (Mt 1:21). Matthew is not saying, "Someone who is 'God' is now physically with us," but rather, "God is acting on our behalf in the person of Jesus."

b. Matthew 12:30 = Luke 11:23

> ὁ μὴ ὢν **μετ'** ἐμοῦ κατ' ἐμοῦ ἐστιν, καὶ ὁ μὴ συνάγων **μετ'** ἐμοῦ σκορπίζει
>
> "The person who is not on my side is against me, and the person who does not join me in gathering, actually scatters."

Originally this may have been an independent "floating logion." In the present context ὁ μὴ ὢν and ὁ μὴ συνάγων refer to the Jewish exorcists (Mt 12:27; Lk 11:19) who cast out demons and therefore seemed to advance the kingdom of God but who rejected Jesus and his message. Jesus is saying, "Those who are not 'on my side' [μετ' ἐμοῦ; cf. BDAG 637a] in my contest with Satan [Mt 12:29; Lk 11:22] are in fact on the side opposed to me [κατ' ἐμοῦ]." As Jesus restates the principle, he may be using an agricultural metaphor drawn from the harvesting of grain (cf. Job 39:12; Mt 3:12), but more probably he is employing a pastoral metaphor referring to the gathering in of a scattered flock (cf. Jer 23:1–4; Eze 28:25).

Jesus is calling for personal alignment and commitment, either to the kingdom of Satan (the "strong man's house" that was destined to be plundered, Mt 12:29; Lk 11:21–22) or to the kingdom of God represented by himself (Mt 12:28; Lk 11:20). In considering Jesus' messianic claims, neutrality was (and is) impossible. Those like the Jewish exorcists or the Pharisees who had accused Jesus of exorcism through the power of Beelzebub (Mt 12:24; Lk 11:15) might appear to be serving the kingdom of God ("gathering"), but they needed to realize that failure to embrace Jesus as Messiah amounted to opposing that kingdom ("scattering").

c. Mark 9:40 (cf. Lk 9:50)

> ὃς γὰρ οὐκ ἔστιν καθ' ἡμῶν, ὑπὲρ ἡμῶν ἐστιν
>
> "Indeed, whoever is not against us is on our side."

This related saying of Jesus at first sight seems to contradict Mt 12:30. In the case of Mk 9:40, however, Jesus is responding to John's complaint that an exorcist was (apparently successfully) invoking Jesus' name in his work without being affiliated with Jesus' disciples or authorized by Jesus. Evidently Jesus regarded the use of his name in exorcism as evidence that *this* exorcist was aligned with him and the work of God's kingdom—that is, was "on our side (ὑπὲρ ἡμῶν)." Matthew 12:30 was spoken to unaffiliated "outsiders" about themselves and was an indirect call for decisive affiliation. Mark 9:40 was addressed to Jesus' disciples about a third party and was part of a direct plea for enlightened tolerance (Mk 9:39).

d. 2 Corinthians 13:13

Ἡ χάρις τοῦ κυρίου Ἰησοῦ Χριστοῦ καὶ ἡ ἀγάπη τοῦ θεοῦ καὶ ἡ κοινωνία τοῦ ἁγίου πνεύματος **μετὰ** πάντων ὑμῶν

"The grace of the Lord Jesus Christ, and the love of God, and the fellowship of the Holy Spirit, be with you all."

As he does at the end of all his letters, Paul uses the preposition μετά in expressing his benedictory wish that a divine person or quality should be "present with" or "experienced by" his addressees and so should constantly fortify them. This contrasts starkly with contemporary letters that often conclude with a generalized wish such as ἐρρῶσθαι ὑμᾶς εὔχομαι, "I pray you may fare well."

Compared with Paul's other closing benedictions, this verse contains two distinctives:

- he refers not only to χάρις but also to ἀγάπη and κοινωνία.
- he refers not only to the Lord Jesus Christ but also to God and the Holy Spirit.

Why, in this embryonic trinitarian formulation, do we find the unexpected order, Christ/God/Spirit?

- Paul begins the benediction with his customary reference to "the grace of [our] Lord Jesus [Christ]" and then expands it.
- Or the order reflects the stages of the believer's experience of God: we come to Christ and so encounter God and then receive his Spirit.

In the first two parts of this triadic structure, the genitives are clearly subjective. Salvation and all its associated blessings (χάρις) were brought (2Co 8:9) and are being brought (12:9) by Christ. Paul is expressing his wish and prayer that the love God has already poured out (Ro 5:5) and demonstrated (5:8) may continue to fortify his readers. Τοῦ ἁγίου πνεύματος could be a subjective genitive in parallelism with the two preceding genitives ("the fellowship with one another engendered by the Holy Spirit" or "the sense of community created by the Holy Spirit"; cf. Eph 4:3), but it could also be an objective genitive ("participation in the Holy Spirit"). Several points support this latter alternative.

1. When κοινωνία is followed by a genitive, it is usually synonymous with μετοχή or μετάλημψις and means "participation in, a partaking of/ sharing in," and the genitive specifies the object in which one partakes (e.g., 1Co 1:9; 10:16).
2. First Corinthians 12:13 affords a close conceptual parallel to this phrase. After speaking of an outward "immersion in the Spirit," the verse speaks of an inward participation in the Spirit. "For indeed we were all baptized in the one Spirit to form a single body — Jews and Greeks, slaves and freemen — and we were all given one Spirit to imbibe."
3. The closest verbal parallel to our phrase is in Php 2:1, εἴ τις κοινωνία πνεύματος, which in all probability means "if any participation in the Spirit."
4. This view suits the context. Common participation in the one Spirit would promote harmony and dispel factionalism (cf. 2Co 12:20; 13:11).

On this view, Paul is expressing a wish (εἴη is to be understood with μετά) that the Corinthians should continue (cf. 2Co 1:7; 12:13) in their common participation in the Spirit's life, power, and gifts (cf. 1Co 12:7; 14:1). Yet this "participation in the Spirit" results in an ever-deepening fellowship among believers (cf. the subjective genitive understanding).

e. 1 John 4:17

ἐν τούτῳ τετελείωται ἡ ἀγάπη **μεθ'** ἡμῶν, ἵνα παρρησίαν ἔχωμεν ἐν τῇ ἡμέρᾳ τῆς κρίσεως, ὅτι καθὼς ἐκεῖνός ἐστιν καὶ ἡμεῖς ἐσμεν ἐν τῷ κόσμῳ τούτῳ

"In our case love finds its full expression when we have confidence regarding the day of judgment, for just as he is, so too is our state in this present world."

The theme of 1Jn 4:16b–18 is the perfecting (τελείωσις; cf. τετελείωται, vv. 17–18; τελεία, v. 18) of human love, which is displayed (1) in confidence about judgment, and (2) in the expulsion of fear about punishment.

If ἐν τούτῳ is retrospective, the sense will be "love is perfected in mutual love and fellowship" (v. 16b). But this phrase is more probably prospective, being defined not by the distant ὅτι but by the immediately following ἵνα (cf. 1Jn 3:8, 11, 23; 4:21; 5:3; 2Jn 6; and esp. Jn 15:8): "in this, love has reached its perfection, namely, that ..." = "love finds its full expression when...." Ἔχωμεν is neither a present that relates to the future nor the equivalent to σχῶμεν (cf. 2:28), but depicts a present reality: "We are confident even now about the day of judgment, that a favorable verdict will be ours, because [ὅτι] just as the exalted Christ [ἐκεῖνος] now enjoys [cf. ἐστιν, not ἦν] in heaven full and perfect fellowship with his Father, so we too enjoy genuine fellowship with the Father [1Jn 1:3b] under the restricted conditions of life on earth [ἐν τῷ κόσμῳ τούτῳ]." The sequence of thought seems to be this: perfected love is shown in confidence regarding judgment, which is based on fellowship.

Μεθ' ἡμῶν has been rendered in three basic ways.

- "among us" (NIV[1,2], NAB[2], NRSV, REB) = "in our community" (Moule 61)
- "in us" (TCNT, Goodspeed, JB, GNB, NJB; cf. ἐν ἡμῖν, 1Jn 4:9, 12, 16) = "in our lives"
- "with us" (RV, Moffatt, RSV, NASB[1,2], HCSB, ESV), "as far as we are concerned" (Barclay), "in our case" (Cassirer)

This third type of rendering is to be preferred since it looks back to v. 12b with its reference to the perfecting (τετελειωμένη ἐστίν) of *God's* love.

D. Εἶναι μετά Denoting "Presence With"

Most NT examples of εἶναι μετά relate to interpersonal relationships. Square brackets around a verse indicate that a form of εἶναι must be supplied.

1. God with Jesus (Jn 3:2; 8:29; 16:32; Ac 10:38)
2. God with humans: through the incarnation [Mt 1:23]
   during the believer's life ([Ro 15:33]; 2Co 13:11; Php 4:9)
   in the final state (Rev 21:3)
   Mary [Lk 1:28]
   Joseph (Ac 7:9)
3. The Lord's hand: with John the Baptist (Lk 1:66)
   with evangelists from Cyprus and Cyrene (Ac 11:21)
4. Jesus with believers: penitent thief (Lk 23:43)
   his followers (Jn 13:33; 14:9)
   Paul (Ac 18:10)
5. The Holy Spirit with believers (Jn 14:16)

There are also the closing benedictions in several of Paul's letters that express the wish (with εἴη understood) that "the grace of the/our Lord Jesus [Christ]" be "with" (μετά) his addressees or their spirits (1Co 16:23; 2Co 13:13; Gal 6:18; Php 4:23; 1Th 5:28; 2Th 3:18; Phm 25; cf. 2Ti 4:22).

This "with-ness" of God or Jesus in relation to humans reflects a variety of purposes for the support.

1. Salvation ([Mt 1:23]; cf. v. 21)
2. Enablement (Mt 28:20; [Lk 1:28]; Jn 3:2; Ac 10:38)
3. Strengthening and prospering (Lk 1:66; Jn 8:29; 14:16; Ac 7:9; 18:10; 2Co 13:11; Php 4:9)
4. Protection (Jn 17:12; Ac 7:9; 18:10)
5. Fellowship (Jn 13:33; 14:9; 16:32; Rev 21:3)

Luke 23:43

καὶ εἶπεν αὐτῷ, Ἀμήν σοι λέγω, σήμερον μετ᾽ ἐμοῦ ἔσῃ ἐν τῷ παραδείσῳ

"And Jesus answered him, 'I can assure you of this, you will be with me this very day in paradise'."

This is the second of seven statements made by Jesus while hanging on his cross. Although one of the criminals crucified with Jesus poured abuse on him and taunted him, the other reprimanded his fellow criminal and then directed a request to Jesus. "Remember me when you come into your kingdom" (reading εἰς τὴν βασιλείαν, v. 42; 𝔓75 B L *al*). By his reply Jesus was not only responding to the man's persistent request (ἔλεγεν, v. 42) but also recognizing his confession of guilt (v. 41) and implied repentance, his assertion of Jesus' innocence (v. 41), and his belief in the afterlife along with Jesus' kingship and rule in that afterlife (v. 42).

It seems incontestable that σήμερον refers to the day of the crucifixion when the man will enter paradise, and that he was granted far more than he had asked. He had requested favorable treatment in the distant or undefined future; he was promised personal companionship (μετά) in the immediate future—σήμερον μετ᾽ ἐμου. In the later Judaism of the NT period three aspects or stages of paradise were distinguished: the first paradise, the garden of Eden; the hidden or intervening paradise of the present, the abode of the righteous departed; and the paradise of the age to come (cf. J. Jeremias, *TDNT* 5:766–68). Here in Lk 23:43 παράδεισος refers to the "hidden" paradise, the dwelling place of the righteous dead, which was located within the third (= highest) heaven, the abode of God (cf. 2Co 12:4), and was a place of transcendent blessedness.

As to the locality of the Christian dead, there are two representations in the NT. From the viewpoint of the living who have witnessed the burial of the dead and have seen them disappear from view, they are resting in the grave (Jn 5:28–29; 1Th 4:16–17; cf. Ac 13:36) or are resident in Hades (Ac 2:27, 31), the invisible realm in the heart of the earth (Mt 12:40) in which all the dead are temporary residents. From the viewpoint of a faith that sees the invisible, they are in proximity to God, whether this be expressed as table fellowship with Abraham

(Lk 16:23); as inhabiting resting places in the Father's house (Jn 14:2) or eternal abodes (Lk 16:9); as fellowship with Christ in paradise (Lk 23:43) or heaven (Jn 12:26; 2Co 5:8; Php 1:23); or, in the case of martyrs, as waiting under the heavenly altar (Rev 6:9).

On the relation between μετά and σύν, see ch. 18 C.

E. Μετά in Compounds

Of the 38 NT compounds involving μετά, 21 are verbs, 16 nouns, and one an adverb (MH 318).

1. Participation/commonality: μετέχω, share, have a share, enjoy; μεταδίδωμι, give a share of, impart
2. Change: μεταβαίνω, pass over; μεταμέλομαι, regret, change one's mind; μετάνοια, change of mind and action, repentance
3. Pursuit: μεταπέμπομαι and μετακαλέομαι, send for, summon
4. Succession: μεταλλάσσω, exchange

Chapter 14

Παρά

A. Basic Sense

With its 194 uses, παρά is twelfth in frequency among the 17 NT "proper" prepositions, although it is fourth in the Ptolemaic papyri and tenth in the LXX (see the chart on p. 32). Its original meaning seems to have been "beside" or "close to [but falling short of]" (Bortone 291; cf. 24, 117, 144, 146). Accordingly:

- with the **accusative** (60x in the NT) παρά designates movement "*to the side of*" (Mk 4:4; Ac 4:35; but cf. Mk 4:1; 10:46, where no idea of movement is implied)
- with the **genitive** (81x), movement "*from the side of*" (Lk 8:49; but note Lk 2:1; 6:19, where παρά follows a verb compounded with ἐκ)
- with the **dative** (53x), rest or position "*at the side of*" (Lk 9:47; Jn 8:38; 19:25, the latter being the only NT use with a thing, not a person)

As W. Köhler puts it, "movement away from proximity (gen.), position in proximity (dat.), and movement into proximity (acc.)" (*EDNT* 3:12c). For a chart that demonstrates the relative frequency of the three cases with παρά and shows the marked contrast between the NT and contemporary Koine in this regard, see Turner 272. Παρά is one of the two NT prepositions (the other is ἐπί) that is regularly used with three cases.

B. Transferred Meanings

By transference from the local sense that παρά bears with the genitive ("from beside"), with the accusative it came to mean "*beyond*" (e.g., 2Co 8:3, παρὰ δύναμιν, "beyond their ability") and then "*contrary to*" (used of that which goes *beyond* specified limits)—this latter meaning being the predominant sense of παρά in Modern Greek (Bortone 254). Consequently, when Paul anathematized anyone who preached a gospel *at variance with* the gospel that he proclaimed and the Galatians had received (παρ᾽ ὃ εὐηγγελισάμεθα ... παρ᾽ ὃ παρελάβετε, Gal 1:8–9), he implies that Judaistic teaching was not conforming to the apostolic norm. The opposite of παρά in this sense is κατά, so that παρὰ φύσιν (Ro 1:26; 11:24) means "contrary to nature, unnatural," and κατὰ φύσιν means "in accord with nature, natural" (see Ro 11:21, 24).

As well as expressing this notion of contrariety, παρά may mark a *comparison* (e.g., παρὰ Μωϋσῆν, "compared to Moses," Heb 3:3; see LSJ [1303b] for Classical Greek usage; Conybeare and Stock [85 – 86] for the LXX; and Rossberg [54] and Mayser [490] for the papyri) by indicating that one thing lies *beyond* and therefore is superior to something else. For instance, in Ro 14:5 Paul observes that "one person regards one day as superior to another" (κρίνει ἡμέραν παρ' ἡμέραν) in the sense of being "more sacred." But in another context the comparison expressed by παρά may suggest inferiority (cf. LSJ 1303b; BDAG 758a): "You made him a little lower than the angels" (**παρ' ἀγγέλους**, Heb 2:7).

Where a comparison is heightened, there is present the idea not merely of preference ("more than") but of exclusiveness ("instead of"; cf. Ps 44:8 LXX; cf. H. Riesenfeld, *TDNT* 5:734). One aspect of Paul's indictment of humankind in Ro 1:18 – 32 is that they reverenced and served created things instead of the Creator (**παρὰ τὸν κτίσαντα**, 1:25). The apostle is not implying, as the rendering "more than the Creator" (KJV) might suggest, that "creature worship" is permissible provided it does not usurp the place of "Creator worship." In a similar way, Lk 18:14 ("this man went home justified before God rather than [or, instead of] the other [**παρ' ἐκεῖνον**]") does not point to two types or degrees of justification ("more than the other"), one of which was experienced by the tax collector, the other by the Pharisee; in fact, only the former gained a right standing before God (cf. BDAG 758a; *TDNT* 5:735).

On the relation of παρά to ὑπο, see below, ch. 20 E.

C. Παρὰ (τῷ) θεῷ

If, in the light of each context, we expand the standard translation of this phrase (i.e., "with God"), a variety of renderings results.

1. "With regard to God": Mt 19:26 (//Mk 10:27; Lk 18:27), παρὰ δὲ θεῷ πάντα δυνατά. This use of παρά is "almost equivalent to the dat[ive]" (BDAG 757b-c)
2. "On God's part": Ro 2:11; 9:14; Eph 6:9; 2Th 1:6; Jas 1:17 (παρ' ᾧ)
3. "From God's perspective": 1Pe 2:4; 2Pe 3:8
4. "Before God": Lk 1:30; 2:52

But the most frequent sense of παρὰ [τῷ] θεῷ is the phrase "in the sight of God" (Ro 2:13; 1Co 3:19 ["before/in the presence of God," LSJ 1302d]; 7:24 ["before God," BDAG 757c; "in the sphere of God, and hence in fellowship with Him," H. Riesenfeld, *TDNT* 5:732]; Gal 3:11; Jas 1:27; 1Pe 2:20; cf. Job 9:2). This usage indicates the ultimate standard — the purity of the divine life and the clarity of the divine vision—by which all aspects of human thought and conduct should now be assessed and will in the end be judged.

D. Παρά and Christology in the Fourth Gospel

1. In the gospel of John the preposition παρά figures prominently in denoting the relation of the Son to the Father. In describing the movement of the Son from the very presence of God (**παρὰ** τοῦ θεοῦ/τοῦ πατρός), three verbs are involved.

(a) Εἰμί + παρά   ὁ ὢν **παρὰ** τοῦ θεοῦ (Jn 6:46)
"be from (beside)"   **παρ**' αὐτοῦ εἰμι (Jn 7:29)
     Cf. the negative statements in Jn 9:16, 33.

(b) Ἐξέρχομαι + παρά   ἐγὼ **παρὰ** τοῦ θεοῦ ἐξῆλθον (Jn 16:27)
"come/go from (beside)"   ἐξῆλθον **παρὰ** τοῦ πατρός (Jn 16:28)
     (ἐκ τοῦ πατρός is read by B C* L X Ψ
     33 al); cf. Nu 16:35, LXX.
     παρὰ σοῦ ἐξῆλθον (Jn 17:8)
     Cf. ἐκ τοῦ θεοῦ ἐξῆλθον (Jn 8:42)
     ἀπὸ θεοῦ ἐξῆλθεν (Jn 13:3)
     ἀπὸ θεοῦ ἐξῆλθες (Jn 16:30)

In Jn 6:46; 8:42; 16:27, 28; 17:8 the speaker is Jesus himself, which suggests that "I came from God/the Father" is the import of "I am from him (= God)"/"the one who is from God." That is, "being from [παρά] God" is the same as "having come from [παρά] God." Moreover, in the case of Jesus, coming from God implied being sent by God (cf. Jn 7:29). John the Baptist, however, was sent from/by God (ἀπεσταλμένος **παρὰ** θεοῦ, 1:6) but did not come from the actual presence of God (cf. BDAG 756b).

(c) Ἐκπορεύομαι + παρά (Jn 15:26): see below

2. Παρά is also prominent in describing the source and, by implication, the accuracy of the message of Jesus. Ἀκούω and ὁράω are the relevant verbs here.

(a) Jesus proclaimed to "the world" what he had heard directly from God (ἃ ἤκουσα παρ' αὐτοῦ, Jn 8:26).
(b) Jesus announced to "the Jews" the truth he had heard straight from God (τὴν ἀλήθειαν ... ἣν ἤκουσα **παρὰ** τοῦ θεοῦ, Jn 8:40), or what he had seen when he was at his Father's side (ἃ ἐγὼ ἑώρακα **παρὰ** τῷ πατρί, Jn 8:38; cf. 6:46).
(c) Jesus made known to his disciples everything he had heard directly from his Father (πάντα ἃ ἤκουσα **παρὰ** τοῦ πατρός μου, Jn 15:15).

What Jesus had seen and heard while (eternally, Jn 1:1, 18) at his Father's side constituted his unique knowledge of God (ἐγὼ οἶδα αὐτόν, 7:29) that perfectly qualified him to reveal the heart of the Father (1:18). At the end of his career his prayer was that the Father would honor him in his own (God's) presence (παρὰ σεαυτῷ) with the glory (now augmented) he had previously enjoyed at his side (παρὰ σοί) before the world existed (17:5).

1. John 1:14

ἐθεασάμεθα τὴν δόξαν αὐτοῦ, δόξαν ὡς μονογενοῦς παρὰ πατρός, πλήρης χάριτος καὶ ἀληθείας

"We have seen his glory, glory such as belongs to the one and only Son who came from the Father and is full of grace and truth."

John has just affirmed the "enfleshment" of the Logos (καὶ ὁ λόγος σάρξ ἐγένετο), his assuming of a new, additional form of existence. To his existence as a fully divine person (θεός, Jn 1:1) was added existence as a fully human person (σάρξ). Then John declares the reality of Jesus' humanity (ἐσκήνωσεν ἐν ἡμῖν, "he lived among us"), his personal splendor, his unique sonship, and his distinctive character.

Μονογενής (from μόνος + γένος) denotes "the only member of a kin or kind" (LSJ 1144a). So in a familial sense it means "of sole descent" (F. Büchsel, *TDNT* 4:738), referring to the only child in a family, a meaning attested in secular Greek literature (e.g., Hesiod, *Op.* 376), the LXX (e.g., Jdg 11:34; Tob 3:15), and other Jewish literature (e.g., Josephus, *Ant,* 1.222; 5.264), and the NT (Lk 7:12; 8:42; 9:38). From the personal application of μονογενής to "the only member of a kin" there developed a nonfamilial and (sometimes) nonpersonal use in reference to "the only member of a kind" (Latin *unicus,* "sole, unique"; cf. μόνος, "alone" and γένος, "species").

But in Johannine usage the conjunction of μονογενής and υἱός (Jn 3:16, 18; 1Jn 4:9) shows that it is not the personal uniqueness of Jesus in itself that John is emphasizing but his being "of sole descent" as the Son of God. He is without spiritual siblings. He is "sole-born" and peerless. No one else can lay claim to the title Son of God in the sense in which it applies to Christ. Certainly, in relation to πατήρ the term μονογενής in Jn 1:18 is likely to mean "the one and only Son" (NIV[2]) rather than "the only One" or "the One and Only" (NIV[1]).

Etymologically, μονογενής is not associated with begetting (γεννάομαι) but with existence (γίγνομαι). Yet it is not surprising that μονογενής soon came to acquire overtones of "being begotten" or "generation," for in 1Jn 5:18 Christ is described as ὁ γεννηθεὶς ἐκ τοῦ θεοῦ, " the One who was born of God." It seems that the impulse to render μονογενής by *unigenitus* (Latin, "only begotten," as in the comparatively late Greek creeds translated into Latin) rather than by *unicus* (as in the earlier Latin renderings) arose from christological dispute and in particular the desire to establish from Scripture the doctrine of the generation of the Son by and from the Father.[1] As far as the evidence of the NT is concerned, μονογενής depicts familial relations, not manner of birth. John does not have in mind either the virgin birth of Jesus or the "eternal generation" of the Son when he uses μονογενής, although F. Büchsel (*TDNT* 4:741) suggests that μονογενής "probably includes also [the idea of] begetting by God."

In the phrase δόξαν ὡς μονογενοῦς, the particle ὡς may indicate the perspective from which the Logos is being viewed (cf. BDAG 1104d; "glory as of the only Son," RSV; "glory in his capacity as the only Son"). Better, ὡς introduces an example (cf. BDAG 1104c for such a usage) — note the repeated δόξαν — and not simply a proverbial example ("such honor as an only son receives from his father," Goodspeed; similarly Moffatt, Barclay), but the prime example, "glory such as belongs to the one and only Son" (taking μονογενοῦς as a possessive genitive).

There is nothing to support the view that παρά is added before πατρός simply to avoid ambiguity: μονογενοῦς πατρός *could* mean "of the only Father." Nor should παρὰ πατρός be seen simply as equivalent to a possessive genitive, "of the Father," as in the rendering "the Father's only Son" (NEB, NAB[2], GNB, REB). Rather, παρὰ πατρός is an abbreviated form of (a) [μονογενοῦς] τοῦ ἐξελθόντος παρὰ πατρός, "who came from the Father" (NIV[1,2]); or (b) τοῦ ἐξερχομένου παρὰ πατρός, "coming from the Father" (BDAG 1104d; similarly NAB[1], Cassirer); or (c) τοῦ ἀπεσταλμένου παρὰ πατρός, "sent from the Father" (TCNT).

For justification for supplying some form of ἐξέρχομαι before παρὰ πατρός, see D.1.(b) above, especially John 16:28 (ἐξῆλθον **παρὰ** τοῦ πατρός).

2. John 15:26

ὅταν ἔλθῃ ὁ παράκλητος ὃν ἐγὼ πέμψω ὑμῖν **παρὰ** τοῦ πατρός, τὸ πνεῦμα τῆς ἀληθείας ὃ **παρὰ** τοῦ πατρὸς ἐκπορεύεται, ἐκεῖνος μαρτυρήσει περὶ ἐμοῦ

"When the Counselor comes, whom I will send to you from the Father, the Spirit who reveals the truth and who goes out from the Father, he will testify about me."

If Jn 1:14 speaks of the Son's coming from the Father (see above), Jn 15:26 affirms the Spirit's coming from the Father. In neither case, it seems, is the evangelist depicting ontological intratrinitarian relations.

(a) The general sense of ἐκπορεύομαι is "come/go out," and in the NT it is often followed by ἐκ (e.g., Mk 13:1), sometimes by ἀπό, εἰς, or ἐπί, but only once (here in Jn 15:26) by παρά (cf. Eze 33:30, τὰ ἐκπορευόμενα παρὰ κυρίου, "the words that proceed from the Lord"). If John was speaking of the Spirit's eternal procession (ἐκπόρευσις = Latin *processio*) from the being of the Father, only ἐκ

---

1. See F. J. A. Hort, *Two Dissertations* (London: Macmillan, 1876), 48–53.

τοῦ πατρός would be appropriate—as the creeds themselves testify, which read τὸ ἐκ τοῦ πατρὸς ἐκπορευόμενον—a combination of Jn 15:26 and 1Co 2:12, τὸ πνεῦμα τὸ ἐκ τοῦ θεοῦ, "the Spirit who is from God." Cf. Rev 22:1, where the river whose waters give life is described as flowing from (= out from within; ἐκπορευόμενον ἐκ) the throne of God and of the Lamb.

(b) Following the forward-looking ὅταν ἔλθῃ and the future πέμψω, and preceding the future μαρτυρήσει, the verb ἐκπορεύεται should probably be taken as a futuristic present rather than a timeless present.

(c) Given John's propensity for "repetition with variation," we can appropriately regard τὸ πνεῦμα τῆς ἀληθείας ὃ **παρὰ** τοῦ πατρὸς ἐκπορεύεται as repeating with variations the preceding clause, ὁ παράκλητος ὃν ἐγὼ πέμψω ὑμῖν **παρὰ** τοῦ πατρός. If so, ὃ **παρὰ** ... ἐκπορεύεται matches ὃν ἐγὼ πέμψω ... **παρά** and both describe the mission of the Spirit.

(d) It seems more likely that **παρὰ** τοῦ πατρός should have an identical sense ("from the Father" = "from the Father's presence") in successive parallel statements than that the first should mean "from the Father's presence" and the second, "[out] from the Father's being."

(e) Just as Jesus was sent by God (Jn 5:37) and therefore could be said to come forth from him (8:42), so the Spirit would be sent by the Father (14:26) and therefore could be said to proceed from him (15:26).

(f) In the context, with its emphasis on the truth of the Spirit's witness to Christ (Jn 15:26c), it would hardly be necessary for John to have indicated the eternal mode of the Spirit's personal and essential subsistence.

I conclude from Jn 15:26 that the Counselor would be sent to believers by Jesus from the Father's presence (**παρὰ** τοῦ πατρός) just as the Spirit who reveals the truth could be said to come forth or proceed from the Father's presence (**παρὰ** τοῦ πατρός). Not only Jesus (16:28), but also the Spirit (cf. 15:26), could say, ἐξῆλθον **παρὰ** τοῦ πατρός.

E. Παρά in Compounds

Of the almost 90 NT compounds involving παρά, 54 are verbs and 26 nouns (MH 319–20). For παρα- compounds in Modern Greek, see Thumb §159.

    1. Proximity
        (a) of rest: παραθαλάσσιος, beside the sea
            πάρειμι, be near
            παρίστημι, place beside; present
        (b) of motion: παρακαλέω, call to one's side
            παρακύπτω, stoop close to look
            παραπλήσιος, coming near; resembling
    2. Movement beyond: παρέρχομαι, pass by; pass away
        παροράω, overlook

3. Deviation: παράβασις, overstepping, transgression
   παραλογίζομαι, delude
   παρανομέω, act contrary to the law
4. Close attention: παρακολουθέω, follow closely
   παρατηρέω, watch closely, observe scrupulously
5. Comparison: παραβάλλω, put beside; compare
   παραβολή, comparison; (model pointing beyond = type)
6. Stealth: παρείσακτος, secretly introduced, smuggled in
   παρεισδύ(ν)ω, slip in stealthily, sneak in

Chapter 15

Περί

A. Basic and Derived Meanings

For frequency among NT "proper" prepositions, περί ranks tenth. Its basic local sense is "around, encircling." Speaking of the circumstances of his conversion, Paul said, "A powerful light from the sky flashed around me [περὶ ἐμέ]" (Ac 22:6). Περί, along with ἐνί, ἐπί, and πρός, are probably old locatives (Bortone 141 n.57). Originally meaning "around in a circle, on all sides," περί replaced ἀμφί ("on both sides," a word never found in the Greek Bible), absorbing its functions (Bortone 160–61, 184, 231). In the NT the genitive with περί is over seven times more common than the accusative after περί and is far more often theologically significant. Unlike Classical Greek (see LSJ 1366c), περί is never found with the dative in the NT or the papyri (Rossberg 10) and occurs only three times in the LXX (Pr 1:9; 3:22; and in some mss., 6:21). On the relation between περί and ὑπέρ, see ch. 19 D.

Prefaced by the definite article, περί can designate a personal point of reference.

(1) ὁ περί + accusative
    usually excludes the central person: Lk 22:49 οἱ **περὶ** αὐτόν "those around him, Jesus' companions/followers"
    sometimes includes the central person: Ac 13:13 οἱ **περὶ** Παῦλον "Paul and his companions"

(2) τὰ περί + genitive, lit., "the things concerning ..." (a common Lukan expression)
    Lk 24:19 τὰ **περὶ** Ἰησοῦ τοῦ Ναζαρηνοῦ "what happened to Jesus of Nazareth"
    Lk 24:27 τὰ **περὶ** ἑαυτοῦ "the passages referring to himself"
    Ac 18:25 τὰ **περὶ** τοῦ Ἰησοῦ "the facts about Jesus," "what Jesus had accomplished" (Cassirer)
    Ac 28:31 τὰ **περὶ** τοῦ κυρίου Ἰησοῦ Χριστοῦ "the truth about the Lord Jesus Christ"

Standing absolutely at the beginning of a sentence, περὶ (δέ) means "[now] concerning/with regard to" (for parallels in the papyri, see MM 504a; Mayser 448–49), and marks a new subject (e.g., 1Co 7:1, 25; 8:1; 12:1; 16:1), a point of importance for reconstructing the Corinthian letter to Paul that he answers in 1Co 7–16.

Since both περί and ὑπέρ can mean "about/concerning," and since both can depict the person or thing on whose behalf or in whose interest something takes place, it is not surprising that each preposition often appears as a variant reading for the other (e.g., Mk 14:24; Jn 1:30; Gal 1:4; Heb 5:1, 3; 1Pe 3:18), and sometimes the two are interchangeable (e.g., Mt 26:28 [περί] compared with Mk 14:24 and Lk 22:20 [ὑπέρ]; Eph 6:18–19); ὑπέρ for περί (meaning "about") is characteristic of Paul (e.g., 2Co 1:7–8; 5:12; 7:4, 14; 8:23–24; 9:3; 12:5 [2x], 8).

1. 1 Thessalonians 4:13

οὐ θέλομεν δὲ ὑμᾶς ἀγνοεῖν, ἀδελφοί, **περὶ τῶν κοιμωμένων**, ἵνα μὴ λυπῆσθε καθὼς καὶ οἱ λοιποὶ οἱ μὴ ἔχοντες ἐλπίδα

"Brothers and sisters, we do not want you to be uninformed about those who have fallen asleep, so that you do not grieve as do the rest of mankind, who have no hope."

One of the purposes of Paul's first letter to the church at Thessalonica was to allay the distress (cf. λυπῆσθε) felt by some owing to their uncertainty concerning the fate of the fellow believers who died before the parousia. Did their death prior to the second advent mean that they had thereby forfeited the right to share in the parousial glory of Christ? Paul responds by asserting that death before the parousia involves no disadvantage at the parousia. If there is any advantage, it belongs to the dead, who will enjoy a temporal precedence—a priority of privilege, not of status—over those who are alive at the parousia in that they will be resurrected before the general "rapture" of both dead and living Christians (1Th 4:15–17).

The verb κοιμάομαι, used by Paul nine times (1Th 4:13–15; 1Co 7:39; 11:30; 15:6, 18, 20, 51), is probably more than a euphemism for death ("pass away") borrowed from conventional religious terminology, since it is applied solely to Christians (ἀποθνήσκω ["die," as, e.g., in 1Co 15:22] is used of the death of people in general). In Pauline usage κοιμάομαι is basically if not exclusively punctiliar in meaning ("fall asleep") rather than linear ("be asleep"). Two apparent exceptions (οἱ κοιμώμενοι here in 1Th 4:13; and οἱ κεκοιμημένοι, 1Co 15:20) mean "those who have fallen asleep" (BDAG 551b) or "those who have passed away" (R. Bultmann, *TDNT* 3:14 n.60), while a third (κοιμῶνται ἱκανοί, 1Co 11:30) means "not a few have died" (Cassirer; cf. BDAG 551b) or "a number are [from time to time] falling asleep." Elsewhere in the NT it is only when the present tense of κοιμάομαι is used, in reference to physical sleep, that a linear sense must be given (Mt 28:13; Lk 22:45; Ac 12:6).

So this verb does not imply that the state between death and resurrection involves a psychopannychitic cessation of consciousness or insensibility. Christians who die "fall asleep" in that they are no longer active in or conscious of the earthly world of time and space, although they are fully alert to their new environment. They are "alive to God" (Lk 20:38), they "live spiritually, as God does" (1Pe 4:6), or, in Pauline diction, they are "with the Lord" (2Co 5:8) or "with Christ" (Php 1:23). Also the verb may possibly allude to the peaceful manner of the Christian's dying, whatever the mode of death (cf. ἐκοιμήθη, Ac 7:60, of Stephen's death under a hail of stones), or to the certainty of awakening to life through the coming resurrection.

2. 1 John 2:27

> καὶ ὑμεῖς τὸ χρῖσμα ὃ ἐλάβετε ἀπ᾽ αὐτοῦ μένει ἐν ὑμῖν καὶ οὐ χρείαν ἔχετε ἵνα τις διδάσκῃ ὑμᾶς, ἀλλ᾽ ὡς τὸ αὐτοῦ χρῖσμα διδάσκει ὑμᾶς **περὶ** πάντων καὶ ἀληθές ἐστιν καὶ οὐκ ἔστιν ψεῦδος, καὶ καθὼς ἐδίδαξεν ὑμᾶς, μένετε ἐν αὐτῷ

> "But as for you, the anointing you received from him remains in you, and so you do not need anyone to teach you. Rather, since his anointing teaches you about everything, and since that anointing is real and not counterfeit, keep in union with him, just as it taught you."

In this verse John develops themes already stated in vv. 20 and 24, namely, that as recipients of the anointing given by the Holy One, all Christians know the truth (v. 20); and that the original Christian truth they once heard and embraced must remain the regulative standard for their belief (v. 24). This is apparently against the counterfeit claims of the secessionists (cf. Jn 2:19) to have fresh truth reserved for the initiated.

Given the references in the fourth gospel to the Holy Spirit as (a) the Paraclete sent by Christ (Jn 15:26), and (b) the Spirit who will reveal the truth (τὸ πνεῦμα τῆς ἀληθείας, 14:17; 15:26; 16:13), guide believers to the whole of the truth (16:13), and teach them all things (14:26), it is likely that τὸ χρῖσμα in 1Jn 2:27 is the gift of the Spirit as the depository of Christian truth. Regarding this "anointing," several affirmations are made.

(a) It is given by Christ (ἀπ᾽ αὐτοῦ ... αὐτοῦ [subjective genitive]; cf. 2:20 ἀπὸ τοῦ ἁγίου).

(b) Received at conversion, it now permanently remains within believers (μένει ἐν ὑμῖν; cf. Jn 14:17).

(c) It affords instruction about everything (διδάσκει ... περὶ πάντων; cf. διδάξει πάντα, Jn 14:26). This instruction is *comprehensive*, is never superseded, and does not need supplementation; it is *real* (ἀληθές), not counterfeit or illusory; and it is *traditional* (καθὼς ἐδίδαξεν ὑμᾶς), not of recent origin.

(d) Receipt of the "anointing" calls for a practical response: "keep in union with Christ" (cf. Jn 15:4–7).

When John rejects the need for new teachers, he is alluding (by the use of τις) to those who were trying to mislead (τῶν πλανώντων, 1Jn 2:26) his readers. He is not denigrating authoritative teaching within the church (cf. Ro 12:7; 1Co 12:28–29; 1Ti 4:11). Similarly, when he affirms that the "anointing" provided by Christ instructs believers "about [περί] everything," he is not, of course, rejecting all human intermediaries in the acquisition of knowledge in general or of Christian knowledge in particular; the referent of πάντα is clearly restricted by the context. It is a case of "everything" that prevents someone from being led astray from the truth (1Jn 2:26); or, to express the point positively and to borrow a Petrine phrase, "everything that promotes true life and godliness/everything needed for a life of piety" (πάντα ... τὰ πρὸς ζωὴν καὶ εὐσέβειαν, 2Pe 1:3).

B. Περὶ ἁμαρτίας/ἁμαρτιῶν

The singular περὶ ἁμαρτίας occurs nine times and the plural περὶ ἁμαρτιῶν five times in the NT. There is no material difference between the singular and plural since περὶ ἁμαρτίας may mean "with respect to sins" (as a generic singular) as well as "in regard to sin" (as in Jn 8:46; 15:22; 16:8, 9), while περὶ ἁμαρτιῶν could mean "with respect to sin" (as a generalizing plural) as well as "in regard to sins."

Where περὶ ἁμαρτίας stands for ἡ θυσία ἡ περὶ ἁμαρτίας (cf. Heb 10:26), "the sacrifice that relates to sin," or ἡ προσφορά ἡ περὶ ἁμαρτίας (cf. Heb 10:18), "the offering that relates to sin," this abbreviated phrase will mean "sin offering(s)."

1. Romans 8:3

Περὶ ἁμαρτίας in Ro 8:3 has been understood in two basic ways:

(1) "to deal with sin" (Moffatt, Barclay, NRSV, REB; similarly JB, GNB, Cassirer; Atkinson 10, "to deal with the question of sin")
"to atone for sin" (BDAG 798a; TCNT; similarly W. Köhler, *EDNT* 3:72c)

(2) "as a sacrifice for sin" (Weymouth, NEB; similarly NJB, NLT)
"to be a sin offering" (NIV[1,2])
"as a sin offering" (RV, Goodspeed, NASB[1,2], NAB[1], HCSB; and, tentatively, H. Riesenfeld, *TDNT* 6:55)

The translations under (2) are to be preferred for three reasons.

(1) There are more than 40 uses of **περὶ** ἁμαρτίας in the LXX in a sacrificial context.

(2) The LXX often renders Hebrew *ḥaṭṭāʾt* (which may mean "sacrifice for sin") by **περὶ** ἁμαρτίας (e.g., Lev 7:37; 16:5) or, less commonly, by τὸ (or τὰ) **περὶ** τῆς ἁμαρτίας (Lev 6:23; 14:19).

(3) **Περὶ** ἁμαρτίας means "sin offering" in Heb 10:6, 8; 13:11 (BDAG 51a; see below)

2. Hebrews

Hebrews 10:6, 8 (citing Ps 39:7 LXX)

ὁλοκαυτώματα καὶ **περὶ** ἁμαρτίας οὐκ εὐδόκησας

"You took no delight in burnt offerings and sin offerings."

Hebrews 13:11 ὧν γὰρ εἰσφέρεται ζῴων τὸ αἷμα **περὶ** ἁμαρτίας εἰς τὰ ἅγια διὰ τοῦ ἀρχιερέως, τούτων τὰ σώματα κατακαίεται ἔξω τῆς παρεμβολῆς

"For the bodies of those animals whose blood is brought into the Most Holy Place by the high priest as a sin offering, are burned outside the camp."

Where either expression (**περὶ** ἁμαρτίας/ἁμαρτιῶν) is used in conjunction with a word denoting sacrifice or sacrificial suffering, the sense of the prepositional phrase is "to atone for sin(s)" or simply "for sin(s)." Thus Heb 5:3; 10:18, 26; 1Pe 3:18; 1Jn 2:2; 4:10.

On the relation between **περὶ** and **ὑπέρ**; see ch. 19 D.

C. Περί in Compounds

Of the 32 NT verbs compounded with **περί** about four-fifths have the sense "around/about" (MH 321).

    1. Movement/position
        "around" — περιπατέω, walk around
            περικεφαλαία, helmet
            περιβάλλω, put on (of clothing)
        "over/beyond" — περιφρονέω, overlook, disregard
            περιεργάζομαι, be a meddler (of "overdoing")
    2. Intensification ("very/exceedingly")
        περιαιρέω, take completely away, remove
        περίλυπος, having excessive sorrow, deeply grieved

Chapter 16

Πρό

A. New Testament Use and Basic Meaning

There are only 47 NT examples of πρό (with the genitive), of which nine are πρὸ τοῦ + infinitive. It is the least common (by far) "proper preposition" in the papyri (Rossberg 8) and the second least common (after σύν) in the LXX (see the chart on p. 32). Most of the NT instances are temporal in sense (as also in its limited Modern Greek use—Bortone 298), but there are four spatial uses (Ac 12:6, 14; 14:13; Jas 5:9) and twice it expresses superiority of importance (πρὸ πάντων, "above everything," Jas 5:12; 1Pe 4:8). It is the "improper prepositions" such as ἔμπροσθεν, ἐνώπιον, ἐναντίον, or ἔναντι (meaning "before, in front of") that serve in place of the spatial πρό (BDF §214; Regard 549; Bortone 187, 227). Both πρό and ἀντί basically mean "in front of," although ἀντί originally signified, more specifically, "opposite, facing."

Πρό figures significantly in passages that describe the divinely established plan of salvation.

> Πρὸ χρόνων αἰωνίων (lit., "before eternal ages"), "before the beginning of time, from all eternity"
> God bestowed his grace on believers in Christ Jesus (2Ti 1:9)
> God promised eternal life to believers (Tit 1:2).
> Πρὸ τῶν αἰώνων (lit., "before the ages"), "before time began, from before all time"
> God foreordained his secret wisdom to be revealed (1Co 2:7).

Also, in a description of the "tenses" of eternity, **πρὸ παντὸς τοῦ αἰῶνος** can allude to "eternity past."

> Πρὸ παντὸς τοῦ αἰῶνος (lit., "before every age"), "before time began" (BDAG 32a), now, and to all eternity (εἰς πάντας τοὺς αἰῶνας), glory, majesty, power, and authority are ascribed to God through Jesus Christ (Jude 25).

B. Notable Uses

1. 2 Corinthians 12:2

οἶδα ἄνθρωπον ἐν Χριστῷ **πρὸ** ἐτῶν δεκατεσσάρων ... ἁρπαγέντα τὸν
τοιοῦτον ἕως τρίτου οὐρανοῦ

"I know a Christian man who, fourteen years ago ... was caught up to
the third heaven."

In 2Co 12:1–7 Paul is describing (reluctantly—note the use of the third
person in vv. 2–3, 5) a visionary ascent into paradise granted to him by the Lord
Jesus that might easily have occasioned spiritual pride were it not for his being
promptly given a "thorn in the flesh."

Πρὸ ἐτῶν δεκατεσσάρων clearly means "fourteen years ago," although the
construction is unusual. John 12:1 affords a close parallel, since **πρὸ** ἓξ ἡμερῶν
τοῦ πάσχα means "properly '6 days ago, reckoned from the passover'" (BDF
§213), that is, "six days before the passover" (= ἓξ ἡμέρας πρὸ τοῦ πάσχα). In
the present instance, perhaps "before fourteen years" implies "counting back-
ward from the time of writing" or, better, **πρό** = πρὸ τοῦ νῦν and is followed
by a genitive of respect, "before the present time by fourteen years" = "fourteen
years ago." For an alternative explanation, see Moule 74. If the vision occurred
fourteen years before the time of writing (AD 56), it took place about AD 43 by
inclusive reckoning, during the decade of Paul's life (AD 35–45) about which
nothing is known other than that some or all of it was spent in Syria-Cilicia
(Gal 1:21).

But why did Paul bother to date his ecstatic experience? Certainly the dat-
ing of the ascent to paradise would have had the effect of confirming the
factuality of the event, but Paul's purpose may have been to draw attention to
his prolonged silence about the episode; it was only his present contest with his
rivals, brought on by the Corinthians' disloyalty to him, that had forced him
to break that silence (cf. 2Co 12:1, 11) and reluctantly mention his privileged
ascent to heaven. Even if the Corinthians already knew of Paul's rapture—
although that is far from certain—they were learning for the first time some
details of that experience. Was he hinting that ecstatic experiences, as private
encounters with God (cf. 5:13), were not to be publicized unnecessarily, and
as God-given privileges, added nothing to a person's standing or role in the
church?

Another reason Paul dated this episode may have been to indicate how long
he had been grappling with his painful and frustrating "thorn in the flesh," for
clearly God gave him this σκόλοψ promptly after this "extraordinary revelation," in order to curb any inordinate pride (v. 7). The weakness in which he
had learned to take pleasure (v. 10) had been a present reality throughout all his
Corinthian ministry and for several years before.

2. Colossians 1:17

καὶ αὐτός ἐστιν **πρὸ** πάντων

"He himself is before all things"

In the hymnic passage, Col 1:15–20, which is marked by extensive parallelism and chiasmus, vv. 15–17 deal with the supremacy of Christ in creation:

πρωτότοκος πάσης κτίσεως, "the firstborn over all creation"
καὶ αὐτός ἐστιν πρὸ πάντων, "and he himself is before all things"; and

vv. 18–20 describe the supremacy of Christ in redemption:

καὶ αὐτός ἐστιν ἡ κεφαλὴ τοῦ σώματος τῆς ἐκκλησίας, "and he himself is
    the head of the body, the church"
πρωτότοκος ἐκ τῶν νεκρῶν, "the firstborn from the dead."

The italicized parallelism and chiasmus illustrate the link between creation and redemption, nature and grace, cosmology and soteriology.

Although some NT uses of αὐτός anticipate Modern Greek, where αὐτός means "he/this/that" and not "himself," in vv. 17a and 18a the wider context indicates that the word is clearly emphatic: "he himself, he and no other." If αὐτος ἐστιν is accented as αὐτὸς ἔστιν, the sense will be "he himself exists before all things" or "he himself exists in supremacy over all things." If it is accented as αὐτός ἐστιν, the meaning will be "he himself is before all things" or "he himself is supreme over all things." Πάντων could be masculine, referring to the θρόνοι κτλ. of v. 16, but the use of τὰ πάντα ("all things" collectively) in vv. 16 (2x), 17b, and 20 suggests it is neuter ("all things, everything" in a distributive sense).

While πρό does not often denote precedence in importance (only in Jas 5:12; 1Pe 4:8), here in Col 1:17 it expresses such a priority of status as well as of time (cf. Moffatt, "he is prior to all"), given the use of πρωτότοκος in v. 15 and of πρωτεύων in v. 18 and the fact that preexistence ("before all things") implies preeminence over all things. Among supernatural potentates (cf. v. 16), Jesus Christ has no rival for the lordship of the universe (v. 17a) and the church (v. 18a). He—and no one else—is before everything in time and rank.

C. Πρό in Compounds

In the sense of "before" in time or place, πρό occurs in five nominal compounds and 49 verbal compounds (of which more than half relate to time; MH 322).

1. Priority: in time—προσάββατον, Friday (the day before the Sabbath)
    προπάτωρ, ancestor
    προοράω, foresee
    in position ("in front of")—προαύλιον, forecourt
    πρόδρομος, going ahead

προάγω, lead the way

2. Extension ("forth, forward"): προβάλλω, put forward, put out (of foliage)

προπέμπω, send on one's way

3. Preference: προαιρέομαι, choose for oneself, commit oneself to

4. Representation: προφήτης, prophet

5. Intensity: πρόδηλος, very obvious

Chapter 17

Πρός

A. New Testament Use and Basic Meaning

In Classical Greek πρός was regularly followed by three cases, but in the NT we find:

- only one instance of the genitive (Ac 27:34, τοῦτο γὰρ **πρὸς τῆς** ὑμετέρας σωτηρίας ὑπάρχει, "for this is essential for your survival"), with only 23 cases in the LXX (HR 1209), and only rare examples in the papyri (MM 544b)
- only seven examples with the dative (Mk 5:11; Lk 19:37; Jn 18:16; 20:11, 12 [2x]; Rev 1:13), all in a spatial sense
- 691 examples with the accusative (see the chart on p. 32).

So then, in comparison with Classical Greek (see LSJ 1496c–99a; Smyth §1695), Biblical Greek is marked by the virtual elimination of πρός with the genitive, the drastic reduction of πρός with the dative, and a dramatic increase in πρός with the accusative (cf. Regard 579). This accords with the rise of the accusative in Hellenistic Greek.

In its basic spatial sense πρός means "near" or "facing" (Robertson 624), so that the expression πρὸς τὴν θάλασσαν ἐπὶ τῆς γῆς (Mk 4:1) means "on the beach at the water's edge" or "on dry land facing the sea." With the accusative πρός means "to/toward the vicinity of," depicting movement toward a location (e.g., Mt 26:57; 1Th 3:6) or approach toward a goal (e.g., Ac 3:10). From this latter sense of mental direction, πρός came to refer to relationships that are *friendly* (e.g., Jn 6:37 [2x]; 2Co 3:16; Gal 6:10; Eph 3:14; 1Th 5:14) or *hostile* ("against"; e.g., Ac 6:1; 1Co 6:1; Eph 6:12 [5x]; Col 2:23). In turn, this notion of psychological orientation led to the use of πρός to express the ideas of:

estimation, "in view of" (Mt 19:8)
purpose, "with a view to" (Jn 13:28; 1Co 10:11), often with the articular infinitive (e.g., πρὸς τὸ θεαθῆναι, Mt 6:1; 23:5)
result, "leading to" (Mt 5:28; Jn 11:4)

conformity, "in accordance with" (Lk 12:47; Eph 4:14)
reference, "in relation to" (Lk 18:1; Gal 2:14)

On the relation between πρός and εἰς, see ch. 8 B.

B. Notable Instances
1. John 1:1

ἐν ἀρχῇ ἦν ὁ λόγος, καὶ ὁ λόγος ἦν **πρὸς** τὸν θεόν, καὶ θεὸς ἦν ὁ λόγος

"In the beginning the Word already existed, and the Word was in fellow-ship with God, and the Word was God by nature."

In itself ἐν ἀρχῇ ἦν ὁ λόγος speaks only of the pretemporality or supratem-porality of the Logos, but by the conjunction of ἐν ἀρχῇ and ἦν John implies the eternal preexistence of the Word whose true sphere was not time but eternity. Having defined the relation of the Word to time, John then specifies his relation to the Father. There can be little doubt that τὸν θεόν designates the Father.

(a) Jn 1:18 expresses a thought similar to 1:1b, using the term πατήρ.
(b) 1Jn 1:2 also affords a close parallel: ἡ ζωὴ … ἦν **πρὸς** τὸν πατέρα.
(c) In Johannine usage ὁ θεός customarily denotes the Father.
(d) The articular ὁ θεός could not refer to the divine essence or to the trinitarian God or to the Spirit.

Five proposals have been made concerning the meaning of ὁ λόγος ἦν **πρὸς** τὸν θεόν.

(1) "The Logos was speaking/was addressing himself to God" ("la Parole parlait [s'adressait] à Dieu"; C. Masson). Masson argues that since a "word" is spoken to a person, one might expect after v. 1a an answer to the question "*To whom* was the word spoken?" rather than "*Where* was the Word?"[1]

However, it is just as reasonable to think that v. 1b answers the question, "What was the relationship of the Logos to the Father at and before the begin-ning?" (cf. 1Jn 1:2). Moreover, Masson is hardly justified in filling out the mean-ing of ἦν πρός on the basis of an accompanying substantive (ὁ λόγος) that here functions as a proper noun.

(2) "The Logos was having regard to/devoted to God" (Abbott §2366). "Probably John combines this spiritual meaning ('devoted to') with the more local meaning ('in converse with') and, in his own mind, the former is predomi-nant" (§2366; but Abbott also suggests "[looking] toward God" §§2308, 2366).

Now it is true that πρός often means "with regard to," but only in the sense

---

1. C. Masson, "Pour une traduction nouvelle de Jean 1:1b et 2," *Revue de Théologie et de Philosophie* 98 (1965): 376–81.

"with reference to," not in the sense "having regard for/being devoted to." What is distinctive about Jn 1:1b is the combination of εἶναι and πρός (see [4], below), whereas Abbott's proposals would comport better with ἔζη πρὸς τὸν θεόν, reflecting the Classical Greek expression ζῆν πρός τινα ("to live in devotion to someone") that Abbott mentions, or even with συνείχετο τῷ θεῷ ("[he] devoted himself exclusively to God"). But one of Abbott's alternative renderings, "in converse with God" (§§2365–66), well captures a conceptual link with λόγος.

(3) "The Word was turned toward (*tourné vers*) God."[2] There can be no objection to this expansion of the meaning of πρός, for this preposition can denote a relationship of orientation and does not in itself suggest reciprocity of action. But the orientation would need to be understood in a dynamic, not a static, fashion.

(4) "The Word was with God." Thus BDF §239 (1); BDAG 875b; MM 544c; MH 467; Regard 552, 556, 579; B. Reicke, *TDNT* 6:722; Moule 53; Turner 274; Turner, *Style* 71; and most EVV, although some emphasize the local sense, "in God's presence" (NAB[1], REB), "by the side of God" (Cassirer), "[The Word] dwelt with God" (NEB). On this view πρός with the accusative is taken to be equivalent to παρά with the dative after εἶναι, denoting position (cf. Jannaris §1658). The preposition does not imply any movement or action on the part of the Logos in his relation to the Father. There are several NT parallels where πρός with the accusative and εἶναι denotes not linear motion but punctiliar rest: Mk 6:3 (= Mt 13:56); 9:19 (= Lk 9:41 but Mt 17:17 has μεθ' ὑμῶν); 14:49 (= Lk 22:53, which has μεθ' ὑμῶν); 1Th 3:4; 2Th 2:5; 3:10; 1Jn 1:2. This usage reflects:

(a) the blurring of the notions of movement and rest in Hellenistic Greek
(b) the reduced use of the dative case and the extension of the accusative case in Hellenistic Greek
(c) "an extension of many classical usages, particularly in such phrases as ἐνθυμεῖσθαι πρὸς αὐτόν" (G. R. Driver, as cited by MH 467)

Winer notes that this usage in which πρός τινα = παρά τινι occurs particularly with personal names (405). But I. de la Potterie points out that elsewhere John uses παρά τινι to express the proximity of one person to another (Jn 1:39; 4:40; 8:38a; 14:17, 23, 25; 19:25) or the nearness of the Son to the Father (Jn 8:38; 17:5).[3]

*(5) "The Word was in fellowship/active communion with God." This rendering differs from (4) only in that it spells out the implication of "with." Milligan and Moulton observe that πρός "denotes not merely being beside, but

---

2. A. Feuillet, *Le prologue du Quatrième Évangile* (Paris: Desclée de Brouwer, 1968), 20, 264–69; idem, *Le mystère de l'amour divin dans la théologie johannique* (Paris: Gabalda, 1972), 65, 107, 182.
3. I. de la Potterie, "L'emploi dynamique de εἰς dans Saint Jean et ses incidences théologiques," *Bib* 43 (1962): 379.

maintaining communion and intercourse with";[4] similarly Robertson 625. When πρός is used of a relationship between persons, it must imply personal intercourse rather than simply denoting spatial juxtaposition or personal accompaniment. If a certain reciprocity of fellowship is necessarily implied since this is an eternal relationship between divine persons, it is only implied, not actually expressed. To give πρός a unilaterally dynamic sense is not to find here an assertion of mutual indwelling or the Son's intratrinitarian "filiation," or to endorse J. A. Bengel's claim that "πρός ... denotes a perpetual, as it were, tendency of the Son to the Father in the unity of essence."[5]

2. 2 Corinthians 5:8

θαρροῦμεν δὲ καὶ εὐδοκοῦμεν μᾶλλον ἐκδημῆσαι ἐκ τοῦ σώματος καὶ ἐνδημῆσαι **πρὸς** τὸν κύριον

"We are confident, I repeat, and prefer to depart from this body and take up residence in the presence of the Lord."

In 2Co 5:1–10 Paul is reckoning with the possibility or probability of his own death before the parousia and is recounting three sources of divine comfort afforded believers who stand within the shadow of death: assurance they will become possessors of a superior form of habitation (vv. 1–2), the present possession of the Spirit as God's pledge of a resurrection transformation (vv. 4–5), and knowledge that death involves departure to Christ and leads to "walking in the realm of sight" (vv. 7–8).

There is no reason to suppose that an interval of time separates the ἐκδημῆσαι ἐκ τοῦ σώματος from the ἐνδημῆσαι **πρὸς** τὸν κύριον. That is, the ἐκδημία of v. 8, like the κατάλυσις of v. 1, occurs at death. This conclusion is confirmed by the two previous verses. First, v. 6 states that residence in a physical body is contemporaneous with absence from the immediate presence of the Lord, clearly implying that when the former ceases, so also does the latter. What v. 6 implies, v. 8 states positively. Second, in v. 7 walking "in the realm of faith" (διὰ πίστεως) and "in the realm of sight" (διὰ εἴδους) are presented as opposites, with no interval posited between them. To cease walking in the realm of faith is to commence life in the realm of sight, which v. 8b defines as an ἐνδημεῖν **πρὸς** τὸν κύριον, which, accordingly, depicts the location of Christians immediately after their death. Since Paul believed that Christ, after his resurrection and ascension, was in heaven (Php 3:20), the "dead in Christ" (1Th 4:16) must also be "located" in heaven.

---

4. G. Milligan and J. H. Moulton, *Commentary on the Gospel of St. John* (Edinburgh: T&T Clark, 1898), 4.

5. J. A. Bengel, *Gnomon of the New Testament* (1750; trans., rev., and ed. A. R. Fausett; 5 vols.; repr. Edinburgh: T&T Clark, 1863), 2:234.

But what of their state? Since the verb ἐνδημέω is purely stative ("be/stay at home"), ἐνδημῆσαι is an ingressive aorist, here denoting entrance upon the state of dwelling (ἐνδημεῖν) with the Lord — thus "make our home" (TCNT, JB, REB) or "take up residence." We have seen that in conjunction with εἶναι, πρός may express position or rest (see above on Jn 1:1b). The same is true when it is used with other verbs: πάρειμι (Ac 12:20; 2Co 11:9; Gal 4:18, 20), γίνομαι (1Co 2:3), κατέχω (Phm 13), θάπτω (Ac 5:10), compounds of μένω — ἐπιμένω (1Co 16:7; Gal 1:18), παραμένω (1Co 16:6), διαμένω (Gal 2:5) — and here with ἐνδημέω.

But when πρός describes an interpersonal relationship, it must signify more than an impassive spatial juxtaposition (as if two objects were being related, as a chair may be said to be "with" a table) and even more than coexistence (as if two persons were being related who were either unacquainted or unfriendly). Although in itself πρός is unidirectional and so does not denote reciprocity of action, when it is applied to a relationship between persons who are known to and esteemed by each other, it implies (but does not express) the dynamic interaction of mutual fellowship. Robertson comments: "It is the face-to-face converse with the Lord that Paul has in mind," πρός being "employed for living relationship, intimate converse" (625; similarly W. Grundmann, *TDNT* 2:64). Paul must be referring to a heightened form of interpersonal communion since he expresses a preference (εὐδοκοῦμεν μᾶλλον) for this ἐνδημεῖν πρὸς τὸν κύριον over living in the earthly form of embodiment, spatially absent from Christ (v. 6), yet in spiritual union with him.

3. 2 Corinthians 5:10

τοὺς γὰρ πάντας ἡμᾶς φανερωθῆναι δεῖ ἔμπροσθεν τοῦ βήματος τοῦ Χριστοῦ, ἵνα κομίσηται ἕκαστος τὰ διὰ τοῦ σώματος **πρὸς** ἃ ἔπραξεν, εἴτε ἀγαθὸν εἴτε φαῦλον

"For all of us must appear before Christ's tribunal, so that each may be duly recompensed for actions, whether good or bad, performed through the body."

In 2Co 5:8–10 Paul gives two reasons for his constant ambition to gain Christ's approval (v. 9) — his destiny of dwelling with the Lord (v. 8), and the future compulsory appearance of all Christians (τοὺς πάντας ἡμᾶς, "the sum total of us" [Turner 201]) before the judicial bench of Christ (v. 10; note διὸ καί and γάρ in vv. 9–10). But accountability and assessment are not en masse but individual (ἕκαστος; cf. ἕκαστος ἡμῶν after πάντες in the parallel passage, Ro 14:10–12). The purpose (ἵνα), and by implication the outcome, of the examination will be the receipt from the Lord (cf. Col 3:24–25) of (lit.) "the things performed [πραχθέντα] by means of the body, in accordance with the things that he has done," that is, "due recompense for actions performed through the body."

Πρός here may mean:

"in accordance with" (Winer 405; BDF §239 (8); Turner 274; TCNT, Weymouth; "according to," RSV, NASB[1,2], GNB, NAB[2]; cf. ZG 544, "corresponding to"), or
"in proportion to" (Moule 53; LN §90.92), or simply
"in relation to"

In each case the emphasis is on the exactitude and (by implication) the impartiality (cf. Eph 6:9; Col 3:25) of the recompense meted out by the divine assessor.

The change from the plural ἅ to the singular ἀγαθὸν ... φαῦλον probably implies that specific actions as reflective of character will be assessed, rather than that conduct will be judged as a whole. The personal character of the retributive process and the fact that recompense might be received for good as well as for bad actions prove that, in Paul's thought, the notions of recompense and reward are not incompatible. Reward may be recompense for good; the "suffering of loss" (ζημιωθήσεται, 1Co 3:15), the forfeiture of reward or privilege, may be part of the requital for evil. Moreover, since the tribunal of Christ is concerned with the assessment of works, not the determination of destiny, it is apparent that the Pauline concepts of justification by grace through faith and recompense in accordance with works may be seen as complementary. Already delivered from ἔργα νόμου, "works done in obedience to law," by justifying faith (Ro 3:28), Christians are presently committed to τὸ ἔργον τῆς πίστεως, "action stemming from faith" (1Th 1:3), that will be assessed and rewarded at Christ's tribunal.

4. Ephesians 2:18

ὅτι δι' αὐτοῦ ἔχομεν τὴν προσαγωγὴν οἱ ἀμφότεροι ἐν ἑνὶ πνεύματι **πρὸς** τὸν πατέρα

"For through him [Christ] we both enjoy access to the Father in the one Spirit."

Ephesians 2:14–18 portrays Christ as the reconciler and peacemaker who by his death on the cross has destroyed the hostility that separated God and humans and also Jews and Gentiles, and he has created in his own person a single new humanity out of the two rival ethnic groups (cf. Gal 3:28; Col 3:11), thereby enabling both groups to have equal and unhindered access (προσαγωγή) to God's immediate presence. Verse 18 affords evidence (ὅτι) of the proclamation (and acceptance) of the good news of peace (v. 17) and of the creation of the one new humanity (v. 15).

All three NT uses of προσαγωγή are Pauline (Ro 5:2; Eph 2:18; 3:12) and probably have an intransitive sense, "access," the freedom and right to enter. The term may allude to the granting of the privilege of admission into the presence of a potentate. Having obtained access (τὴν προσαγωγὴν ἐσχήκαμεν, Ro 5:2), believers now permanently enjoy (ἔχομεν, Eph 2:18; 3:12) this privilege, "emboldened by faith in Christ" (Eph 3:12).

There are four characteristics of this access mentioned in the verse.

(a) It is enjoyed by Jews, "those who were near" (v. 17; cf. Ps 148:14), but also by Gentiles, "those who were far away" (vv. 13, 17; cf. Isa 57:19). Οἱ ἀμφότεροι ("both of us"; cf. vv. 14, 16) implies "without distinction on the basis of race," and "together" in the sense that the two groups now form a single new humanity (v. 15).

(b) Access is "to the Father," that is, to the sanctuary of God's immediate presence (cf. Heb 10:19) or to the enclosure of God's favor (τὴν προσαγωγὴν ... εἰς τὴν χάριν ταύτην, Ro 5:2). In the formal prayer reports in the NT, the addressee is invariably God the Father (e.g., Eph 3:14–15; Php 1:3–4).

(c) Access is made possible "through him [Christ]," that is, "through his cross" (διὰ τοῦ σταυροῦ, v. 16) = "through his blood shed on the cross" (διὰ τοῦ αἵματος τοῦ σταυροῦ αὐτοῦ, Col 1:20). With a different emphasis Eph 3:12 expresses this mediatorial role of Christ in providing and guaranteeing access to God: "In union with him [Jesus Christ our Lord] and through faith in him, we exercise our right of open access [to God] with confidence" (cf. 1Jn 5:14). Referring to the access reflected in prayer, Paul encourages believers to "give thanks to God the Father through him [the Lord Jesus]" (Col 3:17).

(d) Access is experienced "in the one Spirit," that is, "united in one and the same Spirit," or "in the unity of the one body (cf. Eph 2:16; 4:4), created by the Spirit (cf. Eph 4:3)." Clearly there is an intended parallelism between ἐν ἑνὶ σώματι (v. 16) and ἐν ἑνὶ πνεύματι. But it is possible that this latter phrase is instrumental: "enabled/empowered by the one Spirit."

If this πρός–διά–ἐν is the normative pattern for believers' access to God—to the Father, through the Son, in the Spirit—there are two exceptions:

1. *Prayer* is sometimes addressed directly to the Lord Jesus by an individual believer (e.g., Ac 7:59–60; 9:10–17; 22:16, 19; 2Co 12:8) or by a group of believers (Ac 1:24; 9:21; 1Co 1:2; 16:22; Rev 22:20).
2. The Lord Jesus, along with God the Father, is a legitimate object of *worship* (e.g., Mt 14:33; 28:9, 17; Lk 24:52; Jn 9:38; 20:28; Ac 13:2; Php 2:9–11; 2Pe 3:18; Rev 5:12–14).

5. 1 John 5:16–17

Ἐάν τις ἴδῃ τὸν ἀδελφὸν αὐτοῦ ἁμαρτάνοντα ἁμαρτίαν μὴ **πρὸς** θάνατον, αἰτήσει καὶ δώσει αὐτῷ ζωήν, τοῖς ἁμαρτάνουσιν μὴ **πρὸς** θάνατον. ἔστιν ἁμαρτία **πρὸς** θάνατον· οὐ περὶ ἐκείνης λέγω ἵνα ἐρωτήσῃ. πᾶσα ἀδικία ἁμαρτία ἐστιν, καὶ ἁμαρτία οὐ **πρὸς** θάνατον.

"If anyone sees his brother or sister committing a sin that does not lead to death, you should pray and God will give him life. This relates only to those whose ongoing sin does not lead to death. There is, however, a sin that does lead to death. I do not suggest you should make a request about that sin. Every wrong action is sin, and there is a sin that does not lead to death."

In the immediate context (vv. 14–15) John is encouraging his readers to approach God confidently in prayer, knowing he will grant all requests made "according to his will" (cf. 1Jn 3:21–22). Then in vv. 16–17 he applies this general statement about prayer requests made in accordance with God's will to a specific case involving intercession for a brother or sister who persists in a particular (unnamed) sin. If this observable, continuing sin has not led to physical death, intercessory prayer for the sinner's repentance accords with God's will, and in response God will grant such a repentant person the boon of further physical life and renewed spiritual life. But if divine judgment has already fallen on this person in the form of physical death, prayer about that sin is inappropriate; prayer for the dead would be contrary to God's will.

Such an understanding of this difficult passage, which bristles with exegetical problems, assumes a number of solutions to these problems.

(a) The two present tenses, ἁμαρτάνοντα and τοῖς ἁμαρτάνουσιν (v. 16), point to repeated or perpetual sin—sin that was observable (cf. ἴδῃ).

(b) In the crucial phrases, μὴ/οὐ πρὸς θάνατον and πρὸς θάνατον, the preposition is probably consecutive, "that leads to" (so BDAG 51a, 874d; B. Reicke, TDNT 6:725; NASB[1,2], GNB, NIV[1,2], ESV), rather than indicating a tendency, "that tends toward." Cf. Jn 11:4, αὕτη ἡ ἀσθένεια οὐκ ἔστιν πρὸς θάνατον, "this sickness will not end in death," or "this disease is not of the kind that will lead to death" (BDAG 874d). Nor should the repeated phrase πρὸς θάνατον be rendered adjectivally, "mortal" or "deadly."

(c) The subject of both αἰτήσει (an imperatival future) and ἐρωτήσῃ is the indefinite τις. Presumably the request implied by αἰτήσει is for the repentance of the sinning fellow believer.

(d) Since God is the giver of both physical and spiritual life, it is more likely that he is the subject of δώσει rather than the interceding believer (as in TCNT, "he will ask, and so be the means of giving Life to him"; similarly Barclay).

(e) It is difficult to understand ζωή and θάνατος as referring to eternal life and eternal death, since (i) eternal life could scarcely be said to be given to an erring believer as a result of vicarious intercession, and (ii) John is unlikely to have countenanced the idea of sins that do not "tend toward" or "result in" eternal death. Ζωή will refer to the divine gift, given in answer to prayer and as a response to repentance, of both ongoing physical life and revitalized spiritual life. While θάνατος could be that of exclusion from the Christian community

(= excommunication; cf Nu 15:30–31), it is better understood as physical death, regarded as a penalty administered not by humans (cf. Nu 18:22; Dt 22:25–26) but by God (as in 1Co 11:30–32; cf. Ac 5:1–10).

Among the many suggested identifications of the "sin that leads to death," the more probable are:

- the open and deliberate rejection of Christ, involving the denial of his incarnation or messiahship (1Jn 2:22; 4:2–3; 2Jn 7); in other words, apostasy, as evidenced in the promulgation of heretical doctrine (1Jn 2:18–27; cf. Heb 6:4–8)
- blasphemy against the Holy Spirit (Mk 3:28–30), the deliberate rejection of known truth as a way of life, so that repentance is never sought
- deliberate sin (cf. Heb 10:26–31), sin performed "defiantly" (Nu 15:30–31), such as premeditated murder or persistent hatred

C. Πρός in Compounds

Most of the 64 NT compounds involving πρός express some sense of direction (MH 324).

1. Direction/motion toward: προστρέχω, run up (to)
   προσευχή, prayer (addressed to a deity)
   προσλαλέω, speak to (someone)
   προσκαρτερέω, hold fast to, be devoted to
2. Addition ("besides"): προσαναπληρόω, fill up besides
   προσοφείλω, owe (something) besides
   προστίθημι, add to, supply
3. Proximity ("beside")/involvement: προσλαμβάνομαι, take aside, take into one's home
   προσκυνέω, prostrate oneself before
   προστάτις, patron (supportive woman)
4. Opposition ("against"): προσκόπτω, take offense at, strike against

Chapter 18

Σύν

A. Original Meaning and New Testament Incidence

As with other prepositions, the original use of σύν was spatial — "together with" or "jointly with," of literal accompaniment, reinforcing the comitative dative or removing the ambiguity of the plain dative (cf. Bortone 145). Of the 128 NT uses of σύν (14th out of the 17 "proper prepositions"), almost half are found in Luke-Acts, and this preposition does not occur in 2 Thessalonians, the Pastorals, Philemon, Hebrews, 1 Peter, 1–3 John, Jude, and Revelation. There are more NT compounds formed with σύν than with any other preposition (κατά is next).

B. Two Basic Uses

1. Association

- two robbers were crucified "together with" Jesus (σὺν αὐτῷ, Mk 15:27)
- "the chief priests and the teachers of the law including [σύν] the elders came up to him" (Lk 20:1)
- "Ananias, in concert with [σύν] his wife Sapphira" (Ac 5:1; pointing to mutuality and cooperation in an action)
- "Crispus, the synagogue leader, believed in the Lord, along with [σύν] his entire household" (Ac 18:8)
- "the grace of God that was with [σύν] me" (1Co 15:10b) = "that came to my aid" (BDAG 962a; cf. LSJ 1690c; MM 599d–600a and Mayser 400 on the phrases σὺν θεῷ and σὺν θεοῖς)

2. Accompaniment

- "Peter and those with him = his companions [οἱ σὺν αὐτῷ]" (Lk 9:32)
- "while I was still in your company [ἔτι ὢν σὺν ὑμῖν]" (Lk 24:44)
- "they will accompany me [σὺν ἐμοὶ πορεύσονται]" (1Co 16:4)
- "get rid of all bitterness, rage and anger, brawling and slander, as well as every form of malice [σὺν πάσῃ κακίᾳ]" (Eph 4:31)

- "I am with you in spirit [τῷ πνεύματι **σὺν** ὑμῖν εἰμι]" (Col 2:5; of spiritual companionship)

C. Relation to Μετά

In Hellenistic Greek μετά and σύν are "virtually synonymous" (Bortone 151; for LXX usage, see Johannessohn 202–12), notably when they both express association (BDAG 961c), a point well illustrated by Luke 24:29, Μεῖνον *μεθ'* ἡμῶν ... εἰσῆλθεν τοῦ μεῖναι σὺν αὐτοῖς. Bortone calls σύν "a rarer and loftier synonym of μετά" throughout the history of Greek (233; cf. 152). But especially in Hellenistic times μετά was eclipsing σύν, partly because σύν governed the dative, which was on the wane (Bortone 166, 184, 186). As a NT preposition μετά (with the genitive) is more common (364 uses) than σύν (128 uses), and in the fourth gospel, 1–2 John, and Revelation it totally preponderates (Regard 512) whereas Acts prefers σύν over μετά (Turner, *Style* 77). Both prepositions, however, are used in connection with Christian discipleship, fellowship meals, and eschatology (W. Grundmann, *TDNT* 7:794–97, who analyzes NT distribution of the two prepositions [769–70]; see also the chart in Turner 269).

In spite of the general interchangeability of these two words, it is interesting that Paul regularly ends his letters with the wish or prayer that χάρις be "with" (μετά, never σύν) his addressees, whereas he depicts the Christian life as one of identification with Christ and the Christian's destiny as being "with" Christ (σύν, not μετά, in both cases). This would suggest that σύν was more suited to express intimate personal union or close fellowship, and μετά was more suited to denote close association or attendant circumstances or simple accompaniment.

D. Σὺν Χριστῷ and Equivalents in Paul

There are twelve Pauline uses of the phrase σὺν Χριστῷ or its equivalents σὺν αὐτῷ, σὺν Ἰησοῦ, or σὺν κυρίῳ. But not included here are the eleven verbal σύν-compounds that are not accompanied by the actual preposition σύν (these are discussed below under E).

The relevant passages fall into four natural groups.

1. Dying "with" Christ

a. Romans 6:8

Death with Christ (ἀπεθάνομεν **σὺν** Χριστῷ) is the premise for believers'confidence that they will also share his resurrection life.

b. Colossians 2:20

Death with Christ (ἀπεθάνετε **σὺν** Χριστῷ), referring not to believers' self-denial in union with Christ but to their baptismal identification with him in his crucifixion, effects release "from the control of the elemental spirits of the universe" (ἀπὸ τῶν στοιχείων τοῦ κόσμου).

2A. Being Raised "with" Christ—in the Past

a. Colossians 2:13

God made believers alive "together with Christ" (συνεζωοποίησεν ὑμᾶς σὺν αὐτῷ), where σὺν αὐτῷ does not mean "at the same time as" or even "in the same way as," but rather "along with" in the sense of "in the wake of." It is not that the spiritual resurrection of believers occurred at the time of the bodily resurrection of Christ or simply that his resurrection formed the pattern for theirs. Rather, the resurrection of Christians from spiritual deadness to new life is grounded in, and is a consequence of, Christ's own rising from the realm of the dead to immortal life.

b. Colossians 3:3

As a result of believers' dying with Christ in baptism (cf. Ro 6:2–8), their life now "lies hidden with Christ in God" (κέκρυπται σὺν τῷ Χριστῷ ἐν τῷ θεῷ). Σύν indicates that the new spiritual life of believers is experienced in a symbiotic union (cf. ζωὴ ... σύν) with the heavenly Christ. What is more, that life remains concealed in the safekeeping of God in heaven.

2B. Being Raised "with" Christ—in the Future

a. 2 Corinthians 4:14

"For we know that the one who raised Jesus will raise us with Jesus in our turn [καὶ ἡμᾶς σὺν Ἰησοῦ ἐγερεῖ]." It is clear that σύν here cannot signify "at the same time with" or "in conjunction with," for Jesus' resurrection lies in the past, not the future. If this preposition meant "in the company of," referring to the final state of permanent fellowship with Christ, we would have expected εἶναι σὺν Ἰησοῦ ἐγερεῖ ("will raise us to be with Jesus"; cf. Php 1:23; 1Th 4:17). Σὺν Ἰησοῦ may be paraphrased "by virtue of Jesus' resurrection" or "in the wake of Jesus' resurrection," reflecting Paul's belief that Christ or the resurrection of Christ was the firstfruits (ἀπαρχή) of believers' resurrection (1Co 15:20, 23). The two resurrections are essentially one, for the total harvest is representatively and potentially present in the firstfruits.

b. Colossians 3:4

"When Christ appears—he who is your life—then you too will appear with him [σὺν αὐτῷ] in glory." When Christ's glory is manifested at his second advent, believers also will appear "in a blaze of Christ's glory" or "in glorified bodies" (ἐν δόξῃ). Σὺν αὐτῷ will mean either "along with him" at his appearance (cf. Ro 8:17) or "in his train" since he lives in heaven in a "body of glory" (Php 3:20–21) as the paradigm for believers' resurrection transformation.

c. 1 Thessalonians 4:14

"Through the power of Jesus [διὰ τοῦ Ἰησοῦ] God will bring [ἄξει = ἐγερεῖ] with him [σὺν αὐτῷ] those who have fallen asleep." Obviously σὺν αὐτῷ cannot mean "along with him," as if Jesus were not yet raised from the dead. The phrase has the sense "as pledged by the resurrection of Jesus" or "by virtue of their union with the risen Jesus."

d. 1 Thessalonians 5:10

The purpose (ἵνα) of Christ's death on behalf of and in the place of (ὑπέρ) Christians is so that whether they are keeping vigil in life or sleeping in death (εἴτε γρηγορῶμεν εἴτε καθεύδωμεν) at the time of Christ's parousia, they might experience resurrection life "together with him" (ἅμα σὺν αὐτῷ ζήσωμεν)—what the previous verse describes as σωτηρία. Here ἅμα σὺν αὐτῷ may be paraphrased "just as he enjoys resurrection life" (cf. 1Co 15:45; Php 3:21) or "in company with him" (cf. 1Th 4:17).

3. Present Living "with" Christ

a. Romans 8:32

"He who did not spare even his own Son but gave him up for us all—how then can he fail to supply us freely with all things along with him [σὺν αὐτῷ]?" Σὺν αὐτῷ cannot mean "together with" = "including," for God's "not-sparing" of his own Son is already a given, which is the premise for Paul's conclusion (πῶς οὐχὶ καί;). Rather, the phrase is brachylogy for "in Christ's person, who is God's supreme gift."

b. 2 Corinthians 13:4b

"For we also are weak, in union with him [Christ], but in our dealings with you [εἰς ὑμᾶς] we will be fully alive, along with him [σὺν αὐτῷ], because of God's power." Here Paul asserts that Christ's career is the pattern for his own ministry. Just as Christ was crucified because of his "weakness" and now lives because of God's power, so Paul shares the "weakness" of Christ's passion and the effective power of God.

At first sight ζήσομεν σὺν αὐτῷ might express the resurrection hope of living in Christ's presence (cf. Php 1:23; 1Th 4:17), given the use of ζάω in v. 4a in reference to Christ's resurrection life and the use of σὺν Ἰησοῦ in 2Co 4:14 in reference to believers' resurrection. But Paul's focus in the context is on solving the problem of unrepentant believers (12:21; 13:2), not on rejoicing in his final destiny. The apostle is speaking of his imminent visit to Corinth when, *in unison with Christ* (σὺν αὐτῷ) and with God's power, he will act decisively and vigorously (ζήσομεν) against unrepentant evildoers within the congregation.

4. Future Being "with" Christ

a. 1 Thessalonians 4:17b

As a consequence (οὕτως) of the resurrection of the dead (v. 16), the rapture of the living (v. 17a), and their joint meeting with the Lord in the air (v. 17a), all believers, both the resurrected dead and those alive at the parousia, will without interruption be in the Lord's company (πάντοτε σὺν κυρίῳ ἐσόμεθα) in heaven, not only to escape the coming wrath of God (1Th 1:10) but also to enjoy permanent, corporate fellowship with the Lord Jesus. The NT knows nothing of a neoplatonic immortality of "the Alone with the Alone." Resurrection leads to unmediated mutual communion between the individual and his or her Lord but not in isolation from fellow worshipers.

b. Philippians 1:23

συνέχομαι δὲ ἐκ τῶν δύο, τὴν ἐπιθυμίαν ἔχων εἰς τὸ ἀναλῦσαι καὶ σὺν Χριστῷ εἶναι, πολλῷ γὰρ μᾶλλον κρεῖσσον

"I am torn between these two alternatives: I am longing to break camp and so be with Christ, for this is a far, far better state."

As Paul languished in prison awaiting his trial (Php 1:13–14; cf. Ac 28:30) and considered his future, he faced the dilemma of two conflicting desires (cf. vv. 21–22): a personal longing to depart from his present life on earth and so immediately be with his risen Master in heaven, yet also an intense pastoral yearning to promote his converts' spiritual well-being (vv. 23–24). Convinced of the Philippians' need for his pastoral care, Paul expresses his personal conviction that he will in fact continue with them in order to promote their progress and joy in the faith (v. 25).

Paul's distinctive description of Christian existence is embodied in the phrase εἶναι ἐν Χριστῷ (e.g., 2Co 5:17, and see ch. 10 E). There is no evidence in the Pauline corpus that death removes the Christian from ἐν Χριστῷ incorporation: this persists at and after death, as the expression οἱ νεκροὶ ἐν Χριστῷ (1Th 4:16), "the dead [who are] in Christ," indicates. When a believer dies, there is added to ἐν Χριστῷ corporeity a personal and "spatial" dimension σὺν Χριστῷ (Php 1:23). As with πρός in Jn 1:1, when σύν is used to indicate a relationship between two persons who are known to and highly regarded by each other, it points to more than spatial proximity or coexistence; interactive communion between the two parties is implied, although not explicitly expressed. The destiny of believers immediately after death (σὺν Χριστῷ εἶναι, Php 1:23) or at the parousia (σὺν κυρίῳ εἶναι, 1Th 4:17) is to enjoy dynamic, mutual fellowship "with" their risen Lord.

That σύν may bear the sense "in fellowship with" is shown by papyri usage (MM 600; Mayser 399). Deissmann draws attention to a *graffito* from Alexandria, perhaps of the Imperial period, where a deceased person is addressed thus:

"I pray that I might soon be in fellowship with you" (σὺν σοὶ εἶναι, 303 n.1). This parallel to the Pauline use of σύν in Php 1:23 is all the more impressive when one recalls that the person to whose presence the Christian departs at death is not dead but alive. Only if Christ had *not* risen from the grave could Paul have spoken of departed believers as οἱ κεκοιμημένοι σὺν Χριστῷ, "those who have fallen asleep with Christ."

Σὺν Χριστῷ εἶναι is never used to describe the earthly state of Christians. Being primarily an individual and active experience, it is not related to εἶναι ἐν Χριστῷ, essentially a corporate and passive experience, by succession, since οἱ νεκροί remain ἐν Χριστῷ (1Th 4:16). The difference between "the dead in Christ" and living Christians is not in their status (both are ἐν Χριστῷ), but in their somatic state (disembodied vs. embodied), the quality of their fellowship with Christ, and the degree of their proximity to Christ. If we remember that Paul regarded death as a "falling asleep" to this world rather than as an entrance to a "residing in unconsciousness" in the presence of Jesus (see ch. 15 A), there is no tension between his use of κοιμάομαι and the idea of the believer's settled permanent fellowship with Christ at death.

E. Σύν in Compounds

There are more words formed from σύν than from any other preposition.

1. Association: συγχαίρω, rejoice with
   συναθλέω, struggle along with
   σύμμορφος, having the same form
   σύνδουλος, fellow slave
2. Assistance: συνεργέω, work together with, help
   συναντιλαμβάνομαι, (come to) help
   συμφέρω, be profitable, confer a benefit
3. Intensity/perfectivizing: συγκλείω, hem in, imprison
   συγκύπτω, be bent double
   συντηρέω, keep safe, treasure up

Of special significance are eleven verbal σύν- compounds in Paul that are without an accompanying explicit σὺν Χριστῷ (or equivalent), yet with a reference to Christ clearly implied or stated. These eleven verbs may be grouped around two main motifs, two crucial redemptive events, namely, Christ's death and burial, and his resurrection with all its consequences, events that are reenacted in Christian baptism (cf. Ro 6:3–10). These are similar to the expressions discussed in D, above).

At the *beginning* of their Christian experience, believers

- have died with Christ (συναποθνήσκω, 2Ti 2:11)
- were crucified with Christ (συσταυρόομαι, Ro 6:6; Gal 2:19)

- were buried with Christ (συνθάπτομαι, Ro 6:4; Col 2:12)
- were raised with Christ (συνεγείρω, Eph 2:6; Col 2:12; 3:1)
- were made alive with Christ (συζωοποιέω, Eph 2:5; Col 2:13)

Throughout their earthly Christian experience, believers

- are being conformed to Christ's death (συμμορφίζομαι, Php 3:10)
- suffer with Christ (συμπάσχω, Ro 8:17)
- are sitting with Christ in the heavenly realms (συγκαθίζω, Eph 2:6)

At the *consummation* of their Christian experience, believers

- will live with Christ (συζάω, Ro 6:8; 2Ti 2:11)
- will be glorified with Christ (συνδοξάζομαι, Ro 8:17)
- will reign with Christ (συμβασιλεύω, 2Ti 2:12)

But Christians are not associated with aspects of Christ's historical life before his passion. For example, Paul never says believers are baptized with Christ, are tempted with Christ or are transfigured with Christ.

Chapter 19

Ὑπέρ

A. Original Meaning and New Testament Use

The original local sense of ὑπέρ as "[situated] over or above" someone or something, without actual contact, is found in Classical Greek (e.g., Herodotus, *Hist.* 2.6.19) and occasionally in the papyri (Rossberg 40; Mayser 461) but not in the LXX or NT (apart from a variant in Heb 9:5 read by D* E*; most MSS have ὑπεράνω). In frequency of occurrence, ὑπέρ ranks thirteenth out of the seventeen "proper" prepositions in the NT, the LXX, and the Ptolemaic papyri (see the chart on p. 32). Ὑπέρ with the genitive is far more common than ὑπέρ with the accusative, accounting for 87% of the 150 uses. The commonest meaning of this preposition ("on behalf of") seems to have arisen from the image of one person standing or bending *over* another in order to shield or protect him, or of a shield lifted *over* the head that suffers the blow instead of the person (cf. ὑπερασπίζω, "cover with a shield").

B. Ὑπέρ with the Accusative

From the basic spatial sense of "above" three figurative meanings emerge.

1. "Beyond"

1Co 4:6 ἵνα ἐν ἡμῖν μάθητε τὸ μὴ ὑπὲρ ἃ γέγραπται,

"so that you may learn from our example what the saying means, 'Nothing beyond what is written'"

This could be a Pauline slogan (i.e., "Do not go beyond what stands written in Scripture," or "Live according to the rules" [LN §88.95]) or, conceivably, Paul's repudiation of a Corinthian watchword (e.g., "Beyond Scripture!"). See further BDAG 1031b.

1Co 10:13 ὁ θεὸς … οὐκ ἐάσει ὑμᾶς πειρασθῆναι ὑπὲρ ὃ δύνασθε,

"God will not allow you to be tested beyond what you can bear/beyond your power [to resist]" (LN §78.29)

a. 2 Corinthians 11:23[1]

διάκονοι Χριστοῦ εἰσιν; παραφρονῶν λαλῶ, **ὑπὲρ** ἐγώ

"Are they 'servants of Christ'? I am out of my mind when I speak this way — but I am a better servant than they are."

Most grammarians (e.g., Robertson 629; MH 326; Moule 64) and lexicographers (e.g., LSJ 1858b; BDAG 1031c; H. Riesenfeld, *TDNT* 8:516) assume ὑπέρ is here used adverbially, "to a higher degree," supplying διάκονος Χριστοῦ εἰμί (BDF §230). But unambiguous evidence for an adverbial use of **ὑπέρ** is lacking (Caragounis 217 and n.277), so it is preferable to supply αὐτούς after **ὑπέρ** (so BDR §230 [3]; cf. Caragounis 217–18) as well as διάκονος Χριστοῦ εἰμί, "I, beyond them" = "I am a better servant of Christ than they are."

b. Philemon 21

εἰδὼς ὅτι καὶ **ὑπὲρ** ἃ λέγω ποιήσεις

"I know you will do even beyond what I am asking."

Paul was confident of Philemon's compliance (v. 16a) with his specific requests (vv. 17–20): (i) to welcome (προσλαβοῦ) Onesimus as though he were Paul (v. 17b); (ii) to charge Onesimus's debts (ἐλλόγα) to his own account (v. 18b); and (iii) to refresh his heart (ἀνάπαυσον) in Christ (v. 20b). The undefined and climactic "even beyond" or "even more than" (καὶ **ὑπέρ**) may be:

(1) an even more generous reception for Onesimus than Paul had envisaged in v. 17
(2) more specifically, forgiveness for Onesimus and his reinstatement in Philemon's household
(3) most likely, the manumission of Onesimus for Christian service either in Colossae or at Rome with Paul

But although Paul assumes Philemon's compliance with his requests, he leaves him free to follow the dictates of his Christian conscience in determining how his ἀγάπη (vv. 5, 7) should be expressed, and he seriously entertains the possibility that Philemon might decide to retain the services of Onesimus as a slave permanently (vv. 15–16).

2. "Superior to"

Mt 10:24 Οὐκ ἔστιν μαθητὴς **ὑπὲρ** τὸν διδάσκαλον οὐδὲ δοῦλος **ὑπὲρ** τὸν κύριον αὐτοῦ

---

1. Because a number scholars take ὑπέρ in this verse to mean "beyond/even more" (in an adverbial sense), this seems to be the appropriate place to discuss this contested passage.

"A student is not superior to his teacher, nor a slave to his master."

Php 2:9 ὁ θεὸς ... ἐχαρίσατο αὐτῷ τὸ ὄνομα τὸ **ὑπὲρ** πᾶν ὄνομα

"God ... conferred on him the name that is superior to every name."

Phm 16 οὐκέτι ὡς δοῦλον ἀλλ᾽ **ὑπὲρ** δοῦλον, ἀδελφὸν ἀγαπητόν

"no longer regarded as a mere slave but as one who is better than a slave — as a dearly loved brother."

3. *"More than"*

Mt 10:37 ὁ φιλῶν πατέρα ἢ μητέρα **ὑπὲρ** ἐμὲ οὐκ ἔστιν μου ἄξιος

"Anyone who loves their father or mother more than me is not worthy of me."

Heb 4:12 ζῶν γὰρ ὁ λόγος τοῦ θεοῦ καὶ ἐνεργὴς καὶ τομώτερος **ὑπὲρ** πᾶσαν μάχαιραν δίστομον

"For the word of God is alive and active and sharper than any double-edged sword."

The use of ὑπέρ to introduce the second term of a comparison is a feature of Hellenistic Greek not found in Attic Greek (where the genitive would be used) or later Greek (where ἀπό would be used) (Bortone 193). See Conybeare and Stock (84–85) for LXX usage.

C. Ὑπέρ with the Genitive

There are four main meanings for this construction. Because the fourth is especially significant, it is given extended treatment.

1. *"On behalf of, for the benefit of"*

Ro 8:31 εἰ ὁ θεὸς **ὑπὲρ** ἡμῶν, τίς καθ᾽ ἡμῶν;

"If God is on our side, who can prevail against us?"

1Co 4:6 ἵνα μὴ εἷς **ὑπὲρ** τοῦ ἑνὸς φυσιοῦσθε κατὰ τοῦ ἑτέρου

"so that one of you may not be arrogant in favoring one leader over against another"

In both these examples ὑπέρ and κατά stand as opposites.

Col 1:7 ἐστιν πιστὸς **ὑπὲρ** ἡμῶν [𝔓⁴⁶ ℵ* A B G] διάκονος τοῦ Χριστοῦ

"He [Epaphras] is a faithful minister of Christ on our behalf."

2. *"Concerning, in reference to" (see further D, below)*

Jn 1:30 οὗτός ἐστιν **ὑπὲρ** οὗ ἐγὼ εἶπον...

"This is the one about whom I said ..."

Ro 10:1 ἡ δέησις πρὸς τὸν θεὸν **ὑπὲρ** αὐτῶν [τοῦ Ἰσραὴλ] εἰς σωτηρίαν

"My prayer to God for them [the Israelites] is that they may be saved."

2Co 8:23 εἴτε **ὑπὲρ** Τίτου, κοινωνὸς ἐμὸς καὶ εἰς ὑμᾶς συνεργός
"If there is any question regarding Titus, he is my colleague and fellow worker in your service."

In some contexts the "reference" can conceal an aim, "with a view to."
Jn 11:4 αὕτη ἡ ἀσθένεια οὐκ ἔστιν πρὸς θάνατον ἀλλ' **ὑπὲρ** τῆς δόξης τοῦ θεοῦ
"This sickness will not lead to death. Rather, it is to reveal God's glory."
1Co 15:3 Χριστὸς ἀπέθανεν **ὑπὲρ** τῶν ἁμαρτιῶν ἡμῶν
"Christ died to deal with/to atone for our sins" (similarly Gal 1:4 [𝔓⁵¹ B H 33]; Heb 5:1; 7:27).
2Co 12:19 τὰ δὲ πάντα, ἀγαπητοί, **ὑπὲρ** τῆς ὑμῶν οἰκοδομῆς
"Everything, dear friends, is to promote your upbuilding."

3. "Because of, for the sake of"
Ro 15:9 ... τὰ δὲ ἔθνη **ὑπὲρ** ἐλέους δοξάσαι τὸν θεόν
"... and so that the Gentiles might praise God because of his mercy"
Php 1:29 ὅτι ὑμῖν ἐχαρίσθη τὸ **ὑπὲρ** Χριστοῦ ...
"for it has been granted to you [to suffer] for Christ's sake ... "
3Jn 7 **ὑπὲρ** γὰρ τοῦ ὀνόματος ἐξῆλθον
"for they went out for the sake of the Name"

4. "In the place of " (see E, below)

D. Ὑπέρ and Περί
Since both these prepositions can mean "on behalf of" or "concerning," they are sometimes interchangeable (as also in the papyri—Rossberg 40; MM 651c; Mayser 450–54). "The frequent interchange of ὑπέρ and περί is due partly to their affinity, but more particularly to their partial homophony (*iper-peri*)" (Jannaris §1686; cf. §§1684–85). For example:

- τὸ αἷμά μου τῆς διαθήκης τὸ **περὶ** πολλῶν ἐκχυννόμενον (Mt 26:28)
  τὸ ἐκχυννόμενον **ὑπὲρ** πολλῶν (Mk 14:24)
- ἐν πάσῃ προσκαρτερήσει καὶ δεήσει **περὶ** πάντων τῶν ἁγίων καὶ **ὑπὲρ** ἐμοῦ (Eph 6:18–19)
- θυσίας **ὑπὲρ** ἁμαρτιῶν ... προσφέρειν **περὶ** ἁμαρτιῶν (Heb 5:1, 3; cf. 10:12, 26)

This interchangeability is reflected in textual variants that involve these two prepositions (e.g., Mk 14:24; Jn 1:30; Gal 1:4 ὑπέρ 𝔓⁵¹ B H 33; περί 𝔓⁴⁶ ℵ* A D F G 1739 1881).

Ὑπέρ standing for περί ("concerning") (less frequent than περί for ὑπέρ,

BDF §§229 [1], 231 [1]) is characteristic of Paul (e.g., 2Co 1:7–8; 5:12; 7:4, 14; 8:23–24; 9:3; 12:5 [2x], 8). Both in the LXX and in the NT περί is roughly twice as common as ὑπέρ (852:427 and 333:150 respectively). Generally, ὑπέρ is more common with persons and περί with things; e.g., 1Pe 3:18, Χριστὸς ἅπαξ περὶ ἁμαρτιῶν ἔπαθεν, δίκαιος ὑπὲρ ἀδίκων. Not surprisingly, therefore, ὑπέρ often comes across as a more colorful and robust preposition, and περί somewhat colorless and anaemic.

E. Ὑπέρ Meaning "in the place of"

1. Classical Greek

The meaning "in the place of, instead of" for ὑπέρ with the genitive is not common in Classical Greek (see LSJ 1857d; Jannaris §§ 1682–83) except in two contexts.

a. Where the death of one person in the place of another is expressed by the phrase ὑπέρ τινος ἀποθανεῖν (where ἀντί τινος might have been expected).

(1) Xenophon, *Anab.* 7.4.9 ἐθέλοις ἄν, ὦ Ἐπίσθενες, ὑπὲρ τούτου ἀποθανεῖν; "Are you willing, Episthenes, to die instead of this boy?"

(2) Euripides, *Alc.* 700–701 κατθανεῖν ... γυναῖχ' ὑπὲρ σοῦ (cf. line 434, ἀντ' ἐμοῦ).
"for your wife to die in your place"

b. Where one person is speaking or answering as a substitute for another and the phrase ὑπέρ τινος λέγειν/ἀποκρίνεσθαι is used.

(1) Plato, *Theaet.* 162 ἐρεῖ Πρωταγόρας ἤ τις ἄλλος ὑπὲρ αὐτοῦ
"Protagoras or someone else will speak for him"

(2) Plato, *Gorg.* 515c ἐγὼ ὑπὲρ σοῦ ἀποκρινοῦμαι
"I will answer in your place"

2. Hellenistic Greek Literature

E. K. Simpson has assembled impressive evidence from Hellenistic Greek authors to show that ὑπέρ not uncommonly denotes proxyship, "in lieu of" (he cites Lucian, Philo, Plutarch, Dionysius of Halicarnassus, and Appian).[2] Note also the reference of Irenaeus to the Lord who "gave his soul for our souls [ὑπὲρ τῶν ἡμετέρων ψυχῶν] and his own flesh for our flesh [ἀντὶ τῶν ἡμετέρων σαρκῶν]" (*Haer.* 5.1.2).

In the LXX, a substitutionary sense for ὑπέρ is rare. In his *Lexicon* Muraoka

---

2. E. K. Simpson, "Note on the Meaning of ΥΠΕΡ in Certain Contexts," in *The Pastoral Epistles. The Greek Text with Introduction and Commentary* (London: Tyndale, 1954), 112.

does not list "instead of" as a meaning of ὑπέρ, although *GELS* (488a) cites Jdt 8:12, "Who are you to put God to the test today, and to set yourselves up in the place of God [ὑπὲρ τοῦ θεου] in human affairs?" (NRSV; the margin has "above God"). H. Riesenfeld (*TDNT* 8:513 n.31) refers to Dt 24:16 (and the almost identical 4Kgdms 14:6): "Parents shall not be put to death for their children [ὑπὲρ τέκνων], nor shall children be put to death for their parents [ὑπὲρ πατέρων]."

One reason for the rarity of ὑπέρ = "instead of" in the LXX may be the *relative* frequency there of ἀντί (391 uses) in comparison with ὑπέρ (427 uses). With this compare the 22:150 ratio of their relationship in NT usage, where ἀντί is clearly losing ground to ὑπέρ (cf. Wallace 387).

3. Papyri

In the papyri ὑπέρ often stands for ἀντί (Rossberg 41), especially in standardized expressions such as ἔγραψα ὑπὲρ αὐτοῦ ἀγραμμάτου or ἔγραψα ὑπὲρ αὐτοῦ διὰ τὸ αὐτὸν μὴ ἐπίστασθαι γράμματα, with reference to a person who writes a letter or signs a legal document in lieu of someone who cannot write (see MM 6, 651; Mayser 460–61; Deissmann 152–53; Wallace 384–86).[3]

Jannaris sums up the overall situation this way: "Uncommon in [classical] A[ttic period or diction], but not rare in P[ost-classical] compositions, though hardly ever current in uncultivated speech" (§1683).

4. New Testament

a. John 11:50

οὐδὲ λογίζεσθε ὅτι συμφέρει ὑμῖν ἵνα εἷς ἄνθρωπος ἀποθάνῃ ὑπὲρ τοῦ λαοῦ καὶ μὴ ὅλον τὸ ἔθνος ἀπόληται

"You even fail to realize that it is in your interest that one man die for the people than that the entire nation perish."

The high priest Caiaphas is remonstrating with Jewish leaders. It is clear that ὑπέρ here denotes substitution, not simply benefit or representation, since Caiaphas remarks that such a death "for the people" will ensure that "the entire nation" is not destroyed (λαός and ἔθνος both refer to one and the same Jewish nation; cf. ὑπὲρ τοῦ ἔθνους in vv. 51–52). That is, politically the death of the one (as a scapegoat) will be a substitute for the death of the many. As John sees it (vv. 51–52), Caiaphas has unwittingly expressed a theological profundity: Christ's suffering is vicarious and redemptive.

---

3. See also A. T. Robertson, "The Use of ὑπέρ in Business Documents in the Papyri," *The Expositor* 8/19 (1920): 321–27; reprinted in his *The Minister and His Greek New Testament* (Nashville: Broadman, 1977), 35–42.

On 1Co 15:29, see ch. 21 A, where I propose that in this verse **ὑπέρ** [2x] has the dual sense of "in their place" and "for their benefit").

b. 2 Corinthians 5:14

κρίναντας τοῦτο, ὅτι εἷς **ὑπὲρ** πάντων ἀπέθανεν, ἄρα οἱ πάντες ἀπέθανον

"because we have reached this conviction, that one died for all, which means that all died"

In 2Co 5:14–15 Paul is giving the reason why Christ's love governs him in everything. That **ὑπέρ** bears a substitutionary sense here (and in the repeated **ὑπὲρ** πάντων ἀπέθανεν in v. 15a) is shown by the conclusion (inferential ἄρα) Paul draws: "therefore all died." The death of Christ was the death of all human beings (πάντες), because he was dying the death they deserved. He was acting both "on behalf of" and "in the place of" all people. He represented them by becoming their substitute. However, in the case of **ὑπὲρ** αὐτῶν in v. 15b mere representation must be in mind if this phrase qualifies both τῷ ... ἀποθανόντι and [τῷ] ἐγερθέντι (as NASB[1,2]), since Paul never portrays the resurrection of Jesus as being "in the place of" believers.

c. 2 Corinthians 5:20

ὑπὲρ Χριστοῦ οὖν πρεσβεύομεν ὡς τοῦ θεοῦ παρακαλοῦντος δι' ἡμῶν· δεόμεθα **ὑπὲρ** Χριστοῦ, καταλλάγητε τῷ θεῷ

"We are therefore ambassadors for Christ, since God does in fact make his appeal through us. As Christ's envoys, we make this entreaty, 'Get reconciled to God!'"

In relation to the message of reconciliation (2Co 5:18–6:2), Paul recognizes that his role as Christ's ambassador and God's mouthpiece (5:20a) is twofold: evangelistic and pastoral. It involves, first, the universal proclamation of reconciliation in Christ (5:18b, 19b) and the invitation to respond, "Be reconciled to God!" (5:20b). Second, he appeals to those already reconciled to God not to fail to profit from God's grace (6:1–2).

In saying **ὑπὲρ** Χριστοῦ οὖν πρεσβεύομεν, Paul is asserting more than the simple fact that he is "Christ's ambassador" (which would be Χριστοῦ πρεσβεία/ πρεσβευτής ἐσμεν).

As Christ's envoy (πρεσβεύομεν, v. 20a) and also in issuing his impassioned entreaty (δεόμεθα, v. 20b), he acts **ὑπὲρ** Χριστοῦ, both "on behalf of Christ" and "in the place of Christ" (cf. the **ὑπέρ** in 5:14). There is no need here to choose between the notions of representation and substitution for **ὑπέρ**; both concepts are present, in light of the implications of any ambassadorial role. Regarding this twofold ὑπὲρ Χριστοῦ, Winer (383–84) observes that "probably ὑπέρ means both times ... *for* Christ i.e. in his name and behalf (consequently, in his stead)."

d. Galatians 3:13

Χριστὸς ἡμᾶς ἐξηγόρασεν ἐκ τῆς κατάρας τοῦ νόμου γενόμενος ὑπὲρ ἡμῶν κατάρα, ὅτι γέγραπται, Ἐπικατάρατος πᾶς ὁ κρεμάμενος ἐπὶ ξύλου

"Christ ransomed us from the curse invoked by the law by becoming the accursed one for us, for it stands written, 'A curse lies on everyone who is hung on a pole'."

Paul has argued that all those seeking justification by works performed in obedience to the law are under a divine curse (cf. Dt 21:22–23; 27:26) since perseverance in all aspects of the law, while required, is impossible (Gal 3:10)— law-keeping can never impart life (3:21). In v. 13 he affirms that Christ himself has vicariously become the bearer of this curse (κατάρα is "abstract for concrete": bearer of the curse, H. Riesenfeld, *TDNT* 8:509) that is pronounced by the law. Acting both in our place and for our benefit (ὑπὲρ ἡμῶν) when he was "hung on a pole," Christ liberated both Jews and Gentiles (v. 14) from the curse. There was a transference of liabilities from sinners to Christ (cf. 2Co 5:21). Robertson, however, seems to be overpressing the imagery and the significance of ὑπέρ and ἐκ when he comments, "we were *under* the curse [ὑπὸ κατάραν, v. 10]; Christ took the curse on himself and thus *over* us (between the suspended curse and us) and thus rescued us *out from under* the curse" (631, italics his; similarly his *Pictures* 4:294).

e. Philemon 13

[Ὀνήσιμον, v. 10] ... ὃν ἐγὼ ἐβουλόμην πρὸς ἐμαυτὸν κατέχειν, ἵνα ὑπὲρ σοῦ μοι διακονῇ ἐν τοῖς δεσμοῖς τοῦ εὐαγγελίου

"I would have liked to have kept him [Onesimus] with me, so that he could continue helping me in your place while I am imprisoned for the gospel."

As part of his general appeal to Philemon on behalf of Onesimus (Phm 8–16), Paul informs Philemon that he is sending Onesimus back to him with the present letter (v. 12), in spite of the fact that his own preference would be to have kept Onesimus at his side so that he could continue to serve as Philemon's proxy in attending to all Paul's needs during his imprisonment (v. 13). Since, at the time of writing, Philemon is absent from Paul and Onesimus is present with Paul, ὑπὲρ σοῦ naturally means "in your place" (Goodspeed, GNB, HCSB), "as your deputy" (Moffatt), "substituting for you" (similarly NJB), or "as your proxy."

f. 1 Timothy 2:5–6

Χριστὸς Ἰησους, ὁ δοὺς ἑαυτὸν ἀντίλυτρον **ὑπὲρ** πάντων, τὸ μαρτύριον καιροῖς ἰδίοις

"Christ Jesus, who gave himself as a ransom for all people, a fact testified to at its own appointed time."

After affirming the salvific intent (v. 4) of "God our Savior" (1Ti 2:3), Paul reproduces his own or an early Christian confession of faith about the oneness of God, the uniqueness of Jesus Christ as the mediator between God and humankind (v. 5), and the means by which mediation was achieved (v. 6).

Like λύτρον, the term ἀντίλυτρον (a NT *hapax legomenon*) means "ransom price" or "price of deliverance," with the prefix ἀντι- intensifying the idea of substitution already present in λύτρον. We have shown above (ch. 5 E, under Mk 10:45) that the phrase ὁ δοὺς ἑαυτὸν ἀντίλυτρον **ὑπὲρ** πάντων is a reworking of a similar expression found in Mk 10:45 (and Mt 20:28). If this is so, **ὑπὲρ** πάντων is equivalent to the ἀντὶ πολλῶν ("in the place of many") of Mk 10:45. That is, in 1Ti 2:6 ὑπέρ gains a substitutionary sense under the influence of the ἀντι- in ἀντίλυτρον and the ἀντί of Mk 10:45. In the overall context of NT theology, the sense of the verse is this: as enslaved to sin (Ro 6:17) humans are incapable of freeing themselves (Mt 16:26), but Christ's act of self-surrender paid the price for the deliverance of all people.

F. Ὑπέρ as Expressing Both Representation/Advantage and Substitution

In the preceding discussion of 2Co 5:14 and 20 and Gal 3:13 we proposed that ὑπέρ expressed both representation/benefit and substitution. General considerations suggest that the possibility of an occasional dual sense for ὑπέρ should be seriously entertained. Acting on behalf of a person often involves acting in their place. For example, a lawyer who represents a client in court is acting not only on behalf of the client but also in the place of the client, since people are normally permitted to represent themselves in court if they wish to do so.

The preposition ἀντί regularly expresses a substitutionary exchange (see ch. 5 E), "in the place of," while ὑπέρ usually indicates representation ("on behalf of") or advantage ("for the benefit of"). Any of these three meanings may be latent in the ambiguous English preposition "for." Of the two Greek prepositions, ὑπέρ is the broader term, for sometimes the context will show that the manner in which a service is rendered for a person is through assuming their place. That is, sometimes the benefit comes through substitution; ὑπέρ may occasionally express both ideas. Ἀντί is the narrower word, normally confined to expressing substitution, but only implying representation or benefit.

From Tischendorf's slender treatise, *Doctrina Pauli de Vi Mortis Christi Satisfactoria*, R. C. Trench cites (in Latin) a long section at the heart of which Tischendorf observes that "to express the allied senses of advantage and substitution, the Apostle has admirably used the preposition ὑπέρ."[4] This sentiment, which Trench himself endorses, may explain why Paul and other NT writers never say (as one might have expected) that Christ died ἀντὶ ἡμῶν (1Ti 2:6 is the nearest Paul comes—ἀντίλυτρον ὑπὲρ πάντων). Also, ἀντί is "greatly reduced" in usage in the NT (BDF §203), as is evident in its meager 22 NT uses in comparison with the 150 instances of ὑπέρ, so it occasions no surprise that ὑπέρ assumes an expanded role in the NT at the expense of ἀντί.

There are several NT passages describing the redemptive work of Christ in which ὑπέρ may bear the dual sense of representation/advantage and substitution, although it may not inappropriately be rendered by the ambiguous English "for."

- **Ro 5:6** "You see, at the appointed time, while we were still helpless, Christ died for [ὑπέρ] us."
- **Ro 5:8** "But God demonstrates his own love for us by this: While we were still sinners, Christ died for [ὑπέρ] us."
- **Ro 14:15** "Do not by your eating bring ruin on someone for [ὑπέρ] whom Christ died."
- **2Co 5:14–15a** "For Christ's love controls us, because we have reached this conviction, that one died for [ὑπέρ] all, which means that all died. And he died for [ὑπέρ] all...."
- **Gal 3:13** "Christ ransomed us from the curse invoked by the law by becoming the accursed one for [ὑπέρ] us, for it stands written, 'A curse lies on everyone who is hung on a pole'."
- **1Th 5:10** "He [Jesus Christ] died for [ὑπέρ] us so that, whether we are awake or asleep, we may live together with him."
- **1Pe 2:21** "For to this [the patient endurance of unjust suffering] you were called, because Christ suffered for [ὑπέρ] you."
- **1Pe 3:18** "For Christ also suffered once and for all to atone for sins, the Righteous One for [ὑπέρ] for the unrighteous, to bring you to God."
- **1Jn 3:16** "This is how we have come to know what love is: He [Jesus Christ] laid down his life for [ὑπέρ] us."

It is significant that in every case mentioned above, the beneficiary is a person or persons. This suggests that one criterion for taking ὑπέρ in a dual sense may be that it is followed by a personal referent.

---

4. R. C. Trench, *Synonyms of the New Testament* (1880; repr. Grand Rapids: Eerdmans, 1948), 312–13. The original Latin reads (see my translation above): Pro conjunctâ significatione et commodi et vicarii praeclare ab Apostolo adhibita est praepositio ὑπέρ."

G. Ὑπέρ in Compounds

1. Intensity

   ὑπερπλεονάζω, abound exceedingly, overflow
   ὑπερυψόω, raise to a high/the highest position
   ὑπεραυξάνω, grow profusely
   ὑπερνικάω, be completely victorious, prevail completely
   ὑπερήφανος, overbearing, arrogant

2. Excess ("beyond")

   ὑπερεκτείνω, stretch out beyond, overstretch, overreach
   ὑπερλίαν, beyond measure, over and above, extra-special
   ὑπερβαίνω, go beyond, transgress
   ὑπέρακμος, beyond one's prime

"It is characteristic of Paul's temperament that only 3 of 25 occurrences of ὑπέρ-compounds in NT lie outside the *corpus Paulinum*" (MH 326).

Chapter 20

Ὑπό

A. Original Meaning and New Testament Use

The original spatial sense of ὑπό seems to have been "upwards" or "up from under" (Robertson 633, 635) or "out from under" (Winer 368), although another local meaning, "to beneath," seems to have emerged at an early stage (cf. Lk 13:34, "as a hen gathers her chicks under her wings [ὑπὸ τὰς πτέρυγας]").

In frequency of usage ὑπό is 11th in the NT (220 uses) and 12th in both the LXX (498 uses) and the Ptolemaic papyri (364 uses; see chart on p. 32). In the NT the genitive follows ὑπό much more frequently than the accusative (168:52). Although in Classical Greek this preposition was used with the dative (see LSJ 1874b-c) as well as with the accusative and genitive, there are no instances of ὑπό + dative in the LXX (apart from an inferior LXX variant at Job 12:5 A) or in the NT, but there are examples in the papyri (MM 656a; Mayser 512–13). Bortone observes that sometimes there is no appreciable difference in meaning between the three cases with ὑπό in Classical Greek (158–59) or between the two cases in Hellenistic Greek (184).

B. Ὑπό with the Accusative

1. Expressing Motion (answering the question "Where to?")

Mt 5:15 οὐδὲ καίουσιν λύχνον καὶ τιθέασιν αὐτὸν **ὑπὸ** τὸν μόδιον
"nor do people light a lamp and then put it under a bowl"
Eph 1:22 καὶ πάντα ὑπέταξεν **ὑπὸ** τοὺς πόδας αὐτοῦ
"and he [God] has placed everything in subjection beneath his [Christ's] feet" (cf. 1Co 15:25, 27)

2. Expressing Rest (answering the question "Where?")

Jn 1:48 Πρὸ τοῦ σε Φίλιππον φωνῆσαι ὄντα **ὑπὸ** τὴν συκῆν εἶδόν σε
"I saw you while you were still underneath the fig tree before Philip summoned you."

Ac 4:12 οὐδὲ γὰρ ὄνομά ἐστιν ἕτερον **ὑπὸ** τὸν οὐρανὸν τὸ δεδομένον ἐν ἀνθρώποις ἐν ᾧ δεῖ σωθῆναι ἡμᾶς
"For there is no other name under heaven, appointed for mankind, by which we must be saved" (where **ὑπὸ** τὸν οὐρανόν = ἐπὶ τῆς γῆς).

C. Ὑπό with the Genitive

1. Used of Persons (denoting agency)

Mt 4:1 τότε ὁ Ἰησοῦς ἀνήχθη εἰς τὴν ἔρημον **ὑπὸ** τοῦ πνεύματος πειρασθῆναι **ὑπὸ** τοῦ διαβόλου
"Then Jesus was led away by the Spirit into the desert to be tempted by the devil."

Gal 1:11 τὸ εὐαγγέλιον τὸ εὐαγγελισθὲν **ὑπ'** ἐμοῦ
"the gospel that I preached"

2. Used of Things (denoting causation)

Lk 7:24 Τί ἐξήλθατε εἰς τὴν ἔρημον θεάσασθαι; κάλαμον **ὑπὸ** ἀνέμου σαλευόμενον;
"What did you go out into the desert to see? A reed swayed by/as a result of the wind?"

Ro 12:21 μὴ νικῶ **ὑπὸ** τοῦ κακοῦ
"Do not be overcome by evil" (ὑπό is stronger than the simple dative).

2Co 5:4 ἵνα καταποθῇ τὸ θνητὸν **ὑπὸ** τῆς ζωῆς
"so that what is mortal may be swallowed up by life"

A personified ζωή could allude to the resurrected Christ as "a life-giving spirit" (1Co 15:45) or to the Spirit in his revivifying role (Ro 8:2, 11; 2Co 3:6).

In Classical Greek, observes Smyth, "ὑπό with the genitive of a thing personifies the thing. The things so personified are (1) words implying a person, as λόγοι, (2) external circumstances, as ... νόμος, (3) natural phenomena, as χειμών, (4) emotions, as φθόνος" (§1698 n.1). The same is true in the NT, as the following examples illustrate: (1) Col 2:18, **ὑπὸ** τοῦ νοός; (2) Ro 3:21, **ὑπὸ** τοῦ νόμου; (3) Mt 14:24, **ὑπὸ** τῶν κυμάτων; (4) Jas 1:14, **ὑπὸ** τῆς ἰδίας ἐπιθυμίας.

D. Ὑπὸ νόμον

All 11 NT uses of this phrase are Pauline, all are anarthrous, and all are used with a form of εἶναι expressed or implied (except for Gal 3:23, **ὑπὸ** νόμον ἐφρουρούμεθα, and Gal 4:4, γενόμενον **ὑπὸ** νόμον). Efforts to find a consistent distinction between ὁ νόμος and νόμος have not been successful, so that in itself ὑπὸ νόμον could mean "under law/a law/any law" or "under the law." Only the context will indicate whether the reference is to: (1) the Torah/Pentateuch; (2)

the era of the Mosaic law; (3) the OT as a whole; (4) a norm/legislated standard; (5) a legal system; (6) a principle; or (7) legalism/nomism. It is also relevant to remember that the expression ὑπό τινα εἶναι means "be under someone's power" (BDAG 1036c), denoting subordination under some controlling person or personified entity. Accordingly, if (as is probable) Paul regarded ἁμαρτία and νόμος as personified powers, ὑφ᾽ ἁμαρτίαν εἶναι in Ro 3:9 will mean "being under the control of sin" (Goodspeed; "in subjection to sin," TCNT; "under the power of sin," NIV²), and ὑπὸ νόμον εἶναι could mean "be under the control of the law" or "be in bondage to the law."

Here are suggested paraphrases of each of the 11 instances of ὑπὸ νόμον, made in light of the above comments and each distinct context. The first two instances stand in contrast to ὑπὸ χάριν.

Ro 6:14 "For sin shall no longer control you, because you do not live *under the rule of the Mosaic law* but under the sway of God's grace."

Ro 6:15 "What follows, then? Are we to sin because we do not live *under the reign of the law* but under the control of God's grace? Certainly not!"

1Co 9:20 "To Jews I have become like a Jew, in order to win over the Jews. To those *subject to Jewish law* I have become like someone *subject to Jewish law*—though I am **not** *subject to Jewish law* myself—in order to win over those who **are** *subject to Jewish law*."

Gal 3:23 "Before this faith made its appearance, we were held in protective custody and kept prisoners *under the watchful eye of the law*, until this coming faith would be revealed."

Gal 4:4–5 "But when the appointed time had come, God sent his Son, born as a Jewish woman's child and so born as someone *living under Jewish law*, in order to redeem those who stood *under the condemnation of the law*, so that we might receive our adopted status as God's sons."

Gal 4:21 "Tell me this, you who are eager *to have the Mosaic law as your master*: Do you pay no attention to what that law says?"

Gal 5:18 "But if you are led by the Spirit's guidance, you are not *under the restrictive yoke of the Mosaic law*."

E. Ὑπό and Other Prepositions Expressing Agency

There are several ways in which agency is expressed in the NT: ὑπό (1Th 1:4), διά with the genitive (1Co 1:9), ἀπό (2Co 3:18b), ἐκ (Gal 4:4), ἐν (Mt 9:34), the simple dative (Mt 6:1), and possibly (see below) παρά with the genitive.

1. Ὑπό and διά

It cannot be maintained that while διά denotes the inanimate instrument, ὑπό specifies the personal agent, for διά may express personal agency (e.g., δι᾽ ἡμῶν,

2Co 1:19) and ὑπό may be used of inanimate agencies (e.g., ὑπὸ μεριμνῶν, Lk 8:14), nonhuman agents (e.g., ὑπὸ τῶν θηρίων, Rev 6:8), or personified forces (e.g., ὑπὸ ἀνέμων, Jude 12). Where the two prepositions may be distinguished, διά marks intermediate agency and ὑπό ultimate, original, or direct agency. Thus in Mt 1:22 the Lord as the ultimate author (ὑπὸ κυρίου) of the prophetic word is distinguished from the prophet Isaiah, who acted as a mediate agent (διὰ τοῦ προφήτου) in speaking the divine word. Compare the similar distinction between primary origin and subordinate agency in the ἐκ (of God the Father)–διά (of Jesus Christ) contrast in 1Cor 8:6 with regard to creation (see ch. 7 B).

2. Ὑπό and ἀπό

The distinction here, when it applies, is that between immediate and active causation (ὑπό) and more remote and less active causation (ἀπό), between the direct and indirect origination of an action (cf. BDAG 107b), between an internal and an external causal relation (cf. Buttmann 325), or between the efficient cause and the occasional cause ("that from which a result ensued") (Winer 369). In such cases ἀπό may be rendered "at the hands of" (e.g., ἀπὸ τῶν πρεσβυτέρων, Mt 16:21; cf. 2Co 7:13), "by the will/command of" (e.g., ἀπὸ τοῦ θεοῦ, Rev 12:6), or "as a result of" (e.g., ἀπὸ τῶν τριῶν πληγῶν τούτων, Rev 9:18). But that ἀπό occasionally stands for ὑπό seems incontestable (see, e.g., Lk 6:18b; 7:35; 8:43b; Ac 2:22; 15:4, 33; 20:9). On ἀπό in Jas 1:13 see ch. 6 B.

3. Ὑπό and παρά

Whereas παρά traces an action back to its point of departure or source, ὑπό relates an action to its efficient cause (Winer 365). Only rarely does παρά replace ὑπό. Παρὰ κυρίου ἐγένετο αὕτη (Mt 21:42) probably means "the Lord has done this" (as in Ps 117:23 LXX). In Lk 1:45, whether παρὰ κυρίου is construed with τελείωσις or with τοῖς λελαλημένοις, agency may here be expressed by παρά. Then there are the minor textual variants in Mk 10:40, Ac 10:33, and Ac 22:30, where παρά replaces ὑπό. Nevertheless, it is doubtful whether ἄνθρωπος ἀπεσταλμένος παρὰ θεοῦ in Jn 1:6 means "a man sent by God" (so, apparently, Robertson 534, 615; but cf. his earlier Pictures 5:8) as opposed to "a man sent from God" (so most EVV). Similarly in Jn 17:7 πάντα ὅσα δέδωκάς μοι παρὰ σοῦ εἰσιν could be rendered "everything you have given me is [given] by you [= is your gift]" (cf. Robertson 820), but "everything you have given me comes from you" seems a preferable rendering. (However understood, the statement is intentionally tautological, emphasizing Jesus' dependence on his Father).

Observing that ἀπό, ἐκ, παρά, and ὑπό all denote "issuing, proceeding from," Winer ranges these four prepositions in the following order with regard to the degree of intimacy of connection between the objects in question, ἐκ denoting the most intimate and ἀπό the most remote connection: ἐκ, ὑπό, παρά, ἀπό. Only ἀπό and ἐκ directly imply "disjoining"and "removal" (Winer 364–65).

F. Ὑπό in Compounds

Compounds of ὑπό that have survived in Modern Greek have mostly been changed to ἀπο- (e.g., ἀπομονή; Jannaris §1508).

1. Position ("under"): ὑποζύγιον (lit., "under the yoke"), donkey
   ὑπηρέτης, underling, assistant
   ὑπωπιάζω, strike under the eye; wear down, punish
2. Motion ("up"): ὑποζώννυμι, gird up, undergird, brace
   ὑπολαμβάνω, take up, reply, suppose
   ὑποπλέω, sail close up to (= under the lee of an island)
3. Subjection: ὑπείκω, submit (to someone's authority)
   ὑποτάσσω, subordinate
   ὑπέχω, undergo punishment
4. Secrecy (cf. "underhand"): ὑποβάλλω, instigate secretly

Chapter 21

Prepositions with Βαπτίζω

Four prepositions can follow the verb βαπτίζω. The meaning and significance of these prepositions is not substantially altered whether the verb βαπτίζω is taken to mean "dip," "dip under = immerse," or "drench," or whether the appropriate mode of baptism is thought to be immersion, effusion, or aspersion.

A. Ὑπέρ
1 Corinthians 15:29

Ἐπεὶ τί ποιήσουσιν οἱ βαπτιζόμενοι ὑπὲρ τῶν νεκρῶν; εἰ ὅλως νεκροὶ οὐκ ἐγείρονται, τί καὶ βαπτίζονται ὑπὲρ αὐτῶν;

"Otherwise, what do those people imagine they are doing who are baptized for the dead? If the dead are not raised at all, why then are people baptized for them?"

First Corinthians 15:1–34 treat the *that* of resurrection (ὅτι, vv. 4, 12), and vv. 35–58 the *how* of the resurrection (πῶς, v. 35). Paul first enunciates the premise he shares with his opponents, namely, the resurrection of Christ (vv. 1–11), and then proceeds to draw a conclusion from this premise, that the dead in Christ will rise (vv. 12–32). At the end of this latter section he gives two ad hominem arguments supporting this conclusion (baptism for the dead [v. 29]; apostolic peril and labor [vv. 30–32]), and then adds a warning to avoid bad company and conduct (vv. 33–34).

To be satisfactory, any proposed interpretation of the crucial phrases ὑπὲρ τῶν νεκρῶν and ὑπὲρ αὐτῶν must meet two requirements: (a) ὑπέρ should not be given a sense unparalleled in the Greek Bible (since the customary meanings of the preposition afford suitable senses); (b) the resulting meaning of the verse should contribute to Paul's argument in the chapter. It is highly improbable, for example, that ὑπέρ means "in memory of" or "out of respect for"; that ὑπέρ has a local sense, "over [the graves of] the dead"; or that οἱ βαπτιζόμενοι refers to all new converts who were, by their baptismal incorporation into the church, filling up the ranks (ὑπέρ) left depleted by Christian martyrs (οἱ νεκροί).

M. Raeder gives ὑπέρ a final sense: converts to Christianity were having themselves baptized *in order to be united with* their departed relatives and friends at the resurrection.[1] More probably, some baptized Corinthians who had a semi-magical view of baptism were having themselves rebaptized vicariously for certain deceased Christians (the articular οἱ νεκροί presents no difficulty for this view) who were thought to be at a disadvantage because they had not been baptized before being overtaken by death. On this interpretation Paul is using an ad hominem argument in support of a conclusion already established (that the dead in Christ will rise) and is appealing to an aberrant practice (otherwise unknown to us in first-century Christianity), without giving it his approval. (That Paul could argue *ex concessis* is evident from 1Co 8:10; cf. 10:20–21).

The sense of the verse seems to be: "Otherwise [i.e., if there is no resurrection of the Christian dead] what do those people imagine they are doing who are going to the trouble of having themselves baptized in the place of, and so for the benefit of, certain unbaptized deceased believers?" We saw above (ch. 19 F) that when ὑπέρ is followed by a personal referent, it may occasionally express both advantage and substitution.[2]

B. Ὑπό

There are seven instances of βαπτίζεσθαι ὑπό in the NT, all in the Synoptic Gospels (Mt 3:6 [= Mk 1:5], 13, 14; Mk 1:9; Lk 3:7; 7:30), in which the preposition points to the personal agent administering the rite of water baptism and the verb means "be baptized" or (as BDAG 1036a [cf. 164b] proposes for Mt 3:6, 13; Mk 1:5, 9) "allow oneself to be baptized" (cf. Turner 57) = "submit to baptism." It was probably John the Baptist's personal administration of the rite that in part accounted for his title, ὁ βαπτιστής (lit., "the one who dips," Mt 3:1) or ὁ βαπτίζων (Mk 1:4) (Jewish proselytes immersed themselves in the presence of two or [later] three rabbis who constituted a court).

C. Εἰς

1. Two Important Passages

a. Matthew 3:11

ἐγὼ μὲν ὑμᾶς βαπτίζω ἐν ὕδατι εἰς μετάνοιαν

"I indeed am baptizing you in water *on* your [profession of] repentance."

---

1. M. Raeder, "Vikariatstaufe in Kor. 15:29?" *Zeitschrift für die Neutestamentliche Wissenschaft* 46 (1955): 258–60.
2. For the history of the interpretation of this verse, see M. Rissi, *Die Taufe für die Toten* (Zürich: Zwingli, 1962), and, more recently, A. C. Thiselton, *The First Epistle to the Corinthians* (NIGTC; Grand Rapids: Eerdmans, 2000), 1242–49, who himself supports "ὑπέρ as final."

From a grammatical point of view, εἰς here may be:

- telic — "with a view to, for"
- consecutive — "resulting in"
- *temporal (εἰς = ἐν) — "on [your profession of]" (cf. Mt 3:6, where the participle ἐξομολογούμενοι suggests the simultaneity of baptism and confession of sin [= repentance] in John the Baptist's baptism)
- referential — "with regard to" (elsewhere John's baptism is termed a "baptism of [= relating to/marked by] repentance," a "repentance baptism," βάπτισμα μετανοίας, Mk 1:4; Lk 3:3; Ac 13:24; 19:4)

b. Acts 2:38

μετανοήσατε καὶ βαπτισθήτω ἕκαστος ὑμῶν ἐπὶ τῷ ὀνόματι Ἰησοῦ Χριστοῦ **εἰς** ἄφεσιν τῶν ἁμαρτιῶν ὑμῶν

"Repent and be baptized, each one of you, in the name of Jesus Christ *upon* the forgiveness of your sins."

From a grammatical point of view, εἰς (which qualifies both μετανοήσατε and βαπτισθήτω) here may be:

- telic — "with a view to, for"
- consecutive — "resulting in"
- *temporal (εἰς = ἐν) — "on/upon" (in this case forgiveness is being regarded as *conceptually* [but not necessarily chronologically] coincident with repentance and baptism)
- referential — "with regard to"

From the book of Acts we may deduce that there are five components in the brief or prolonged process of Christian initiation — repentance, faith, baptism, forgiveness of sins, and receipt of the Spirit. Each element is an essential ingredient in the whole, which forms a single conceptual unity. Accordingly, when any one or two elements are mentioned in Scripture, apparently in isolation, the others are presupposed. For example, in Ac 16:31, 33 ("Believe in the Lord Jesus, and you will be saved — you and your household … he and all his family were baptized"), the Philippian jailer's repentance is presupposed and presumably his being "saved" involved forgiveness and receipt of the Spirit. Similarly, in 1Pe 3:21 ("baptism now saves you") the readers are assumed to have experienced the other four aspects of Christian initiation.

In seeking to formulate the relation between the five elements, we are probably wiser to speak in terms of concomitance rather than causation (as if, e.g., baptism as a rite automatically produced salvation), since salvation from first to last results from God's action. But whereas repentance and faith are prerequisites for receiving forgiveness and the Spirit (cf. Ac 20:21), baptism seems to be a natural and necessary concomitant of repentance and faith and therefore of the receipt of forgiveness and the Spirit. See the summary of the data of Acts in the chart below that shows the variation in the relation of baptism to receipt of the Spirit in the early spread of Christianity.

The Five Elements in Acts (by sequence)

Passage	Repentance	Faith	Baptism	Forgiveness	Spirit
2:38	1		2	3	4
2:41		1	2		
3:19 (cf. Lk 24:47)	1			2	
8:12, 14–17		1	2		3
9:17–18		1	3		2
22:14–16		1	2	3	
10:44–48		1	3		2
16:31–34		1	2		
19:1–6		1	2		3

2. Two Key Phrases

a. (Βαπτίζεσθαι) εἰς τὸ ὄνομά τινος

There are three principal views about the significance of this phrase, summarized here in descending order of probability.

(1) It may denote the establishment of a relationship of belonging and possession, and so a transference of ownership, as when money is paid "[in]to the account of" an individual whose name stands over the account or is credited "to the name" of someone in banking transactions or commercial sales. The person who is baptized is transferred into the possession of another.[3]

(2) The phrase arose as a Greek rendering of a Semitic expression (Heb. *ľšēm* or Aram. *ľšûm*) used in the OT, Mishnah, and Talmud, with the basic meaning "with respect to," but with a wide variety of applications (see SB 1:1054–55). It denotes the fundamental reference or purpose of some thing, rite, or action (εἰς is regularly used this way). Baptism "with respect to" Jesus was a "Jesus baptism," a baptism fundamentally determined by the person and work of Jesus, which distinguished Christian baptism from other rites, especially John the Baptist's baptism.[4]

---

3. See W. Heitmüller, *Im Namen Jesu* (Göttingen: Vandenhoeck & Ruprecht, 1903), 100–127.

4. See L. Hartman, "'Into the Name of Jesus': A Suggestion concerning the Earliest Meaning of the Phrase," *NTS* 20 (1973–74): 432–40; idem, "Baptism 'Into the Name of Jesus' and Early Christology: Some Tentative Considerations," *Studia Theologica* 28 (1974): 21–48; *EDNT* 2:522b.

(3) Since the salvific work of Jesus is inextricably linked to his name, "to baptize into the name of the Lord Jesus" means to endow a person through baptism with the benefits of the salvation accomplished by Jesus Christ.[5]

So then, when the phrase εἰς τὸ ὄνομα is used with βαπτίζω, the person being baptized is viewed as passing into the secure possession and "dedicated protection" (BDAG 713b) of the triune God (Mt 28:19) or the Lord Jesus (Ac 8:16; 19:5; cf. 1Co 1:13, 15, where a putative baptism into Paul's name is equated with belonging to Paul). These are the five NT uses of the phrase.

It is a remarkable fact that the NT records no case of baptism in the triune name, only of baptism "into the name of the Lord Jesus" (Ac 8:16; 19:5) or "in the name of Jesus Christ" (2:38; 10:48). We may explain this apparent anomaly by observing that the Lukan formulas, abbreviated forms of the Matthean, may not indicate the precise words used in Christian baptisms — actually the trinitarian form — but rather may highlight the point that in the baptismal "transference of ownership" a person becomes the property of Christ and his slave (cf. Ro 1:1; 1Co 6:19b–20; 7:22–23) and may reflect the fact that in the baptismal ceremony, "the name of Christ is pronounced, invoked and confessed by the one who baptises or the one baptised (Ac 22:16) or both" (A. Oepke, *TDNT* 1:539–40).

b. (Βαπτίζεσθαι) εἰς Χριστὸν (Ἰησοῦν)

This expression, found in Ro 6:3 and Gal 3:27a, may simply mean "with reference to Christ," pointing to the invocation of Christ by the person being baptized (Ac 22:16) and/or the baptizer. Both כְּ (BDB 512c–16d; see above, 2.a) and εἰς (BDAG 291a) can mean "with reference to." But more probably the phrase should be taken as brachylogy for:

- "into the body of Christ," the church (cf. 1Co 12:12, where ὁ Χριστός = the body of Christ)
- *"into the name of Christ," where εἰς Χριστόν = εἰς τὸ ὄνομα τοῦ Χριστοῦ, just as in commercial usage ἐν with the name can be a substitute for εἰς [τὸ] ὄνομα (H. Bietenhard, *TDNT* 5:245, 275, referring to Mayser 415)
- "into union/fellowship with Christ." Support for this expansion may be found in the immediate context of Galatians 3, where εἰς Χριστόν is redefined, first as "putting on Christ" (3:27b), then as "being in Christ" (3:28).

The second view, which corresponds to 2.a.(1) above, is to be preferred. If so, the ideas of belonging, protection, and submission that are attached to the full phrase εἰς τὸ ὄνομα also adhere to the abbreviated version, εἰς Χριστόν.

---

5. See G. Delling, *Die Zueignung des Heils in der Taufe* (Berlin: Evangelische Verlagsanstalt, 1961), esp. 97.

3. Other Uses of Βαπτίζεσθαι εἰς

Mk 1:9 εἰς τὸν Ἰορδάνην may denote the element into which Jesus was plunged, but more probably εἰς = ἐν ("in the Jordan").

Ro 6:3b To be baptized "into the death " (εἰς τὸν θάνατον) of Christ Jesus is to participate in all the benefits of his "death in relation to sin" (τῇ ἁμαρτίᾳ ἀπέθανεν, Ro 6:10).

1Co 10:2 Whether we read ἐβαπτίσθησαν or ἐβαπτίσαντο (see Metzger 493), εἰς τὸν Μωϋσῆν indicates that identification with Moses or allegiance to him as leader was the goal and outcome (εἰς) of the Israelites' baptism or submission to baptism.

1Co 12:13 ἡμεῖς πάντες εἰς ἓν σῶμα ἐβαπτίσθημεν. First, since ἓν σῶμα cannot refer only to the church at Corinth, ἡμεῖς πάντες will not mean "all you Corinthians and I," but must refer to all believers, including Paul. Second, since the one body *with its many parts* did not exist before the baptism of all believers ἐν ἑνὶ πνεύματι (on this phrase see D, below), εἰς in 12:13 will mean "so as to form," not "so as to participate in." Incorporation into the one body of Christ is the purpose and effect, the "aim sought and accomplished" (A. Oepke, *TDNT* 1:539) (εἰς), of "baptism in the Spirit."

D. Ἐν

Generally ἐν has a local sense when it is used with βαπτίζω:

- ἐν τῷ Ἰορδάνῃ, "in the [river] Jordan" (Mt 3:6; Mk 1:5 [= εἰς τὸν Ἰορδάνην, Mk 1:9])
- ἐν τῇ ἐρήμῳ, "in the desert" (Mk 1:4)
- ἐν Αἰνών, "in Aenon" (Jn 3:23)
- ἐν τῇ νεφέλῃ καὶ ἐν τῇ θαλάσσῃ, "in the cloud and in the sea" (1Co 10:2)

Ἐν ὕδατι denotes the element *in* which the baptized were "immersed" or *with* which they were "drenched" (Mt 3:11; Jn 1:26, 31, 33; cf. the simple dative ὕδατι in the following places—Mk 1:8.; Lk 3:16; Ac 1:5; 11:16).

So also with the phrase (ἐν) πνεύματι (ἁγίῳ), which is generally contrasted with (ἐν) ὕδατι (Mt 3:11; Mk 1:8; Lk 3:16; Jn 1:33; Ac 1:5; 11:16): believers are either immersed *in* the Spirit or drenched *with* the Spirit.

1 Corinthians 12:13 (also see C. 3, above)

καὶ γὰρ ἐν ἑνὶ πνεύματι ἡμεῖς πάντες εἰς ἓν σῶμα ἐβαπτίσθημεν, εἴτε Ἰουδαῖοι εἴτε Ἕλληνες εἴτε δοῦλοι εἴτε ἐλεύθεροι, καὶ πάντες ἓν πνεῦμα ἐποτίσθημεν

"For indeed we were all baptized in the one Spirit to form one body—whether we are Jews or Gentiles, whether slaves or free—and we were all given one and the same Spirit to imbibe."

EVV are evenly divided in their rendering of ἐν ἑνὶ πνεύματι:

- "by [the] one Spirit" (KJV, TCNT, Moffatt, RSV, NASB[1,2], GNB, NIV[1,2] [with a footnote, "Or *with*; or *in*"], Cassirer, NLT, HCSB; instrumental ἐν expressing agency)
- "in (the) one Spirit" (RV, Weymouth, Goodspeed, NAB[1,2], NEB, JB, NJB ["in a single Spirit"], NRSV, REB, ESV; locatival ἐν expressing the sphere or realm). It is noteworthy that the NRSV has replaced the RSV's "by" with "in"

There is no doubt that ἐν πνεύματι can express the agency of the Spirit in Paul (Ro 2:29; 1Co 12:3 [2x]; 14:16; Eph 2:22; 3:5; 4:30), but there are several reasons for preferring the second translation. To doubt whether ἐν is instrumental in 1Co 12:13 is not, of course, to deny the personality of the Spirit.

1. Elsewhere ὑπό expresses personal agency with βαπτίζεσθαι (see B, above).
2. There is no certain instance of an instrumental ἐν with βαπτίζεσθαι. In the other examples of ἐν πνεύματι with βαπτίζεσθαι, the parallel with (ἐν) ὕδατι dictates that ἐν should mean "in" or "with," not "by [means of]" — denoting the "sphere" or "material" (Mt 3:11; Mk 1:8; Lk 3:16; Jn 1:33; Ac 1:5; 11:16), but not the agent.
3. In the logia of John the Baptist regarding "Spirit baptism," it is always Jesus who is the baptizer, never the Spirit. Accordingly, in 1Co 12:13, the agent should be taken as implied (i.e., Jesus Christ).
4. In the one place Paul uses ἐν with βαπτίζω (1Co 10:2), the preposition is local in sense ("in the cloud and in the sea").
5. The following phrase, "and we were all given one and the same Spirit to imbibe," suggests an inward participation in the Spirit to which a preceding outward "immersion in the Spirit" would correspond. The Spirit is both around believers (v. 13a) and within them (v. 13b; cf. Eph 5:18).
6. The parallel ἐν ἑνὶ πνεύματι in Eph 2:18 cannot be an instrumental use of ἐν, since δι' αὐτοῦ (= Christ) precedes. However, ἐν τῷ ἑνὶ πνεύματι in 1Co 12:9 is undoubtedly instrumental in sense, in light of the preceding διὰ τοῦ πνεύματος (12:8; cf. vv. 7, 8b, 11).

The focus in the verse is on believers' common and universal experience (πάντες ... πάντες) of the Spirit that creates unity out of diversity (cf. v. 12). Verse 13 explains how the many diverse parts of the body of Christ are constituted a single entity — it is by their immersion in one and the same Spirit (ἐν ἑνὶ πνεύματι) and by their deriving spiritual nourishment from a single source, the Spirit (ἓν πνεῦμα).

E. Ἐν/ἐπὶ τῷ ὀνόματι

Some scholars find no distinction between εἰς τὸ ὄνομα, ἐν τῷ ὀνόματι, and ἐπὶ τῷ ὀνόματι after βαπτίζω,[6] each meaning "in the name of." Others distinguish εἰς (= Heb. *lᵉ*, "with regard to") both from ἐν (= Hebrew *bᵉ*, "on the authority of") and from ἐπί ("resting on" or "devoted to" the name [= person] of Christ).[7]

A mediating position between these two extremes is defensible. We have dealt with the probable meaning of εἰς τὸ ὄνομα above (C.2.a), i.e., "into the name of" = " into the possession and protection of." The other two phrases, ἐν τῷ ὀνόματι (Ac 10:48; cf. 2:38 *v.l.*) and ἐπὶ τῷ ὀνόματι (2:38), often have an identical meaning in the LXX, especially with verbs such as "bless," "swear," or "speak." For example, with λαλέω we find ἐπὶ τῷ σῷ ὀνόματι (Ex 5:23) and ἐν ὀνόματι κυρίου (Zec 13:3); or ἐπὶ τῷ ὀνόματί μου is closely followed by ἐν τῷ ὀνόματι Δαυίδ in 1Kgdms 25:5, 9.

Similarly, when these two expressions are used with βαπτίζω in the NT, no distinction between them should be pressed: both mean "in the name of" = "with use of the name of"/"while naming the name of" (cf. BDAG 713a, 713d–14a), referring to the baptismal candidate's calling on the name of Jesus Christ in a confession of faith and also to the administrant's invocation of Jesus as the authenticating authority for and witness to the rite. If this is the case, both ἐν and ἐπί here describe an accompanying circumstance, so that these two prepositional expressions depict the administration or operation of the baptismal rite, just as εἰς τὸ ὄνομα portrays its nature and goal. Two other passages are relevant at this point.

1. Acts 22:16

ἀναστὰς βάπτισαι καὶ ἀπόλουσαι τὰς ἁμαρτίας σου **ἐπικαλεσάμενος τὸ ὄνομα αὐτοῦ**

"Get up, have yourself baptized, and get your sins washed away, *as you invoke his* [the Lord's] *name.*"

Ἐπικαλεσάμενος is not a modal participle attached only to ἀπόλουσαι; rather, it depicts circumstances attendant on both the baptism (βάπτισαι) and the removal of sin (ἀπόλουσαι).

2. Ephesians 5:20

εὐχαριστοῦντες πάντοτε ὑπὲρ πάντων **ἐν ὀνόματι** τοῦ κυρίου ἡμῶν Ἰησοῦ Χριστοῦ τῷ θεῷ καὶ πατρί

"always giving thanks to God the Father for everything, *while naming the name of the Lord Jesus Christ*" (BDAG 713c; cf. Jas 5:14)

---

6. E.g., S. New, "The Name, Baptism, and the Laying on of Hands," in *The Beginnings of Christianity* (ed. K. Lake and H. J. Cadbury; London; Macmillan, 1933), 5:123 n.3.
7. E.g., R. Abba, "Name," in *Interpreter's Dictionary of the Bible* (ed. G. A. Buttrick; Nashville: Abingdon, 1972), 3:507a.

Chapter 22

Prepositions with Πιστεύω and Πίστις[1]

Apart from the many instances where πιστεύω is used absolutely (a rare use in the LXX; e.g., Isa 7:9; 28:16) — either in a religious sense (= πίστιν ἔχειν, "have faith," e.g., Mk 5:36; 9:23–24; 2Co 4:13; or "have faith [in Christ]," e.g., Jn 3:18b; Ac 2:44; 2Th 1:10) or in a nonreligious sense ("give credence," Mk 13:21; Lk 22:67) — there are a number of constructions with this verb and noun that occur in the NT.

A. Nonprepositional Constructions

1. **Accusative of the thing**, where the verb means "believe, convinced of" (Jn 11:26b; 1Co 11:18; 13:7; 1Jn 4:16) or "entrust" (Lk 16:11; and with the "retained accusative" after a passive, Ro 3:2; Gal 2:7; 1Th 2:4; 1Ti 1:11; Tit 1:3) or **accusative of the person**, where the verb means "entrust" (Jn 2:24)
2. **Accusative and infinitive** (Ac 8:37 *v.l.*; cf. 15:11)
3. **Infinitive** (Ro 14:2), where πιστεύει means "has confidence" or "has [sufficiently strong] faith [to eat]"
4. **Ὅτι** (= Heb. *heʼᵉmin kî*), with the verb signifying "believe that, be convinced that" (Lk 1:45; Jn 20:31a; Ro 6:8; 10:9; 1Th 4:14; Jas 2:19a)
5. **Dative with ὅτι** following (Jn 4:21; Ac 27:25)
6. **Dative** (= Heb. *heʼᵉmin lᵉ or bᵉ;* see Johannessohn, 1:60–61) of the thing believed (Lk 1:20; Jn 4:50; Ac 24:14) or the person believed. In the latter category the sense of πιστεύω will range from "give credence to [the testimony of]" men or God (e.g., Mk 11:31; Jn 6:30; Ac 8:12;

---

1. For a convenient analysis of the meaning of πιστεύω and πίστις in Classical Greek, the LXX, and the Pseudepigrapha, see Burton, *Commentary on the Epistle to the Galatians,* 475–78. A chart that classifies NT constructions used with πιστεύω (when it is not used absolutely and does not mean "entrust") may be found in Moulton 68 n. 2, although some of the statistics mentioned below differ slightly.

26:27a; 1Jn 5:10b) to "entrust oneself to" God (Ac 16:34; Tit 3:8) or Christ (e.g., Jn 8:31; 2Ti 1:12)

B. Prepositional Constructions

1. **Περί** with ὅτι following (Jn 9:18).

2. **Πρός**. In Phm 5 it is probable that the εἰς phrase modifies τὴν ἀγάπην and πρὸς τὸν κύριον Ἰησοῦν modifies τὴν πίστιν in an instance of chiasmus (ABBA; so BDF §477[2]; Robertson 1200; Turner, *Style* 97): "your love for [εἰς] all of God's people and the faith which you have in [πρός] the Lord Jesus" (GNB). Again, in 1Th 1:8 the phrase πρὸς τὸν θεόν depicts the object of πίστις, although such a construction is rare in the LXX (4Mc 15:24; 16:22). Πρός is never used with πιστεύω in Biblical Greek.

3. **Ἐν**. Each of the three possible instances of ἐν with πιστεύω is contested. (a) It is unlikely that πιστεύετε is absolute in Mk 1:15 (πιστεύετε ἐν τῷ εὐαγγελίῳ), with ἐν meaning "in the sphere of"[2] or "by means of" or "on the basis of" since there are several LXX instances (Jer 12:6; Pss 77:22, 32 *v.l*; 105:12; Da 6:24 Theod.; cf. 1Kgdms 27:12) in which ἐν after πιστεύω introduces the object of faith. The verse may be translated "believe the good news" or "put your trust in the Good News" (Cassirer). Regard (339) paraphrases thus: believe "in the truth of the substance of the Gospel."

(b) The uncertainty in Jn 3:15 (ἵνα πᾶς ὁ πιστεύων ἐν αὐτῷ ἔχῃ ζωὴν αἰώνιον) is both textual and exegetical. 𝔓75 B Wsupp 083 0113 *al* read ἐν αὐτῷ, while ἐπ' αὐτῷ is read by 𝔓66 L; εἰς αὐτόν has wide geographical support, and ἐπ' αὐτόν is the reading of 𝔓63vid A. In addition, ἐν αὐτῷ may be taken with what precedes or what follows. The textual choice is between εἰς αὐτόν and ἐν αὐτῷ, but the strong proto-Alexandrian combination of 𝔓75 B favors the latter reading (cf. Metzger 175).

On the exegetical issue, ἐν αὐτῷ probably belongs with ἔχῃ ζωὴν αἰώνιον, since (i) εἰς regularly follows πιστεύω in the fourth gospel (33x; note esp. Jn 3:16b), but ἐν never follows πιστεύω elsewhere; (ii) πιστεύω often stands absolutely in this gospel (see BDAG 817d); and (iii) Jn 20:31 is a close parallel: ἵνα πιστεύοντες ζωὴν ἔχητε ἐν τῷ ὀνόματι αὐτοῦ, "that through believing you may have life in reliance on his name." So Jn 3:15 may be rendered "that everyone who believes may have eternal life in reliance on him."

(c) Finally, in Eph 1:13 ἐν ᾧ καί should be construed not with πιστεύσαντες but with ἐσφραγίσθητε ("Through your very union with him [Christ] you were sealed with the Holy Spirit of promise when you believed"), since (i) in v. 11 also ἐν ᾧ καί is attached to the finite verb, not the participle; and (ii) πιστεύω ἐν is not used elsewhere in Paul.

(d) In the four clear cases where ἐν is to be construed with πίστις (Eph 1:15;

---

2. G. A. Deissmann, *Die neutestamentliche Formel "In Christo Jesu"* (Marburg: Elwert, 1892), 46–47; and note Moulton's change of mind on the matter (Moulton 67–68; MH 464).

Col 1:4; 1Ti 3:13; 2Ti 3:15; but probably not in Ro 3:25 and Gal 3:26 [see RV, NRSV, and REB on these two verses]), the prepositional phrase is as likely to mark the sphere or realm in which faith was operative and evident as to specify the actual object of faith (cf. Moule 81). For example, in Col 1:4, τὴν πίστιν ὑμῶν ἐν Χριστῷ Ἰησοῦ may be rendered "your faith in/directed toward Christ Jesus" (= πίστιν εἰς Χριστὸν Ἰησοῦν = πίστιν Χριστοῦ Ἰησοῦ), but since Paul expresses the object of faith unambiguously in Col 2:5 by τὸ στερέωμα τῆς εἰς Χριστὸν πίστεως ὑμῶν, and in Phm 5 by τὴν πίστιν ἣν ἔχεις πρὸς τὸν κύριον (cf. 1Th 1:8) and seems immune from the Hellenistic Greek tendency to confuse ἐν and εἰς (see ch. 8 C), perhaps the sense is "your faith as those who are in Christ Jesus" or "your faith experienced in fellowship with Christ Jesus."

4. Διά. (a) In reference to *persons*, διά with the genitive (δι᾿ αὐτοῦ or δι᾿ ὧν) expresses the human or divine agent by which persons come to faith in Christ or God.

- With πιστεύω: Jn 1:7, of John the Baptist, and 1Co 3:5, of Paul and Apollos: both with Christ as the implied object of faith
- With πίστις: Ac 3:16, of Jesus, with God as the implied object of faith (cf. 1Pe 1:21, [ὑμᾶς] τοὺς δι᾿ αὐτοῦ πιστοὺς εἰς θεόν)

(b) In reference to *things*, διά with the accusative expresses the reason or basis for belief.

- **Jn 4:41** "Because of his words [διὰ τὸν λόγον αὐτοῦ] many more became believers"
- **Jn 4:42** "We no longer believe simply because of what you said [διὰ τὴν σὴν λαλιάν]"
- **Jn 14:11** "Or at least believe on the basis of the works themselves [διὰ τὰ ἔργα αὐτά]"

5. Ἐπί with dative. Four times this construction (with πιστεύω) is used with a personal object (Ro 9:33; 10:11; 1Pe 2:6 [these three verses being citations of Isa 28:16 LXX]; 1Ti 1:16; see also the textual variants in Mt 27:42 and Jn 3:15), once with an impersonal object (Lk 24:25 where ἐπί means "on the basis of," BDF §187[6]). In the former four cases, πιστεύω ἐπί denotes the placing of one's complete reliance and trust on a person (Christ) who affords a firm support or a solid foundation (ἐπί = "resting on").

6. Ἐπί with accusative. The idea of metaphorical movement (ἐπί = "directed toward," Regard 465) implied in the seven instances that occur with πιστεύω (Mt 27:42; Ac 9:42; 11:17; 16:31; 22:19; Ro 4:5, 24; cf. Wis 12:2) and the one example with πίστις (Heb 6:1) may derive from the notion of turning away from former objects of devotion that brought disappointment to a new personal object of faith in whom one has confidence. It usually refers to the initial act of conversion. Wisdom 12:2 and Isa 28:16 are the only LXX uses of πιστεύω ἐπί.

7. **Εἰς with accusative.** Examples of this construction with πιστεύω, which is perhaps modeled on the Hebrew *he'emin b* (not on the Greek ἐπιστρέφω ἐπί or πρός), are lacking in Classical Greek, the LXX (but see Sir 38:31),[3] and the papyri (Mayser 257); πιστεύω εἰς "is an original NT construction" (A. Oepke, *TDNT* 2:432). In the NT it is a characteristically Johannine idiom, with only nine of the 45 NT uses being found outside the fourth gospel and 1 John (Mt 18:6; Mk 9:42; Ac 10:43; 14:23; 19:4; Ro 10:14; Gal 2:16; Php 1:29; 1Pe 1:8). Ἐπί never follows πιστεύω in the Johannine corpus, but elsewhere it is used with πιστεύω more frequently (12x) than εἰς (8x).

In John's gospel πιστεύω εἰς occurs in reference to

• God (12:14; 14:1)
• Jesus (12:11): "him" (e.g., 2:11; 3:16; 16x total), "me" (e.g., 6:35; 7:38; 10x total), "the Son" (3:36; cf. 1Jn 5:10a), "the Son of Man" (9:35), "the Light" (12:36), "his name" (1:12; 2:23; 3:18; cf. 1Jn 5:13), "the one the Father sent" (6:29)

There is no doubt that John occasionally uses the dative with the same sense as εἰς with the accusative (e.g., Jn 5:24, 38; 8:31; cf. 8:30, εἰς αὐτόν), but it ought not be assumed that the two constructions are completely interchangeable, for πιστεύω with the dative of the person believed sometimes means simply "give intellectual credence to"(Jn 4:21; 5:46 [2x], 47 [2x]; 8:45–46; 10:37, 38a; 14:11a; 14:11b *v.l.*), a meaning πιστεύω εἰς never bears (cf. 6:29–30). Furthermore, it is clear that for John πιστεύω εἰς is intimately connected with ἔρχομαι εἰς (5:40; 6:37, 44–45, 65; 7:37; and esp. the parallelism in 6:35), and with πιστεύω εἰς τὸ ὄνομα (1:12; 2:23; 3:18; 1Jn 5:13; cf. 1Jn 3:23, τῷ ὀνόματι). This latter phrase (πιστεύω εἰς τὸ ὄνομα) probably means (by metonymy) "believe in the person of," but it could possibly be related to the formulaic βαπτίζω εἰς τὸ ὄνομα and so imply a transference of ownership, resulting in a new allegiance (although this view is scarcely possible in Jn 2:23; cf. 2:24). However, Jn 3:18 shows that πιστεύω εἰς τὸ ὄνομα may simply be a variant of πιστεύω εἰς and that the absolute πιστεύω may stand for either.

In Gal 2:16 it would appear that πιστεύω εἰς Χριστὸν Ἰησοῦν = πίστις Ἰησοῦ Χριστοῦ. The objective genitive after πίστις may stand in the place of (1) εἰς after πιστεύω, and (2) πίστις εἰς (a phrase found in Ac 20:21; 24:24; 26:18; Col 2:5; 1Pe 1:21b).[4]

It follows that εἰς after πιστεύω denotes, as a minimum, the object of faith (Regard 341–42) or the direction of faith. But more seems to be implied. Πιστεύω [or πίστις] εἰς Χριστόν depicts the commitment of one's self to the person of Christ (*fiducia*), something more than an intellectual acceptance of the

---

3. Πάντες οὗτοι εἰς χεῖρας αὐτῶν ἐνεπίστευσαν, "all these [artisans] rely on their hands."
4. On the contested issue of the meaning of the expression πίστις Χριστοῦ, see the bibliographies in BDAG 819b; G. Barth, *EDNT* 3:91b–92a.

message of the gospel or a recognition of the truth about Christ (*assensus*, which may be expressed by πιστεύω ὅτι or πιστεύω with the dative). But these two aspects — commitment and recognition — are intimately related. Since the person of Christ is the essence of the message that is proclaimed and accepted, to accept the message concerning him involves accepting him. That is, πιστεύω ὅτι naturally becomes πιστεύω εἰς or ἐπί, as Jn 20:31 and Ro 10:9–11 clearly establish. An εἰς (*fiducia*) presupposes a ὅτι (*assensus*), while a ὅτι ideally leads to an εἰς. So then, τὸ εἰς αὐτὸν [Χριστὸν] πιστεύειν (Php 1:29), "constantly believing in Christ," describes the Christian condition, while entrance into that state is denoted by εἰς Χριστὸν πιστεῦσαι (cf. Ro 10:14; Gal 2:16), "to come to faith in Christ."

C. Concluding Observations

1. As used in profane Greek, πιστεύω (πίστις) with the dative emphasized the element of intellectual apprehension or simple credence. The twofold moral emphasis in the Hebrew use of *he'ᵉmin* (i.e., personal trust and confident reliance) is reflected in the Christian use of the phrases πιστεύω εἰς (denoting personal trust and dedication) and πιστεύω ἐπί (with the accusative, denoting confidence; with the dative, denoting reliance). It is true the dative case was on the wane in the NT period (see ch. 10 A), but this fact in itself cannot account for the coinage (in the case of πιστεύω εἰς) and wide use of these two prepositional phrases. If no new connotation were intended by NT writers in using εἰς and ἐπί after πιστεύω, one might have expected ἐν after πιστεύω to be far more frequent (it is found only in Mk 1:15 — see above, B 3), for one tendency of Hellenistic Greek was for ἐν to be added to the simple dative case.

2. Nowhere is πιστεύω εἰς followed by a human object of faith and only once is the expressed object impersonal (1Jn 5:10c), and even there εἰς ... τὴν μαρτυρίαν signifies God's testimony concerning his Son (cf. Jn 12:36). In NT usage "believing" connotes the total and confident trust and reliance that individuals place in a divine person, not merely the simple credence they give to verifiable facts. It involves not only recognition and acceptance of the truth but also adherence and allegiance to the truth as embodied in Jesus (Jn 14:6) and dedication to living by his teaching (Jn 8:31).

3. The fact that God is (relatively speaking) so infrequently held up as the object of faith (Jn 12:44c; 14:1a; Ac 16:34; Ro 4: 3, 5, 17, 24; Gal 3:6; 1Th 1:8; Tit 3:8; Heb 6:1; 1Pe 1:21) and Christ so frequently indicates that it is in Christ that God meets the individual in salvation. There are not two competing objects of human faith.

Chapter 23

"Improper" Prepositions

A. Nomenclature and Classification

Earlier we noted (ch. 1 B) a distinction is traditionally drawn between "proper" and "improper" prepositions, with the adjective "improper" describing those prepositions that do not function as prefixes. This description is not apt, since it defines such prepositions negatively in relation to other prepositions that can be prefixed to certain words. This problem of nomenclature seems intractable. For example, if prepositions that can be prefixed were termed "prefixable," the dilemma would still remain, for other prepositions would then have to be termed "nonprefixable"! Any positive qualification of one term necessitates a negative qualification of the other.

Little is gained by speaking of "true" (Turner 258), "regular" (Robertson 637), or "genuine" (*echt*, Mayser 160) prepositions (= "proper" prepositions); or by describing "improper" prepositions as "adverbial prepositions" or "prepositional adverbs" (Robertson 554, 557, 636–37), since "proper" prepositions were originally adverbial. So I will rest content with the customary terminology.

While "proper" prepositions are traditionally classified into three groups, according to the number of cases with which they can be used (one, two, or three), "improper" prepositions have no such subgroups, since they are all followed (or on occasion, preceded) by the genitive case, except for ἅμα (Mt 13:29) and παραπλήσιον (Php 2:27), which take the dative, while ἐγγύς (cf. BDAG 271b) takes both the genitive and the dative. Another difference between the two categories of prepositions is that "proper" prepositions are monosyllabic or disyllabic whereas "improper" prepositions are disyllabic or polysyllabic.

But two ways of classifying "improper" prepositions may be mentioned, the first by function and form, the second by concept.

1. Mayser (160, 518, 526, 538) uses three headings:
    (a) nongenuine or improper prepositions (e.g., ἄνευ, ἕως, μέχρι)
    (b) adverbial prepositions, also used as adverbs (e.g., ἐκτός, ἐντός)

(c) combinations of genuine prepositions with adverbs (e.g., ἐπάνω, ὑποκάτω)

2. Baldwin (30–48) identifies three categories of relationship:
(a) spatial—internals (e.g., ἔσω), externals (e.g., ὑπεράνω), relatives (e.g., ἔμπροσθεν)
(b) logical—causatives (e.g., ἕνεκα), associatives (e.g., ἅμα), comparatives (ὑπερεκπερισσοῦ), extent (e.g., μέχρι), degree (ἐγγύς)
(c) temporal—e.g., ἕως

B. "Improper" Prepositions in Hellenistic Greek

Hellenistic Greek is marked by an increase in the use not only of prepositions in general but also of "improper" prepositions (Bortone 179–81, 194).[1] Moreover, since "improper" prepositions are generally longer than "proper" prepositions, their widespread use in Hellenistic Greek reflects its preference for longer forms as part of a general tendency toward fuller expression (cf. Zerwick §§83, 481; Mayser 538).

The *new* "improper" prepositions that appear in Koine:
(1) can be equivalent to old "proper" prepositions; e.g.,

Homeric	ὑπὸ ποσσί (*Iliad* 2.784), "under the feet" (dative)
Classical	ὑπὸ τοὺς πόδας (Xen. *Oec.* 18.5), "under the feet" (accusative)
Koine	ὑποκάτω τῶν ποδῶν (Mk 6:11), "under the feet" (genitive) (Bortone 187)

(2) tend to replace old prepositions; e.g.,

ἄντικρυς, (κατ)έναντι, κατενώπιον, and ἀπέναντι (all meaning "in front of") replace πρό (which had replaced ἀντί in a spatial sense)
ἐ-/ἀπάνωθεν, ὑπεράνω ("above") replace ὑπέρ
κυκλόθεν ("around") takes the place of περί (Bortone 187)

(3) tend to bear a spatial sense; e.g.,

in Biblical Greek ἐν is both spatial and nonspatial, whereas the new "improper" preposition ἐντός is only spatial
ἄπωθεν and ὀπίσω are only spatial (Bortone 188–89, 194)

In Modern Greek "improper" prepositions "denote mostly spatial relations, rarely temporal or other relations" (Thumb §169; see his whole treatment of "improper" prepositions in Modern Greek, §§169–74).

---

1. Bortone (188 n.35) refers to the 1884 study of F. Krebs (*Die Präpositionsadverbien in der späteren historischen Gräcität*, Part I [Munich: Lindauer, 1884]) who found no fewer than 61 "improper" prepositions in literary Hellenistic Greek.

Chart Showing Frequency of
New Testament "Improper" Prepositions[2]

Preposition	Meaning as a preposition	NT use as a preposition[3]	Total NT use	Total LXX use
ἅμα	simultaneously with	1	10	124
ἄνευ	without, apart from	3	3	48
ἄντικρυς	opposite	1	1	1
ἀντιπέρα	on the opposite side	1	1	0
ἀπέναντι	in the presence of, opposite, against	5	5	98
ἄτερ	without, apart from	2	2	1
ἄχρι(ς)	up to, until	44	49	4
ἐγγύς	near, close to, on the verge of	12	31	59
ἐκτός	outside, except	4	8	26
ἔμπροσθεν	in front of, in the presence of, before	44	48	162
ἔναντι	before, in the presence of	2	2	263
ἐναντίον	before, in the judgment of	5	8	432
ἕνεκα, ἕνεκεν, εἵνεκεν	for the sake of, because of	26	26	138
ἐντός	within, among	2	2	8
ἐνώπιον	in the presence of, in the judgment of	94	94	558
ἔξω	outside, out of	19	63	109
ἔξωθεν	from outside, outside	3	13	49
ἐπάνω	upon, above	16	19	127
ἐπέκεινα	beyond	1	1	18
ἔσω	inside	1	9	19
ἕως	as far as, to the point of	90	146	1565
κατέναντι	opposite, before, in the sight of	7	8	87
κατενώπιον	before, in the presence of	3	3	6
κυκλόθεν	round, about	2	3	92

---

2. The totals for NT use come from C-K (s.v.) and the totals for LXX use are from GELS (s.v.).

3. These figures should not be regarded as definitive, because textual variants are sometimes involved and because it is sometimes unclear whether a word is a preposition or a conjunction.

κύκλῳ	round	3	8	234
μέσον	in the middle	1	58	432
μεταξύ	between, among	7	9	4
μέχρι(ς)	up to, as far as	16	17	69
ὄπισθεν	behind, after	2	7	41
ὀπίσω	behind, after	26	35	461
ὀψέ	after	1	3	4
παραπλήσιον	near to	1	1	0
παρεκτός	except, apart from	2	3	0
πέραν	beyond, to the other side	15	23	107
πλήν	except, apart from	4	31	248
πλησίον	near	1	17	224
ὑπεράνω	far above, over	3	3	22
ὑπερέκεινα	beyond	1	1	0
ὑπερεκπερισσοῦ	far beyond	1	3	0
ὑποκάτω	beneath	11	11	92
χάριν	for the sake of, because of	9	9	117
χωρίς	without, apart from, besides	40	41	20

C. An Annotated Alphabetical List of All 42 New Testament "Improper" Prepositions

1. Ἅμα

Used as a preposition with the dative (once in Mt 13:29, although this construction is "not unusual" in the papyri [MM 24d]) and regularly as an adverb meaning "at the same time" (e.g., Phm 22) or "together" (e.g., Ro 3:12). In 1Th 4:17; 5:10 it is linked with σύν ("apparently pleonastic[ally]," BDAG 49b) to form a virtual compound preposition, "together with" (cf. Regard 678), and in Mt 20:1 it is linked with the temporal adverb πρωΐ to mean "early in the morning" or "at dawn."

2. Ἄνευ

Only three NT examples, all in a nonspatial sense (cf. Bortone 154 n.72). This word is virtually synonymous with ἄτερ and χωρίς, which also mean "without, apart from," although LN tentatively suggests "that χωρίς differs from ἄνευ and ἄτερ in focusing upon a greater degree of separation or lack of involvement" (§89.120 n.22).

> a. Of persons: ἄνευ τοῦ πατρὸς ὑμῶν. A sparrow will not fall to the ground "without your Father's [knowledge and permission]" (Mt 10:29, on which see ch. 24 A).

b. Of things: ἄνευ λόγου. By their submissive behavior Christian wives could win over their husbands who reject the message [ἀπειθοῦσιν τῷ λόγῳ] of the gospel "without a word being spoken" (1Pe 3:1); ἄνευ γογγυσμοῦ: "Show hospitality to one another without complaining" (1Pe 4:9).

3. Ἄντικρυς

Originally an adverb meaning "straight on," this compound word (MH 328) later meant "opposite" (LSJ 157b) = ἀντίκρυ σέ or ἀπό in Modern Greek. It is used (as a preposition) only once in the NT (ἄντικρυς Χίου, "opposite Chios," Ac 20:15) and only once in the LXX (ἄντικρυς ἀνακλῖναι αὐτοῦ, "to recline opposite him," 3Mc 5:16).

4. Ἀντιπέρα

This compound (ἀντί + the adverb πέρα, "beyond, across") is used only once in the NT: ἀντιπέρα τῆς Γαλιλαίας, "opposite Galilee" (Lk 8:26) = right across Lake Gennesaret from Galilee (i.e., on the eastern shore of the lake).

5. Ἀπέναντι

Three "proper" prepositions (ἀπό, ἐν, and ἀντί) make up this compound word. The five NT uses represent three distinct meanings:

a. "before, in the presence of" (Mt 27:24; Ac 3:16; Ro 3:18)
b. "opposite, over against" (Mt 27:61)
c. "contrary to, against" (Ac 17:7), an exceptional nonspatial use (Bortone 188–89)

6. Ἄτερ

Both NT examples have the sense "apart from, without": ἄτερ ὄχλου (Lk 22:6), "apart from the crowd" = "when no crowd was present" (NIV[1,2]) or "without causing a public disturbance" (Cassirer); ἄτερ βαλλαντίου (Lk 22:35), "without purse."

7. Ἄχρι(ς)

In addition to the five uses of ἄχρι as a conjunction meaning "until" (all found in Revelation), this preposition regularly means "until" (e.g., Ac 20:11, ἄχρι αὐγῆς, "until sunrise"; Php 1:5, ἄχρι τοῦ νῦν, "until now"), or sometimes "up to the point of" (e.g., Rev 2:10, πιστὸς ἄχρι θανάτου, "faithful to the point of death") or "as far as" (e.g., Ac 11:5, ἄχρι ἐμοῦ, "right down to me"; Heb 4:12, ἄχρι μερισμοῦ, "even to dividing"). BDAG (160d–61a) classifies ἄχρι(ς) οὗ, "until the time when" (7x in NT) as a conjunction, but whether this compound expression is an ellipsis for ἄχρι χρόνου ᾧ or for ἄχρις ἐκείνου τοῦ χρόνου ἐν ᾧ, formally ἄχρι is here prepositional (so also Moule 82).

8. Ἐγγύς

This word regularly functions as an adverb (19x; e.g., Mt 24:32, ἐγγὺς τὸ θέρος) and once adjectivally (Eph 2:17, εἰρήνην τοῖς ἐγγύς). It is prepositional 12 times: 10 times followed by the genitive (e.g., Jn 19:20, ἐγγὺς ... τῆς πόλεως) and twice by the dative (Ac 9:38, ἐγγὺς ... τῇ Ἰόππῃ; 27:8).

9. Ἐκτός

The adverb ἐκτός is formed from ἐκ + the ablatival suffix–τος (MH 329). The four prepositional uses are ἐκτὸς τοῦ σώματος, "outside the body" (1Co 6:18; 2Co 12:2; on these two verses see ch. 24 B), ἐκτὸς τοῦ ὑποτάξαντος, "excluding the One who subjected [all things to Christ]" (1Co 15:27), and οὐδὲν ἐκτὸς ... ὧν, "nothing except the things which" (Ac 26:22). Once ἐκτός is used substantivally (Mt 23:26, τὸ ἐκτὸς [μέρος], "the outside [part]") and three times as a conjunction in the pleonastic negative ἐκτὸς εἰ μή, "unless" (1Co 14:5; 15:2; 1Ti 5:19). But in Mt 23:26 τὸ ἐκτὸς αὐτοῦ could conceivably mean "the outside-it-[part]," in which case ἐκτός would be prepositional (see below on ἐντός and ἔξωθεν).

10. Ἔμπροσθεν

By formation this preposition is ἐν + πρός + the ablatival suffix–θεν (see Bortone 114, 128). Four times it is an adverb of place (e.g., Php 3:13, τοῖς ... ἔμπροσθεν, "what lies ahead"), but usually (44x) it functions as an "improper" preposition that is almost always spatial (cf. Regard 625) and that refers to people (e.g., Mt 27:11, ἔμπροσθεν τοῦ ἡγεμόνος, "before the governor"), position (e.g., Mt 5:24, ἔμπροσθεν τοῦ θυσιαστηρίου, "in front of the altar"), or even status (Jn 1:15, 30, ἔμπροσθέν μου γέγονεν, "he has taken precedence over me," on which see ch. 24 C).

11. Ἔναντι

In Hellenistic Greek ἔναντι, along with ἔπροσθεν and ἐνώπιον, takes over the spatial sense of πρό, which is "almost always used non-spatially" (Bortone 189; cf. 187). Never adverbial, ἔναντι occurs twice: ἔναντι τοῦ θεοῦ, "in God's presence" (Lk 1:8), "in God's estimation" (Ac 8:21; cf. 7:10 v.l. 𝔓⁷⁴ ℵ).

12. Ἐναντίον

The five uses of ἐναντίον as an "improper" preposition ("before, in the sight/ judgment of") are all Lukan and all refer to persons (Lk 1:6; 20:26; 24:19; Ac 7:10; 8:32). Three times it occurs as an articular adverb τοὐναντίον, "on the other hand" (2Co 2:7; Gal 2:7; 1Pe 3:9).

13. Ἕνεκα

This word is found in three forms (see BDAG 334c-d): ἕνεκα is the Attic form (MH 67, 329), found only four times in the NT; from the third century BC on ἕνεκεν became increasingly dominant, as it is in the LXX and NT; while εἵνεκεν is rare, with only two certain NT examples (Lk 4:18; 2Co 3:10). The words are always nonspatial (Bortone 170), never adverbial, and twice postpositive (Lk 4:18; Ac 19:32). They usually express cause (e.g., ἕνεκα τούτων, "for this reason, that is why," Ac 26:21; εἵνεκεν τῆς ὑπερβαλλούσης δόξης, "on account of the glory that surpasses [it], 2Co 3:10"). Of the three uses of ἕνεκεν in 2Co 7:12, the first two are causal, expressing two negative reasons, whereas the third is final (so also BDAG 334d), describing a positive purpose.

14. Ἐντός

In one of the two NT uses, this preposition is probably adverbial: τὸ ἐντὸς τοῦ ποτηρίου, "what is inside [with reference to] the cup" (Mt 23:26), i.e., its contents, in contrast with τὸ ἐκτὸς αὐτοῦ, "the outside," but it is not impossible that even here ἐντός is prepositional, "the inside-the-cup" (cf. Robertson 641). A variety of renderings has been proposed for ἐντός in the other NT occurrence, ἐντὸς ὑμῶν (Lk 17:21): "within/inside," "among," "in the midst of," "within the grasp of" (see ch. 24 D).

15. Ἐνώπιον

With its 94 NT uses, this word is the commonest by far of the seven "improper" prepositions that can mean "before" (see κατενώπιον below). It was unknown in Classical Greek (Regard 640) but is found in the papyri in the sense "in person" (Deissmann 213; MM 220b). In addition to meaning "before" (e.g., Rev 4:10, ἐνώπιον τοῦ θρόνου) and "in the presence of" (e.g., 1Ti 6:12, ἐνώπιον πολλῶν μαρτύρων), this preposition can mean "in the eyes/opinion of" (e.g., Ac 6:5, ἐνώπιον παντὸς τοῦ πλήθους; cf. BDF §214 [6]) and "on behalf of" (e.g., Rev 13:14, ἐνώπιον τοῦ θηρίου) or even "against" (Lk 15:18, ἐνώπιόν σου).

16. Ἔξω

This adverb of place (e.g., Mk 3:31) is sometimes used substantivally (e.g., Col 4:5, τοὺς ἔξω, "outsiders" = unbelievers) or adjectivally (e.g., Ac 26:11, τὰς ἔξω πόλεις, "the outside [= non-Jewish] cities"). As a preposition it is used only of places, either answering the question "Where?" (e.g., Heb 13:12, ἔξω τῆς πύλης, "outside the gate") or "Where to?" (e.g., Mk 5:10, ἔξω τῆς χώρας, "out of the district").

17. Ἔξωθεν

By form ἔξωθεν is ἔξω + the ablatival suffix –θεν (thus "from outside"). There are only three prepositional uses of this adverb of place: ἔξωθεν τοῦ ἀνθρώπου, "from outside a person" (Mk 7:15); ἔξωθεν τοῦ ναοῦ, "outside the temple" (Rev 11:2); ἔξωθεν τῆς πόλεως, "outside the city" (14:20). But it is possible that in Mt 23:25 ἔξωθεν is prepositional (cf. ἐντός and ἐκτός, above): τὸ ἔξωθεν τοῦ ποτηρίου, "the outside-the-cup."

18. Ἐπάνω

Apart from three adverbial uses ("above, more than") (Mk 14:5; Lk 11:44; 1Co 15:6), the other 16 NT occurrences of ἐπάνω are prepositional, denoting (a) *position* (e.g., Mt 21:7, ἐπάνω αὐτῶν [= τὰ ἱμάτια], "(up)on them"; Mt 27:37, ἐπάνω τῆς κεφαλῆς αὐτοῦ, "above his head"); in this spatial sense ἐπάνω is often equivalent to ἐπί—compare ἐπάνω ὄρους (Mt 5:14) and ἐπὶ τοῦ ὄρους (Mt 24:3, an example cited by Bortone 181); (b) *superior status* (e.g., Jn 3:31, ἐπάνω πάντων ἐστίν, "[the one who comes from above] is above all").

19. Ἐπέκεινα

By form ἐπέκεινα is ἐπί + ἐκεῖνα [μέρη], "beyond those [parts]." The only NT use is in Ac 7:43 (a citation of Am 5:27): ἐπέκεινα Βαβυλῶνος, "beyond Babylon."

20. Ἔσω

This is an adverb of place (e.g., Jn 20:26, ἦσαν ἔσω, "[his disciples] were within" = in the house) but with the article it becomes substantival (e.g., 1Co 5:12, τοὺς ἔσω, "those within [the company of believers])." Mark 15:16 is the only NT prepositional use: ἔσω τῆς αὐλῆς, "inside/into the palace."

21. Ἕως

As well as being a conjunction meaning "until" (e.g., 1Co 4:5), ἕως is often used as a preposition, being the most common NT "improper" preposition after ἐνώπιον. Its many uses may conveniently be classified by meaning.

    a. "Until": with a noun (e.g., ἕως τέλους, "until the end," 1Co 1:8)
        with a temporal adverb (e.g., ἕως ἄρτι, "until now," Mt 11:12)
        with οὗ (e.g., ἕως οὗ ἔτεκεν υἱόν, "until she had given birth to a son," Mt 1:25) (see ch. 24 E); this use assumes ἕως οὗ = ἕως τοῦ χρόνου ᾧ (cf. BDAG 423b-c)
        with ὅτου (e.g., ἕως ὅτου τελεσθῇ, "until it is completed," Lk 12:50)

    b. "As far as": with an indication of place (e.g., ἕως τρίτου οὐρανοῦ, "to the third heaven," 2Co 12:2; ἕως κάτω, "[from top] to bottom," Mt 27:51)
        with another preposition (e.g., ἕως πρὸς Βηθανίαν "as far as

Bethany," Lk 24:50) or an adverb (e.g., ἕως ἔξω τῆς πόλεως, "out of the city," Ac 21:5)

c. "To the point of": e.g., ἕως θανάτου, "to the point of death" (Mk 14:34)

d. "Up to": e.g., ἕως μεγάλου, "[from small] to great" = "both high and low" (Ac 8:10)

e. "While": with οὗ (e.g., ἕως οὗ ἀπολύσῃ, "while he dismissed" (Mt 14:22)

with ὅτου (e.g., ἕως ὅτου εἶ, "while you are" (Mt 5:25)

22. Κατέναντι

In form this preposition is simply a combination of three preposititons—κατά, ἐν, and ἀντί. Its meanings, which largely overlap with those of ἀπέναντι, are all spatial: "in the sight of" (e.g., κατέναντι θεοῦ, "in God's sight," 2Co 2:17); "before/over against" (e.g., κατέναντι ὑμῶν, "[the village] facing you," Mt 21:2; κατέναντι τοῦ ἱεροῦ, "opposite the temple," Mk 13:3).

23. Κατενώπιον

This is the last of seven "improper" prepositions that can mean "before" (see end of this chapter). Awareness of divine accountability lies behind each of the three NT uses of κατενώπιον: Jude 24, κατενώπιον τῆς δόξης αὐτοῦ, "before/face-to-face with his [God's] glorious presence"; Eph 1:4; Col 1:22, κατενώπιον αὐτοῦ, "before himself/in his own [God's] presence" (for this reflexive use of the personal pronoun, see Robertson 681). In the latter two passages the reference is to "someone who is viewed as having jurisdiction, whether visibly present or not" (BDAG 531a).

24. Κυκλόθεν

Once this word is adverbial (Rev 4:8, "all round") and twice prepositional (κυκλόθεν τοῦ θρόνου, "around/encircling the throne," 4:3–4).

25. Κύκλῳ

In form κύκλῳ is the locatival dative of κύκλος ("circle"), thus "in a circle." In the NT five times it is adverbial (e.g., Ro 15:19) or adjectival (e.g., Mk 6:36), and three times prepositional (κύκλῳ τοῦ θρόνου, "around the throne," Rev 4:6; 5:11; 7:11).

26. Μέσον

In form this is the neuter singular of the adjective μέσος ("middle") that appears in many adverbial phrases such as ἀνὰ μέσον (see ch. 4 B) and ἐν μέσῳ. It occurs by itself only once in the NT: Php 2:15, μέσον γενεᾶς σκολιᾶς, "in the midst of a crooked generation," although one textual variant (א C K L P *al*) in Mt 14:24 reads μέσον τῆς θαλάσσης, "in the middle of the lake."

27. Μεταξύ

This compound (μετά + ξύν [σύν]) adverb and preposition is once adverbial (Jn 4:31) and once adjectival (Ac 13:42) in the NT. In its other seven uses, all prepositional, it indicates *position*, either of people (e.g., **μεταξὺ** δύο στρατιωτῶν, "between two soldiers," Ac 12:6) or of places (e.g., **μεταξὺ** τοῦ ναοῦ καὶ τοῦ θυσιαστηρίου, "between the temple and the altar," Mt 23:35), and *reciprocity* (e.g., **μεταξὺ** σοῦ καὶ αὐτοῦ μόνου, "between you and him in private," Mt 18:15).

28. Μέχρι(ς)

There is only one NT use of μέχρι as a conjunction (Eph 4:13), assuming that μέχρις οὗ (Mk 13:30; Gal 4:19) = μέχρις τοῦ χρόνου ᾧ and therefore is prepositional (see ἄχρι and ἕως, above). As a preposition μέχρι has three meanings: (a) "until" (e.g., Ro 5:14, **μέχρι** Μωϋσέως, "until [the time of] Moses"); (b) "to the point of" (e.g., Php 2:8, **μέχρι** θανάτου, "right up to his death"); (c) "as far as" (Ro 15:19, **μέχρι** τοῦ Ἰλλυρικοῦ, "as far as Illyricum").

29. Ὄπισθεν

In addition to its five adverbial uses (e.g., Rev 5:1, ἔσωθεν καὶ **ὄπισθεν**, "[a scroll with writing] inside and on the back"), ὄπισθεν twice functions as a preposition, meaning "after": **ὄπισθεν** ἡμῶν, "[she keeps crying out] after/from behind us" (Mt 15:23); or "behind": **ὄπισθεν** τοῦ Ἰησοῦ, "[to carry the cross] behind Jesus"(Lk 23:26).

30. Ὀπίσω

Twice this word is adverbial (Mt 24:18; Lk 7:38) and seven times it becomes substantival by means of the article: τὰ ὀπίσω, "what lies behind" (e.g., Php 3:13). As a preposition it usually relates to persons and has two meanings: (a) "behind," as in ὕπαγε **ὀπίσω** μου (Mt 16:23), "Get behind me!" = "Get out of my sight!" (Goodspeed); (b) "after," of place, as in **ὀπίσω** μου ἐλθεῖν (Mt 16:24), "to come after me," where "come after" = "follow"; and of time, as in ὁ **ὀπίσω** μου ἐρχόμενος (Jn 1:15, 27), "the one who comes after me."

31. Ὀψέ

As an adverb the word means "late in the day" (Mk 11:19; 13:35). The one NT prepositional use may be **ὀψὲ** ... σαββάτων (Mt 28:1) if this means "after the Sabbath" (as BDAG 746c; Turner 278, "just after"), but not if the meaning is "late on the Sabbath." Like Moulton (72–73), Robertson equivocates: "If Matthew has in mind just before sunset, 'late on' would be his idea; if he means after sunset, then 'after' is correct" (646).

32. Παραπλήσιον

This is the neuter of an adjective (παραπλήσιος, "coming near") formed from παρά and πλησίος. Its one use in Biblical Greek is in Php 2:27 in reference to Epaphroditus: ἠσθένησεν **παραπλήσιον** θανάτῳ (ℵ² B P Ψ *al* read θανάτου), "he was ill—at the point of death."

33. Παρεκτός

Its one adverbial use is in 2Co 11:28: χωρὶς τῶν **παρεκτὸς** [γινομένων], "apart from what I leave unmentioned" (BDAG 774d, as one option). The two prepositional uses are: **παρεκτὸς** λόγου πορνείας, "except for the reason of immorality" (Mt 5:32); and **παρεκτὸς** τῶν δεσμῶν τούτων, "apart from these chains" (Ac 26:29).

34. Πέραν

Eight times πέραν is adverbial in the expression εἰς τὸ πέραν, "to the [land on the] other side" (e.g., Mk 4:35). The other 15 NT uses are prepositional, where εἰς τὸ πέραν or πέραν is qualified by a genitive (e.g., Mk 5:1), or where the standard phrase πέραν τοῦ Ἰορδάνου ("on the other side of the Jordan") is found (e.g., Jn 1:28), an expression that sometimes "functions as an indecl[inable] name for the territory on the other (eastern) side of the Jordan, i.e. *Perea*" (BDAG 797a).

35. Πλήν

In the NT this word is often an adversative conjunction ("but, nevertheless, except"; e.g., **πλὴν** ἐφ᾽ ἑαυτὰς κλαίετε, "but rather weep for yourselves," Lk 23:28), but on four occasions it is prepositional: e.g., **πλὴν** τούτων τῶν ἐπάναγκες, "apart from these necessary requirements" (Ac 15:28); **πλὴν** τοῦ πλοίου, "except the ship" (Ac 27:22).

36. Πλησίον

Apart from 16 uses of the substantival ὁ πλησίον, "the person who is near" (= "my neighbor"; e.g., Mt 5:43), there is only one prepositional use: **πλησίον** τοῦ χωρίου, "near the place" (Jn 4:5). Even in Lk 10:29 (μου **πλησίον**) and 10:36 (**πλησίον** ... τοῦ ἐμπεσόντος εἰς τοὺς λῃστάς), the anarthrous πλησίον is substantival rather than prepositional: "my neighbor" and "neighbor to the man who had fallen into the hands of robbers" (so also Robertson 646).

37. Ὑπεράνω

This compound of ὑπέρ and ἄνω displaces the simple ὑπέρ in its three NT (prepositional) uses, the first denoting status and the other two place: ὑπεράνω πάσης ἀρχῆς (Eph 1:21), "high above any other source of rule" (Cassirer); ὑπεράνω πάντων τῶν οὐρανῶν (4:10), "far above all the heavens"; ὑπεράνω ... αὐτῆς [τὴν κιβωτόν] (Heb 9:5), "above [the ark]."

38. Ὑπερέκεινα

A compound of ὑπέρ and the pronoun ἐκεῖνα (cf. ἐπέκεινα, above), this preposition occurs only once in the Greek Bible, at 2Co 10:16: τὰ ὑπερέκεινα ὑμῶν [μέρη], "the areas that lie beyond you."

39. Ὑπερεκπερισσοῦ

This word meaning "very far in excess of" (Moule 86) or "quite beyond all measure" (BDAG 1033a) serves twice as an adverb: ὑπερεκπερισσοῦ δεόμενοι, "praying with the greatest earnestness" (1Th 3:10); and ἡγεῖσθαι αὐτοὺς ὑπερεκπερισσοῦ, "hold them in the highest possible regard" (1Th 5:13). Once it is a preposition: ὑπὲρ πάντα ... ὑπερεκπερισσοῦ ὧν αἰτούμεθα ἢ νοοῦμεν, "immeasurably more than all we could ask or conceive" (Eph 3:20). Here ὧν = τούτων ἃ and is a genitive of comparison (BDAG 1033a) or respect.

40. Ὑποκάτω

As a newer (postclassical) "improper" preposition, ὑποκάτω tends to supersede the older ὑπό (Bortone 187–88). All 11 NT uses are prepositional: e.g., ὑποκάτω τῆς συκῆς, "beneath the fig tree" (Jn 1:50). Five times we find ὑποκάτω τῶν ποδῶν, "under the feet" (e.g., Mt 22:44; Mk 12:36, citing Ps 110:1).

41. Χάριν

In its nine NT uses, χάριν (the accusative of χάρις, "thanks") is postpositive except for 1Jn 3:12 (see the chart in Turner 278). It may express a *purpose* ("for the sake of"): e.g., τῶν παραβάσεων χάριν (Gal 3:19), "[the law was added] for the sake of transgressions," that is, in order that transgressions may be brought into the open; or a *cause* ("on account of"): e.g., οὗ χάριν, "for this reason" (Lk 7:47).

42. Χωρίς

To illustrate his statement that "newer 'improper' prepositions seem to oust even some older 'improper' items," Bortone observes that "χωρίς and later δίχα appear instead of ἄνευ and πλήν" (188), adding that "the chronological order of appearance πλήν/ἄνευ to χωρίς to δίχα is also interesting for Modern Greek, since πλήν and ἄνευ are now very archaic, χωρίς standard, and δίχως ['without'] colloquial" (188 n.36). Only one of the 41 NT uses of χωρίς is adverbial ("apart," in Jn 20:7), and all are prepositive except for οὗ χωρίς, "without which [= holiness]," in Heb

12:14. As a preposition it is used of (a) *persons*: e.g., οὔτε γυνὴ **χωρὶς** ἀνδρὸς οὔτε ἀνὴρ **χωρὶς** γυναικὸς ἐν κυρίῳ, "in the Lord woman is not independent of man, nor is man independent of woman" (1Co 11:11); **χωρὶς** Χριστοῦ, "separated from Christ" (Eph 2:12); and (b) *things*: e.g., **χωρὶς** ἁμαρτίας, "apart from [= not to deal with] sin" (Heb 9:28, on which see ch. 24 F); ἡ πίστις **χωρὶς** ἔργων νεκρά ἐστιν, "faith without actions is dead" (Jas 2:26).[4]

It is noteworthy that there are seven "improper" prepositions (ἀπέναντι, ἔμπροσθεν, ἔναντι, ἐναντίον, ἐνώπιον, κατέναντι, κατενώπιον) that can mean "before" (cf. MH 465). Only the context will indicate which of the following senses of "before" is applicable in each use of each preposition: "in the [physical] sight of," "in the [personal] presence of," "in front of [spatially]," or "in the eyes/ evaluation of" (cf. Baldwin 37). Often there is an allusion to divine omniscience or to ultimate human accountability to God.

---

4. Some authorities (e.g., MH 332; BDAG 691b) regard ὁδόν in Mt 4:15 (ὁδὸν θαλάσσης) as an "improper" preposition; thus "toward the sea." But this accusative (not found in the LXX at Isa 8:23), which is unexpected after the nominatives, γῆ ... γῆ , (a) is a literal translation of the Hebrew *derek hayyām* in Isa 9:1, where *derek* is the object and the whole phrase is titular, "the Way of the Sea" (NIV²); and (b) may be classified either as adverbial, "lying to the sea" (Moffatt; the Mediterranean Sea or the Sea of Galilee) or as an accusative of extent of space (BDF §1611.), "along the road to the sea" (Goodspeed).

Chapter 24

Notable Uses of Selected "Improper" Prepositions

As was the case with "proper" prepositions, the choice of passages for special consideration is rather arbitrary, but each contains some significant theological issue.

A. Ἄνευ
Matthew 10:29

Οὐχὶ δύο στρουθία ἀσσαρίου πωλεῖται; καὶ ἓν ἐξ αὐτῶν οὐ πεσεῖται ἐπὶ τὴν γῆν **ἄνευ** τοῦ πατρὸς ὑμῶν

"Is it not true that two sparrows are sold for a penny? Yet not one of them will fall to the ground apart from your Father."

At the beginning, center, and end of Mt 10:26–31 Jesus admonishes the Twelve not to be afraid, in spite of his announcement of their certain persecution (vv. 16–25):

- v. 26a μὴ **οὖν** φοβηθῆτε αὐτούς, where "them" refers to the persecutors of vv. 16–23
- v. 28a μὴ φοβεῖσθε, where the persons not to be feared are "those who can kill the body but cannot kill the soul"
- v. 31a μὴ **οὖν** φοβεῖσθε, where no object is explicit

But embedded within the center of this paragraph (v. 28) is a positive admonition: φοβεῖσθε δὲ μᾶλλον τὸν δυνάμενον καὶ ψυχὴν καὶ σῶμα ἀπολέσαι ἐν γεέννῃ. "Rather, hold in awe the one who has power to destroy both soul and body in hell." The whole pericope, then, deals with appropriate and unwarranted objects of fear.

Some EVV render **ἄνευ** τοῦ πατρὸς ὑμῶν in a literal manner: "without your Father" (RV) or "apart from your Father" (NASB[1,2], NRSV, ESV), giving **ἄνευ** the sense it bears ("without, apart from") in its other NT uses (1Pe 3:1; 4:9).

But since the phrase is clearly elliptical (in no sense does the Father fall when a sparrow falls), most EVV supply from the context an appropriate expansion. "Apart from your Father's help" (cf. ἄνευ τοῦ θεοῦ, "without God's help," Ge 41:16) is inappropriate, as is "without your Father's command" (cf. ἄνευ κυρίου, "without the Lord's direction," 4Kgdms 18:25; Isa 36:10). Four options remain.

a. "Without your Father's knowledge" (TCNT, NAB[2], REB), "without your Father knowing" (JB, NJB; similarly Barclay, NLT). Support for this view may be found in three directions.
   • The next verse (Mt 10:30) speaks of the divine omniscience: "Why, even the number of the very hairs on your head is known to God."
   • The parallel passage in Lk 12:6 reads, "Yet not one of them [the sparrows] has escaped God's notice."
   • The colloquial ἄνευ ἡμῶν can mean "without our knowing" (cf. Mayser 520; MM 42b).

b. "Without your Father's consent" (NAB[1], GNB, Cassirer, HCSB), "without your Father's leave" (Weymouth, NEB). A linguistic parallel for this sense is found in Ge 41:44 (LXX), where Pharaoh assures Joseph "I am Pharaoh, but ἄνευ σοῦ ['without your permission,' Muraoka 36a] no will lift up his hand in all Egypt."

c. "Unless your Father wills it" (Moffatt), "without your Father's will" (RSV), "apart from the will of your Father" (NIV[1]). Whereas b. alludes to the "permissive/concessive will" of God, this view adverts to the "directive will" of God. But whether God in any sense actively wills the death of any of his creatures must remain doubtful. Perhaps these EVV equate God's will with his permission.

*d. "Without the knowledge and consent of [your Father]" (BDAG 78a). That a dual completion of an ellipse after ἄνευ is legitimate is suggested by two papyri: "the associates [the verb is missing] nothing without the knowledge and wish of the secretaries" (ἄνευ τῶν ἀντιγραφέως; Rev. L. 10.5, cited by Mayser 519); "nothing happens without the cognizance and permission of the gods" (ἄνευ τῶν θεῶν οὐθὲν γίνεται, P Par 45[4], BC 153).

Verses 29–31 form a potent a fortiori argument. If God as creator knows about and consents to the death of one of his apparently insignificant creatures, how much more is God as an all-knowing Father concerned about his infinitely more valuable children, especially when they face death by martyrdom (cf. v. 28). The idea of God's concern and sovereign control belongs to the second part (vv. 30–31), not the first part of the argument (*pace* TNIV, NIV[2], "outside your Father's care," 10:29b). The assumption is that if God knows and consents, he also protects from ultimate harm. If there is an allusion to Am 3:5 (LXX) —

πεσεῖται ... ἐπὶ τὴν γῆν ἄνευ is common to both passages—there is an implied contrast between the deadly intent of a human fowler and the beneficent control of a divine Father.

On this understanding, in 10:26–31 Jesus is giving three reasons why his disciples should not fear their persecutors (cf. 1Pe 3:14; Rev 2:10).

- God will make apparent to all on the last day the truth of the good news (v. 26), so the secrets of the kingdom that Jesus was quietly entrusting to his disciples should be boldly and widely and fearlessly proclaimed (v. 27).
- Persecution affects what is outward and temporal, but it cannot touch what is inward and eternal, whereas God has power over both body and soul, and therefore it is he who should be "feared" (v. 28).
- Every aspect of the lives of God's children, including the trauma of persecution, is known to him and is included within his providential consent and sovereign care (vv. 29–31).

B. Ἐκτός
1. 1 Corinthians 6:18

v. 18a φεύγετε τὴν πορνείαν
v. 18b πᾶν ἁμάρτημα ὃ ἐὰν ποιήσῃ ἄνθρωπος ἐκτὸς τοῦ σώματός ἐστιν
v. 18c ὁ δὲ πορνεύων εἰς τὸ ἴδιον σῶμα ἁμαρτάνει

v. 18a "Make it your habit to flee from sexual immorality.
v. 18b Every sin a person may commit is taking place outside the body,
v. 18c except that the person who sins sexually is sinning against his own body."

In 1Co 6:12–20 Paul is countering certain libertines at Corinth who apparently believed, on the basis of the premise that matter was inherently evil, that actions involving the physical body were morally indifferent. So their watch cries or slogans seem to have been: "I have the right to do anything I want" (v. 12; cf. 10:23); "food is meant for the stomach, and the stomach for food" (v. 13a), from which some Corinthians probably inferred that the satisfaction of other physical appetites, such as the sexual drive, was equally inevitable and desirable, that "the body ... is meant for illicit sex" (cf. v. 13b). All this, as they sought to justify their actions in visiting prostitutes.

The apostle enumerates a succession of reasons, some direct, some indirect, why sexual immorality must be ruthlessly repudiated (cf. μὴ γένοιτο, "Perish the thought!," v. 15c; φεύγετε τὴν πορνείαν, v. 18a).

- The body is meant to honor the Lord (v. 13b).

- Resurrection involves the body (v. 14).
- The bodies of Christians are "members" (= limbs and organs) of Christ (οὐκ οἴδατε ὅτι, v. 15).
- Physical unity with a prostitute is incompatible with spiritual unity with the Lord (οὐκ οἴδατε ὅτι, vv. 16–17).
- Sexual immorality is a sin against one's own body (v. 18).
- The body is a sanctuary in which the Holy Spirit resides (οὐκ οἴδατε ὅτι, v. 19a-b).
- As purchased property, Christians do not belong to themselves; purchase leads to ownership (vv. 19c–20a).
- Christians are obliged to honor their new owner, God, with their whole personality, including their body (v. 20b).

Paul's primary prohibition in the passage is φεύγετε τὴν πορνείαν (v. 18a), which, being asyndetic, is an urgent and forceful charge. It is reminiscent of Joseph's dramatic rejection of the sexual advances of Potiphar's wife: "He left his cloak in her clutches, fled from her, and dashed outside" (καταλιπὼν τὰ ἱμάτια αὐτοῦ ἐν ταῖς χερσὶν αὐτῆς ἔφυγεν καὶ ἐξῆλθεν ἔξω, Ge 39:12). Yet this prohibition is simply the negative corollary of his positive exhortation, "Let your bodies serve to glorify God" (Cassirer; v. 20b).

Before we examine the overall meaning of v. 18b-c,[1] several technical matters need to be considered.

a. We assume v. 18b is Paul's own composition, although some (e.g., Moule 196–97, tentatively) have regarded it as another Corinthian libertine slogan that Paul cites and then counteracts.

b. Πᾶν ἁμάρτημα does not here mean "every sin (without exception)" for the following adversative δέ (v. 18c) introduces the one and only exception to what appears to be an absolute statement: "ἄλλος is sometimes omitted where we would add 'other'" (BDF §306 [5]), thus "every other sin" (so many EVV).

c. At first sight, εἰς τὸ ἴδιον σῶμα might seem to correspond precisely to ἐκτὸς τοῦ σώματος, as if here εἰς = ἐν = "within," the opposite of ἐκτός, with the elliptical sense, "[arising from desires] within his own body." But ἁμαρτάνω εἰς regularly means "sin against" (see, e.g., 1Co 8:12 [2x]; BDAG 50a), and elsewhere Paul never confuses εἰς and ἐν (see ch. 8 C). The most we can say is that in this context ὁ δὲ πορνεύων εἰς τὸ ἴδιον σῶμα ἁμαρτάνει implies (but is not equivalent

---

1. See the useful classification of exegetical options in the chart on pp. 542–43 of the article by B. N. Fisk, "ΠΟΡΝΕΥΕΙΝ as Body Violation: The Unique Nature of Sexual Sin in 1 Corinthians 6.18," NTS 42 (1996): 540–58.

to) ὁ δὲ πορνεύων ἐν τῷ ἰδίῳ σώματι ἁμαρτάνει, "the person who sins sexually sins by means of his own body."

d. The presence of ἴδιον in the phrase εἰς τὸ ἴδιον σῶμα shows that σῶμα does not refer to the body of Christ.

We suggest that when Paul affirms that any and every sin, apart from sexual immorality, is "outside the body" (ἐκτὸς τοῦ σώματός), he means that all other sins do not involve the whole person, σῶμα and πνεῦμα, as the sexual act uniquely does. Sins such as drunkenness, gluttony, or drug abuse certainly affect the physical body but they belong to a different class of sin. For Paul, *the uniqueness of sexual sin* resided in the fact that its stain on the personality as a repudiation of God's intent for sexual relations was deep and permanent. That is, it adversely affects the character more severely than all other transgressions, and it is irreversibly damaging in its effects. Paul saw the sexual act as more than an outward physical encounter involving only bodily organs. It is an outward and inward personal bonding, involving both body and spirit, a reciprocal communication between two individuals on both a physical and a spiritual plane. To be joined to a prostitute was to become not only ἓν σῶμα or μία σάρξ with her (v. 16) but in some real sense ἓν πνεῦμα with her (v. 17).

Any sexual liaison with someone other than one's spouse (cf. Eph 5: 22–33) was "against one's body" (εἰς τὸ ἴδιον σῶμα), not only in the self-destructive sense indicated above but also in the sense that it amounted to a violation of the believer's already established union with the Lord in spirit (τῷ κυρίῳ ἓν πνεῦμα εἶναι, v. 17), and it involved taking what was Christ's (v. 19c) and giving it to an illegitimate and immoral competitor and making it an instrument of sin. Believers have already chosen to surrender irrevocably their whole selves, body and spirit, to the Lord.

2. 2 Corinthians 12:2

οἶδα ἄνθρωπον ἐν Χριστῷ πρὸ ἐτῶν δεκατεσσάρων, εἴτε ἐν σώματι οὐκ οἶδα, εἴτε ἐκτὸς τοῦ σώματος οὐκ οἶδα, ὁ θεὸς οἶδεν, ἁρπαγέντα τὸν τοιοῦτον ἕως τρίτου οὐρανοῦ

"I know a Christian man who, fourteen years ago — whether he was in the body, I do not know, or out of the body, I do not know (God knows) — was caught up as far as the third heaven."

As Paul boasts of things that demonstrate his weakness (cf. 2Co 11:30), he cites in 12:1–7 a second celebrated instance. There was not only his ignominious nocturnal escape from Damascene plotters (11:32–33), but also his painful and incapacitating physical malady, his "thorn in the flesh," that was his constant, tormenting companion (12:7). But to explain why God gave him this σκόλοψ, he needed to recount, in outline form, his privileged journey to paradise some fourteen years earlier (12:2–4).

This ascent "all the way to [ἕως] the third heaven … into [εἰς] paradise" (vv. 2c, 4a) was merely one of Paul's "visions and revelations granted by the Lord [Jesus]" (κυρίου, subjective genitive). That Paul himself is the "man in Christ" is clear from several facts. (a) He knows the exact time in the distant past when the revelation took place (v. 2) and that its content was beyond words, even if it were permissible to try to communicate it (v. 4). (b) The revelation was directly related to the receipt of a "thorn, that was given, says Paul, "to me" (μοι, v. 7). (c) The reference to a lack of awareness as to whether or not this "man" was in the body (vv. 2–3) points to a personal experience. (d) It would not have been relevant for Paul to relate a remarkable experience of some Christian unknown to the Corinthians but known to him. Paul chooses to objectify his experience probably because he is embarrassed at needing to engage in fruitless boasting (v. 1), and because he wishes to avoid suggesting he is in any sense a special kind of Christian or that this distinctive experience in any way enhances his apostolic status.

That the whole statement εἴτε ἐν σώματι οὐκ οἶδα, εἴτε ἐκτὸς τοῦ σώματος οὐκ οἶδα, ὁ θεὸς οἶδεν in v. 2 is parenthetical is indicated by the otiose and resumptive τὸν τοιοῦτον ("such a man/this man of whom I am speaking") that looks back to ἄνθρωπον ἐν Χριστῷ. If there had been no parenthesis, τὸν τοιοῦτον would not have been needed. In the two prepositional phrases ἐν σώματι and ἐκτὸς τοῦ σώματος, it is the present physical body that is being spoken of in a generic sense: "in the body" (not "in his body") and "out of the body" (not "out of his body"), that is, "in an embodied state" and "in a disembodied state." (It is no difficulty for the generic sense that σώματι is anarthrous [the phrase being a colloquialism] and σώματος articular.)

Whether we translate ἐκτός by "out of" or "apart from" or "independent of," the sense is the same—that of total dissociation (note the precisely parallel χωρὶς [𝔓⁴⁶ B D*] τοῦ σώματος in v. 3; see Mayser 529 on the synonymity of ἐκτός and χωρίς). Although Paul was certain that he was transported to heaven (ἁρπαγέντα points to a sudden rapture, not a gradual ascent; cf. Ac 8:39), he professed ignorance whether his body was actually carried up or whether his spirit or soul was wafted to the heavenly realm while his body remained on earth (in a comatose state?).

These two references to the σῶμα should not be treated as basic building blocks for a reconstruction of Paul's anthropology, but he does seem in this passage to envisage the possibility of sentient and rational experience (cf. v. 4) in a disembodied state, albeit temporarily. That is, he can conceive of temporary disembodiment during one's lifetime in exceptional circumstances created by God, and therefore he could probably also envisage noncorporeal yet sentient experience in an interim state between death and resurrection. But whatever judgment is passed on these inferences, he emphatically insists that the final state of believers is one of embodiment (2Co 5:1) — in a σῶμα πνευματικόν, a body comparable to Christ's resurrection body (Php 3:21) and perfectly adapted to the ecology of heaven (cf. 1Co 15:42–44).

Over against his own unawareness of his bodily state during his revelatory vision, Paul sets divine knowledge (ὁ θεὸς οἶδεν, vv. 2–3; cf. 11:11), either knowledge he is not lying (cf. 11:31) in claiming ignorance, or (more probably) knowledge of his actual somatic state during the whole experience. Why in vv. 2–3 Paul so emphatically denies knowledge of his physical circumstances during the episode remains uncertain. Perhaps he is emphasizing that direct encounter with the realities of the heavenly realm is so overwhelming and awe-inspiring that consciousness of the physical world is totally eclipsed. And, at least indirectly, he is suggesting that embodiment (cf. ἐν σώματι, vv. 2–3) is no impediment to spiritual experience (cf. 2Co 5:6–7).

C. Ἔμπροσθεν
John 1:15 (cf. 1:30)

Ἰωάννης μαρτυρεῖ περὶ αὐτοῦ καὶ κέκραγεν λέγων, Οὗτος ἦν ὃν εἶπον, Ὁ ὀπίσω μου ἐρχόμενος ἔμπροσθέν μου γέγονεν, ὅτι πρῶτός μου ἦν

"John testified about him and called out with the words, 'This was the one about whom I said, "The one who comes after me has taken precedence over me, because he existed before me"'."

If the prologue of John's gospel (Jn 1:1–18) describes the mission of the Logos, its last section (1:14–18) depicts a crucial aspect of his mission — his unique role as the Logos-Son who reveals the Father. Within this section v. 15 records John the Baptist's testimony to the preeminence of his principal, the Father's only Son (μονογενής, v. 14), Jesus the Messiah.

The central affirmation of the verse falls into three clear parts, each defining a relationship between Jesus and John (μου, three times).

1. Ὁ ὀπίσω μου ἐρχόμενος. Although ὁ ἐρχόμενος was a current title for the Messiah when used absolutely (Lk 7:19–20; Heb 10:37), here it is verbal rather than titular in import since it is qualified by ὀπίσω μου (see ch. 23, C.30), where this adverb is prepositional and temporal: "the One who comes after me" (with regard to time). John is a forerunner.

2. ἔμπροσθέν μου γέγονεν. Ἔμπροσθεν ("before, in front of"), originally an adverb of place, here functions as a preposition denoting not time ("before me," which would make the following clause tautological) but rank (so BDAG 325c; Robertson 640). As an example of ἔμπροσθεν with the sense "ahead of," denoting status, Muraoka (179b) cites Ge

48:20, ἔθηκεν τὸν Ἐφραὶμ ἔμπροσθεν τοῦ Μανασσῆ, "he set Ephraim ahead of Manasseh." Γέγονεν could be present or aoristic in sense, but more probably is perfective; lit., "he has become [before me]" = "he has taken precedence over me."

3. ὅτι πρῶτός μου ἦν. The superlative πρῶτος ("first") stands for the comparative πρότερος ("earlier, prior"; BDF §62): "he was earlier than me [μου, genitive of comparison]" = "he was before me" (BDAG 893a) or "he existed before I did."

Three affirmations are therefore made about the Logos-Son in relation to John: his posteriority with regard to time, his precedence in status, and his priority with regard to time. It is logical and occasions no surprise that a forerunner would declare himself to be inferior to his principal, but this is not the basis for John's assertion of Jesus' superiority. For John the Baptist, the absolute preeminence of Jesus the Messiah was based on and evidenced by (ὅτι) his "preexistence," which in the context of the Christology of John's gospel must refer not merely to his antedating John but to his pretemporal and eternal existence (cf. 1:1; 8:58; 17:5). The one who came after John the Baptist in time surpassed him in rank and importance because he existed before him in time.

D. Ἐντός
Luke 17:21

ἰδοὺ γὰρ ἡ βασιλεία τοῦ θεοῦ ἐντὸς ὑμῶν ἐστιν

"No, in fact the kingdom of God is in your midst."

Luke 17:20–37, which describes the signs of the arrival of the kingdom of God, begins and ends with a question posed to Jesus. In v. 37 his disciples ask him, "Where, Lord?"; that is, "Where [will the rescued ones be taken; cf. vv. 34–35], Lord?" To this he enigmatically replies, "Where there is a corpse, there the vultures will gather"; that is, they will be assuredly "gathered" to the Son of Man (cf. v. 34). In v. 20a certain Pharisees ask Jesus when the kingdom of God will come, and his response (vv. 20b–21) relates not to timing but to false and true ways of determining the kingdom's arrival: it is not by studious observation of ambiguous signs (v. 20b) or by following other people's competing suggestions (v. 21a; cf. v.23), but by recognizing its unambiguous presence (v. 21b).

A clear indication of the scholarly uncertainty about the meaning of ἐντός in this verse may be gained from the fact that of the 25 major EVV, ten have a footnote giving an alternative rendering, four give two alternatives, and one (REB) lists three.

There are three main proposed renderings of ἐντὸς ὑμῶν.[2]

1. **"Within you"** (KJV, RV, TCNT, Weymouth, Goodspeed, Barclay, GNB, NIV[1]; LSJ 577a ["in your hearts"]; Robertson 641; Turner, *Insights* 61–63). "Within" is undoubtedly the essential meaning of ἐντός (see LSJ 577a-b; Mayser 530 for the papyri; and note ἐντός μου, "within me," in Pss 38:4; 108:22, LXX). But even if ὑμῶν is generic, the primary referent is the Pharisees, and it seems unlikely, in light of Lk 11:37–54 (esp. vv. 52–54), that Jesus is paying them "the compliment of allowing that within their hearts too the Spirit and the kingdom were at work" (*Insights* 62). And nowhere else does Luke speak of the kingdom as an internalized, subjective reality; people enter the kingdom rather than the reverse.

2. **"Among you"** (NEB, JB, NJB, NAB[2], Cassirer, NRSV, REB, NLT, HCSB, TNIV/NIV[2]; H. Riesenfeld, *TDNT* 8:150). BDAG suggests ἐντὸς ὑμῶν "is probably patterned after ἐν σοί (= [God] is among you)" in Isa 45:14 (340d).

3. **"In your midst"** (Moffatt, RSV, NASB[1,2], NAB[1], ESV; BDAG 340d; H. Riesenfeld, *TDNT* 8:150). It is true that elsewhere Luke expresses this sense by ἐν μέσῳ ὑμῶν (as in Lk 22:27; Ac 2:22), but parallels for this meaning of ἐντός may be found in SS 3:10 (in the midst of [ἐντός] King Solomon's carriage was a mosaic pavement) and Polycarp, *Pol* 3:3 ("If anyone is in the midst of these [faith, hope, love] [τούτων ἐντός] = is engrossed in these virtues, he has fulfilled the commandment of righteousness").

On this third view, which is to be preferred, Jesus is directing a challenge to the Pharisees and soliciting a response. "I myself embody the kingdom you are enquiring about (cf. Lk 10:9, 11; 11:20); it is right here before your very eyes." He is saying in effect, "Look at what lies in front of you," to borrow a Pauline expression (τὰ κατὰ πρόσωπον βλέπετε, 2Co 10:7). They do not need to search elsewhere for signs of the kingdom's presence.[3]

---

2. For a history of interpretation, see B. Noack, *Das Gottesreich bei Lukas: Eine Studie zu Luk. 17, 20–24* (Lund: Gleerup, 1948) 3–38; for bibliographical data, see BDAG 341a; *EDNT* 1:460 c-d. Ἐν σοί ἐστι certainly can mean "it is in your power" (Jannaris §1560), but in 17:21 no EV has "within/in your grasp" in the text although four mention this translation in a footnote (NEB, REB, NLT, ESV). However, Bortone notes that ἐντός is one of the "improper" prepositions that " are *almost* always spatial throughout antiquity" (169; his italics), while "in Biblical Greek, the old ἐν ... is both spatial and non-spatial, while its new counterpart ἐντός is only spatial" (189). Both NEB and REB give "suddenly will be among you" as one of their footnote alternatives (similarly GNB).

3. Admittedly, the difference between "among you" and "in your midst" is slight, but in reference to persons the translation "in your midst" more readily coheres with the ideas of recognition and easy accessibility.

E. Ἕως οὗ
Matthew 1:25

καὶ οὐκ ἐγίνωσκεν αὐτὴν **ἕως οὗ** ἔτεκεν υἱόν· καὶ ἐκάλεσεν τὸ ὄνομα αὐτοῦ Ἰησοῦν

"But he had no sexual relations with her until she had given birth to a son. And Joseph named him Jesus."

After establishing the Davidic ancestry of Joseph, the foster father of Jesus, by tracing the genealogy of Jesus (Mt 1:1–17), Matthew proceeds in 1:18–25 to describe the circumstances of Jesus' birth, while developing one of the dominant themes of his gospel, namely, the life of Jesus as the fulfillment of scriptural prophecy (vv. 22–23). The focus in vv. 24–25 is on Joseph's immediate and complete obedience to the directions given by the angel of the Lord. Verse 25a states the one qualification (introduced by adversative καὶ οὐκ ἐγίνωσκεν αὐτήν) to the statement "he took Mary home as his wife" (v. 24b; cf. v. 20).

Some classify ἕως οὗ as a conjunction (e.g., MGM 449c–50b), but here I am treating ἕως as a preposition (as also BDAG 423b-c) on the basis that ἕως οὗ is elliptical for ἕως τοῦ χρόνου ᾧ, "until the time when" (with ᾧ being attracted into the case of its antecedent, which is then omitted; cf. ZG 2 and ἕως τῆς ἡμέρας ἐκείνης ὅταν in Mt 26:29).

Matthew's purposes in v. 25 would seem to be threefold.

1. In v. 25b he shows that Jesus is of Davidic lineage because by naming Mary's child, Joseph is formally and publicly acknowledging that Jesus is his lawful son. Joseph "fully respected the legal character of the paternity imposed on him by the divine will" (NAB[1] footnote on Mt 1:25).

2. In v. 25a Matthew again makes it clear that Joseph was not responsible for the conception of Jesus (cf. the earlier πρὶν ἢ συνελθεῖν αὐτούς, v. 18).

3. Also in v. 25a Matthew clarifies that there was not only a virginal conception (v. 18) but also a virginal birth. During the period from conception to birth Joseph did not have sexual relations with Mary (γινώσκω was a euphemism for sexual intercourse, BDAG 200c; cf. Lk 1:34). The imperfect οὐκ ἐγίνωσκεν points to an unbroken period of sexual abstinence: "He had no relations with her at any time before she bore a son" (NAB[1]); "... but kept her a virgin until she gave birth to a Son" (NASB[1,2]). But it is scarcely appropriate to claim (as ZG 2) that the (constative) aorist would have been required to express termination of Joseph's action.

Is Matthew implying the perpetual virginity of Mary in v. 25a? That this is not being explicitly asserted is clear; Matthew's attention is focused solely on the period up to the birth of Jesus, not on what may or may not have occurred thereafter. There is no exact parallel in the NT for the construction found in

v. 25a, i.e., a negated imperfect + ἕως οὗ + aorist. But with regard to the use of ἕως οὗ or ἕως ὅτου or ἕως ἄν or simply ἕως after a negated verb, there could be an implication—but only an implication—that the negated action continued after the point of time indicated. For instance, in Ge 28:15 (οὐ μή σε ἐγκαταλίπω ἕως τοῦ ποιῆσαί με πάντα ὅσα ἐλάλησά σοι) we may fairly assume that God did not desert Jacob after the fulfillment of his promises.

But far more frequently it is the *opposite* of the negated action that may be assumed to occur. In Ge 8:7 (καὶ ἐξελθὼν οὐχ ὑπέστρεψεν ἕως τοῦ ξηρανθῆναι τὸ ὕδωρ ἀπὸ τῆς γῆς), for example, the implication is (in the LXX) that the raven did return to the ark when the water had dried up from the earth. Similarly, note Mt 16:28 (ἕως ἄν); 17:9 (ἕως οὗ); Jn 9:18 (ἕως ὅτου); 13:38 (ἕως οὗ); Ac 23:12, 14, 21 (ἕως οὗ); in all these cases the negated activity ends at the point of time indicated by the ἕως clause and the implication is that the opposite then occurs.

As these data are applied to Mt 1:25a, there are two opposite but equally legitimate inferences that may be drawn: after the birth of Jesus Joseph continued to refrain from all sexual relations with Mary (which would point to her perpetual virginity); or he began to have normal marital relations with Mary after Jesus' birth. Of these two inferences, the latter seems more probable.

1. In most cases where ἕως or some combination with ἕως follows a negated verb, the implication is clear that the opposite action takes place after the time marked by the ἕως clause.
2. If Matthew believed in the perpetual virginity of Mary, he would not likely have expressed himself in a way that linguistically leaves open the possibility that after Jesus was born, Joseph began to have sexual intimacy with Mary. Certainly, if he had wished explicitly to assert Mary's permanent virginity, he could have simply added ἤ ἀπὸ τότε ("or from that time on") or the equivalent after υἱόν.
3. There are subsequent references in Matthew to Jesus' ἀδελφοί (Mt 12:46, [47, text]; 13:55) and ἀδελφαί (Mt 13:56), which most naturally refer to Jesus' siblings. Considerations such as these are probably behind two recent renderings of Mt 1:25a. "[He took his wife to his home] while yet refraining from being on terms of intimacy with her until after she had given birth to her son" (Cassirer), and "But he did not consummate their marriage until she gave birth to a son" (NIV[2]).

F. Χωρίς
Hebrews 9:28

… οὕτως καὶ ὁ Χριστὸς ἅπαξ προσενεχθεὶς εἰς τὸ πολλῶν ἀνενεγκεῖν ἁμαρτίας, ἐκ δευτέρου χωρὶς ἁμαρτίας ὀφθήσεται τοῖς αὐτὸν ἀπεκδεχομένοις εἰς σωτηρίαν

"... so Christ was once for all offered in sacrifice in this respect, that he took upon himself the sins of many people; and to those who are eagerly awaiting him he will appear a second time, not to deal with sin, but to bring them salvation."

In Heb 9:23–28 the author speaks of Christ's entering heaven with his once-for-all sacrifice that achieved the annulment of sin and final salvation for his people, as part of the overall purpose of the letter to demonstrate the finality and superiority of Christ and Christianity. At the heart of this passage are references to three "appearances," expressed by three different Greek verbs (ἐμφανισθῆναι, v. 24; πεφανέρωται, v. 26; ὀφθήσεται, v. 28), which here all mean "appear" (BDAG 325d, 1048b, 719d, respectively). Elsewhere in the NT this third "appearance" is described by the terms παρουσία (e.g., 1Co 15:23), ἐπιφάνεια (e.g., 1Ti 6:14), and ἀποκάλυψις (e.g., 1Pe 1:13). The first and the third "appearance" (vv. 26 and 28), chronologically speaking, take place on earth, while the second (v. 24) occurs in heaven in God's presence (v. 24; cf. Ex 28:29–30).

Of the four qualifiers of ὀφθήσεται ("he will appear"):

1. ἐκ δευτέρου ("a second time") sets up a crucial contrast with the first "appearance" and its purpose, εἰς ἀθέτησιν κτλ. (v. 26).
2. χωρὶς ἁμαρτίας depicts the circumstances surrounding the second "appearance" on earth, which is called "the Day" in 10:25 and is commonly known as "the second advent."
3. τοῖς αὐτὸν ἀπεκδεχομένοις defines the recipients of this second "appearance" (see BDAG 719d for this dative).
4. εἰς σωτηρίαν states the purpose and result of this "appearance."

Χωρὶς ἁμαρτίας has been understood in three ways.

1. "*Without sin*" (KJV). The only other NT occurrence of this phrase is in Heb 4:15b, where Jesus, believers' empathetic high priest, is described as "one who has been tempted in every way, exactly as we are—yet without sinning" (χωρὶς ἁμαρτίας). In a context that stresses the ability of Jesus, a great high priest, to empathize with human weaknesses (v. 15a), "without sin" is unlikely to mean that during his incarnate life he was devoid of sinful inclinations arising from within that might have prompted temptation, true though that was. Rather, he was "without sin" in being totally free of sinful actions that resulted from succumbing to temptation, whatever its source ("without committing any sin," BDAG 1095d; Goodspeed); he was ἄμωμος, "unblemished, without fault" (Heb 9:14), ἄκακος, ἀμίαντος, "blameless, undefiled," and consequently κεχωρισμένος ἀπὸ τῶν ἁμαρτωλῶν, "set apart from sinners" (7:26). If the phrase has this meaning in 9:28 (the intent of the KJV translators is not known, although they placed no comma

after "the second time"; but note RV "apart from sin"), the sense is: as at his first appearance on earth, so also at his second and beyond, he will be "sinless." Again, although this will be true, this understanding overlooks the contrast in v. 28 between Christ's assumption of sins (ἁμαρτίας, plural) upon himself at his first appearance and the absence of sin (ἁμαρτίας, singular) at his second.

2. *"Sin being no more"* (NJB), *"sin done away"* (NEB), *"sin having been done away with"* (Cassirer). This perfectly legitimate understanding of "apart from sin" maintains the "then-now" contrast in v. 28 and resonates with Paul's correlation between sin and death (e.g., Ro 5:12; 1Co 15:56) and his assertion that death, the last enemy, will be destroyed at the end (1Co 15:24–26; cf. Rev 21:4, 27). On this view, then, the second advent marks the final demise of sin.

3. *"Not to deal with sin"* (Moffatt, RSV, Barclay ["this time … "], GNB, NRSV, REB, ESV; similarly JB, NLT), *"not to bear sin"* (NIV[1,2], TNIV, HCSB), *"not to take away sin"* (NAB[1,2]).

All these renderings are appropriate contextual expansions of a literal translation of **χωρὶς** ἁμαρτίας: "without any relation to sin" (BDAG 1095d, "i.e. not w[ith] the purpose of atoning for it") or "without *reference to* sin" (NASB[1,2]). In this case "not to deal with sin" corresponds negatively to two positive Pauline statements of the purpose of the atonement: Ro 8:3, περὶ ἁμαρτίας, which may be rendered "to deal with sin" (Weymouth) or "atone for sin" (TCNT); and 1Co 15:3, ὑπὲρ τῶν ἁμαρτιῶν ἡμῶν, "in order to deal with our sins." No further dealing with sin is necessary since Christ has already offered one final acceptable sacrifice (Heb 9:12, 14; 10:12); **χωρὶς** ἁμαρτίας underlines the "once-for-all-ness" of Christ's vicarious sacrifice. Εἰς σωτηρίαν is contrasted not only with εἰς τὸ πολλῶν ἀνενεγκεῖν ἁμαρτίας but also with **χωρὶς** ἁμαρτίας: with regard to its purpose, Christ's second advent is "not to deal with sin," but positively to consummate his people's salvation (cf. Heb 1:14; 2:10; 1Pe 1:5), that is, to deliver them from adverse divine judgment (cf. Heb 9:27; 12:23) and bring them safely to their promised eternal inheritance (9:15).

Index of Biblical References

- references in **bold italics** indicate detailed discussion of the verse or passage in question
- references in *italics* indicate that a translation is given or an exegetical comment is made on the verse or passage being discussed
- references in roman type are merely citations of a verse or passage that documents or illustrates or parallels the grammatical or exegetical point being made
- * = Septuagint

Old Testament

Genesis

1:2 41
1:6 – 8 41
*4:23 . . . . **91**
*4:25 50
*9:11 66
12:1 – 3 99
13:1 99
15:4 – 5 99
*15:6 . . . . **98 – 99**
16:1 – 16 151
21:1 – 21 151
22:1 – 18 99
*22:13 50
*22:18 49
*28:15 263
*37:17a 84
*39:12 . . . . *256*

*41:16 . . . . *253*
*41:44 . . . . *254*
*44:33 . . . . *50*
*48:20 . . . . *259 – 60*

Exodus

3:14 67
*4:21 84
*5:23 232
*8:5 62
14:31 98
19:5 – 6 71
19:10 – 11 154
21:23 – 25 49
21:30 52
24:3 – 8 71
28:29 – 30 . . . . *264*
*29:30 . . . . *50*
30:11 – 16 51
30:12 . . . . . . *51, 52, 53*

30:12b *51*
30:13 – 16 . . . . *53*
30:13 – 14 . . . . *53*
30:15 – 16 . . . . *53*
30:16 . . . . *51*
34:34 65

Leviticus

*6:23 183
*7:37 183
*14:19 183
*14:20 145
16:1 – 34 154
*16:5 183
18:6 – 18 143

Numbers

14:33 143
15:30 – 31 197
*16:35 173

18:22 197
*22:3 66
35:31 52
35:32 52

Deuteronomy
*1:29 36
6:4 74
*7:29 36
21:22 – 23 214
*21:23 144
22:13 – 21 143
22:25 – 26 197
*24:1 143
*24:16 212
27:26 214

Joshua
*7:22 84

Judges
*11:34 174

**1 Samuel
(1 Kingdoms)**
*25:5 232
*25:9 232
*27:12 234

**2 Samuel
(2 Kingdoms)**
*2:13 138
*19:1 50
19:22 49

**1 Kings
(3 Kingdoms)**
2:19 107
22:19 107

**2 Kings (4
Kingdoms)**
*14:6 213
*18:25 253
20:5 154

Nehemiah
10:32 – 33 51

Job
*9:2 172
*12:5 (Codex A) . . . 219

Psalms
*2:2 . . . . 138 – 39
*3:7 36
*15:10 . . . . **84 – 85**
*33:4 138
*38:4 261
*44:8 172
49:7 – 9 . . . . 53 – 54
*75:7 66
*77:22 234
*77:32 234
*77:62 91
*85:11 134
*101:28 95
*105:12 234
*108:22 261
*109:1 106
*109:4 96
110:1 . . . . 106, 250
*117:16 107
*117:23 222
148:14 195

Proverbs
*1:9 179
*3:22 179
*6:21 179
6:35 52
13:8 52

Song of Songs
*3:10 61

Isaiah
4:4 44
*7:9 233
*7:14 164

*8:8 164
*8:10 164
*8:23 251
*9:1 251
*28:16 . . 133, 233, 235
30:28 44
36:10 253
*45:14 261
52:13 – 53:12 53
53:4 – 6 154
*53:4 . . . . 53, 144
*53:5 81
53:7 53
53:9 53
53:10 – 12 154
53:10 53
*53:11 – 12 53
*53:11 . . . . . . 53, 55, 81
*53:12 . . . . 53, 81, 144
57:19 195

Jeremiah
*9:23 . . . . 129, 132 – 33
9:24 132
*12:6 234

Ezekiel
*33:30 175
36:25 – 27 111
*37:10 121

Daniel
6:24 Theodotion . . 234
7:9 107

Hosea
6:1 – 2 154

Amos
*3:5 . . . . 254 – 55
*5:27 246

Nahum
*1:7 66

Habakkuk
*2:4 . . . . 43, 108

Zechariah
*13:3 232

Old Testament Apocrypha
2 Maccabees
3:34 62

3 Maccabees
5:16 243

4 Maccabees
15:24 234
16:22 234

Sirach
38:31 236

Wisdom of Solomon
12:2 235

New Testament
Matthew
1:1–17 262
1:18–25 262
1:18 262
1:20 262
1:21 . . . . 61, 169
1:22–23 262
1:22 . . . . 164, 222
1:23 . 164–65, 168–69
1:24–25 262
1:24b 262
1:25 . . . . 246, 262–63
1:25a 262–63
1:25b 262
2:6 118
2:22 . . . . 51, 138
3:1 226

3:6 . . . . . 226, 227, 230
3:7 138
3:11 . . . . . . .44, 84, 91,
226–27, 230–31
3:12 165
3:13–17 79
3:13 226
3:14 226
3:15 79
3:16 58
4:1 220
4:4 . . . . 69, 138
4:13 85
4:15 251
5:11 41
5:14 296
5:15 219
5:21–22 33
5:24 244
5:25 247
5:28 . . . . . 36, 118, 189
5:32 . . . . 143, 249
5:34–36 84
5:35 84–85
5:37 41
5:38 49
5:43 249
6:1 . . . . 189, 221
6:7 . . . . . . .36, 117, 120
6:13 41
6:13b 41
7:16 35
7:24 138
8:17 53
8:32 147
9:34 . . . . .117, 221
10:9 84
10:15 119
10:16–25 253
10:16–23 253
10:24 208–9
10:26–31 . . . . 253, 255

10:26 255
10:26a 253
10:27 255
10:28 . . . . .36, 253,
254–55
10:28a 253
10:29–31 254–55
10:29 . . . 242, 253–55
10:29b 254
10:30–31 254
10:30 254
10:31a 253
10:37 209
10:41–42 91
10:41a 90
10:41b 90
10:42 90
11:12 . . . . 58, 246
11:19 . . . . . 58, 59, 248
11:26 36
12:18 85
12:24 165
12:27 165
12:28 . . . . 138, 165
12:29 . . . . 63, 165
12:30 . . . . 165, 166
12:32 94
12:40 169
12:41 90
12:46 263
12:47 263
13:19 41
13:25 45
13:29 . . . . 239, 242
13:33 44
13:38 41
13:55 263
13:56 . . . . 191, 263
14:22 247
14:24 . . . . 220, 248
14:26 66
14:31 90

14:33 195
15:23 248
16:16 – 17 141
16:16 . . . . .141 – 42
16:17 . . . . .141 – 42
16:18 – 19 141
16:18 . . . .138, *141 – 42*
16:19 142
16:21 . . . . *59*, 222
16:23 . . . . 60, *248*
16:24 . . . . *248*
16:26 215
16:27 152
16:28 263
17:9 263
17:17 191
17:24 – 27 51
17:27 . . .50, *51 – 52, 56*
18:6 236
18:7 58
18:15 . . . . *248*
18:18 142
19:5 – 6 . . . . *37*
19:8 189
19:9 . . . . *142 – 43*
19:26 172
19:28 . . . . *41*
20:1 . . . . *242*
20:9 – 10 . . . . *46*
20:20 . . . . *163*
20:21 107
20:23 107
20:28 . . . . . .50, *52 – 54*,
215
21:2 . . . . *247*
21:7 . . . . *246*
21:42 . . . . 37, 222
22:21 60
22:34 139
22:44 . . . . 106, *250*
23:5 189
23:25 . . . . *246*

23:26 . . . .*244 – 45*
23:35 . . . . *248*
24:3 246
24:18 . . . . 34, 248
24:22 80
24:30 . . . . *163*
24:32 244
26:28 . . . . .34, 53,
180, 210
26:52 . . . . . . .113, 119
26:57 189
26:64 107
26:67 – 68 113
27:11 – 14 113
27:11 . . . . *244*
27:14 147
27:24 243
27:27 – 31 113
27:37 . . . . *246*
27:42 235
27:51 . . . . *246*
27:57 53
27:61 243
28:1 . . . .*248 – 49*
28:2 103
28:9 195
28:13 181
28:17 195
28:18 70
28:19 . . . . *229*
28:20 . . . . *163*, 169

Mark
1:4 . . .44, 226 – 27, 230
1:5 . . . . 226, 230
1:8 . . . . .230 – 31
1:9 . . . . . 84, 226, *230*
1:10 . . . . *58*
1:13 . . . . *163*
1:15 . . . . 234, 237
1:39 84
2:1 . . . . *69*

2:27 80
3:3 85
3:23 . . . . *119*
3:28 – 30 197
3:28 94
3:28a 94
3:29 . . . . *93 – 94*
3:31 245
4:1 . . . . 171, 189
4:4 171
4:35 249
5:1 249
5:2 36
5:10 . . . . *245*
5:11 189
5:14 84
5:25 86
5:34 . . . .*84 – 85*
5:36 233
5:38 – 39 . . . . *35*, 83
6:3 191
6:8 84
6:36 247
7:15 246
8:31 . . . . *59*
9:2 111
9:7 111
9:9 111
9:19 191
9:20 137
9:23 – 24 233
9:39 166
9:40 . . . . *165 – 66*
9:42 236
10:10 84
10:27 . . . . *172*
10:37 107
10:40 222
10:43 – 44 53
10:45 . . . . .50, *52 – 54*,
215
10:46 171

11:31 233	2:34 109	10:1 . . . . *46*
12:17 . . . . *138*	2:40 138	10:7 134
12:36 . . . . *250*	2:41 . . . . *155*	10:9 . . . . 138, 261
13:1 175	2:49 . . . . *118*	10:11 261
13:3 . . . . 84, *247*	2:52 . . . . *172*	10:21 . . . . *36*
13:9 84	3:2 138	10:31–32 . . . . *249*
13:16 . . . . 34, 84	3:3 227	10:36 . . . . . *84–85*, 249
13:21 233	3:7 226	11:7 84
13:30 . . . . *248*	3:16 230–31	11:11 . . . . *51*
13:35 . . . . *248*	3:20 . . . . *138*	11:15 165
14:5 . . . . *246*	4:1 . . . . *120*	11:19 165
14:24 . . . . . 52, *53*, 180,	4:18 . . . . 27, 245	11:20 . . . . 165, 261
210	4:21 45	11:21–22 165
14:34 . . . . 65, *247*	4:23 84	11:22 165
14:35 137	4:44 84	11:23 . . . . **165**
14:36 66	5:5 . . . . *138*	11:32 . . . . *90*
14:49 191	6:8 85	11:37–54 261
14:60 85	6:18b 222	11:44 . . . . *246*
14:62 106–7	6:19 171	11:52–54 261
15:7 . . . . *119*	6:44 . . . . *35*	12:3 49
15:16 . . . . *246*	7:12 174	12:4 . . . . *36*
15:27 . . . . . . .107, 199	7:19–20 259	12:6 254
15:34 90	7:24 . . . . *220*	12:10 . . . . *254*
16:2 156	7:30 226	12:14 137
16:19 107	7:35 . . . . 58, 222	12:29 161
	7:38 248	12:42 137
Luke	7:47 . . . . *250*	12:44 . . . . 137, *138*
1:6 244	7:50 . . . . . . *40, 84–85*	12:47 . . . . *190*
1:8 . . . . *244*	8:14 222	12:50 . . . . *246*
1:17 . . . . *121*	8:26 . . . . *243*	12:51 121
1:20 . . . 49, 84–85, 233	8:34 84	12:56 90
1:28 168–69	8:42 174	13:9 . . . .*84–85*
1:30 . . . . *172*	8:43b 222	13:34 219
1:34 262	8:48 . . . .*84–85*	14:8 84
1:45 233	8:49 171	14:10 84
1:66 168–69	9:4 191	14:31 117
2:1 171	9:22 . . . . *59*	15:18 . . . . *245*
2:4 . . . . *57*	9:32 199	16:9 . . . . . 58, *104,* 170
2:6 . . . . *119*	9:38 174	16:11 233
2:11 . . . . *118*	9:47 171	16:22–23 88
2:25 60	9:50 165	16:23 170
2:26 138	9:61 84	17:20–37 260

17:20a 260
17:20b–21 260
17:20b 260
17:21 . . . *245, **260–61***
17:21a. 260
17:21b 260
17:23 260
17:25 . . . . *59*
17:34–35 260
17:34 260
17:35 139
17:37 . . . . *260*
18:1 190
18:14 . . . . *172*
18:25 69
18:27 . . . . *172*
18:30 . . . . *94*
19:3 . . . . *58*
19:29 83
19:37 189
19:44 49
20:1 199
20:26 244
20:36 72
20:38 181
21:16 . . . . *36*
21:37 84
22:6 . . . . *243*
22:19 . . . . ***97–98***
22:20 . . . . 34, 119, 180
22:22 152
22:27 261
22:35 . . . . *243*
22:37 . . . . *163*
22:45 . . . . 66, 181
22:49 . . . . 36, 117,
119, *179*
22:52 . . . . *163*
22:53 191
22:67 233
22:69 107
23:26 . . . . *248*

23:28 . . . . *249*
23:41 169
23:42 169
23:43 . . . .168, ***169–70***
23:53 117
24:19 . . . . *179*, 244
24:25 235
24:27 . . . . *179*
24:29 . . . .*200*
24:31 . . . . . .31, ***62–63***
24:44 199
24:46 154
24:47 228
24:50 . . . .*246–47*
24:51 . . . . *63*
24:52 195

John
1:1–18 259
1:1 . . . 39, 86, 173–74,
190–92, 203, 260
1:1b 87, 191, 193
1:3 70
1:6 . . . . 172, *222*
1:7 235
1:10 70
1:12 236
1:12a 106
1:12b 106
1:12c 106
1:12c–13 . . . . ***106***
1:13 . . . . .105, 111
1:14–18 259
1:14 . . . .***174–75***, 259
1:15 . . . . *40, 244, 248,*
259–60
1:16 . . . .*54–55*
1:17 55
1:18 . . . . . . .39, *71, 84,*
86–88, 173–74,
190
1:26 . . . . 79, 230

1:27 . . . . *248*
1:28 . . . . 51, *249*
1:30 . . . . .*40*, 180, *209*,
210, 259
1:31 . . . . 79, 230
1:32 . . . . 134, 137
1:33 . . . . . .79, 230–31
1:39 . . . . 134, 191
1:44 58
1:48 . . . . *219*
1:50 . . . . *250*
2:11 236
2:19–20 . . . . *119*
2:19 181
2:23 236
2:24 . . . . 233, 236
3:1–15 110
3:2 168–69
3:3 . . . . . . 106, 110–11
3:5 . . . *43–44*, 79, *105*,
106, *110–11*
3:6 . . . . *105*, 111
3:7 106
3:8 . . . . *105*, 111
3:13 . . . . ***118***
3:15 . . . . . 43, ***234***, 235
3:16 . . . . 174, 236
3:16b 234
3:18 . . . . 174, 236
3:18b 233
3:21 . . . . *134*
3:22 79
3:23 330
3:26 79
3:31–32 88
3:31 . . . . *246*
3:35 . . . . *84*, 121
3:36 . . . . 109, 134, 236
4:1–2 79
4:5 . . . . *249*
4:6 . . . . 58, *104*
4:21 . . . . 233, 236

4:23–24 133
4:31 248
4:40 191
4:41 . . . . *235*
4:42 . . . . *235*
4:47 103
4:50 233
5:24 236
5:26b 73
5:28–29 169
5:37 176
5:38 . . . . 136, 236
5:40 236
5:46 236
5:47 236
6:21 137
6:27 134
6:29–30 236
6:29 236
6:30 233
6:33 . . . . *57*
6:35 236
6:37 . . . . 189, 236
6:38 . . . . *57*
6:44–45 236
6:46 . . . . 87, 173
6:51 94
6:56 . . . . **125**, 135
6:56b 134
6:57 85
6:57a *73*
6:58 . . . . *94*
6:65 . . . . . 58, *104*, 236
7:9 134
7:17 . . . . *105*
7:23 . . . . *119*
7:29 173
7:37 236
7:38 236
7:41–42 . . . . *57*
8:15 147
8:26 173

8:29 168–69
8:30 236
8:31 . . . . 136, 234,
236–37
8:35 . . . . *94*
8:38 . . . . . 171, 173, 191
8:38a 191
8:40 . . . . 63, 173
8:42 . . . . . *105*, 173, 176
8:45–46 236
8:46 182
8:47 . . . . *105*
8:58 260
9:1 58
9:7 85
9:16 173
9:18 . . . . 234, 263
9:33 173
9:35 236
9:38 195
10:11 79
10:15 79
10:17–18 79
10:18 63
10:32 . . . . *105*
10:37 236
10:38 . . . . *125*
10:38a 236
11:1 58
11:4 . . . . . 189, 196, *210*
11:26b 233
11:42 80
11:50 . . . . **212**
12:1 . . . . 31, 186
12:11 236
12:14 236
12:26 170
12:30 80
12:36 236–37
12:44c 237
12:46 136
13:3 . . . . *35*, 173

13:23–26 88
13:23 86–87
13:28 189
13:33 168–69
13:38 263
14:1 236
14:1a 237
14:2 170
14:6 237
14:9 168–69
14:10–11 . . . . *125*
14:10 . . . . *136*
14:10c 135
14:11 . . . . *235*
14:11a 236
14:11b 236
14:16 . . . . . *94*, 168–69
14:17 . . . . 134, 181, 191
14:20 . . . . *125*
14:23 191
14:25 191
14:26 181
15:4–7 182
15:4–5 . . . . *125*
15:4 . . . . *118*, 135
15:4a 134
15:5 135
15:5b 134
15:6 . . . . 135, 181
15:7 135–36
15:8 167
15:9–10 136
15:9 135
15:10c 135
15:15 173
15:22 182
15:26 . . . . 173, *175–76*
15:26c 176
16:8 182
16:9 182
16:13 . . . . *121*, 181
16:17 . . . . *36*

16:20 37
16:27 . . . . *35*, 173
16:28 . . . .*35*, 173,
175–76
16:30 . . . . *120*, 173
16:32 168–69
17:5 . . . . .*173*, 191, 260
17:7 . . . . *222*
17:8 173
17:12 169
17:15. 41
17:17 . . . . . . 133, *134*
17:19 . . . . . . 133, *134*
17:21 . . . . . . *125*, 135
17:23 . . . . *125*
18:16 189
19:13 . . . . *84*, 87
19:20 244
19:25 . . . .*171*, 191
19:34 . . . . *79*
20:1 156
20:3–6. 83
20:3 . . . . *35*
20:4 . . . . *35*
20:5b *35*
20:7 . . . . . . 84, 87, *250*
20:8 . . . . *35*, 83
20:11 189
20:12 189
20:19 . . . . 85, 156
20:26 . . . . 85, *246*
20:28 195
20:29 79
20:31 . . . . 234, 237
20:31a 233
21:4 85
21:6 66
21:10 . . . . *60*

Acts
1:3 . . . .*69–70*, 162
1:3a 70

1:5 230–31
1:8 138
1:9 63
1:15 139
1:24 195
2:1 . . . . *139*
2:5 . . . . 66, 84, 125
2:16–17 117
2:17–18 . . . . . . *60*, 138
2:22 . . . . . *35*, 222, 261
2:23–32. 154
2:27 . . . . . .*84–85*, 169
2:31 . . . . 84, 169
2:32–33. 70
2:33 . . . . *107*
2:34 106
2:36 142
2:38 . . . . . *91*, **227–28**,
229, 232
2:40 . . . . *61*
2:41 . . . . *228*
2:44 . . . . *139*, 233
2:46 . . . . *120, 139, 155*
2:47 . . . . *139*
3:10 189
3:16 . . . . *138, 235, 243*
3:19 . . . . *228*
4:3 84
4:5 84
4:12 . . . . *220*
4:26 139
4:35 171
4:36 . . . . *69*
5:1–10. 197
5:1 199
5:10 193
5:30 144
5:31 107
5:42 . . . . *155*
6:1 189
6:3 . . . . *138*
6:5 . . . . *245*

6:9 . . . . 58, *109*
7:4 84
7:9 168–69
7:10 244
7:12 84
7:29 36
7:43 . . . . *246*
7:53 . . . .*84–85, 90*
7:55–56. 107
7:59–60. 195
7:60 181
8:2 66
8:10 . . . . *247*
8:12 . . . . *228*, 233
8:14–17. . . . . *228*
8:16 229
8:21 . . . . *244*
8:32 244
8:37 233
8:38–39. 58
8:39 258
8:40 84
9:1–2. 150
9:10–17. 195
9:17–18. . . . . *228*
9:17 118
9:21 . . . . 84, 195
9:22 . . . . 142, 150
9:27 118
9:28 84
9:38 244
9:42 235
9:43 134
10:11 137
10:22 63
10:30 126
10:33 222
10:38 168–69
10:39 144
10:40 . . . . *63*
10:41 . . . . *63*, 161
10:43 236

10:44–48 . . . . *228*
10:45 138
10:48 . . . . . . 229, 232
11:2 . . . . *110*
11:5 . . . . 126, *243*
11:16 230–31
11:17 235
11:21 168
11:28 78
12:1 58
12:2 119
12:6 . . . . .181, 185, *248*
12:14 . . . . 58, 185
12:20 . . . . *59,* 193
12:23 49
13:2 195
13:13 . . . . *179*
13:24 227
13:31 . . . . *70*
13:34–37 154
13:36 169
13:42 . . . . .*84–85,* 248
13:48 . . . . *89*
14:13 185
14:23 . . . . . . *155,* 236
14:25 84
15:4 . . . . 34, 222
15:5 58
15:9 69
15:11 233
15:20 143
15:28 . . . . *249*
15:29 143
15:33 . . . . *85,* 222
16:12 126
16:24 84
16:31–34 . . . . *228*
16:31 . . . . . . 227, 235
16:33 227
16:34 . . . . . . 234, 237
16:36 . . . . *40,* 85
17:3 . . . . 142, 150

17:7 . . . . *243*
17:30–31 . . . . *120*
17:31 119
18:5 142
18:8 199
18:10 168–69
18:23 156
18:25 . . . . *179*
18:28 142
19:1–6 . . . . *228*
19:3 84
19:4 . . . . 227, 236
19:5 229
19:14 126
19:21 . . . .*77–78*
19:22 . . . .*84–85*
19:27 37
19:32 . . . . 27, 245
20:7 156
20:9 222
20:11 . . . . *243*
20:14 84
20:15 . . . . *243*
20:18–35 71
20:20 155
20:21 . . . . 227, 236
20:22–23 . . . . .*77–78*
20:22 78
20:28 . . . . 71, 120
21:4 . . . .*77–78*
21:4b 78
21:5 . . . . *247*
21:9 78
21:11 78
21:12 78
21:13 . . . . 78, 84
22:3 43
22:5 84
22:6 179
22:11 66
22:12 66
22:14–16 . . . . *228*

22:14 118
22:16 . . . 195, 229, *232*
22:19 195
22:30 222
23:11 84
23:12 263
23:14 263
23:21 263
23:31 69
24:14 233
24:16 36
24:24 236
25:4 84
26:9–11 150
26:11 . . . . *245*
26:16 118
26:18 236
26:19 118
26:22 . . . . *244*
26:27a 234
26:29 . . . . *61, 249*
27:8 244
27:14 147
27:15 . . . . *60*
27:17 . . . . *60*
27:22 . . . . *249*
27:25 233
27:34 189
28:30 203
28:31 . . . . *179*

Romans
1:1 . . . . 159, 229
1:3–4 . . . .***111–12***, 148
1:3 149
1:4 100
1:7 62
1:16 108
1:17 . . . . . . *43, 107–8,*
            112
1:18–32 172
1:20 . . . . 84, 90

1:24 36
1:25 . . . . 95, *172*
1:26 172
2:6 152
2:7 72
2:11 . . . . *172*
2:13 . . . . *172*
2:17 . . . . *132*
2:23 . . . . *131*
2:26 . . . . *37*
2:27 . . . . *77*
2:28 – 29 150
2:29 . . . . *105*, 231
3:2 233
3:7 . . . . *92*
3:9 . . . . *221*
3:12 242
3:18 . . . . *243*
3:20 . . . . *44*
3:21 – 31 112
3:21 220
3:22 – 23 113
3:22 . . . . 78, 112
3:24 . . . . 113, *123*
3:25 – 26 . . . *34, 84*, 112
3:25 – 26a . . . . . ***80 – 81***
3:25 . . . 78, *80 – 81*, 113,
 119, *120*, 235
3:26 . . . . *109*, 112
3:28 . . . . 99, 194
3:30 . . . . . *34*, ***112 – 13***
4:1 – 25 99
4:1 149
4:3 . . . . 37, *99*, 237
4:5 . . . . . . 99, 235, 237
4:6 . . . . *99*
4:9 . . . . *99*
4:11 . . . 77, *90*, 99, 113
4:12 . . . . *109*
4:13 . . . . *99*
4:14 . . . . *110*
4:16 . . . . . . 80, *90, 110*

4:17 237
4:18 . . . . 43, *90*
4:20 . . . . *91*
4:22 99
4:23 . . . . *99*
4:24 . . . . 235, 237
4:25 . . . . ***81 – 82***
4:25a *81*
4:25b *81*, 82
5:1 112
5:2 . . . . .194 – 95
5:3 . . . . *132*
5:5 166
5:6 . . . . *216*
5:8 . . . . 166, *216*
5:9 – 10 81
5:9 . . . . . . .70, 119 – 20
5:10 . . . . 89, 125
5:11 . . . . *132*
5:12 – 21 140
5:12 . . . . 126, *139 – 40*,
 265
5:14 . . . . *248*
5:15 52
5:18 – 19 140
5:19 52
6:2 – 8 201
6:3 – 10 204
6:3 . . . . 61, 72, *229*
6:3b *230*
6:4 . . . . 78, 205
6:5 61
6:6 204
6:8 . . . . . .61, *200*, 205,
 233
6:9 66
6:10 230
6:11 . . . . *124*
6:14 . . . . *221*
6:15 . . . . *221*
6:17 215
7:5 90

7:8 . . . . *118*
7:17 – 18 . . . . *118*
7:20 . . . . *118*
8:1 . . . . *123*
8:2 . . . . 44, 73, 220
8:3 . . . . 36, 75, 111,
 182 – 83, 265
8:4 – 5 . . . . ***151***
8:4 158
8:5 149
8:10 125
8:11 . . . . . *72 – 73*, 100,
 220
8:17 . . . . 201, 205
8:18 – 25 163
8:20 . . . . *138*
8:23 100
8:29 – 30 64
8:29 100
8:30 117
8:31 . . . . 164, 209
8:32 . . . . . . 71, 81, 111,
 202
8:33 – 34 81
8:34 . . . . 98, 107
8:39 . . . . *124*
9:1 – 3 148
9:1 122
9:3 . . . . *59, 60 – 61*, 149
9:4 – 5 148
9:5 . . . 74, *95*, ***147 – 48***,
 149
9:6 . . . . *109*
9:8 37
9:14 – 21 89
9:14 . . . . *172*
9:15 . . . . *125*
9:17 99
9:18 89
9:22 . . . . ***89***
9:23 . . . . *89*
9:24 89

9:30 . . . . 99, 112
9:32 112
9:33 . . . . 133, 235
10:1–4 150
10:1 209
10:4 . . . . 43, 90
10:5 43
10:9–11 237
10:9–10 90
10:9 . . . . 150, 233
10:11 . . . . . . 133, 235
10:12–13 150
10:14 236–37
10:17 113
11:21 172
11:24 . . . . 33, 172
11:28a 80
11:32 91
11:33–36 73
11:33 48
11:36 . . . . . 70, 73, 76,
83, 89, 95,
105, 106, 109
12:2 . . . . . . .64–65, 90
12:3 73
12:5 123–24
12:7 182
12:16 93
12:17 50
12:21 220
13:4 90
14:2 233
14:5 172
14:10–12 193
14:14 130
14:14a 130
14:15 . . . . . . 134, 216
15:1–3 127
15:7 92
15:9 210
15:15 73
15:17 133

15:19 . . . . .31, 247, 248
15:26 . . . . 152, 156
15:33 168
16:3 122
16:5 155
16:7 124
16:8 130
16:9 124
16:12a 130
16:19 85
16:25–27 42
16:26 99
16:27 95

1 Corinthians
1:2 . . . . 122, 195
1:3 62
1:4 124
1:8 246
1:9 . . . . . . .70, 167, 221
1:10 127
1:13 229
1:15 229
1:17 109
1:23 109
1:26–29 133
1:26 . . . . 59, 149
1:28 59
1:30 . . . . .58–59, 105
1:31 . . . . . 129, 132–33
2:3 193
2:7 185
2:12 . . . . 105, 176
3:1 122
3:3 78
3:5 235
3:8 152
3:11 142
3:13 43,119
3:15 . . . . 69, 194
3:19 172
3:21 132

4:5 246
4:6 . . . . . 121, 207, 209
4:15a 124
4:17 128
4:18–19 156
4:21 36
5:1 143
5:12–13 150
5:12 246
6:1 189
6:2 120
6:5 46
6:6 164
6:12–20 255
6:12 255
6:13a 255
6:13b 255
6:14 . . . . 100, 256
6:15 256
6:15c 255
6:16–17 256
6:16 257
6:17 257
6:18 . . . . 244, 255–57
6:18a 255–56
6:18b-c 256
6:18b 255–56
6:18c 255, 256
6:19a-b 256
6:19b–20 229
6:19c–20a 256
6:19c 257
6:20 120
6:20b 256
7:1 180
7:5 . . . . 104, 139
7:7 105
7:14 . . . . 36, 125
7:15 122
7:18 120
7:22–23 229
7:22 . . . . 128, 129

7:23 . . . . *120*
7:24 . . . . *172*
7:25 179
7:26 31
7:39 . . . . 128, *130*, 180
8:1 179
8:4–6. 74
8:4 . . . . *74*
8:6 . . . **70–71, 74–75,**
  76, 89, *105*, 106,
  109, 222
8:10 226
8:12 . . . . *256*
9:1 . . . . *129*
9:2 . . . . *130*
9:10 . . . . *138*
9:14 . . . . *104*
9:15 . . . . *121*
9:16–17 155
9:20 . . . . *221*
10:2 . . . . *125, 230*, 231
10:11 189
10:13 . . . . *207*
10:16 167
10:18 149
10:20–21 226
10:23 255
10:25–26. 74
10:31–11:1 127
10:31 . . . . *92*
11:9 . . . . *41*, 80
11:11 . . . . . *129, 251*
11:12 . . . . *41, 105*
11:15. . . . . *49–50*
11:17–34 98
11:17 . . . . *90*
11:18 . . . .139, 149, 233
11:20 . . . . . 21, 98, *139*
11:23–25 . . . . . . *63*, 98
11:23 . . . . . .31, **63–64**
11:24–25 . . . . . . *97–98*
11:25 120

11:26 98
11:30–32 197
11:30 . . . . *180*
11:34 . . . . *90*, 98
12:1 179
12:3 231
12:7 . . . . .167, 231
12:8 231
12:8b 231
12:9 . . . . *231*
12:11 231
12:12 . . . . . . *123*, 129,
  229, 231
12:13 . . . **167, 230–31**
12:13a 231
12:13b 231
12:28–29 182
13:7 233
14:1 167
14:5 244
14:16 231
14:23 . . . . *139*
14:27 . . . . *46, 156*
15:1–34 225
15:1–11 225
15:2 244
15:3–4 . . . . . . **153–54**
15:3 . . . . . 64, *210*, 265
15:4 225
15:5–8 70
15:6 . . . . 180, *246*
15:9–11 40
15:10 40
15:10b 199
15:12–32 225
15:12 225
15:17 81
15:18 . . . . *123*, 180
15:20 . . . 112, *180*, 201
15:22 . . . *124*, 140, 180
15:23 . . . 112, 201, 264
15:24–26 265

15:27 . . . . *244*
15:29 . . . 213, **225–26**
15:30–32 225
15:33–34 225
15:35–58 225
15:35 225
15:43–44 65
15:43 122
15:44 128
15:45 . . . . . .37, 44, 73,
  202, 220
15:49 . . . . 64, 100
15:51 . . . . 65, 180
15:52 . . . . *119*
15:53–54 100
15:56 265
15:58 . . . . *130*
16:1 156
16:2 . . . .*156–57*
16:2b 156
16:4 199
16:5–6. 156
16:6 193
16:7 193
16:19 . . . . *130, 155*
16:22 195
16:23 168

2 Corinthians

1:2 62
1:7–8 . . . . 180, 211
1:7 167
1:12 149
1:14 58
1:15–16 83
1:17 . . . . **149**
1:17a. 149
1:17c. 149
1:19 222
1:20 92
1:21 85
1:22 121

1:24 . . . . 75, 149
2:4 104
2:5 58
2:7 244
2:9 85
2:12 . . . . . 41, 128, 129
2:15 108
2:16 108–9
2:17 . . . . . 105, 155, 247
3:5 . . . . 41, 105
3:5c 41
3:6 . . . . 73, 220
3:7 64
3:10 245
3:11 40
3:13 64
3:14 123
3:15 137
3:16–17 44
3:16–17a 65
3:16 189
3:17a 65
3:17b 65
3:18 . . . . . . 44, 64–65,
          73, 100, 108
3:18b 221
3:18c 65
4:1–6. 75
4:2 155
4:4 118
4:5 75
4:13 233
4:14 . . . . 201, 202
4:15 92
4:16 . . . . 64, 100
4:16b 100
5:1–10. . . . . 140, 192
5:1–2. 192
5:1 . . . . 105, 192
5:2–4. 141
5:2 141
5:3 141

5:4–5. 192
5:4 . . . 139, 140–41, 220
5:4b 141
5:5 . . . . . 99–100, 141
5:5b 100
5:6–7. 259
5:6 . . . . . . .79, 192–93
5:7–8. 192
5:7 . . . . . . .78–79, 192
5:8–10. 193
5:8 . . . . . . 79, 170, 181,
          192–93
5:8b 192
5:9–10. 193
5:9 193
5:10 193–94
5:12 . . . . 132, 150,
          180, 211
5:13 186
5:14–15 213
5:14–15a 216
5:14 . . . . . 28, 213, 215
5:15a. 213
5:15b 213
5:16 . . . . . 43, 149–50
5:16a 149–50
5:17 . . . . 105, 123, 203
5:18–6:2 213
5:18–19 89
5:18 . . . . . 71, 105, 126
5:18b 213
5:19a 125–26, 127
5:19b 213
5:20 . . . . 89, 155,
          213–14, 215
5:20a 213
5:20b 213
5:21 . . . . 124, 214
6:1–2. 213
6:4b–10. 116
6:4b–7a. 116
6:4b–5. 116

6:4b 116
6:5 116
6:6–7a. 116
6:6 . . . . 42, 116
6:7 116
6:7a 116
6:18 37
7:1 151
7:4 . . . . 180, 211
7:8 153
7:9–11a 153
7:9–10. 90
7:9 . . . . 35, 104
7:9a 153
7:9b 153
7:10a 153
7:10b 153
7:11a. 153
7:12 245
7:13 . . . . 138, 222
7:14 . . . . 180, 211
8:1 121
8:2 147
8:3 . . . . 152, 171
8:6 90
8:7 104
8:8 156
8:9 . . . . . 75, 127, 166
8:10 . . . . 34, 156
8:11 . . . . 104, 157
8:12 157
8:16 . . . . .117, 121
8:19 92
8:23–24. . . . . 180, 211
8:23 210
9:2 34
9:3 . . . . 180, 211
9:7 . . . . 58, 156
9:13 . . . . 73, 138
10:1–2. 113
10:1 . . . . 93, 127
10:2b–3. 150

10:2 78
10:2a 150
10:3 . . . . . 147, 149–50
10:7 261
10:10–11 113
10:13–16 133
10:15 132
10:16 . . . . 91, 250
10:17 . . . . 129, 132–33
11:2 61
11:3 61
11:4a 61
11:4b 61
11:4c 61
11:9 193
11:10 155
11:11 259
11:12 132
11:18 149
11:20–21 113
11:23 208
11:28 . . . . 156, 249
11:30 . . . . . . 113, 257
11:31 . . . . 95, 259
11:32–33 257
12:1–7 . . . . . 186, 257
12:1 . . . . 186, 258
12:2–3 . . . 186, 258–59
12:2–4 258
12:2 . . . . 124, 186–87,
      244, 246, 257–59
12:2c 258
12:3 258
12:4 . . . . 169, 258
12:4a 258
12:5 . . . . 132, 180, 186,
      211
12:7 . . . . .186, 257, 258
12:8 . . . . .180, 195, 211
12:9–10 113
12:9 . . . . 132, 138, 166
12:10 186

12:11 186
12:13 167
12:18 78
12:19 210
12:20 167
12:21 . . . . . . 155, 202
13:2 202
13:3 155
13:4 113
13:4a 202
13:4b 113, 202
13:5 125
13:7 155
13:8 155
13:9–10 113
13:9b 155
13:11 . . . . 167–68, 169
13:13 . . . . 166–67, 168

Galatians

1:3 62
1:4 . . . . . . 94, 180, 210
1:5 95
1:8–9 171
1:11–12 63
1:11 220
1:16 118–19
1:18–19 63
1:18 193
1:22 . . . . . 123–24, 125
1:23 125
2:1 31
2:4 . . . . 124, 151
2:5 193
2:7 . . . . . 155, 233, 244
2:9 83
2:12 110
2:14 190
2:16 . . . . . .44, 78, 112,
      236, 237
2:17 123
2:19 204

2:20 . . . . . .65, 125, 150
3:2 . . . . 44, 99
3:5 . . . . 44, 99
3:6–14 99
3:6 . . . . 99, 237
3:7 . . . . 99, 109
3:8–9 125
3:8 112
3:9 109
3:10 . . . . 44, 214
3:11 . . . . . . 43, 99, 172
3:13 . . . . 144, 214, 215,
      216
3:14 . . . . 99, 214
3:17 . . . . 90, 152
3:19 . . . . 85, 250
3:21 214
3:23 . . . . 220, 221
3:26–29 150
3:26 . . . . 112, 235
3:27 65
3:27a 229
3:27b 229
3:28 . . . . 112, 124, 229
4:4–5 221
4:4 . . . 75, 111, 220–21
4:7 70
4:8–9 61
4:18 193
4:19 248
4:20 193
4:21–31 151–52
4:21 221
4:23 152
4:23a 152
4:23b 152
4:24 152
4:25 152
4:26 152
4:29 152
5:1 151
5:6 70

5:10 . . . . *129*
5:13 . . . . *138*
5:13b 75
5:16 . . . . 78, *134*
5:17 . . . . **154**
5:18 . . . . *221*
5:19 151
5:22 – 23a 158
5:22 151
5:23 . . . .**157–58**
6:4 . . . . *91*
6:8 . . . . 100, *151*
6:10 . . . . *129*, 150, 189
6:13 . . . . *132*
6:14 . . . . 109, *132*
6:18 168

Ephesians
1:2 62
1:3 – 14 . . . . . **100–101**
1:4 . . . . *247*
1:5 100
1:6 . . . . 42, 100
1:7 120
1:9 . . . . *101*
1:10 . . . . . .*40, 88, 101,*
123
1:11 . . . . *101*
1:12 . . . . *92, 101*
1:13 . . . . *101*, 155, **234**
1:14 . . . . . *92*, 100, *101*
1:15 234
1:20 . . . . .107, *118*
1:21 . . . . *250*
1:22 . . . . *219*
2:1 33
2:2 78
2:3 – 5 . . . . **89**
2:3 89
2:5 205
2:6 . . . . 107, 205
2:7 . . . . *94*

2:8 112
2:10 138
2:11 – 21 150
2:12 . . . . *57, 251*
2:13 . . . . 120, 195
2:14 – 18 194
2:14 195
2:15 – 16 . . . . *123*
2:15 195
2:16 . . . . 89, 195
2:17 . . . . 195, 244
2:18 . . . . **194–95**, *231*
2:20 . . . . 107, 142
2:22 231
3:5 231
3:12 . . . . 194, *195*
3:14 – 15 195
3:14 189
3:20 . . . . *250*
4:1 . . . . *130*
4:3 . . . . .167, 195
4:4 195
4:5 74
4:6 74
4:10 . . . . *250*
4:13 248
4:14 190
4:15 85
4:16 117
4:17 . . . . 122, *130*
4:21 122
4:30 . . . . 100, 231
4:31 199
4:32 . . . . *123*
5:8 . . . . *129*
5:18 231
5:20 . . . . *232*
5:22 – 33 257
5:31 49
6:2 . . . . *121*
6:5 149
6:9 . . . . *172*, 194

6:12 189
6:18 – 19 . . . . . .*35*, 180,
210
6:22 99

Philippians
1:1 155
1:2 62
1:3 – 4 195
1:5 . . . . *85, 243*
1:9 – 11 . . . . *92*
1:10 90
1:13 – 14 203
1:21 – 22 203
1:22 150
1:23 – 24 203
1:23 . . . . 170, 181,
201 – 2,
203–4
1:25 203
1:29 . . . . *210*, 236, *237*
1:30 . . . . *125*
2:1 167
2:5 . . . . .123, *124,*
126–27
2:5b 127
2:6 – 11 . . . . 73, 126
2:6 . . . . 75, 93
2:7 93
2:8 . . . . . . 93, *113, 248*
2:9 – 11 . . . . . . 93, 195
2:9 209
2:10 – 11 . . . . . . **92–93**
2:12 . . . . *163*
2:13 . . . . 33, 43
2:15 . . . .*247–48*
2:19 . . . . *130*
2:22 . . . . *85*
2:26 125
2:27 . . . . *138*, 239, *249*
2:29 . . . . *130*
3:1 128

3:3 . . . . *132–33*
3:5 . . . . *104*
3:9 . . . 43, 99, *105*, 108,
138
3:10 205
3:12 . . . . *139–40*
3:13 . . . . *244, 248*
3:20–21. 201
3:20 192
3:21 . . . . .65, 100, 122,
128, 202
4:1–2. 128
4:1 . . . . *129*
4:2 . . . . *129*
4:9 168–69
4:10 . . . . *139–40*
4:20 . . . . *95*
4:22 . . . . *109*
4:23 168

Colossians
1:4–5. . . . . .72, *75–76*
1:4 . . . . *235*
1:5 . . . . 134, 155
1:7 . . . . 63, 209
1:10–12. 158
1:10 . . . . 78, 158
1:11 . . . . *119, 158*
1:13 127
1:15–17 . . . . *187*
1:15 . . . . 127, 187
1:16 . . . . . **88–89**, 187
1:16c *70*
1:17 . . . . *42, 187*
1:17a. 187
1:17b 88, 187
1:18–20. . . . . *187*
1:18 . . . . 112, 187
1:18a 187
1:19–20. 88–89
1:19 . . . .*123*, 126,
127–28

1:20 . . . . . *88, 94*, 120,
126, 128, 187, *195*
1:21 . . . . 36, *120*
1:22 . . . . 126, 128, *247*
1:27 125
1:28 122
2:4–8. 159
2:4–7. 159
2:5 . . . . 151, 199,
235–36
2:7c 117
2:8 . . . . **158–59**
2:9 . . . .*123*, 126,
127–28
2:10 . . . . *124*
2:12 205
2:13 . . . . *201*, 205
2:14–15 145
2:14 . . . . **154**
2:16 . . . . *121*
2:18 220
2:20 . . . .**61**, 65,
200–201
2:23 . . . . 35, 189
3:1 . . . . . 107, 118, 205
3:3 . . . . *201*
3:4 . . . .**122, 201**
3:9 . . . . *93*
3:10 . . . . . 65, 90, **101**
3:12 144
3:14 . . . . **143–44**
3:16 . . . . 43, *122*
3:17 195
3:18 . . . . *129*
3:22 . . . . **148**, 149
3:24–25. 193
3:25 194
4:1 148
4:2c 117
4:5 . . . . *130, 245*
4:8 99
4:15 . . . . *155*

1 Thessalonians
1:1 . . . . *62, 122*
1:3 194
1:4 221,
1:8 . . . . . *234*, 235, 237
1:10 203
2:4 233
2:6 . . . . *40*
2:12 78
2:13 63
3:4 191
3:6 189
3:8 . . . . *129*
3:10 . . . . *250*
4:1 . . . . . . 63, 128, *130*
4:7 . . . . 122, 138
4:13–18. 153
4:13–15 180
4:13 . . . . **180–81**
4:14 . . . . . 43, **202**, 233
4:15–17 180
4:16–17 169
4:16 . . . .*123*, 192,
203, *204*
4:17 . . . . . .*201–3, 242*
4:17a. 203
4:17b **203**
5:10 . . . . **202**, *216, 242*
5:12 . . . . *130*
5:13 . . . . *250*
5:14 189
5:15 50
5:28 168

2 Thessalonians
1:1 . . . . *122*
1:2 62
1:6 . . . . *172*
1:8 . . . . *61*
1:9 . . . . **61**
1:10 233
2:4 85

2:5 191
2:10 49
2:13 – 14 . . . . *101*
2:13 89
3:4 . . . . *129*
3:10 191
3:12 . . . . *122, 130*
3:18 168

1 Timothy
1:2 . . . . *62*
1:9 – 10 158
1:11 233
1:16 . . . . . 80, *121*, 235
1:17 . . . . *95*
2:3 215
2:4 215
2:5 – 6 . . . . *215*
2:6 . . . . . . *52–53*, 215
2:7 . . . . *121*
2:15 . . . . *42*
3:13 . . . . 122, 235
3:16 81
4:1 . . . . *57*
4:11 182
4:14 . . . . *42, 77*
5:19 . . . . *138*, 154, 244
6:6 . . . . *163*
6:12 . . . . *245*
6:14 264
6:16 72
6:17 . . . . *94*

2 Timothy
1:2 . . . . *62*
1:6 . . . . *77*
1:9 . . . . *185*
1:12 234
2:10 . . . . *124*
2:11 . . . .*204–5*
2:12 . . . . 163, 205
2:25 . . . . *91*
2:26 . . . . *44, 91*

3:1 117
3:15 235
4:18 . . . . *41, 95*
4:22 168

Titus
1:1 . . . . *159*
1:2 . . . . *138, 185*
1:3 233
1:4 76
2:13 74
3:6 138
3:8 . . . . 234, 237
3:14 . . . . *91*

Philemon
2 155
3 62
5 . . . . 83, 208, *234*, 235
6 85
7 . . . . *138*, 208
8 – 16 214
8 . . . . *123*
12 214
13 . . . . . . *35*, 193, *214*
15 – 16 208
15 80
16 209
16a 208
17 – 20 208
17 208
17b 208
18b 208
20 . . . . *130*
20b 208
21 . . . . *208*
22 242
25 168

Hebrews
1:2 . . . . *35*, 117
1:3 . . . . . . 76, 95, 107
1:3b 81

1:7 – 8 . . . . *41–42*
1:8 . . . . *96*, 107
1:12 96
1:12b 95
1:13 106
1:14 265
2:7 172
2:9 . . . . *43*
2:10 . . . . . . *70, 76*, 265
2:15 65
2:18 36
3:3 172
4:12 . . . . *209, 243*
4:14 – 15 95
4:15a 264
4:15b 264
5:1 . . . . 180, 210
5:3 . . . . . .180, 183, 210
5:6 . . . . *74*, 96
5:7 . . . . .31, *65–66*, 95
6:1 . . . . 235, 237
6:4 – 8 197
6:6 90
6:18 . . . . *56*
6:20 . . . . *94*, 96
7:16 . . . . *96*
7:17 . . . . *94*, 96
7:24 – 25 . . . . 95, *96*
7:24 . . . . *94*, 95
7:26 . . . . 95, *264*
7:27 145
8:1 . . . . . . .76, 106–7
9:3 . . . . *161*
9:5 . . . . 207, *250*
9:11 43
9:12 . . . . 120, 265
9:14 . . . . *264*, 265
9:15 265
9:23 – 28 264
9:24 264
9:25 . . . . 36, 155
9:26 264

9:27 265
9:28 . . . . .*251*, **263–65**
10:1 155
10:3 . . . . .97, 155
10:6 . . . . **183**
10:8 . . . . **183**
10:12 . 106–7, 210, 265
10:18 182–83
10:19 . . . . 120, 195
10:25 264
10:26–31. 197
10:26 . . . . 182–83, 210
10:37 259
11:3 90
11:7 . . . . *65*
11:9 85
11:25 . . . . *56*
11:26 . . . . *56*
11:35 . . . . *104*
12:1 . . . . *56*
12:2 . . . . . .**55–56**, 107
12:7 . . . . *91*
12:14 . . . .*250–51*
12:16 . . . . *50*
12:23 265
12:28 . . . . *65*
13:7 95
13:8 . . . . . . **95–96**, 97
13:11 . . . . **183**
13:12 . . . . 120, *245*
13:20 60
13:21 . . . . *95*
13:24 31

James
1:4 121
1:9 132
1:13 . . . . **59**, 222
1:13a *59*
1:13b *59*
1:14 220
1:17 . . . . 59, *172*

1:27 . . . . 59, 172
2:14–26. . . . . . . 70, 99
2:16 . . . . *40*, 85
2:19a 233
2:21 . . . . 99, 145
2:22 99
2:23 . . . . **99**
2:26 . . . . *251*
3:3 90
3:4 14
4:7 59
4:15 . . . . *51*
4:16 . . . . *131*
5:3 . . . .**117–18**
5:4 . . . . 59, *60*
5:9 185
5:12 . . . . *185*, 187
5:19 59

1 Peter
1:3–5. . . . . **101**
1:3 . . . . . .*101*, 112, 162
1:4 . . . . 76, *101*
1:5–7. 163
1:5 . . . . 162, 265
1:7 162
1:8 . . . . 79, 236
1:9–10. 162
1:9b–10a. 162
1:10–12. 162
1:10 162
1:11 . . . . . **89, 162–63**
1:12 162
1:13 . . . . 162, 264
1:17 152
1:18 162
1:20 117
1:21 . . . . 162, 235, 237
1:21b 236
1:23 . . . . **40**
1:25 . . . . *94*
2:4–6. 142

2:4 . . . . *172*
2:5 145
2:6–8. 109
2:6 235
2:8 . . . . **89**
2:11 154
2:20 172
2:21 . . . . *216*
2:23 113
2:24a **144–45**
3:1 . . . . *243, 253*
3:7 153
3:9 . . . . *50*, 244
3:14 255
3:18 . . . . 162, 180, 183,
211, *216*
3:20 . . . . **42**, 85
3:21 . . . . 162, 227
3:22 . . . . .107, 162
4:6 . . . . . **153**, 181, 187
4:8 . . . . *185*
4:9 . . . . . . *93, 243, 253*
4:11 . . . . *95*
4:12–13. 163
4:13 162
4:14 . . . . 138, 163
5:1 162
5:4 162
5:11 . . . . *95*
5:12 . . . . *85*
5:14 127

2 Peter
1:3 . . . . *182*
1:4 . . . . .31, 42, **71–72**
1:8 . . . . *85*
1:17 . . . . *85*
1:19 96
1:20–21. . . . . *60*
1:20 60
1:21 . . . . *60*
2:2 . . . . *134*

2:10 162
3:4 72
3:5 . . . . *41*
3:8 . . . . 96, *172*
3:9 72
3:10 . . . . 72, 96
3:12 – 13 72
3:18 . . . . **96**, 195

1 John
1:1 87
1:2 190–91
1:3b 168
1:5 63
1:6 . . . . *134*
1:7 . . . . 79, *134*
1:8 136
2:2 . . . . 79, 183
2:5 – 6 135
2:6 135–36
2:10 136
        2:14 136
2:17 . . . . *94*
2:18 – 27 197
2:19 . . . . . 79, 134, 136
2:20 181
2:22 197
2:24 . . . . . 135–36, 181
2:24b 135
2:26 182
2:27 135–36,
          181–82
2:28 . . . . 135, 168
2:29 . . . . *105*
3:2 – 3 72
3:6 135
3:8 167
3:9 . . . . *105*, 136
3:11 167
3:12 250
3:14 136
3:15 136

3:16 . . . . 79, *216*
3:17 136
3:18 . . . . *40*, 133
3:21 – 22 196
3:23 236
3:24 . . . . . *125*, 135–36
4:2 – 3 197
4:2 . . . . 79, *105*
4:4 . . . . *105*
4:6 . . . . *105*
4:7 . . . . *105*
4:9 . . . . 168, 174
4:10 . . . . 79, 183
4:12 . . . . 135, 168
4:12b 168
4:13 . . . . *125*, 135
4:14 79
4:15 – 16 . . . . *125*
4:15 135
4:16b – 18 167
4:16 . . . . 135–36, 168,
          233
4:16b 167
4:17 – 18 167
4:17 . . . . **167–68**
4:18 167
4:21 167
5:1 . . . . *105, 248*
5:3 167
5:4 . . . . *105*
5:6 . . . . *35, 79–80*
5:10 . . . . *91*
5:10a 236
5:10b 234
5:10c 237
5:12 – 14 195
5:13 236
5:14 – 15 196
5:14 195
5:16 – 17 . . . 84, **195–97**
5:16 196
5:18 . . . . *105*, 174

5:19 . . . . *105, 118*
5:20 . . . . *119*, 122

2 John
1 133
2 136
3 . . . . 62, 66, 133
4 . . . . *133*, 134
6 . . . . *134*, 167
7 . . . . **40**, 197
9 136

3 John
1 133
3 . . . . *133*, 134
4 . . . . *133*, 134
7 . . . . *210*
11 . . . . *105*

Jude
8 162
12 222
24 . . . . *247*
25 . . . . **96–97**, 185

Revelation
1:4 – 5 . . . . . . *62, 66–67*
1:4 . . . . 31, 97
1:5 120
1:7 66
1:8 . . . . *48*, 67, 76
1:9 122
1:10 156
1:11 85
1:13 189
1:17 76
2:8 76
2:10 . . . . *243*, 255
2:23 152
3:21 . . . . . . *47*, 107, *118*
4:2 137
4:3 – 4 . . . . *247*
4:6 . . . . **46**, 47, *247*
4:8 . . . . . *46*, 67, 97, *247*

4:9 137	7:15 137	21:4 265
4:10 . . . . . 107, 137, 245	7:17 . . . . . . .44, 46–47	21:5 137
5:1 137	9:18 222	21:6 . . . . 48, 76
5:6 47	11:2 245	21:21 46
5:7 . . . . 47, 137	11:11 121	21:22 48
5:9 . . . . 71, 120	11:17 67	21:27 265
5:11 . . . . 47, 247	12:6 . . . . 59, 222	22:1 . . . . . .48, 107, 176
5:13 . . . . 48, 137	12:11 120	22:3 . . . . 48, 107
6:6 47	13:10 119	22:7 67
6:8 . . . . 36, 222	13:14 245	22:12 67
6:9 170	14:20 245	22:13 . . . . 48, 76
6:16 137	16:5 67	22:14 144
7:9 48	16:10–12 58	22:19 84
7:10 137	19:4 137	22:20 195
7:11 247	20:4 163	
7:14 120	21:3 . . . . 168, 169	

Index of Greek Words and Expressions

αἷμα, 71, 79, 119–20
αἰών, 94–97
ἅμα, 241–42
ἀμφί, 45, 179
ἀνά, in compounds, 48
　　NT uses, 45–46
ἀνὰ μέρος, 46
ἀνὰ μέσον, 45–48
ἀνάμνησις, 97–98
ἄνευ, 241–43, 253–55
ἀνθ' ὧν, 49, 56
ἀντί, basic idea and NT use, 49
　　expressing equivalence, 49–50
　　expressing exchange, 50
　　expressing substitution, 50–51
　　important NT uses, 51–56
　　in compounds, 56
　　relation to ὑπέρ, 215–16
ἄντικρυς, 240–41, 243
ἀντίλυτρον, 52, 215
ἀντίπερα, 241, 243
ἀπέναντι, 240–41, 243
ἀπό, ellipses with (pregnant), 60–61
　　expressing "indirect origination," 59–60
　　in compounds, 67
　　in Paul's epistolary salutations, 62
　　other notable uses, 36, 62–67

relation to εἰς, 64
relation to ἐκ, 57–58
relation to ὑπό, 222
ἀπὸ θεοῦ, 58–60
ἄτερ, 241, 243
ἄχρι(ς), 241, 243–44

βαπτίζεσθαι εἰς, 226–28
βαπτίζεσθαι εἰς τὸ ὄνομά τινος, 228–29
βαπτίζεσθαι εἰς Χριστὸν ('Ιησοῦν), 229
βαπτίζεσθαι ἐν, 230
βαπτίζεσθαι ἐν/ἐπὶ τῷ ὀνόματι, 232
βαπτίζεσθαι ὑπέρ, 225–26
βαπτίζεσθαι ὑπό, 226
βλασφημεῖν εἰς τὸ πνεῦμα τὸ ἅγιον, 93–94

διά, attendant circumstances and manner, 77–80
　　cause or ground, 72–76
　　in compounds, 82
　　means/instrument/agent, 70–72
　　origin and basic idea, 69
　　purpose?, 80–82
　　relation to εἰς, 88
　　relation to ἐν, 79–80

relation to ὑπό, 221–22
temporal, 69–70
δικαιοσύνη, 98–99, 107–8
δόξα, 64–65, 96–97, 100–101, 122, 201

ἐγγύς, 241, 244
εἶναι εἰς, 37
εἶναι ἐν, 122–31
εἶναι μετά, 168–70
εἵνεκεν, 241, 245
εἰς, ambiguity of meaning 101–2
    causal?, 90–92
    consecutive/ecbatic, 90
    in compounds, 102
    origin and NT use, 83
    relation to διά, 88
    relation to ἐν, 35, 84–88, 121
    relation to πρός, 83–84
    significant phrases using εἰς, 37, 92–100
    significant successive instances of εἰς, 100–101
    telic, 88–89
εἰς αὐτὸ τοῦτο, 99–100
εἰς δικαιοσύνην, 43, 90
εἰς ὄνομα, 90–91
εἰς (τὴν) δόξαν (τοῦ) θεοῦ (πατρός), 92–93
εἰς τὴν ἐμὴν ἀνάμνησιν, 97–98
εἰς τὸ ὄνομα, 228–29
εἰς τὸν αἰῶνα, 94–95
εἰς τοὺς αἰῶνας, 95
εἰς τοὺς αἰῶνας τῶν αἰώνων, 95
ἐκ, basic signification, 103
    important constructions using ἐκ, 105–10
    in compounds, 113
    other significant instances, 110–13
    partitive, 36
    range of figurative uses, 103–5
    relation to ἀπό, 57–58

ἐκ δεξιῶν τοῦ θεοῦ/μου, 106–7
ἐκ … εἰς, 103, 107–9
ἐκ πίστεως, 34, 43, 112–13
ἐκ (τοῦ) θεοῦ, 105–6
ἐκτός, 241, 244, 255–59
ἔμπροσθεν, 36, 241, 259–60
ἐν, agency, 120
    attendant circumstances 120–21
    causal, 120
    encroachment on other preposi-
        tions, 117–18
    exegetical ambiguities, 122
    extended NT use, 26, 115–16
    in compounds, 136
    instrumental, 119–20
    key phrases, 122–36
    locatival, 118–19
    relation to δία, 79–80
    relation to εἰς, 35, 84–88, 121
    respect, 121
    temporal, 119
    ultimate disappearance, 115–16
    versatility, 116–17
ἐν αὐτῷ (= ἐν Χριστῷ), 127–28
ἐν μέσῳ, 46–47
ἐν σαρκί, 150
ἐν (τῇ) ἀληθείᾳ περιπατεῖν, 133–34
ἐν τῷ αἵματι τοῦ Χριστοῦ, 119–20
ἐν (τῷ) κυρίῳ Ἰησοῦ, in Paul, 128–31
ἐν τῷ ὀνόματι, 232
ἐν (τῷ) Χριστῷ (Ἰησοῦ), in Paul, 122–28
ἔναντι, 241, 244
ἐναντίον, 241, 244
ἕνεκα, 241, 245
ἕνεκεν, 241, 245
ἐντός, 240–41, 245, 260–61
ἐνώπιον, 241, 245
ἔξω, 241, 245
ἔξωθεν, 241, 245–46
ἐπάνω, 241, 246
ἐπέκεινα, 241, 246

ἐπί, basic meaning, 137–38
  important constructions using ἐπί,
    138–41
  in compounds, 145
  other notable uses, 141–45
  versatility, 138
ἐπὶ τὸ αὐτό, 138–39
ἐπὶ τῷ ὀνόματι, 232
ἔσω, 241, 246
ἐφ᾽ ᾧ, 139–41
ἕως, 241, 246–47
ἕως οὗ, 262–63

θέωσις, 71–72
θρόνος, 46–48, 137

κατά, ambiguous examples, 157–60
  basic meaning, 147
  denoting correspondence or con-
    formity, 152–54
  denoting opposition, 154
  distributive, 155–57
  in compounds, 160
  phrases involving κατά, 147–52
κατὰ θεόν, 153
κατὰ μίαν σαββάτου, 156
κατὰ πνεῦμα, 151–52
κατὰ σάρκα, 59, 147–52
κατὰ τὰς γραφάς, 153–54
κατέναντι, 240–41, 247
κατενώπιον, 240–41, 247
καυχᾶσθαι ἐν, 131–33
κοιμάομαι, 180–81, 204
κυκλόθεν, 240–41, 247
κύκλῳ, 46–47, 242, 247

λογίζεσθαι εἰς, 98–99
λύτρον, 52–54, 215

μένειν ἐν in John, 134–36
μένειν ἐν and εἶναι ἐν, 136
μέσον, 242, 247–48
μετά, εἶναι μετά denoting "presence
  with" 168–70

in compounds, 170
  original meaning and NT use, 161
  with accusative, 161–63
  with genitive, 163–68
μεταξύ, 242, 248
μέχρι(ς), 242, 248
μονογενής, 174–75

ὁ/οἱ ἐκ, 109–10
ὅ ἐστιν, 144
ὄπισθεν, 242, 248
ὀπίσω, 240, 242, 248
ὀψέ, 242, 248–49

παρά, and Christology in the fourth
  gospel, 173–76
  basic sense, 171
  in compounds, 170
  relation to ὑπό, 222–23
  transferred meanings, 171–72
παρὰ (τῷ) θεῷ, 172–73
παράδεισος, 169
παραπλήσιον, 242, 249
παρεκτός, 242, 249
πάρεσις, 81
πέραν, 242, 249
περί, basic and derived meanings, 45,
  179–80
  in compounds, 183
  relation to ὑπέρ, 210–11
περὶ ἁμαρτίας/ἁμαρτιῶν, 182–83
πέτρα/πέτρος, 141–42
πιστεύω/πίστις διά, 235
πιστεύω/πίστις εἰς, 236–37
πιστεύω/πίστις ἐν, 234–35
πιστεύω/πίστις ἐπί, 235
πιστεύω περί, 234
πίστις πρός, 234
πλήν, 242, 249
πλησίον, 242, 249
πρό, in compounds, 187–88
  notable uses, 186–87
  NT use and basic meaning, 185

πρός, in compounds, 197
  notable instances, 190–97
  NT use and basic meaning,
    189–90
  relation to εἰς, 83–84
  relation to παρά, 190–92
πρόσωπον, 37

ῥύεσθαι ἀπό/ἐκ, 41

σύν, expressing accompaniment,
    199–200,
  in compounds, 204–5
  expressing association, 199
  original meaning and NT inci-
    dence, 199
  relation to μετά, 200
σὺν Χριστῷ and equivalents in Paul,
    200–204
σωματικῶς, 128

ὕδωρ, 79
ὑπέρ, expressing both representation
  and substitution, 215–16

in compounds, 217
  meaning "in the place of," 211–15
  original meaning and NT use, 207
  relation to ἀντί, 215–16
  relation to περί, 210–11
  with the accusative, 207–9
  with the genitive, 209–10
ὑπεράνω, 240, 242, 249–50
ὑπερέκεινα, 242, 250
ὑπερεκπερισσοῦ, 242, 250
ὑπό, in compounds, 223
  original meaning and NT use, 219
  relation to διά, 221–22
  relation to other prepositions
    expressing agency, 221–23
  with the accusative, 219–20
  with the genitive, 220,
ὑποκάτω, 240, 242, 250
ὑπὸ νόμον, 220–21

χάριν, 242, 250
χρῖσμα, 181–82
χωρίς, 242, 250–51, 263–65

Subject Index

access to God, 194–95
accusative case, preference for in Hellenistic Greek, 33–34
agency, ways of expressing, 221–23
"anointing," the, 181–82
atonement money, 51

baptism, for the dead, 225–26
in Mark and Matthew, 58,
in the one Spirit, 230–31
in the triune name, 228–29
into (the name of) Christ, 229
prepositions with βαπτίζω, 225–32
relation to repentance, faith, forgiveness, and receipt of the Spirit in Acts, 226–28
belief, 75–76, 78–79, 233–37
blasphemy against the Holy Spirit, 93–94
blurring of motion/rest distinction in Hellenistic Greek, 35, 191
boasting, proper and improper, 132–33
body, the physical, and sexuality, 255–57

chart showing frequency of "improper" prepositions, 241–42

chart showing frequency of "proper" prepositions, 32
classical Greek and Hellenistic Greek, 33–35
continuity between OT and NT, 60, 99, 132–33, 154, 162
creation, Christ's role in, 74–75, 88, 187, 222

dangers to be avoided in exegeting prepositions, 39–44
dative case and its ultimate demise, 34, 115–16, 237
death, physical, for believers, 169–70, 180–81, 192–93, 203–4
deity of Christ, 47–48, 62, 93, 95–97, 128, 148, 187
diagram showing basic spatial meanings of NT "proper" prepositions, 29
divorce, 142–43
disembodiment, 258–59
distinctions in prepositional use, 40–41
double entendre, 41–43
doxologies, 95–97, 185

ecstatic experience, 186
ellipses with ἀπό, 60–61
epistolary salutations, Paul's, 62
eternity, 94–97, 185

fellowship, between Father and Son, 135, 191–92
of the Holy Spirit, 166–67
with Christ at death, 192–93, 203–204
"for ever (and ever)," 94–97

God, as cause, 73–76
as goal, 73–75
as judge, 172–73, 251
as source, 73–76, 105
glory of, 92–93, 96–97, 100–101, 185
Greek, NT, characteristics of, 33–35
Greek, Biblical, 25, 115, 117, 119, 121, 189, 261,
Classical, 25, 34, 39–40, 45, 84, 115, 121, 161, 179, 189, 191, 211, 219–20, 236, 245
Hellenistic/Koine, 25, 31, 39–40, 57, 84, 86, 171, 191, 200, 209, 211–12, 219, 240, 244
Medieval/Byzantine, 25, 57
Modern, 25–27, 34, 116, 161, 171, 185, 187, 223, 240, 243, 250
phases of the language, 25–26

Hellenistic/Koine Greek, characteristics of, 33–35
sources for, 25
hope, 76
house churches, 155

"in Christ," 122–28
"in the Lord," 128–31
Indo-European language, putative, 115
"interchange"/"overlap" of prepositions, 34–35, 58, 84, 117–18, 137–38, 180, 200, 210–11

Jesus Christ, and creation, 70–71, 74–75, 88, 187, 222
and John the Baptist, 259–60
as μονογενής, 174–75,

blood of, 71, 119–20132–33
boasting in, 132–33
"coming of," 79–80
death of, 79–81, 98, 213
deity of, 47–48, 62, 93, 95–97, 127–28, 148, 187
eternality of, 96–97, 185
exaltation of, 70, 106–107
humanity of, 128
in Revelation, 46–48
in the fourth gospel, 86–88, 173–76, 190–92
lordship of, 75
mediatorial role of, 74–75, 97
parousia of, 61, 96, 263–65
preexistence of, 97, 190
relation to the Father, 70–71, 74–75, 86–88, 92–93, 125–28, 173–75, 190–92
"remaining in," 134–36
resurrection of, 111–12
resurrection appearances of, 63, 69–70
sufferings of, 89, 162–63
supremacy of, 74–75
worship of, 48, 93
Joseph and Mary, sexual relations of?, 262–63

kingdom of God, 260–61
kōper, 51,

lamb and the throne on Revelation, 46–48
laying on of hands/ordination, 77,
localistic hypothesis regarding prepositions, 28–30
Lord's Supper, 97–98

mutual indwelling, 125, 135

nouns, order of, after prepositions, 44

Paul and slavery, 75, 148

Paul and the law, 220–221
Peter and the church, 141–42
preaching, results of, 108–9
prepositions, ambiguity of, 101–2,
    122, 130–31, 157–60, 168
    and adverbs, 27, 34
    and cases, 28
    as "governing" cases, 28
    as removing ambiguity, 28
    as substitutes for simple cases, 33
    basic spatial meaning of, 27–30
    distinctions in use, 40–41
    distinctive features of NT use of,
        33–37
    endings of, as originally case
        inflections, 28
    exegeting, techniques for, 31–32
    figurative uses of, 30
    frequency of NT, 33
    "improper," 27, 33–34, 239–65
    localistic hypothesis about, 28–30
    lists of NT, 32, 241–42
    meaning in compounds, 14, 48,
        56, 67, 82, 102, 113, 136,
        145, 160, 170, 176, 183, 187,
        197, 204, 217, 223
    "overlap"/"interchange" of, 34–35,
        58, 84, 117–18, 137–38,
        180, 200, 210–11
    possible Semitic influence on use
        of, 36–37, 119–20
    "proper," 27, 32, and passim
    repetition/nonrepetition of, 37,
        43–44, 62, 79, 110–11
    the term, 26–27
    versatility of, 30, 34, 116–17, 138
    word order with, 44
principles of choice for detailed treat-
    ment of specific verses, 30–31

ransom, 51–54, 215
reconciliation, 88–89, 125–26,
    213–14

regeneration, 110–11
"remembering," 97–98
resurrection, 100, 140–41, 201–2
reward, 194

salvation, 101, 162
Semitic influence, possible, on NT
    prepositional use, 36–37,
    119–20
Shema, 74
"sin that leads to death," 195–97
sin-offering, 182–83
spatial meaning of prepositions,
    28–30
Spirit, the Holy, and baptism,
    230–31
    and resurrection, 72–73, 100
    and the "anointing," 181–82
    as pledge, 100
    fellowship of, 166–67
    "procession of," 175–76
stewardship, principles of, 156–57
stylistic variation, 35, 40
substitution, and representation,
    53–54, 215–16
    expressed by ἀντί, 51–54
    expressed by ὑπέρ, 211–16

temple tax, 51, 53
temptation, 59
throne in Revelation, 46–48
tradition, 63–64, 159
transformation of believers, 64–65

unidirectionality hypothesis concern-
    ing prepositions, 28

Verhältniswort, 27

walking in the truth, 133–34
will of God, 77–78, 253–55
"with Christ," being, 203–4
    dying, 200–201
    living, 202
    raised, 201–2

Questions and Rhetoric in the Greek New Testament

An Essential Reference Resource for Exegesis

Douglas Estes

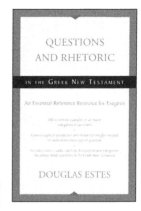

While there are almost 1000 questions in the Greek New Testament, many commentators, pastors, and students skip over the questions for more 'theological' verses or worse they convert questions into statements to mine them for what they are saying theologically. However, this is not the way questions in the Greek New Testament work, and it overlooks the rhetorical importance of questions and how they were used in the ancient world.

Questions and Rhetoric in the Greek New Testament is a helpful and thorough examination of questions in the Greek New Testament, seen from the standpoint of grammatical, semantic, and linguistic analysis, with special emphasis on their rhetorical effects. It includes charts, tools, and lists that explain and categorize the almost 1000 questions in the Greek New Testament. Thus, the user is able to go to the section in the book dealing with the type of question they are studying and find the exegetical parameters needed to understand that question.

Questions and Rhetoric in the Greek New Testament offers vibrant examples of all the major categories of questions to aid the reader in grasping how questions work in the Greek New Testament. Special emphasis is given to the way questions persuade and influence readers of the Greek New Testament.

Available in stores and online!

Advances in the Study of Greek

New Insights for Reading the New Testament

Constantine R. Campbell

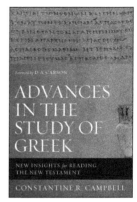

Advances in the Study of Greek offers an introduction to issues of interest in the current world of Greek scholarship. Those within Greek scholarship will welcome this book as a tool that puts students, pastors, professors, and commentators firmly in touch with what is going on in Greek studies. Those outside Greek scholarship will warmly receive Advances in the Study of Greek as a resource to get themselves up to speed in Greek studies. Free of technical linguistic jargon, the scholarship contained within is highly accessible to outsiders.

Advances in the Study of Greek provides an accessible introduction for students, pastors, professors, and commentators to understand the current issues of interest in this period of paradigm shift.

Available in stores and online!

Printed in the USA
CPSIA information can be obtained
at www.ICGtesting.com
JSHW011012120824
67797JS00009B/74

9 780310 116943